Thinking through China

Thinking through China

Jerusha McCormack and John G. Blair

ROWMAN & LITTLEFIELD
Lanham • Boulder • New York • London

Published by Rowman & Littlefield
A wholly owned subsidary of The Rowman & Littlefield Publishing Group, Inc.
4501 Forbes Boulevard, Suite 200, Lanham, Maryland 20706
www.rowman.com

Unit A, Whitacre Mews, 26-34 Stannary Street, London SE11 4AB, United Kingdom

British Library Cataloguing in Publication Information Available

Library of Congress Cataloging-in-Publication Data

McCormack, Jerusha.
  Thinking through China / Jerusha McCormack and John G. Blair.
    pages cm
  Includes bibliographical references and index.
  ISBN 978-1-4422-4791-8 (cloth : alk. paper) — ISBN 978-1-4422-4792-5 (pbk. : alk.
paper) — ISBN 978-1-4422-4793-2 (electronic) 1. China—Civilization. 2. China—
Intellectual life. I. Blair, John G. II. Title.
  DS721.M44 2015
  951—dc23
                                                                    2015010140

∞™ The paper used in this publication meets the minimum requirements of American
National Standard for Information Sciences—Permanence of Paper for Printed Library
Materials, ANSI/NISO Z39.48-1992.

Printed in the United States of America

This book is dedicated to our students,
past, present, and to come.

We see the world not as it is but as we are.

—The Talmud

The Greek: What is the Truth?
The Chinese: Where is the Way?

—Angus Graham

There should be no premature closing of our account with reality.

—William James

Contents

Introduction

Entering a Chinese World

IMAGINE

Imagine you are entering a place that strikes you as entirely horizontal. Although you see the sky, sky here means simply "the heavens." Here there is no heaven where earth's highest reality resides—no God, no choirs of angels, and no eternal souls. Nor do any ideal forms or first principles lurk in this beyond, informing all that is on the earth below. Here you have entered a City of Man—a place without a "City of God" in either thought or imagination.[1] In this place, the values of the people reside in their relations with others. For this reason, they invest enormous energy not in an imagined afterlife or in referring to an invisible realm of higher principles but in creating and sustaining human relations within their families and networks of friends and colleagues. Convinced that tomorrow is uncertain, they concentrate on the present, while hoping and working for a better future on this earth. While we in the West may believe in unchanging realities, in this world people expect unrelenting change. Therefore, they pay a great deal of attention to practical matters, giving little weight to large systematic principles. Decisions are made according to the degree of trust in those around them, not in regard to abstract rules. The people in this place do not often ask why. Their urgency, in this transient world, is to know how—as in "how to cope" with the shifting world about them.

If you think this is an impoverished world, you are wrong. Although only imagined, that place might be taken as a rough outline of what is, in fact, the oldest continuous civilization in the world and thus among the richest and most complex cultures in existence. It may be taken to represent the world of China, both of yesterday and today.

INTERPRETING CHINA TO THE WEST

Of course, the imagined world described above is a Westerner's idea of China.[2] Used to living within clear definitions, Westerners[3] often find the categories that matter in the Chinese world to be disturbingly permeable. Distinctions that are routinely made in the West—such as those between self and others, body and spirit, or this world and the next—tend in China to merge and overlap in confusing ways. For, in this Chinese world, bodies can think; self and others are imbricated in a complex nexus; large impersonal forces govern the way things happen; and ghosts of ancestors or "immortals" may move in and out of vaguely defined realms, neither fully alive nor quite dead—in a Western sense of these words.

Still, this portrayal of an imagined, largely horizontal world is less hyperbolic than that routinely offered by Western books about China—if only because most such books about China decipher it through Western mindsets. They ask Western questions and respond with Western answers, typically finding China lacking in one or another attribute. They trust to Western methods of analysis and rely on Western constructions such as "fact" to describe a world in which "the facts" are often factitious. What they are likely to miss is that Western categories—especially the big words with capitals such as God, Truth, Freedom, Rights, or Justice—do not help a Westerner to understand how Chinese look at the world. We know that the Chinese experience the world differently because their *categories* are different; they see the world differently because they approach it with very different presumptions. What we are tracking here are precisely those differences.

Accordingly, this book proposes ten key Chinese categories central to the way Chinese people understand their world. In explaining the meaning—and use—of these key words and the way they relate to each other, this book seeks to account for that invisible web that the French call a culture's "mentality." We do so comparatively, noting how, despite their divergent trajectories, there are occasional and startling convergences in the way both civilizations see the world. Finally, we deploy this Chinese lexicon to respond to four persistent Western questions about China, enabling a response to these questions, for once, in Chinese terms.

Perhaps not surprisingly, that response changes the perspective on these questions, sometimes in quite drastic ways. Why are such fundamental issues not taken into account by Western books on China? Perhaps this is so because the way people think about the world is itself largely invisible—not only to outsiders but also often to Chinese and Westerners as well. In fact, most humans never feel the need to think much about the civilization they inhabit. Like fish, they do not know water; they simply live in it. The Chinese have their own way of saying this: a famous poem about a sacred mountain concludes, "When on the slopes of Lushan / One cannot see Lushan."[4] To view the mountain, one has to get off the mountain. In other words, it may take an actual encounter with a distant way of life, such as that of China, for people to begin thinking about their own unspoken presumptions about the world in which they live and move and have their being.

COMPARATIVE STUDIES

Moving off the mountain allows for viewing it from another perspective, that is, viewing it from a distance. Comparative study as between China and the West is still a relatively new, and still highly contested, area; yet it has already generated fresh perspectives rich with possibility. While throwing unexpected light on how we normally see China, such studies require us, at the same time, to reevaluate our own origins in relation to it. More significantly, such studies also require us to reevaluate our own relationship with ourselves.

One recent foray into this field has all the ring of manifesto. In "No (More) Philosophy without Cross-Cultural Philosophy," Karsten J. Struhl argues that, while "philosophy is a radical inquiry whose task is to interrogate the fundamental assumptions of some given activity, discipline, or set of beliefs," it cannot do so without attempting to "create a distance not only from the assumptions under investigation but also from its own assumptions, which is to say, that it must be able to raise questions about its own method." Such self-reflexivity requires an alternative vantage point, as otherwise its assumptions will remain so deeply imbedded within its given culture that a serious critique is impossible. Hence, "the only way to step outside the boundaries of these cultural presuppositions is to reflect on the given problem from the vantage point of another culture's philosophical tradition."[5] Thus, he argues, cross-cultural study is necessary to go beyond the invisible limits of one's own acculturation if one is to observe the imperatives of a true intellectual inquiry. The comparator used for his study is, significantly, Asian philosophy, in particular, Indian Hindu-Buddhist narratives. In short, Struhl too believes that to see the mountain, one has to get off the mountain. What holds for comparative philosophy applies all the more to the broad-gauge cultural comparisons proposed here.

And in one sense, many of us are all already involved in such processes. In our own everyday world, all of us—as we read the news, search the Internet, travel further, and meet more people (whether formally or informally) from radically different cultures—are in fact engaged in comparative studies as, inevitably, we are forced into awareness of *otherness*. Most of the time these comparisons are scattered and unsystematic. What the domain of comparative cultural studies seeks to do is to make such comparisons systematic and thereby more fruitful. What these comparisons yield are possibilities for new paradigms and, with them, new concepts that will help us devise a language appropriate to negotiations across such cultural divides. Most importantly, what these comparisons do for us is to make our own boundaries, and our own presumptions, as clear to us as if subjected to an X-ray.

WHY TODAY'S CHINA IS NOT TODAY'S WEST

To hold up China against the West is to undertake exactly such a large-scale comparative exercise. But in doing so, it is important to remember that China and the

West have arrived at today by different routes and on different schedules. Not only does modernity not occur simultaneously in both these worlds, but also it does not even occur simultaneously in different domains within each world. What may be defined as "modernity" is thus not tied to any specific dates but can be best understood as an ongoing series of processes issuing in quite different modernities. In both civilizations, these take off when long-held traditional values and practices are called seriously into question. Such processes typically go on for centuries and can still be seen at work today. Such an approach to a definition of "modernity" calls particular attention to the sixteenth and seventeenth centuries in the West when such processes clearly began to emerge. That is why historians of Europe have come to call this period "early modern." In the case of China, however, major challenges to traditional patterns began only in the second half of the nineteenth century, marked by defeats in wars against foreign powers along with diverse resistances to the declining Qing dynasty.[6]

When modernity is understood as signaled by cultural self-questioning, it loses its conventional association with the West. All too many Westerners unthinkingly presume that in China "modernizing" really means "Westernizing," or perhaps even "Americanizing." But a culturally alert definition of "modernity" must first of all acknowledge the particular traditions actually in place before being brought under challenge. When modernizing changes do begin, by this definition they modify above all those practices and credences that dominated prior to that time. It follows that, although one can cite similarities between medieval Europe and traditional China before the twentieth century, the two can be seen, on examination, to be based on very different premises and ways of thinking. Similarly, as China and the West come from different pasts, no one should expect Chinese modernity to replicate Western (or American) versions of modernity except on the most superficial of levels.

In fact, recent Chinese leaders have consistently limited reliance on Western-style models. Starting with Deng Xiaoping's reforms in the late 1970s, they have instead tried hard to appropriate only those aspects of Western life that can fit most profitably into the Chinese situation. These include certain visible aspects of free-market capitalism, for example, direct foreign investment, partial opening of state-owned enterprises to competition, and heavy investment in university-level institutions of learning, as well as entry-level social security systems for pensions and health care. For elites, they might also include prestige for imported emblems of Western high culture: classical music, art works, and luxury goods. But despite importing such Western practices and despite the new rich indulging a taste for Western brand names, what has not changed substantially is the way Chinese people assimilate such ideas or products. In short, despite welcoming Western goods, Western styles, and even some Western concepts, China still remains recognizably Chinese.

Simultaneously, the grand Chinese tradition is also being tested for relevance to today's newest New China. This trend reverses the emphasis of Mao Zedong's thirty years of blanket condemnation of Chinese traditions as "feudal." These two processes—of selective importation and simultaneous reassessment of native traditions—are combining to help China maintain its momentum as the most dynamic nation on earth. Nonetheless, given all the complexities of modernizing processes, no one should claim that either China or the West is monolithic.[7] China, though less so than Europe, has many different subcultures and language groups. There is no magical "essence" to China any more than there is to "the West." And it is necessary to recall that, between the strong desire of China to promote a unified sense of agreed values and the strong desire of the West to have a clear and comprehensible reading of China, generalizations about either are bound to simplify the diverse and often untidy ways their values manifest themselves in practice.

Yet rethinking China from a Western perspective demands some such large-scale distinctions, even if arbitrary, just as it entails simplifications of often messy and diverse practices. Clarity can be expensive. But without undue sacrifice, certain credible generalizations may be advanced on the basis of deep and underlying assumptions that channel the way each civilization works.

CREDIBLE GENERALIZATIONS

What does "a credible generalization" amount to? Here is a quick example from China that concerns the ways words may be seen to interact with events.[8] As every Mandarin speaker knows, words may influence, by their utterance alone, what is likely to happen. For instance, the word *sì*, meaning *four*, sounds very much like *sǐ*, meaning *death*—with only a difference of intonation. On this basis, a few years ago automobile drivers in two populous provinces, Guangdong (capital Guangzhou, aka Canton) and Jiangsu (capital Nanjing), complained vigorously about the possible implications of this homophone. After all, who would want to drive around just inviting trouble? In 2004, the provincial authorities finally yielded to popular pressure by banning the number four on their license plates. Homophones—words pronounced identically, such as "pair," "pear," and "pare"—can cause unease in China. Although educated Chinese may think of themselves as too "modern" to take such traditional associations seriously, everyone acknowledges that homophonic puns *can* have the power to release good or bad energies into the larger world.[9]

How can we be sure that what might be an isolated linguistic anxiety actually constitutes a trait of cultural significance? Look to the markets. Within China such a belief sustains widely differing prices, for instance, for mobile telephone numbers. Numbers with identical functionality may vary in price by a factor of ten or more, depending in part on whether they include a number four (other numbers, such as eight, have positive resonances, also for homophonic reasons).[10] Thus watching the trouble a Chinese newcomer to the West takes in selecting a mobile phone number is puzzling—until one understands its logic. In the West, all the numbers carry the same price. But for the Chinese customer, paying no more for a "good" number is like getting free luxury goods—prompting a predictable scramble (obscure to the Western shopkeeper) for the "best" (that is, the luckiest) numbers.

This small example suggests how we can best approach Chinese mentalities at work—with language at its heart. On this basis, responsible comparisons may be made, even though attitudes toward language itself differ radically as between these two civilizations. For instance, in the West, words are understood to be part of a distinct domain called "language." There words are expected to refer to or to represent the real world, but they always remain "just" words. For as Westerners we tend to believe that actions follow from words only when humans decide to implement them: sticks and stones may break my bones, but words will never hurt me.[11] In Mandarin, on the other hand, words may quite involuntarily inflect events, sometimes promoting good fortune, at other times threatening harm. Grasping this linguistic feature might help us to understand why State leaders in China today seem to react so strongly to any and all words in public space that might imply some form of critique. This political sensitivity extends to Chinese homophones or puns. To evade censors, bloggers have referred to the dissident artist Ai Weiwei by using the Chinese characters for "love the future," an approximate homonym of his name. Such bloggers are now the target of a new penalty system that, if they continue their game, may shut down their websites.[12]

LANGUAGE AS A KEY

Language, then, offers valuable primary evidence for how the Chinese organize their experience. To assess such cultural implications does not require mastering Mandarin, but it does ask for thoughtful attention to linguistic differences. To take a position on the long debates on this issue, we side with Guy Deutscher, one of the latest observers to reflect on how language may affect thinking, who argues that

> language forces you to be attentive to certain details in the world and to certain aspects of experience that speakers of other languages may not be required to think about all the time. And since such habits of speech are cultivated from the earliest age, it is only natural that they can settle into habits of *mind* that go beyond language itself, affecting one's experiences, perceptions, associations, feelings, memories and orientation in the world.[13]

To support this argument, one revealing example Deutscher gives concerns gender. If one wants to say, "I had dinner last night with a neighbor," French and German (among other languages) would force you into confessing whether the neighbor was a man or a woman—whereas in English (and Chinese) that information would remain private. In fact, Chinese almost always leaves gender unmarked. As Deutscher concludes, we can do better than pretending that when we employ different languages, we will all still think in the same way.[14]

One does not have to learn a great deal of Mandarin, for instance, to realize that it has no articles (no *the* or *a*). What does that imply? In English these are the most common words one uses, because they clarify the category status of what one is talking about: "*an* idea" or, in a case of a particular instance, "*the* idea." Chinese nouns, however, do not work within such distinctions. Hence, one cannot, as in English, automatically turn a noun into a principle, in the way that "truth" can easily become "the Truth" or "a god" can become "God"—with implications of "the one true God." Without articles, Chinese nouns activate a semantic field that does not differentiate between general and particular or masculine and feminine or even between singular and plural. These are indicative differences that tend to block Western expectations, such as the ability to move easily from the particular to the abstract or to discern immediately what amounts or degrees of things/people are involved in a certain transaction or reference.

Although this is only one instance of many, it concurs with Deutscher's thesis that, while native speakers of every language can (at least hypothetically) find ways of expressing any idea they can conceive of, certain ways of thinking will seem to come more naturally in one language than another. These are the kinds of differences we want to highlight. In the present context, attempting to define key Chinese concepts to those habituated to Western languages can prove tricky because such words in Chinese may function in context as a noun, a verb, or an adjective. Under such conditions meaning blurs and clear-headed Western-style thinking becomes elusive, if not at times almost impossible.

FROM LANGUAGE TO MENTALITIES

Moving from language to mentalities involves a logical leap that may always remain contentious, even though that process is now emerging as a rich field for research. One suggestive study is Richard E. Nisbett's *The Geography of Thought: How Asians and Westerners Think Differently—and Why*. In one segment, Nisbett brings together extensive research on language acquisition, particularly among young children. It does not fit perfectly with our current concerns, since his tests involve not only Chinese but also other East Asians from Korea and Japan. Nonetheless, the cumulative recorded differences are striking, as when East Asian mothers show up as teaching their children language primarily by emphasizing verbs and relationships (Mommy gives to you; you give to Mommy) as opposed to American mothers who focus the child's attention on nouns and how they relate to each other through the medium of abstract categories (This is a dog; this is a panda. These are animals).[15]

What habits of mind would such linguistic enculturation encourage in both worlds? Can we trace to such early experience the Chinese habit of seeing everything as connected in a world of continuous exchange? Or can we trace the Western habit of thinking of the world in terms of isolated things belonging to abstract categories posited as having a stable, unchanging essence? In other words, is the world to which the child is being attuned a world privileging verbs—or nouns?

In another study Nisbett illustrates how, from a very early age, Asian and Western children tend to construct very different mental worlds. Here Chinese and American four-year-olds are shown three pictures, such as a chicken, some grass, and a cow.

They are then asked (1) If you were to place two objects together, which would they be? and (2) Why do these two seem to belong most easily together? What the study showed is that most American children preferred to group objects according to a (transcendental and invisible) category, placing both the chicken and the cow together under the label of "animal." The Chinese children, on the other hand, preferred to group the objects on the basis of (visible, this-worldly) relationship. And indeed, what relationship could be more intimate than that of one (the cow) eating the other (grass)?[16]

From Nisbett's reports of research on language learning, it is now possible—thanks to a scholar coming from Chinese origins—to venture further into mentalities, a notoriously difficult concept to pin down. Qi Wang, trained at Peking University and then Harvard, is now professor of human development at Cornell's College of Human Ecology. Her research shows how differently fully acculturated individuals in China and the United States process and remember experience.[17] In their cognitive functioning, whether focused on personal experience or on an anonymous narrative text, Euro-Americans distinguish and remember more episodes than comparable Chinese or other East Asians. Euro-Americans also, in processing their experience in more and more detailed segments, tend to highlight their own individual role in these episodes. The Chinese, however, segment experience into fewer and more general episodes, highlighting activities in general rather than emphasizing personal involvement. These observations are not surprising, given our comparisons of China and the West; but prior to this study there was no solid research to clarify just what cognitive differences might characterize two such different mentalities.

Confirming the utility of this approach are the observations of Gish Jen's 2012 lectures at Harvard.[18] As an American-born Chinese seeking to understand her father's natively Chinese mentality, Jen opens by confessing that she does not understand why her father seemed to leave himself out of his own autobiography, even though such apparently depersonalized accounts were often her own preferred mode of telling a story. Enlightenment came when she discovered the analyses of Qi Wang. There Jen was startled to learn that, when Chinese people tell stories about their past, "personal events are not forgotten. Rather, they are never mentally filed away to begin with because they are filtered out before they can be."[19] What Qi Wang's study did was to help Gish Jen become more conscious of the two distinct ways of thinking about the world—one Chinese, one American—which she was trying, through her own storytelling, to bridge.

For those who work in the emerging discipline of comparative cultural studies, what such research does is to establish formally that Americans and East Asians *do in fact think very differently* from their very first enculturation. But sometimes such differences seem easy to deny experientially; since humans go on learning all their lives, their experience may also lead to broadening out in their ways of thinking. For example, in Nisbett's tests, Asian Americans tended to score midway between the East Asian and the American subjects, thus blurring (or combining) cultural distinctions. Similarly, it is clear that immigrants can, over time, absorb the ways of thinking common to their new surroundings, so that they may be able to think in more than one modality. Hence the differences are undeniably real, but depending on cross-cultural experience, they can easily become less pronounced over time, making clear distinctions between mentalities more difficult to assess.

WORKING WITH KEY WORDS

Working between these two modalities is thus a precarious business. For that reason, rather than simply assert large cultural generalizations, this book seeks to work through specific categories. As most travelers are aware, cultural exchanges do not work well if words are treated merely as a currency transaction, as if they had equivalent value in the other civilization. Few words or categories ever emerge as fully equivalent across civilizations; at times, they are not even commensurate. But when key categories are recognized as having something in common, it becomes possible to measure the distance between them. For instance, we all have "bodies," and we might casually assume they are all alike. But that is not the way, in these two worlds, they are actually understood. In fact, traditional Chinese assumptions about the body and how it operates turn out to be radically different from those of the modern West.[20]

Similarly, when Westerners approach China through a familiar list of their own prized concepts—such as *democracy, freedom* (aka *liberty*), *equality* (aka *social justice*), *free markets, the rule of law, religion*, or *science*—they are apt to assume that in China these words are used in similar ways and mean roughly the same thing. In fact, although apparently equivalent translations may well appear in the other's dictionaries, these words commonly carry quite different meanings—or they may mean little at all beyond a certain formulaic rhetoric. Others are simply alien. While *mianzi* (face) and *guanxi* (relationships) may be shown to have Western cognates, for instance, Chinese categories such as *qi* (vital energy), *yi* (change), *yin* and *yang*, or *Dao* (a name for the underlying order of things) are manifestly not commensurate to anything in the Western world. Then how can one proceed?

SUSPENDING WESTERN EXPECTATIONS

First of all, in undertaking this exercise, it is important to suspend our own cultural assumptions about the world. We gain nothing by wrenching Chinese experience into Western categories any more than forcing Western experience into those from China. For millennia, China has been not merely a nation but also a civilization, organized along its own, distinctively non-Western, lines and following its own trajectories. Only a very pure Western arrogance could still believe that Western modes of thinking must be "universal," applying to all things at all times and in all places. Not only does such an assumption distort and shrink the experience of other worlds, but also it constitutes the worst form of cultural imperialism. Thus to challenge the

Chinese world because it does not promote Western-style "democracy" or "human rights" or to believe that there is something inherently immoral in a world that does not believe in a creator-god is to indulge in the crudest forms of intellectual colonialism. The consequences of such discourse, as evidenced in Western Cold War rhetoric, block any attempt to understand (much less negotiate with) those from another, and in this case, specifically Chinese, world.

As a way of negotiating such potential blockages, this book seeks to set out for Westerners a China that is presented on its own terms. We do so even while conceding that, as foreigners, we cannot possibly capture all the resonances of these key words in Mandarin. Instead these basic Chinese concepts are deployed here in an instrumental way: as an aid in helping Western readers to step aside from their own frames of reference in order to look at the ways in which the Chinese themselves frame their experience. For these purposes, comparisons are indispensible.

HOW WE PROCEED

Accordingly, Part I focuses on ten key concepts that keep coming up when Chinese people explain how they think about things. In each case we clarify the etymology of the word and the extent to which equivalents exist in English. Because in China such categories are used in a fluid way—without the clear definitions or boundaries we seek for such words in the West—it is necessary to situate each concept in relation to traditional Chinese culture and assess its relevance under the changing conditions of China today. Where possible, we also track how some of these Chinese presumptions are beginning to manifest themselves in the West. By the end of this section, the reader will have learned the ten Chinese words most revealing of Chinese views of the world.

To a Western mind, these words easily group themselves into clusters. The first group presents words that focus on persons and their relations with others: *xiao*, *mianzi*, and *guanxi*. These ideas are constantly at work in shaping Chinese social life.

In second place come words focused on the nature of human beings and of the natural world: *xin*, *qi*, *yi*, and *Dao*. Though Chinese worldviews do not give great importance to deciphering the nature of things, Westerners seeking to make sense of China need to know its dominant affirmations about human nature and the wider world we call "nature" or "reality."

Third in place are words that highlight Chinese protocols, personal and national: *he* and *luan*. These stand for "harmony" and "chaos" insofar as they function as carrot and stick to keep the Chinese people in line under the Communist Party's direction.

The last word, *celüe* or "strategizing," represents the cumulative outcome of the preceding nine. All Chinese people see themselves as trying to cope strategically with the changing circumstances they encounter every day. Their investment in devising ways of coping may be seen as perhaps the most pervasive characteristic shared by Chinese people today.

Only ten words in all: but understood comparatively, these will open for a Western reader new ways of entering the Chinese world. While it is difficult to see how others think, by invoking these words we can now recognize the factors that will frame what they think and why, in our terms, they tend to act the way they do.

In Part II, we ask those questions most frequently put to China watchers by Westerners who interrogate what they learn about China. Then, by drawing on these ten keywords, we seek to respond to them in Chinese rather than Western terms. Our point is that dominant Chinese views do not result from today's political or ideological assertions as much as from the fundamental orientations of Chinese culture. The selected keywords, taken together, ground Chinese understandings of that aspect under question. By taking these categories as our primary frame of reference, we can reorient our own perspective on these issues—showing how they tend to play out within a Chinese, rather than a purely Western, context.

Part III, "Rethinking the West," opens with new insights as to how, in world terms, the West is WEIRD (Western, Educated, Industrialized, Rich, and Democratic) but not necessarily *right*.[21] Based on research across a number of domains, it demonstrates how much of an outlier the West really is in terms of its thinking. Certainly the rising profile of China, along with an intensive deconstruction of our own Enlightenment values, has tended to put Western orthodoxies to the test. Could this provide an insight into those radically different modes of thinking said to define the rest of the world? In other words, do we have something to learn from China?

At the very least it is clear that our becoming open to such questions is now critical. Both China and the West, for different reasons, have arrived at a point where their own values are, of necessity, being reformulated. At the same moment, they have tried to resolve what is a crisis of civilizational values by emphasizing the necessity of economic growth. But economic growth along established lines cannot continue indefinitely. The human enterprise has now collectively reached the point where earth's natural equilibriums have been pushed to—and increasingly even beyond—their breaking point. At the same time no single nation or region can ensure its future viability, given the known limitations of earth's resources. Thus unprecedented forms of collaboration are now indispensable. Imagining a context within which dialogue can take place, as this book seeks to do, may offer a first step toward the only direction that makes sense.

Such a commitment does not imply that China must become more like the West. Many Western observers seem fixated on Chinese dissenters as if their actions might initiate a magical transformation of the People's Republic of China (PRC) into something more Western in orientation. This is unlikely. While the Chinese aspire to prosperity, they are not attracted by the side effects of Western lifestyles. Even taking into account visible signs of "Westernization," it appears that the vast majority of Chinese alive today are content to live within the restraints currently imposed on them—in return for the promises of ongoing prosperity for their families along with a return to greatness for the nation as a whole. Rather than imitating the West, China often presents a trenchant critique of our own world. From a Chinese point of view, Western cultures tend to produce ill-disciplined children and destructively individualistic mindsets, plus chaotic political and economic management, enabled by shortsighted, self-seeking factions at every level of decision making. Sometimes, from a Chinese perspective, Western-style democracy can appear like a young and very fragile experiment. If this view of our world is disconcerting, it is one worth contemplating, if only to underline just how special our view may be and how much, in intellectual terms, we may have to learn about ourselves from Chinese ways of seeing the world.

NOTES

1. For the lack of a transcendental world in Chinese thought, see David L. Hall and Roger T. Ames, "Transcendence and Immanence as Cultural Clues," in *Thinking from the Han: Self, Truth, and Transcendence in Chinese and Western Culture*, 189–269 (Albany: State University of New York Press, 1998).

2. What, then, do we mean by "China"? As the oldest nation/state/civilization in the world, China seems pretty well defined geographically, with borders that largely reflect the expansive Qing Empire that ended in 1911. But despite official "One China" policies, China is also many different places, with distinctive peoples, dialects, customs, cuisines, and climates. There are important distinctions to be made between traditional and modern China—although, compared to the West, China has maintained remarkable continuity in its dominant civilizational values across the millennia.

3. As to "the West," for the purposes of this book, we define it rather arbitrarily. In its simplest and most obvious terms, the core of "the West" includes Europe, North America, Australia, and New Zealand, with the United States often providing the extreme examples of Western tendencies. Russia and Latin America remain borderline "Western," depending on how one reads their trajectories. Other regions such as South Asia, the Middle East, or Africa maintain their own ways of life—along their own lines of thinking.

4. The Song dynasty poet, Su Shi (1036–1101) wrote of this famous mountain (translated literally here):

bù shí lú shān zhēn miàn mù, 不 识 庐 山 真 面 目，	Lushan's true features I cannot see,
zhǐ yuán shēn zài cǐ shān zhōng, 只 缘 身 在 此 山 中。	because I am in its midst.

5. Karsten J. Struhl, "No (More) Philosophy without Cross-Cultural Philosophy," *Philosophy Compass* 5, no. 4 (2010): 287. From a somewhat different perspective, Zhang Longxi, evaluating diverse efforts at cross-cultural readings of China and the West, sharply criticizes comparisons that insist on incommensurability between these two entities, including some commentators we value greatly such as François Jullien. Zhang Longxi, "The Complexity of Difference: Individual, Cultural, and Cross-Cultural," *Interdisciplinary Science Reviews* 35, nos. 3–4 (2010): 341–52. Nonetheless we concur with his final approbation of Benjamin Schwartz's formulation that "difference is ever present but it is not inaccessible" (350).

6. In fact, modernizing ideas entered China largely through Japan in the late nineteenth century. The linguistic impetus to such transfers is well studied in Lydia Liu, *Translingual Practice: Literature, National Culture, and Translated Modernity—China, 1900–1937* (Stanford, CA: Stanford University Press, 1995).

7. These concepts are subject to variable definitions, as spelled out in notes 2 and 3, above.

8. Here we treat these homophones as a linguistic matter. It is also important to note that in Chinese written words may also carry resonance, as for example, when carved into mountain cliff faces where emperors declare themselves in characters assumed to have, effectively, timeless influence. Later on in the book, within the context of *qi* energies, we will seek to make clear how traditional Chinese worldviews affirmed a language that works through such acoustic resonances (see chapter 5, "The Energy Unifying the World: *Qi*").

9. Though one may feel tempted to dismiss such associations as "superstition," they are better understood as a function of the Chinese language. Western-style superstition shows up in nervousness about the number thirteen. But what carries the ominous charge is the *idea* of the quantity thirteen, not the word for it in any Western language. In Chinese, it is the sound of the words that seems to resonate beyond language, hence their phonics functioning through homophones. See John G. Blair and Jerusha McCormack, *Comparing Civilizations: China and the West; A Sourcebook* (New York: Global Scholarly Publishing, 2013), CD, 610–13 (hereafter *CCCW* [604 pages] and *CCCW*, CD [1,680 pages; CD issued alongside sourcebook]).

10. Nines are valuable for other reasons: as the highest integer in the number system to the base ten, nines have long been associated with emperors and hence powerful presences.

11. This saying, of course, presumes that only physical hurt is worth considering. Social hurts, especially to people heavily reliant on social media, may prove much more damaging. Most Chinese understood that long before concerns about the effects of social media became an issue in the West.

12. Such ploys may be punished with an announced regime of penalty points, which could ultimately disqualify the abuser from using the Internet legally. Michael Wines, "Crackdown on Chinese Bloggers Who Fight the Censors with Puns," *New York Times*, May 28, 2012.

13. Guy Deutscher, *Through the Language Glass: Why the World Looks Different in Other Languages* (New York: Metropolitan Books, 2010), 234.

14. Guy Deutscher, "Does Your Language Shape How You Think?" *New York Times*, August 26, 2010, accessed March 25, 2013, http://www.nytimes.com/.

15. Richard E. Nisbett, *The Geography of Thought: How Asians and Westerners Think Differently—and Why* (London: Nicholas Brealey, 2003), 150.

16. Nisbett, *Geography of Thought*, 140–41.

17. Qi Wang, "Are Asians Forgetful? Perception, Retention, and Recall in Episodic Remembering," *Cognition* 111 (2009): 123–31. Her earlier research focused on comparing autobiographical memories among Chinese and American children. See Qi Wang, "Culture Effects on Adults' Earliest Childhood Recollection and Self-Description: Implications for the Relation between Memory and the Self," *Journal of Psychology and Social Psychology* 81 (2001): 220–33. *CCCW*, CD, 774–75. From there she observed important differences in the accounts the two groups produced.

18. Gish Jen, *Tiger Writing: Art, Culture, and the Interdependent Self* (Cambridge, MA: Harvard University Press, 2013), 68. Jen usefully reprints two images related to Qi Wang's research that contrast how differently an American and a Chinese person mark episodes in the same narrative text.

19. Gish Jen, *Tiger Writing*, 66.

20. See the section "Why the Chinese Do Not Have Bodies: MWM versus TCM," in chapter 5, "The Energy Unifying the World: *Qì*."

21. For example, recent social science research suggests that the West must be understood in global terms as an outlier that is unlike just about everybody else in the world. See discussion in Part III, "Rethinking the West."

To the Reader

This book is one of a kind. While there are many other books about China, few take today's China on its own terms. *Thinking through China* seeks to do exactly that. By isolating ten key concepts through which Chinese people habitually frame the world, it compares these with the way most of us, as Westerners, think about our own world. The broad range of theoretical concerns that enables cultural comparisons has been assembled in a recent book, *Comparison: Theories, Approaches, Uses*, edited by Rita Felski and Susan Stanford Friedman (Baltimore: Johns Hopkins University Press, 2013). Among the Chinese essays, this observation by Zhang Longxi is particularly welcome: "Since comparison is something we always do anyway, all the talk about whether to compare is but idle talk. The question is not whether, but how; it is a matter of the relevance or reasonableness of the comparison we make, and of its consequences and implications."[1] Such bridging work allows those who have no deep or detailed knowledge of China—but know it is important—to obtain a working knowledge of how Chinese people tend to think. It helps explain, in other words, what is uniquely Chinese about China.

In undertaking this work, we rely on the observations and analyses of many other scholars to illuminate our own extensive experience of China. Over the last decade and more, teaching Western Civilization at some of its most prestigious universities, we discovered that the most effective method was to begin where the students begin: with their home culture. This task, however, proved difficult. For many reasons, not least the long-term effects of the Cultural Revolution, Chinese students tend to be unfamiliar with their own cultural grounding. Thus began an adventure, seeking to reconstruct both civilizations through key readings in cognate domains. Its eventual outcome is a sourcebook of representative readings, now going into its fourth edition in China and its first in the United States, under the title *Comparing Civilizations: China and the West.*[2] That opus provides the underpinning for many of the comparisons made here, as well as amplifying their larger implications.

Although comprehensive, as a guide to how Chinese culture has evolved, that book proved too big and heavy to help those embarking on Chinese adventures. Here we condense it into something more accessible—not only more compact but also more richly composite, as one that weaves our own experience into its web of key concepts. The result we trust to be lively, relevant, and useful for those seeking to understand a China more deeply than merely informational guides can offer.

METHODOLOGY AND LIMITATIONS

As this book is one of a kind, there are bound to be questions about its methods. To divide up any civilization into ten concepts, however central, may seem, on the face of it, dangerously arbitrary.[3] Yet, despite appearances, there are cogent reasons behind our choices. The number ten is useful, as both civilizations discovered long ago in using decimal systems. Ten may be taken as a basis for both simple and very complex calculations and, in doing so, serve to explore concepts that are both basic and comprehensive. Taken one by one, these ten concepts exemplify key elements in a worldview. Joined with others, with which they are often coextensive, these concepts gain cumulative resonance as well as compounded value. Thus the virtues of "respect for elders" or *xiao* enforces hierarchies in both family and state as well as grounding the significance of worldviews, such as the Confucian, which crucially depend on acknowledging the full presence of other persons.

But if the number ten is seen as both core and comprehensive, there will still be disagreements on which concepts should be chosen as central. Here everyone who knows something about China will want to add, subtract, or substitute different categories. This poses a dilemma: if proliferating concepts risks thinness and superficiality, then severely limiting their number could easily become reductive. In the end, what is crucial about these ten concepts is that they cover many, if not all, of the issues that are significant in establishing for Western readers the cultural differences that define today's China. Hence we see the limit of ten key words as offering a viable compromise.

Further contention might involve just how these concepts are organized. For instance, while we lodge *yin* and *yang* under *qi* as the two modes of expression of its vital energy, we acknowledge that they also inevitably relate to the more comprehensive category of *dao*. Other key categories, such as that for *becoming human* or *ren* (仁), are so fundamental that they tend to emerge almost everywhere. In this regard, we ask for the reader's patience; Chinese concepts don't respond to the kind of rigid circumscription of Western definitions; thus overlap—and with it repetition—may sometimes occur as a result of the complex exchanges initiated by any one designated Chinese word.

Another point of contention will certainly also involve definitions: what is this "China," and what is the "West" with which it is to be compared? As asserted in the introduction, China can be a slippery notion as it involves both a nation-state and a civilization, and not just any civilization but one that is, in its core values and practices, the most long-standing in human history. For this reason, the use of "China" often covers many values (such as *xiao*) that are enjoined in texts centuries old—yet in practice may still be observed today. Because these practices also became important within China's sphere of historical influence (as in Japan, Korea, Vietnam, or Singapore) we define them as "Chinese," though not necessarily as limited to the nation-state that now defines itself as China. Where only the nation-state is involved, we focus our observations on the PRC or the People's Republic of China.

Arguably the use of "the West" might be seen as more problematic. At the core of this usage is Euro-America, with the United States, in terms of the comparative spectrum, usually supplying extreme versions of what it means to be "Western." As the point of the book is to define what is Chinese about China, to involve Russia, the Middle East, Africa, or India would complicate the issues fatally. But that having been said, the fault lines are not always so very clear. Italian families, for instance, in many ways resemble the Chinese more closely than the American. In both civilizations, one can find countercultures (such as the Romantic Movement in the West) that are native but cognate to the other civilization—or have actually been adapted from the other, as with the American discoveries of Zen Buddhism after 1945 or of Mao Zedong's *Little Red Book* in the 1960s. Sometimes even these become significant influences in the adopting culture, as in the wholesale praise of Western models of science and democracy widespread in early postimperial China.

"WHO HAS A RIGHT TO SPEAK ABOUT CHINA?"

Perhaps the strongest objection to this whole enterprise—one we have encountered before—is that we are not China "specialists": by which is meant philologically grounded sinologists. Scholars such as Marcel Granet, Angus Graham, Joseph Needham, Benjamin Schwartz, François Jullien, Roger Ames, or Tu Weiming (among many others) have generated interpretive studies of Chinese culture more profound than this present enterprise. Instead this book moves beyond such specialized work—which so often confines itself to one domain or another—to give a comprehensive insight into the kind of thinking that underlies all of them, thereby making what has been called "cultural China" accessible in a way not always possible for more linguistically sophisticated experts.

The phrase "cultural China" belongs to Tu Weiming, a scholar and distinguished neo-Confucian thinker. At a recent conference on comparative cultural studies, he posed the question, "Who has a right to speak about China?" Anyone, Tu Weiming responded, with an interest in China and who is prepared to learn about and from its civilization.[4] Clearly this is a battle cry for a new kind of conversation, one that liberates Chinese studies from specialized, particularistic domains into an informed interrogation of what it means, in fact, to be Chinese. Given that academia is colonized by specialists, many of its China experts may in fact recoil from the kinds of generalizations being made in this book. Just as many, we believe, will welcome the effort to get past our native habit of shoehorning China into Western categories or subdividing it to fit into narrowly defined sinological disciplines. Our goal is to take China as a whole way of life and on its own terms. Inevitably, specialist scholars will debate the details. Perhaps none will endorse this venture wholeheartedly. But we consider this book a significant contribution to the field of Chinese studies if only as a catalyst for what has become a most necessary conversation, both within the Western academy and between those who wish to encounter China through its own way of thinking.

That conversation is necessary because, at present, despite much commentary, there is little understanding in the West of how Chinese people perceive the world. Worse, there are not even the right conditions for creating such understanding, as the West has traditionally insisted that its ways of conceiving of the world are the only correct ones—and that others need Western concepts because their own thinking is underdeveloped or simply erroneous. Recent history suggests otherwise. Where the rest of the world has adopted Western thinking—for instance, in an almost exclusive emphasis on economic growth—the results, now being played out in such countries as China, are verging on the disastrous. Due to the breakneck speed of its economic expansion, much of China's soil, air, and water are heavily polluted. In other words, translating the "American Dream" into Xi Jinping's mantra of the "Chinese Dream" is resulting in a daily nightmare for its citizens, who cannot—much of the time— confidently drink the water, comfortably breathe the air, or trust the food they eat.[5]

Yet we believe that each civilization has the resources to counter this latest, most urgent challenge to the way we live now. The West has many assets—financial, technological, and scientific—to counter its own escalating environmental problems. But it suffers from a powerful humility deficit. Lacking openness to the warnings of its climate scientists, how can it encourage China to tackle its own escalating problems? Or how can it comprehend that, in our newly globalized world, no crisis is any longer merely national? It is within this context that we seek, through the medium of this book, to propose a new kind of solidarity: one based on the recognition that ultimately, although we have radically different perspectives, we are neither Western nor Chinese but simply human. The coming era is so stark that our choices of how to conduct our lives will determine how—or even whether—future generations in any given part of the world can, or even will, continue to survive.

EDITORIAL NOTES

Chinese words are consistently given in *pinyin*, at present the most common world-available system for representing Mandarin sounds in Roman letters.

"Party" is always capitalized as a proper noun. As the only established party in power, it calls for the definite article. In accordance with general Western convention, we refer to the Chinese Communist Party by its acronym of CCP.

In the endnotes to each chapter, *CCW* is used as an abbreviation for *Comparing Civilizations: China and the West*, the American edition of our sourcebook (formerly published only in China by Fudan University Press). This collection of selected readings from Chinese and Western civilizations over the last three thousand years or so provides a ready repository of evidence for many of our arguments and observations. For details on *CCW*, see listing on Amazon.com or http://www.gsp-on line.org/index.php?page=shop.product_details&category_id=10&flypage=flypage .tpl&product_id=116&option=com_virtuemart&Itemid=64&vmcchk=1&Ite mid=64.

NOTES

1. From his chapter "Crossroads, Distant Killing, and Translation: On the Ethics and Politics of Comparison," in *Comparison: Theories, Approaches, Uses*, ed. by Rita Felski and Susan Stanford Friedman, 46–63 (Baltimore: Johns Hopkins University Press, 2013), 51.

2. References to this publication appear in the notes under *CCW*.

3. The working title of this book, originally *China in Ten Words*, was changed after the publication of the Yu Hua book under that title in 2012.

4. In Tu Weiming's words, "Cultural China includes an increasing number of people, who are connected with China neither by birth, nor by marriage, so they are foreigners. When I first proposed that, some people in Hong Kong were very puzzled. But now everybody accepts it, because if you talk about China as a culture, those people who study China, who analyze China, earn the right to talk about China. Sinologists to be sure: they are more qualified to talk about China than the overwhelming majority of Chinese people because they have studied. Culture is an attainment, is an achievement; culture is not naturally born, but we have to learn the language, learn the values, learn the basic ideas, to be a member of the culture tradition." First conference of the International Association for the Comparative Study of China and the West, Peking University, July 12, 2013.

5. Elizabeth Economy assembles a devastating overview of environmental China's problems in "Environmental Governance in China: State Control to Crisis Management," *Daedalus* 143, no. 2 (Spring 2014): 185–87.

I

WHAT MAKES CHINA CHINESE?

Ten Key Words

孝

Xiào

1

Binding Families

Xiào 孝

Families are not democracies.

—A Harvard professor on becoming a parent

As visiting professors in one of the elite universities in China, we had much to learn. Inadvertently one of our brightest students gave us a master class. Having left a short message by e-mail that he had won a scholarship to graduate school at Cambridge University (based partly on our recommendation), he came by our campus apartment a few days later. On arrival, he brought an abrupt halt to our congratulations. "My parents do not want me to go to Cambridge," he said flatly.

"But your parents must be very proud of you," we countered, trying to respond in a Chinese register. "You would bring great honor to the family." "They are very proud of me," he replied rather stiffly, "so they want me to join the Foreign Ministry. You see, they both have high positions, one in the government, the other in the Party." There was a pause. "I took the necessary exams a few months ago. I have just learned that I have passed them. So now I must refuse the offer from Cambridge."

"But that's your dream," we objected—in pure disbelief.

"I'm sorry," he said. Then he looked at us sorrowfully, as if we were exceptionally slow students. "This is what it means to be Chinese."

Can one imagine such a compliant response from a young man in the West? There, to be so dictated to by one's parents would be seen as a gross insult to one's growing independence: at best, humiliating; at worst, threatening to one's personal autonomy. Although other factors might be at work, clearly something applies here that is off the scale of Western experience, at least in living memory. How does one explain such a conversation to people in the West today?

The key is a Chinese word, *xiao*, for which there is no adequate equivalent in English. While the dictionaries give a standard translation as "filial piety," neither of those words carries much resonance in the Western world today. A better translation is "family reverence," used by Roger Ames and Henry Rosemont Jr. in their translation of the *Xiaojing* (the classic from more than two thousand years ago devoted to promoting *xiao* practices).[1] Perhaps the most contemporary understanding is offered by a close Chinese colleague who says that, for her, *xiao* means nothing less than "the duty of love" toward one's parents (and grandparents).

In many ways this locution is superior to "reverence," which carries connotations that do not fit well in a world where religion, as a category, is problematic.[2] In China, the vast majority does not believe in a creator-god. Instead children understand their parents to be the origin of the gift of life. Understandably, then, all the gratitude that a Western Christian might direct to God is directed instead to those parents and, more indirectly, to the ancestors who, in turn, gave life to them. What surprises most Western observers is how persistently this gratitude translates into lifelong obligations.

Given this context, in China one is *always* a child—and a child devoted to its parents. The Western tradition is different. Its standard, taken from the Ten Commandments, is to "honor your father and your mother." In comparison to Chinese expectations, this injunction pales. In the West, explicitly in both the Old and the New Testaments, young people who marry are enjoined to cling to each other, leaving their parents behind.[3] At that point if not before, they are assumed to have become adults: their focus is now on their new family and future offspring. As we often have to explain to our Chinese colleagues (concerned that we were far away from elderly parents), for Westerners, the general idea is to pass parental love on or down to the next generation, not to pay it back to the one preceding.

XIAO IN WESTERN TRADITION

Yet there was a time in the West when such a demonstration of duty toward parents was held up as a cultural ideal. In Chinese, the written character for *xiao* (孝) uses the sign for "elder" sitting on top of the sign for "younger." Mirroring exactly the verticality of that written character is the Bernini sculpture (1618–1619) of "pious Aeneas" carrying his father away from burning Troy.

"Pius Aeneas" was the Latin phrase Virgil used in the *Aeneid*, the foundation story of Roman Civilization—and indeed our own.[4] For centuries, the image of the warrior Aeneas—with his aged father on his shoulders (in turn carrying the household gods, the *lares* and *penates*, along with an urn of ancestral ashes) with his young son clinging to his tunic—provided a model to the West of what it meant to be a man as well as a hero. For centuries schoolboys memorized the *Aeneid* as moral preparation for service to the Roman and, later, to the British Empire. Yet attempting to explain the resonances of *xiao* indicates just how outmoded this value is in today's West.

The Chinese character for *xiao*, with the sign for elder above, younger below.

Bernini statue (1618–1619) of Aeneas with his father and son fleeing burning Troy. *Source:* Special Collections, Fine Arts Library, Harvard University.

How many children do we describe as "pious" or "filial"? How many of our children do we enjoin to "reverence" parents? In the West even the word "duty," at least in regard to parental obligation, seems nearly as dead as the dodo. Yet in China, *xiao* might be seen as *the* central core value, even today. The fact that states and schools with very different economic and political systems (such as Hong Kong, Taiwan, and mainland China) all promote *xiao* shows its importance as a value in Chinese culture.

What does this imply?

XIAO AS RECIPROCAL OBLIGATION

As the Chinese character for *xiao* vividly illustrates, the elder is on top and the younger below. The vertical dimension is significant. But how can it be read in relation to actual power structures? Does the elder dominate the child? Or does the child support the elder? Or both?

At first, it may look as if *xiao* enforces a simple top-down hierarchy. Even today, for most Chinese, *xiao* is very often followed by *shun* (顺), meaning "obedient." In the words of one Chinese colleague, "When your parents say something you don't agree with, you do not argue with them. When they ask you to do something, you stand up and do it." Yet, as our student taught us by heading into the Chinese foreign service instead of into graduate school, such deference does not imply a simply robotic obedience to authority. Freely and thoughtfully given, it is the very core of devotion to the parent.

In China this duty of love endures—even if the parents are neglectful or abusive. What that tells us is that *xiao* is unconditional, in force as a value *despite the actions of parents, as long as they shall live and even after their death.* In that event, rituals of solicitude will still persist, for dead parents are never altogether cut off from the living.[5] They continue to be regarded as a resource, to be petitioned on a regular basis. Paper money burned at funerals and annual tomb-sweeping ceremonies in the spring aim to provide for the needs of those who now live in the shadowy realm of spirits. The reasoning is that, if the spirits of the intimate dead are happy, they will help to further the plans and ambitions of the living. But the opposite may apply as well; if the spirits of the dead are unhappy, misfortune may strike their descendants—all the more reason to attend to their well-being after death. Even today the intimate dead—particularly if they achieved public prominence in their lifetime—may be honored by house shrines or private rituals for many years thereafter. It is no coincidence that a secondary meaning for *xiao* is "mourning," as in those practices that continue to demonstrate a child's attachment to parents, even if deceased.

What these practices make clear is that *xiao* is not merely a top-down authoritarian affair enjoined by parents—but a feeling deeply ingrained in all children that parents (and by extension, other elders) should be treated with nothing less than sustained devotion. Nor does it imply blind obedience; texts such as the *Xiaojing* emphasize that if parents do something morally wrong, the child has an obligation to criticize the parents (even texts such as *Dizigui*, meant for young children, make this point).[6] In other words, *xiao* works as much from the bottom up as much as from the top down; the Chinese character allows for both.

From our own perspective, the Chinese concept of *xiao* throws into high relief how confused we in the West can be about what we expect from our children. At minimum, most of us parents insist on "respect." But any such emphasis implies that family relations must, by definition, be hierarchical and therefore more or less authoritarian. To some (such as our Harvard professor cited in the epigraph) this comes as a surprise—particularly where children have been raised within a pervasive discourse of "equality" and individual "rights." But even if enforced, such "respect" in the West is certainly not equivalent to the emotional reciprocities of *xiao*. Few parents in the West would feel it right to enjoin their children to "give back" the unconditional devotion and care they have lavished on them. Nor would Western parents feel it right or fair to impose on their children what in China is an intense, lifelong demonstration of solicitude and obedience.

Yet, over hundreds of years, China has inculcated in its children, from the earliest age, just such injunctions. With lines memorized long before they are understood, the *Three-Character Classic* (*Sanzijing*, 三子经) contains such short, sharp lessons as

> It is not right if a child does not learn [or does not study].
> If the young do not learn, what will happen to them when they are old?
> In its natural state, jade is of no use.
> Someone who has not learned will not know how to live properly.
> While young, one should . . . form close friendships, become engaged with teachers, and learn the proper way to behave in all respects.
> Nine-year-old Xiang knew how to perform household duties.
> Children should be very filial towards their parents.
> Four-year-old Rong gave the best pears to his family.
> One of the first things to know is the proper way for younger people to relate to older people.
> The very first thing to learn is filial duty and fraternal love, then learn other things.[7]

Another classic tool of enculturation is *The Twenty-Four Filial Exemplars* (二十四孝 by Guō Jūjìng 郭居敬, flourished fourteenth century). As a text that has served as popular training in *xiao* for Chinese children for the last seven centuries, it has been out of print only during the thirty years when Mao Zedong dominated China. Many of its parables involve miraculous rewards for extreme filial sacrifices to aid parents, roughly comparable to medieval saints' lives in the West (and like them, designed to impress even the uneducated). Told (like fairy tales in the West) to very young children from a very early age—they are then invoked as models to guide behavior.

As such, these stories offer what Jerome Bruner calls a *template* for the way Chinese people tend to organize their experience[8]—as well as providing a rich source of exemplars from which to draw in making crucial decisions. As models they often illustrate not merely strategies but also the high ideals of Chinese society (such as those dealing with *xiao* loyalties). In Bruner's phrase, such stories provide people with "root metaphors" for the way one makes sense of life—and how to make the best way through it. They would not be seen as "old" and therefore "irrelevant," if only because, in China, history tends to be seen not as linear but as cyclical.[9] So, according to Chinese ways of thinking, any of these classic stories may be called up at any time, depending on the occasion, and would still be seen to apply.

To pick one, an exemplary tale, while it involves no miracles, could never be imagined as credible in the Western world. Here's the story: Lao Laizi's parents, in their nineties, were depressed at how old they were getting. Their son, already

Lao Laizi amuses his aged parents.

seventyish himself, finally thought of a way of distracting them; dressing up as a child, he pranced around pretending to be still a small boy. Amused, his parents were encouraged to think that, if their son could still act so young, they themselves could not be so very old.

The Yuan dynasty text ends with a verse in his honor:

> He cut a comic caper, and played the merry fool,
> The Spring breeze fluttered his flower-drum gown.
> The old folks laughed with toothless glee;
> The sounds of their delight filled the air with joy.[10]

As this example makes clear, *xiao* devotion need not involve material comfort or money but should involve any measures that might improve the parents' sense of well-being. Although this admirable son cannot change his parents' age, he can invent a way of consoling them—even in his own gray-bearded years.

From this perspective, the character for *xiao* may be correctly interpreted as a child supporting an elder—while simultaneously depicting the elder as being "over" the child in terms of authority. Yet such relations are more than a matter of mere authority. Chinese parents habitually do everything they can to further the lives of their children—but not quite in the same spirit of making them comfortable or happy. A famous story that illustrates how *xiao* responsibilities weigh on parents—again from centuries ago—tells how the widowed mother of Mengzi (the Confucian sage whose Latinized name is Mencius[11]) moved house three times so that her young son would have the right environment in which to study. Today Chinese parents may dip deep into hard-won savings to buy an apartment that would establish residence in the district of a prestigious public school, later perhaps to help a son or daughter attend university or to buy their own apartment. Typically their concerns are less with the individual offspring than with the family and its future standing.

Even more seriously, in the absence of a creator-god—or of heaven, hell, and all the related superstructures that Western civilization has invested in—most Chinese see "immortality" as the ability of the family to prolong itself in time, generation after generation. Thus the sacrifices of the present generation are readily justified in the expectation that the next generation will flourish to an unprecedented extent. No wonder the only children resulting from the "one-child policy" of the last thirty years often feel intense pressure to ensure the prolongation of the family. But such pressure is not just recent; more than two thousand years ago, the sage Mengzi already defined the worst sin against *xiao* to be that of not producing an heir.[12] Today any Chinese person tempted *not* to have a child faces enormous pressure—because such a decision would deprive not only the parents but also all of the ancestors of their own prolongation through time.

Thus there is huge anxiety that these precious only children marry while still at childbearing age. The pressure might be less if a sibling already has a child, but the one-child policy dating back to 1979 means that most Chinese under thirty are now only children. There are other anxieties at work. Long before the one-child policy, the felt necessity of having a son led to long-standing traditional arrangements such as polygamy, concubinage, and even adopting or "buying" a boy child.[13] In fact, monogamy is a recent development in Chinese society, instituted early in the People's Republic of China (PRC) by the Marriage Act of 1950 (which also abolished the traditional practices associated with arranged marriages).[14] While nowadays finding a spouse is nominally left to the young people themselves, there are numerous reports of parents placing ads or seeking out "suitable" partners for their one child—often on the pretext that the young people are "too busy" to find one for themselves. By the age of thirty (the age about which Kongzi wrote that he was "established"[15]) young people are normally expected to have married and to be ready to produce the child.[16] Consensus on this matter is so overwhelming that it often appalls Westerners, used to the freedom of choosing when to marry and when to have children, if any. For many, the observance of *xiao* and what it entails is thus an enduring shock for the newcomer to China.

FROM FAMILIES TO CHINESE HIERARCHIES

One reason *xiao* is the most pervasive and enduring value of Chinese civilization is that it applies to more than families. Over many centuries, the family in China has been taken as a model for the larger public sphere. Officially this goes back to the second century BCE when the Emperor Han Wudi established the Confucianist ideal of the family as the core structure of the State. From even before his time, the classic text articulating these values has been the *Xiaojing* (*The Classic of Filial Piety* 孝 經), which remained for many centuries an obligatory text for memorization among children.[17] This text, written in simple language, begins with a character named "Confucius"[18] extrapolating on the radical demands of *xiao*, extending even to the ownership of one's own body:

> Your physical person with its hair and skin are received from your parents. Vigilance in not allowing anything to do injury to your person is where family reverence begins; distinguishing yourself and walking the proper way [*dao*] in the world; raising your name high for posterity and thereby bringing esteem to your father and mother—it is in these things that family reverence finds its consummation.[19]

The social implications of this point are many. Piercing and tattoos, for instance, are regarded as a mutilation of the perfect body given to you by your parents. Today, it also helps to explain popular resistance to organ donation.

If not even one's body belongs to oneself, neither do one's achievements. Instead of personal goals, worldly success is encouraged as a means of honoring one's family. By extension, as the *Xiaojing* also asserts, the "service of parents . . . proceeds to the service of the ruler." This intimate linking of family matters with political and social structures is typical of Chinese holism: the expectation being that, as everything is connected, so the "private" life of individuals and families feeds seamlessly into the "public" life of communities and authority structures. This is sometimes hard for outsiders to grasp, as modern Western thinking enjoins a sharp distinction between the "private" realm of families and "public" governance.[20] Still, even in the West, there are certain exceptions to this way of thinking. In a pioneering essay, George Lakoff analyzes American child-rearing practices in relation to political affiliations. He does so by dividing families today into two sharply distinguished ideal types: the "strict-father" family and the "nurturant-parent" family. As part of their quite distinctive values and lifestyles, Lakoff argues, the former tend to vote for conservative candidates, the latter for progressivists. Could the radical polarization of American politics in recent years confirm the relevance of this analysis?[21] But against this pioneering analysis of political affiliation, even conservatives in the West today would resist what they would see as an intrusion of "family values" into the public domain (except perhaps when they become a campaign slogan, as under Ronald Reagan). While in the West, one can think of one's family as being *against* the world, in China the family is routinely taken as a model *for* the world. While American feminists used to argue that the "personal is political," within the Chinese system, the "political" *is* the "personal."

If some Westerners regard this metaphor as merely sentimental—as when the Chinese speak of the nation as a "big socialist family"—it is exactly that model that allows traditional hierarchies to flourish. As a deeply held value among ordinary

Chinese people, *xiao* provides the Party with a reservoir of popular feeling from which to reinforce deference and even obedience. In other words, the political use of *xiao* is not only top down but also empowered from the bottom up. The Party is adept at requisitioning grassroots sentiment to mobilize its various campaigns. If it were not so, the Party would simply not succeed in imposing order on more than 1.3 billion people. If one sees these practices of deference to those on top as merely an anachronism, a quick look at recent Chinese history will show how persistently they have been reinvented by the Powers That Be.[22]

CHINESE HIERARCHIES VERSUS WESTERN EQUALITY

What Westerners do not always understand about *xiao* may be exemplified by what happened in an earlier attempt to reform the old hierarchies. During the first phase of the PRC under Mao Zedong in the 1950s, its rhetoric of "comrades" and "equality" aggressively aimed to abolish class and gender distinctions. But it did so through propaganda campaigns that boldly extended *xiao* to a new entity: the Party. As one famous revolutionary song decreed: "The Party is a mother. . . . The Party is my family." Thus, in the name of a larger *xiao*, the Party officialized an abolition of class and hierarchy through a violent inverting of them both: with peasants put in control over landlords and all other social classes similarly turned upside down by a new system of official categories privileging peasants and workers.[23]

An even more violent overturning of *xiao* was instituted during the decade of the "Cultural Revolution" (1966–1976), when the young were given encouragement to attack all in authority, including bureaucrats, teachers, and even elders within their own families. How could this happen? By transferring the obligations of *xiao* to the Party, the Chinese Communist Party (CCP) fostered an intense emotional attachment that, by definition, overrode one's loyalties to the actual family. In this way, *xiao* became *zhong* (忠), literally, loyalty to the center. The mass hysteria at news of Mao's death, and the continued veneration of his body (entombed in Tiananmen Square), prolong this metaphor of Party as family with Mao as its venerated ancestor.

Today, many Chinese see the Cultural Revolution as a turning point for China, one that destroyed an important trust within society. Since then, they believe, Chinese society has found no way to recover that trust. What this history illustrates is that the Party neither rose nor flourished in a vacuum. It has built on, some would say exploited, the traditional and deeply held values of *xiao*. Now the old model of *xiao*, which has, after all, worked effectively in China for hundreds of years, is again back in official favor. Once again one hears public statements to the effect that the family should be taken as a model for governance. As, by definition, the family (as our Harvard professor discovered) cannot be a democracy, so the old hierarchies are once again being reinforced. And once again, "Confucius" has been pressed into service.[24] In terms of hierarchy, his authority is used to invoke the traditional five relationships or *five bonds* (*wǔlún* 五倫), metaphorically extending the authority of superiors as ruler to ruled; father to son; husband to wife; elder brother to younger brother; and friend to friend.

Note that *every one* of these relationships necessitates *xiao*, in terms of deference from inferiors and obligations of care from superiors. In China (as the Westerner will discover) escape from hierarchies is almost impossible as, among these five relationships, the only one open to "equality" might be that between friends.[25] Even here, one friend is likely to be older, richer, or more distinguished, thus once again introducing an implicit rank order. It would be noted too that these hierarchies remain dominantly male, and this is still a problem for many women in China—for whom Mao's saying that "women hold up half the sky" may now be repeated only in a tone of irony. Yet, coming from a world in which "equality" is honored (at least rhetorically), it is hard for Westerners to appreciate the extent to which hierarchy permeates all relations in the Chinese world. This is partly because an imported Marxist discourse of "equality" still circulates in China as well. But even when lip service is paid, equality is not operative in most relationships in China; it should be recognized (as the Chinese do) as merely gestural.

There are compensations. If hierarchies imbue every relationship in China, at least within this vertical dimension everyone can find a place, however high or low. In this sense they minimize conflict, whereas horizontal relations, which by definition lack established lines of authority, often invite it.[26] For this reason, even while using the rhetoric of "equality," Chinese people tend to distrust it—and wonder at the Western defense of such a tricky concept. And, indeed, in teaching about Western values, rationalizing equality as it occurs in practice is often difficult, as our students wonder how such a principle can actually play out—within families, between students and teachers, within careers, or in relation to leaders.

REASSESSING EQUALITY

Their questioning has a point. While "equality," along with "freedom," is held fast as a "universal" value in the West, it is of course relatively recent here—and almost always a point of contention. As part of our Enlightenment heritage, the two are often linked and seldom questioned. That is now beginning to change. Late in 2012, Stephen Asma, who teaches philosophy and Buddhism in Chicago, published *Against Fairness*—an exemplary reevaluation of Western traditions. What he seeks to demonstrate are the limitations of our widespread emphasis on egalitarian principles. In his pursuit of this concept into far-flung disciplines, he seeks scientific confirmation for "equality" as a basic human impulse. What he discovers is what we know as a matter of fact: most of the world has myriad ways of playing favorites. It routinely expects us to defend family against all comers. When possible, it deploys nepotism, expecting and respecting the inequalities involved in hierarchies. Asma grounds these widespread practices as biological, citing recent research on how bonding affects newborns, not just in various animal species but also in humans themselves. We humans are thus hardwired, he argues, to recognize intimate family members and to build out from there as our lives become more complex, a view Chinese readers would find not merely congenial but also indisputably "natural."

Not surprisingly, there is a Chinese backstory here. Stephen Asma speaks often of his Chinese wife and their son, whose encounters with schools in diverse parts of the world provide him with sharp examples of Asian meritocracies versus American same-treatment-for-all policies. The family, for instance, lived for a year in a section of Shanghai largely free of foreigners. Asma also taught Buddhism for a time in Cambodia, where he identified not only Chinese but also Indian influences, which again favor the hierarchical. Emerging from such a context, the goal of his argument is clearly not to remake us as Chinese but to show the degree to which egalitarian ideology in the West, particularly in the United States, needs to be contested as inconsistent with a wider and deeper understanding of humanity. Equality of opportunity can never guarantee equality of outcomes. Hierarchies exist in all enterprises, along with their inherent demands for deference or *xiao*—even though they tend, in the Western world, to be obscured or even vigorously denied.

In raising such issues, Asma's thinking seeks to move beyond accepted ideology to identify a more fundamentally human nature. Perhaps nothing less will provide grounds for China and the West to initiate a creative dialogue on what constitutes genuinely moral action.[27]

WILL *XIAO* SURVIVE AS A CENTRAL CHINESE VALUE?

As China's longest-surviving value and its most pervasive, can *xiao* survive the multiple challenges of modernity? All present evidence suggests that *xiao* continues to show remarkable resilience.[28] Almost a century ago, *xiao* came under explicit attack under the first sustained attempt to modernize China, as exemplified by the work of Hu Shi, a major player in the May 4th movement of 1919. Returning to China two years earlier with a new doctorate from Columbia University, Hu Shi published his simplified funeral rituals for the death of his mother. There he explicitly identified the traditionally elaborate *xiao* mourning rituals as outmoded "Confucianist" practices.[29]

More powerful attacks were launched during the revolutionary phase of the PRC led by Mao Zedong. Their target was all backward "feudal" practices, including the traditional practices of *xiao*. In particular, during the Cultural Revolution, young Red Guards were encouraged to turn in their parents if they lacked revolutionary enthusiasm. The fact that some did so shows the short-term efficacy of Mao's campaign to overturn clan-based *xiao* through a rhetoric of larger loyalty to the Party. In that sense, one might argue that the Party's redirection of *xiao* fueled the Cultural Revolution. That linkage between Party and family, however, is in many ways wearing thin. As former Red Guards reach retirement age, confessions and self-condemnations abound. Today, although one still meets people who refer to the Party as their "family," *xiao* has contracted for most people to actual blood relations—enhanced by that larger set of relations defined as one's network or *guanxi*.[30]

Within this context, *xiao* endures remarkably well, still widely acknowledged as a touchstone for continuity within Chinese life. Nevertheless, ongoing modernity continues to pose significant challenges to this most enduring of Chinese values. Where is *xiao* most severely tested today? Most strenuously in the countryside as young people, especially young women, leave home to work in the burgeoning coastal factories in such cities as Shenzhen (near Hong Kong) or Dongguan (near Guangzhou).[31] In her book *Factory Girls*, Leslie T. Chang reveals much about these young women, who typically leave home in their late teens.[32] Obtaining factory jobs, they now have, for the first time in their lives, access to cash income. They work long hours, often to the point of exhaustion, but they have salaries. After minimal living expenses and sending some home, the little that is left still gives them a taste for independent living. While some return home after a time—to marry mates chosen by or at least approved by the family—many resist returning more often than for Spring Festival time at the Chinese New Year. Some have even been known to rent a boyfriend to accompany them home for those few days as a way of fending off *xiao* pressures to marry.

Yet, despite this break with tradition, there is not much encouragement in Chinese culture for such young women to become independent individuals as understood in the West. Having left home, these young women still look outside themselves for substitute parental advice. They are ready consumers, for instance, of self-help magazines and books. As Peter Hessler recounts in *Oracle Bones*, many look for advice to late-evening radio broadcasts by and for young women like themselves.[33] A common question is whether or not it is okay to live with someone without being married.

In the long run most of these young women will no doubt marry—a man of their own choice—and they will stay in the cities. The open question for the future is how they will raise their one child. Having escaped the direct generation-to-generation transmission of *xiao*, will they then try to enforce it as parents? Certainly for rural families the factory life opens a breach in Chinese continuity that is unprecedented. But if the young people become typical urban parents, they will join the upwardly mobile urban families around them—who regard *xiao* practice as necessary and inevitable in raising the precious only child.

IN THE COUNTRYSIDE

As Leslie Chang's book on factory girls suggests, *xiao* as a presumptive underlying value may be severely tested among the families of those who leave the rural half of the population to go to the cities, not only single girls but also married men in large numbers. In little more than fifty years, China has moved from a largely rural to a dominantly urbanized country.[34] Considering that the same transition took the West on average about two hundred years, it is not surprising that this, the biggest peaceful migration perhaps in human history, has a significant (if largely undocumented) impact on Chinese families.[35]

One reason it remains largely undocumented is that the migrants are often classified—and treated—as if they were only temporary workers. They are the source of China's cheapest labor, coming from rural areas to build China's cities and roads, work in the shops, and mind the children. Although the *hukou* (or official residency permits) operate differently in different cities, migrant workers are in many cases not offered all the benefits of city living (such as free education or health care that would accompany permanent residence there). At the same time, they leave their families behind them; if both husband and wife emigrate to the cities to find work, they abandon their children to be raised by their own parents. Once a year, during the Spring Festival, they will be expected to return, with money and gifts and tales of their new life elsewhere. Whether or not the folks back home are coping tends to vary a great deal.

Perhaps it is not surprising then that the highest rates of suicide in China are among rural women—double the rates common in Western countries. Why? They are isolated, often carrying the entire responsibility for raising children as well as looking after elderly parents. They have little or no status in the community. They rarely see their husbands if the latter have headed off to seek jobs in the city. They have little money. Yet one of the most widespread reasons for rural women to commit suicide is not lack of material support but lack of something much more intangible and important: *respect*, the *xiao* that anticipates needs before they are articulated. One recent study of suicide cites a rural woman who pinpoints the key issue: "I am unlike other parents who directly ask money from their children. I only want them to give me money voluntarily. You know, the money I ask from them is different from the money they give me."[36] As the author points out, this sensitivity echoes across 2,500 years Kongzi's dictum that "those today who are filial are considered so because they are able to provide for their parents. But even dogs and horses are given that much care. If you do not respect your parents, what is the difference?"[37]

Thus *xiao* is intimately bound up with social stability, perhaps the highest priority for the Party. But *xiao* is a value of the encultured heart and thus not amenable to the force of law. Nonetheless recent legislation stipulates that elderly people now have a legal right to be looked after "physically and mentally" by their children.[38] How realistic is its implementation? China at present is dealing with the problems of a growing elderly population (an eighth of its population is now over the age of sixty, with more than half of those living alone). As young people, along with older but able-bodied adults, abandon their villages for work in cities, migration and work pressures are fracturing family ties. Rural villages have often been left to the old people, to struggle along on minimal pensions, their health deteriorating, without money for medical care or even, at times, food. Now without wider family support, whether financial or emotional, these old people feel abandoned in a world whose values they no longer recognize, lamenting the collapse of that *xiao* deference that they would, in former times, have normally expected from their offspring.

From the perspective of their migrant-worker children, *xiao* attention is simply no longer practical in the world they live in today. Decades of China's one-child policy have left fewer workers supporting more and more elderly relatives. Distances are long, salaries and time off work are not sufficient to make long journeys back. Considering the new law, one report (with typical Chinese wisdom) concludes, "It would be better to strengthen moral education than to force people to do something legally."[39] A more cynical response comes from those who accuse the Party of attacking the traditional values of *xiao* (except where it applies to Party loyalty) while at the same time shirking their duties to look after the most vulnerable: those in rural areas, particularly the sick and the elderly.[40] Is this another example of the State reconfiguring Confucian values for its own purposes? Or worse, perhaps it is another sign that these traditional values, as legislating for them might imply, are fading for the present generation of China's migrating offspring.

Yet insofar as most of today's factory girls will in time become tomorrow's urban mothers, they will be under great pressure to impose on their children many of the *xiao* disciplines they experienced in their own rural childhoods. If they wish their child to be able to compete, the compliances implicit in *xiao* must be rigorously enforced.

TYPICAL URBAN FAMILIES TODAY

With urban families, the problems tend to be different. Many observers of such families today complain about "little emperors": spoiled only children who appear to dominate their elders. In satirical exaggerations this precious only child, in a classic reversal of *xiao*, may be seen as central to his or her elders.

There is a reason behind their central status. These single children carry more cultural weight than their counterparts in the West; they are, after all, the only vehicle

Yang Liu, "The Child." *Source:* Yang Liu, *Ost trifft West* [East meets West], 10th ed. (Mainz, Germany: Hermann Schmidt Verlag, 2014). Used by permission.

for the "immortality" or prolongation of their families through time. Families such as these are thus caught up in a 4-2-1 pattern: the single child becoming the primary focus of all the hopes and fears of two parents and up to four grandparents. In China, these grandparents also have a special status. Often the one child is turned over to the grandparents to raise while both parents work. As the child's earliest, most intimate caregivers, the grandmothers in particular serve an important role in transmitting traditional values, most particularly those of *xiao*. One might even wonder if a key to the remarkable continuity of Chinese civilization might be due to this widely accepted child-rearing practice.

Once these children reach school age, however, heavy expectations descend. Early schooling in China claims as its primary goal that of "cultivating good habits," which means the spoiled "little emperors" who arrive expecting to be the center of attention "must learn to observe rules and regulations, be polite to teachers, follow rules in games, and think about others." That is, they must learn to live collectively, according to a society that continues to require that children be courteous and polite, respect their parents and elders, and treat their friends kindly. Thus "training children to observe these rules and behave accordingly is a major task at day-care centers" as well as for the early years at school.[41]

The importance of this key intervention in early childhood cannot be overstated. Of its significance, none is so adamant as Lucian Pye, unique among China experts in tracing back to childhood what he sees as the psychological roots of its political ethos.[42] "The secret of the survivability of Chinese culture," he writes, "lies in the intense self-consciousness of the socialization process by which young Chinese are brought up by their families and guardians. Little is left to chance as Chinese children are taught correct behavior and the importance of loyalty to the group."[43] In locating such continuities between family and public structures, Pye stresses how, after a short period of intense indulgence, relentless suppression of impulses toward aggression or sexuality has often had dramatic consequences. These are played out, as he analyzes them, in China's alternation between periods of stoic endurance and unmitigated brutality, such as those forces unleashed in the Cultural Revolution.

But school is only one marker for this period of intense socialization. Chinese elders understand their crucial role in civilizing their child. Once they are at school, parents at home do not see their role as to indulge, compensate, or comfort the children for the rigors of their new regime but to continue it: knowing that, if their children are to aspire to white-collar status, their lives must be tightly controlled. Thus they load the hours outside of school with extra activities or classes designed to improve chances for higher education, which is seen as the key to rising in the world.[44] In May 2006, *Beijing This Month* magazine suggested that Chinese parents think of two models for educating their child: "Force-feeding a duck" (*tiányā* 填鸭) or "letting a sheep eat freely in a pasture" (*fàngyáng* 放羊).[45] The latter may suffice in the West—but not for good parenting Chinese style. In most urban families the "force-feeding" tendency is enforced: children who distinguish themselves bring honor to their family as a whole (a dominant theme in the *Three-Character Classic*). Inversely, children who perform poorly disgrace their family as a whole. Under such pressures, Chinese schoolchildren tend to devote to schoolwork about twice the hours per week as their Western counterparts.[46] Nonetheless, as a concession, some traditional acquisitions, such as memorizing classic texts or mastering Chinese calligraphy, may well be left aside in favor of "modern" skills such as extra English lessons or playing the piano or violin. In all this, the authority of parents remains central: Chinese parents tend to be very directive, allowing little if any time for casual play or wider, undirected experimentation.

Today, tiger motherhood is characteristic of most of China's upwardly mobile urban classes. Although not unknown in the West, when it does surface, such exceptionally strict Chinese-style parenting tends to be seen as shocking. In *Battle Hymn of the Tiger Mother*, Amy Chua lists all the diversions (TV, playdates, sleepovers, school plays, etc.) that she as a Chinese American mother banned for her two daughters, accusing many American parents of simply being "lazy."[47] The book roused huge controversy in the media, dramatizing as it does central questions about parenting styles in the two cultures—clearly very different in most cases. In Western terms, the fun part of Chinese childhood is short, surviving only sporadically after schooling begins at age four or five.[48] It seems true that Chinese methods can result in extraordinary performances—but often at the expense of creativity, if not also of what most Westerners value as their idea of childhood.[49]

XIAO IN COMPARATIVE CULTURAL CONTEXTS

Meanwhile, many Chinese adults deplore what they see as a loss of *xiao* among the younger generation. They are no doubt correct to do so, based on their own experience of growing up some decades ago.[50] Newspapers and other popular media recount again and again the stories of unfilial sons or faithless daughters or abandoned elderly parents. But these stories retain news value precisely because they violate the ongoing expectations of most Chinese people.[51] Most such stories would not be considered newsworthy in the West. There, by and large, children are expected to pursue their own self-interest, though in all Western countries individuals alive today can recall a time when respect or even fear of parents was much stronger than today.

By comparison with the evolution of these dominant Western practices, in China *xiao* as deference and *shun* as obligation have so far survived recent challenges with remarkable persistence. There have been unfilial children in every Chinese generation, and laments on the subject abound in Chinese writing. Even so, the expectation of filial deference persists. From such a perspective, one can still say with confidence that *xiao* remains the primary bonding force of its society—a crucial factor in maintaining China as the oldest continuous civilization in our world today.

NOTES

1. Roger T. Ames and Henry Rosemont Jr., *The Chinese Classic of Family Reverence: A Philosophical Translation of the* Xiaojing (Honolulu: University of Hawaii Press, 2009), 105.

2. See chapter 11, "Question One: Christianity?"

3. See Genesis 2:24 and Mark 10:7.

4. The rich resonance of Virgil's story throughout Western civilization to date is well traced by Richard A. Waswo in *The Founding Legend of Western Civilization: From Virgil to Vietnam* (Middletown, CT: Wesleyan University Press, 1997).

5. While Roman Catholics may still pray for their ancestors, hoping to reduce their years in Purgatory, the difference is that the Chinese pray directly to the ancestors themselves, offering them symbolic comforts such as money for the afterlife and asking help for those of the family still living.

6. For the *Xiaojing*, see *CCCW*, 61, 119–20. *Dizigui* (弟子规, *Standards for Being a Good Pupil and Child*) was written during the reign of the Kangxi emperor (reigned 1661–1722) by Li Yuxiu. Strictly Confucianist, it emphasizes the basic requisites for being a good person and guidelines for living in harmony with others. Like the other children's text quoted in the text, the *Sanzijing* (the *Three-Character Classic*) the *Dizigui* is written in simplified three-character verses.

7. These are the dominant themes in the *Sanzijing* (三子经), a Song dynasty text from a thousand years ago that has been reintroduced in Chinese elementary schools in recent years. Excerpts from the *Sanzijing* appear in *CCCW*, 47–49, with the original Mandarin in *CCCW*, CD, 63–65.

8. Jerome Bruner, *Making Stories: Law, Literature, Life* (Cambridge, MA: Harvard University Press, 2002), 7, 34–35, 60. See also Paul A. Cohen, "Conclusion: Cross-Cultural Perspectives," in *Speaking to History: The Story of King Goujian in Twentieth-Century China*, 228–40 (Berkeley: University of California Press, 2008). In this book, Paul Cohen shows how the ancient story of King Goujian, a fifth-century BCE monarch, spoke powerfully to the Chinese during China's turbulent twentieth century. In doing so, Cohen explores on a more general level why such stories often remain sealed up within a culture, unknown to outsiders. Labeling this phenomenon "insider cultural knowledge," Cohen inquires why, at certain moments in their collective lives, the Chinese have returned repeatedly to a story from twenty-five centuries ago.

9. See the section "Organizing *Yi*: History in China and the West," in chapter 6, "Chameleon Reality: *Yi*."

10. Guo Jujing, *The Twenty-Four Paragons of Filial Piety*, accessed November 24, 2012, http://www.rice.edu/.

11. Mengzi was the second classical sage to be accorded a Latinate name by the Jesuit missionaries headed by Matteo Ricci in the late Ming dynasty. As in the case of Kongzi, they wanted a name like Mencius to sound familiar enough that it could help them assimilate the classical Chinese tradition to the Catholicism they were preaching. This missionary movement is commented on in more detail in chapter 11, "Question One: Christianity?"

12. More precisely, Mengzi was calling for sons, articulating the enduring Chinese preference for male offspring that underlies today's sex ratio problem cited below.

13. The imbalanced sex ratio at birth is an underlying problem for China as recent surveys report that there may be as many as 119 male births for every 100 live female births. See *CCCW*, 187.

14. See the 1950 marriage law, one of the first laws passed by the newly independent PRC. *CCCW*, 175–78.

15. Roger T. Ames and Henry Rosemont Jr., trans., *The Analects of Confucius: A Philosophical Translation* (New York: Ballantine, 1998), 2.4, in *CCCW*, 40.

16. Despite the fact that homosexuality was decriminalized in the PRC as of 1997 and removed from the official list of mental illnesses in 2001, everyone in a Chinese family recognizes that, in this context, a gay child is a disaster. Hence the usual response is to go into denial. Often the gay son or daughter marries—and produces the one child—before either divorcing or perhaps reaching some kind of understanding with his or her partner about future arrangements. In any case, being gay is still largely an underground activity in today's PRC, leading to the kinds of dilemmas explored in the film *The Wedding Banquet* (1993) directed by Ang Lee; this film was responsible for similar explorations—this time within a Western context—in his *Brokeback Mountain* (2005).

17. *CCCW*, 61, 119–20. See note 6 above.

18. This book maintains a distinction between Kongzi and Confucius, taking advantage of the existence of his Latin name, as bestowed by Jesuit missionaries who arrived in China in the late sixteenth century. In this text "Kongzi" refers to the historical sage and to writings directly attributed to him, basically the *Analects*. "Confucius" (or "Confucianist") applies to writings or campaigns that try to exploit his status to promote the goals that became important later and in other contexts.

19. Ames and Rosemont, *Chinese Classic*, 105. This injunction caused particular problems in the days of eunuchs who as boys were castrated to fit them for service in the Imperial Palace. Out of respect to their parents, their severed body parts were preserved in mercury to be buried alongside their bodies when the time came.

20. Of course, in this new era of intrusive media, the line between private and public conduct has become increasingly blurred, especially in the case of prominent figures who, like Princess Diana or President Clinton, have become celebrities.

21. George Lakoff was warmly received for an extended lecture series in Beijing in 2004, partly because his insights fit well with Chinese views on families as models. See his *Ten Lectures in Cognitive Linguistics* (Beijing: Beihang Linguistics Lecture Series, 2004), 176–83. *CCCW*, 161–65.

22. This supremely vague designation for top leaders seems especially appropriate to the Chinese world where "government" is diffusely defined and where crucial decisions are made behind closed doors under ill-defined complexities of influence.

23. Early in the PRC earlier hierarchies were "revolutionized" by simply inverting their categories. See *CCCW*, CD, 1389–91.

24. The attempt to exploit Confucianist models for contemporary influence is examined in some detail in chapter 8, "Thinking in Harmony: *Hé*."

25. The trust implicit among friends as equals, often cemented among classmates, can be exemplified by the 2007 suicide of Zhang Shuhong. The owner of a toy factory, he found that his exports were recalled due to being contaminated with lead paint, leading to ruination. The paint, wrongly labeled as lead free, had been supplied by the factory of his classmate and best friend. This trust had been fatally betrayed. "Chinese Toy Factory Boss Commits Suicide over Lead Paint Scandal," *Guardian*, August 13, 2007, accessed February 4, 2013, http://www.guardian.co.uk/.

26. The most articulate justification for Chinese hierarchies comes from Xunzi late in the Warring States Period during the third century BCE. See *CCCW*, 406–8.

27. Stanley Fish has already signed on as an admirer of someone not afraid to acknowledge the importance of in-group connections for us all. "Favoritism Is Good," Opinionator, *New York Times*, January 7, 2013, accessed March 24, 2013, http://opinionator.blogs.nytimes .com/.

28. Multiple aspects of the survival value of *xiao* are treated in the essays assembled in *Filial Piety: Practice and Discourse in Contemporary East Asia*, ed. Charlotte Ikels (Stanford, CA: Stanford University Press, 2004). This book confirms that, at least up to the end of the 1990s, despite a loosening of bonds, *xiao* continues as a dominant influence in most Chinese families.

29. *CCCW*, 165–70. Ironically Hu Shi called for less ritual but more sincerity, thereby reinforcing one of Kongzi's original concerns. In the Chinese world it is harder to avoid Confucianist models than one might think.

30. See chapter 3, "The People Network: *Guānxi*."

31. A different kind of testing occurs when both parents leave the countryside seeking work in cities, leaving children in the charge of grandparents who may or may not be able to maintain discipline. See the next section in this chapter, "In the Countryside."

32. Leslie T. Chang, *Factory Girls: Voices from the Heart of Modern China* (New York: Spiegel and Grau, 2008).

33. Peter Hessler, "At Night You're Not Lonely," in *Oracle Bones*, 149–68 (New York: HarperCollins, 2006).

34. Depending on how urban centers are defined, it is estimated that 51.2 percent of China's population lives in cities as of 2011; this should be compared to the figure of 26 percent for 1990.

35. For an intimate account of the lives of these migrant workers, see Michelle Dammon Loyalka, *Eating Bitterness: Stories from the Front Lines of China's Great Urban Migration* (Berkeley: University of California Press, 2012).

36. Wu Fei, "Suicide: A Modern Problem in China," in *Deep China: The Moral Life of the Person; What Anthropology and Psychiatry Tell Us about China Today*, by Arthur Kleinman et al., 213–36 (Berkeley: University of California Press, 2011), 222.

37. Ames and Rosemont, *Analects*, 2.7, in *CCCW*, 131.

38. One editorial for the *South China Morning Post* argues that the "Tradition of Filial Piety Needs the Force of Law" (July 2, 2013) on the grounds that "society is changing fast on the mainland—so fast that laws are needed to protect age-old traditions. The coming into force on Monday of a legal requirement for children to visit and take care of elderly parents shows just how far culture has shifted. But as much as the move is about preserving family values, it is also a necessity for a nation that is quickly aging while still developing. Putting it in place is a timely and welcome decision."

39. "China Law to Make Children Visit Parents," *BBC News*, January 6, 2011, accessed April 8, 2015, http://www.bbc.co.uk/.

40. A piece by Yu Hua for the *New York Times* (July 7, 2013), "When Filial Piety Is the Law," tells the story of how he read, as a young child, a smuggled copy of the Confucianist classic, *Twenty-Four Paragons of Filial Piety*, proscribed during the Cultural Revolution. As he writes, "China's imperial dynasties stressed the importance of being loyal to one's ruler and country and dutiful to one's parents, but when the 'Paragons' was banned, it meant that, of loyalty and filial piety, only loyalty remained—loyalty to the Communist Party. While the Communist Party now promotes filial piety, it ignores its own history of suppressing it and blames individual behavior for the breakdown of ethical norms, then comes out with a ridiculous legal clause as it fudges its own responsibility as the Party in power for the last 63 years."

41. Lee C. Lee, "Day Care in the People's Republic of China," in *Child Care in Context: Cross-Cultural Perspectives*, ed. Michael E. Lamb, Kathleen J. Sternberg, Carl-Philip Hwang, and Anders G. Broberg, 355–92 (Hillsdale, NJ: Lawrence Erlbaum, 1992), 382–83.

42. Lucian Pye, "The Psychological Roots of China's Opposing Political Cultures," in *The Mandarin and the Cadre: China's Political Cultures*, 36–74 (Ann Arbor: University of Michigan Center for Chinese Studies, 1988).

43. Lucian Pye, preface, in *Mandarin and the Cadre*, x.

44. For a satirical portrait of the pressures on parents, see "Raising a Child in Today's China," *Peoples' Daily Online*, English edition, December 2, 2004, http://en.people.cn/.

45. Linda Schueler, "More Options Than Ever: Educating Your Child in Beijing," *Beijing This Month*, May 23, 2006, accessed August 29, 2011, http://www.btmbeijing.com/.

46. See the 2007 film *Two Million Minutes* for a graphic comparison of representative high school students from India, China, and the United States: *Two Million Minutes* (documentary), directed by Chad Heeter (Arlington, VA: Broken Pencil Productions, 2007), accessed November 24, 2012, http://www.2mminutes.com/. Two million minutes turns out to be the time consumed in a typical four-year secondary-school career.

47. Amy Chua, *Battle Hymn of the Tiger Mother* (New York: Penguin, 2011). This model of child-rearing has already been spelled out long ago in the *Three-Character Classic*: "Hard work pays off; there is no positive result from play. Guard against this waste! Do your utmost to better yourself." *CCCW*, 49.

48. Modern China has not experienced the upward revaluing of childhood that began with eighteenth-century Romanticism in the West and continues in large measure today. *CCCW*, CD, 1075–76.

49. Howard Gardner, after observing both systems with a critical eye, concludes that Chinese education does enhance performance but at a considerable cost in creativity. The Chinese want basic skills to take priority, whereas Americans often worry that if creativity is once discouraged, it may never be recovered. There is no surefire winner in such debates. See *To Open Minds: Chinese Clues to the Dilemmas of Contemporary Education* (New York: Basic, 1989). A short excerpt appears in *CCCW*, 101–4.

50. Our view of cultural change is relevant here. We agree with those who observe extreme volatility in Chinese culture since 1949 (and indeed for many decades before then). For example, Stanley Rosen in 2000 identified five experientially distinct "generations" during the first half century of the PRC (*CCCW*, 178–82). Many in China today feel a need to identify a sixth and even a seventh generation, as more of those born in the 1980s and then in the 1990s seem to respond so differently to the challenges of growing up in the PRC. These differences are real but relatively superficial compared to the long-term continuities we aim to track. While changes must of course be acknowledged, in our view these Chinese young people remain clearly Chinese in their values and thinking, even if their parents deplore a diminished attention to *xiao*.

51. For example, *China Daily* on November 1, 2011, under the title "Civil Servant Sorry for Beating Parents," reported how a city official in Shenzhen, who had physically beaten his parents from the Hunan countryside, later knelt before them to ask forgiveness. Even more revealing of the status of *xiao* today was the survey carried out by sina.com.cn in response to this incident. Of 2,207 respondents to the survey, 1,649 (about 75 percent) said they thought the man's behavior was too abominable to be forgiven, while 1,141 (about half) said they did not consider him qualified to be a civil servant. Accessed November 18, 2012, http://www.chinadaily.com.cn/.

面子

Miànzi

2

Locating a Self through Others

Miànzi 面子

We met our host at the restaurant. When we arrived, we were guided to a private room upstairs, the table elaborately set. After introductions to the other guests, high-ranking colleagues from his organization, the food began to arrive. And arrive. And arrive. The appetizers were followed by vegetable and then meat dishes, all different, each amazing. After making our way, with elaborate praise, through the first three courses, we were beginning to flag. After the fifth course, we signaled defeat—and sued for amnesty—just as the most lavish centerpiece, consisting of lobsters and shellfish arrived. And then a large fish. Then, finally, soup. We nibbled and slurped politely over the next interminable hour, waiting for the inevitable argument over the bill; the nominal host was challenged, and then outsmarted, by his colleague, who slipped out on excuse of using the toilets and paid behind his back.

Although at least a third of the food still remained untouched, no one would ask for dabao (a "doggy bag"). This display of what Thorstein Veblen once called "conspicuous waste" was a gesture signifying here not only wealth but also a reaffirmation of our host's now augmented social importance or "face."[1] It was, we knew by then, once more a question of mianzi.

When we asked a Chinese teaching colleague at our university to help us find a text on "face," she looked confused. "I don't think I could find such a document," she confessed. "It is not something we think much about, certainly don't write about." If a value is so central to a culture that everyone lives with it but few consciously articulate it, then we know it to be crucial. *Mianzi* is one such key to a whole way of life. But just as it is difficult for a Chinese person to explain it to a Westerner, so it may be hard for a Chinese person to explain it to him- or herself because, in some radical sense, *mianzi is* that self.

INNER AND OUTER SELVES, IN THE WEST AND CHINA

What seems to be at stake here is the relation between inner and social selves, the realm where face resides.

The pair of contrasting images below was created by Yang Liu, a graphic designer who was born in Beijing but raised in Berlin. Yang Liu depicts the stereotypical Westerner as thinking "apples" and saying "apples"—whereas the Chinese person, thinking "pears," says (possibly to agree with his Western other) "apples." Protecting face involves a series of defensive strategies well recognized in the Chinese world. One of the first is that you *don't* say what you mean.

In the West, we commonly think we should express our feelings openly as a show of *sincerity*. "Sincerity" originally meant "purity," implying "unmixed." At least since the term gained currency in the late eighteenth century, "sincerity" has implied being transparently honest in expressing publicly what is felt privately.[2] In any case, the Western direction is clear: what you see is what you get. Hence one should feel free to speak one's mind, unless of course discretion calls for a polite evasion. The Chinese tendency is exactly contrary; one must always exercise reserve, revealing inner thoughts only to a select few, if any, while actively disguising feelings of frustration, irritation, or anger.

Why this difference? There are many factors involved in what the Chinese call *mianzi*—normally translated as "face." This may be a misleading translation because, in the West, we commonly think of "face" as the appearance we see in the mirror, that is, our social self, as in T. S. Eliot's line about preparing "a face to meet the faces that you meet."[3] Privately, we distinguish this sense of "face" from what is "behind" or "beneath" the image in the mirror, that is, our *real* or *authentic* selves. We often think of our social self as a mask, to be taken on or off at will. This is not threatening as Westerners consider that, although our outward appearance may change, we remain basically the same person underneath.

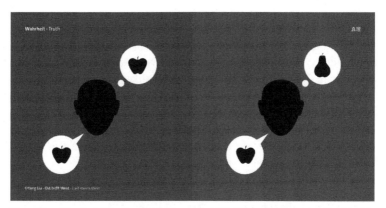

Yang Liu, "Truth." *Source:* Yang Liu, *Ost trifft West* [East meets West], 10th ed. (Mainz, Germany: Hermann Schmidt Verlag, 2014). Used by permission.

Furthermore, to the confusion of many Chinese people, we in the West commonly consider it a virtue to express this hidden self—we think of erupting into anger, for instance, as a sign of passion or, at least, of authenticity. Such transparency often dismays not only Chinese but also Asian people in general. One of the cardinal rules for all those going to China is, whatever happens, do not lose your temper. Do not show strong feelings openly and certainly don't express them verbally. To do so is seen as very confrontational, and confrontation inevitably means that someone must lose face—that is, feel humiliated. As such, confrontation damages relationships.

In such a world, face does not have to do with *asserting* a social self as much as *protecting* it; to quote an old Chinese saying, "A person needs face as a tree needs bark."[4] If the bark is stripped off, the tree dies. In China, if face is lost, you risk losing your only viable self. For this reason, *mianzi* needs to be considered in all relations, both with oneself and with others.

In terms of one's own presentation of self, what needs to be protected is the social self or *mianzi* from the inchoate eruptions from within. In contrast to the usual Western response, Chinese people under strong emotional stress try to keep their face expressionless—hiding beneath its surface. To hide strong emotion, they may actually smile if deeply upset.[5] For this reason, Westerners often call Chinese people "inscrutable." This reading is not altogether wrong. Most Chinese shy away from revealing underlying feelings. Nor do they believe that expressing strong negative feelings is a good thing. In becoming openly angry one loses face because it is perceived as a loss of self-control. Also in attacking others, thereby causing them to lose face, you too risk being humiliated. Furthermore, one can never be sure what others might do if they become aware of your innermost feelings and hopes. In terms of expressing emotions and/or thoughts then, *mianzi* implies both "keeping one's cool" and "keeping up appearances."

MIANZI AS SOCIALLY CONSTRUCTED SELF

In seeking to understand *mianzi*, one needs to think of how we actually perceive ourselves. For instance, in the course of everyday life, you cannot see your own face. If you do suddenly see your face—say, in a shop window—you might not instantly recognize yourself. "Can that old woman who looks like my mother (one might ask) actually be *me?*" Even if we avoid mirrors, inevitably we are brought face-to-face with ourselves through the reaction of others. From the way they look at us, and the way they treat us, we take our bearings. Are we accepted? Well liked?[6] Respected? For the Chinese, this is exactly what face means: a constructing of one's own sense of worth through the responses of those around us.

Thus, though "inner feelings" might be acknowledged, there is little sense of a *real self* understood as lurking inside, threatening to break through to the surface. Here what counts most are the responses of others. Without other people, no real sense of self would exist, because here, to a large extent, your public self or *mianzi defines* your

"real self." One might go so far as to say that, in China, without face, in some basic sense you no longer exist. You are a nobody, a nonperson, invisible—and powerless.

Living with such a conception of self, one becomes radically dependent on others, cradled in their response. For such an "interdependent" (as opposed to the "independent" self of the West), trust is crucial—for if you depend on others for face, you are depending on them for that recognition that literally makes you into a person.[7] As they, in turn, must depend on you.

Such criteria for selfhood might well appall Westerners—schooled from an early age to believe that they are born to be fully independent selves (if not as fully independent bodies). For instance, when teaching Jean-Jacques Rousseau to our Chinese students, we began with his resounding assertion: "Man is born free, and is everywhere in chains."[8] This statement provoked confusion. What does it mean to be "born free"? Surely Rousseau (they responded), like all of us, was born as a baby, as a helpless human being, completely dependent on its family. In what sense could such a creature be defined as born "free"?[9]

There is a firm basis for their confusion. In China, one is not born as a person at all; there it is assumed that one must *become* a person. This is a social process, something to be achieved—and one that cannot be pursued by going, as Henry David Thoreau did, to "find oneself" in isolated woods around Walden Pond. In China, one can only become a person *through a relationship with at least one other person.* One cannot (as Kongzi implied) become "human" on one's own.[10]

Such is the implication of the Chinese character for "human-ness" (*ren* 仁), which combines the sign for "person" with the number "two."[11] Achieving personhood, according to this model, involves being part of a group, such as a family, hence evolving through a series of ongoing relationships. Because one cannot become a person on one's own, one is always "in relation." It is therefore (by definition) an intensely moral world, if one understands the "moral" as a value that must always involve a relationship with another. Because it presumes such radical interdependence, versions of the Golden Rule have been key sayings in China about as long as they have been in the West.[12]

Meanwhile, in the West, the "self" functions as a kind of absolute noun: an inner self or "essence" that will, in the sense of soul, always *be the same*. In other words, in the West *you are what you are*.[13] But in China, *mianzi* is a kind of collective noun that acts more like a verb: *what you are* is largely a function of *what you do* and *what you do* involves others; *we are what others make us*. In other words, *mianzi* encourages, by its very nature, what might be called a "we-awareness." In this context, Western-style oppositions between "self and society" or "individual and group" remain abstract and disembodied, whereas "we-awareness" involves a performance always conscious of the reactions of others, even if one is alone.

Of course, this kind of consciousness does exist in the Western world as well. Once, during an interview before a concert, we asked the performer, "How difficult is it to play this Mozart concerto while conducting the orchestra as well—as you propose to do tonight?"

He smiled broadly.

> In fact, what I am doing is quite new for me.
>
> Ordinarily, I worked at "simply" preparing the solo piano part. I would sit down and start to practice from my first solo entry rather than examining in sufficient detail what the orchestra played before I came in. So I would make decisions on tempo/dynamic/articulation based on my own part rather than on the whole piece.
>
> But when I undertook to conduct the orchestra as well as to play my part, a lot of things changed. Suddenly I had to pay a lot of attention to everything else that was happening right from the start to the very end of the piece. I no longer felt like a soloist; my part was knitted into other parts. I had to listen to it from other sites in the orchestra: how would it sound against the violins? Against the brass? In the end, this resulted in a more holistic, unified approach—which makes sense, really, because Mozart conceived the piece to be performed this way. It was, in short, a revelation to me.[14]

What the young pianist discovered—in an exclusively Western context—was another way of thinking. Although a social psychologist from the West might regard his discovery as fairly mainstream thinking in his own field, the fact is, for this musician, it was a *discovery*. Even social psychologists limit their experiments to occasions of social interaction, implying that a self exists quite independently of these interactions. And indeed most Westerners are raised to concentrate only on their own solo part, practicing without reference to a wider context. In so doing, they normally think of composing themselves from the inside out—at times in resistance to the "outside" influences of family, friends, or society at large. But in China, most people habitually think of themselves as composed by others, becoming oneself *through relations* with family, with friends, and by extension (although much more tenuously), through one's relations to society at large. Thus, in this world, it would be almost impossible to consider one's own performance in isolation from its impact on others. The distinction might be put even more sharply: whereas in the West one commonly seeks to distinguish oneself *from others*, in China, one seeks to identify oneself *through others*.

VERSIONS OF CHINESE IDENTITY

Hence the kinds of self-awareness as between Chinese and, say, an American may well be defined, at the furthest end of the spectrum, as radically and substantially distinct. However, there *is* a spectrum; one can always find people from the middle of the scale or those who have learned to negotiate life through both modalities. A writer such as Gish Jen, the child of Chinese immigrants to America, is one person who tends to write exactly about such issues.[15] In this context, what would be most accurate to say is that each civilization, Western and Asian, provides a template against which people define their sense of selfhood, according to different degrees of compliance or resistance. Thus one can find very individualistic Chinese people as well as very collectively oriented Westerners. Some might even argue that, in the West, women tend more toward the Chinese model of selfhood while men tend to work toward the Western one.[16] But, as Richard Nisbett observes, "Variations between and within societies, as well as within individuals, should not blind us to the fact that there are very real differences, substantial on the average, between East Asians and people of European origin."[17]

With this in mind, it is fair to say that it is loosely this stress on "we-awareness" that helps define a representative Chinese sense of identity. For instance, in China, family names come first, implying that the family is the key identifier of who you are. Before the introduction of the single-child policy, your given name or names might well have accorded with your birth order and gender: as First Son, Second Daughter, and so forth. That designation also defined your role for life and, with it, your first loyalties. After your family, you would then identify yourself through reference to your work unit or profession or by place of origin. All of these acquired identities would then crystallize into what constitutes you as in "individual." But the idea that you could discover or even create a personal identity belongs to the fantasies of celebrity culture. Certainly an "identity crisis" along Western lines seems very foreign to Chinese teenagers, who are above all concerned during their adolescence with school grades and exams. And even today in China the notion that you are somehow an "individual" with goals and desires radically independent from those of your family might easily be condemned as "selfish."

Such distrust of "individualism" (as it is called in China) can be very threatening to Westerners, for whom a unique self is indispensable. It is, after all, part of their

Drummers at the opening ceremony of the Beijing Olympics (28). *Source:* Photo by Jonathan Ferrey, with the permission of Getty Images.

inheritance from a long tradition, both Greek and Christian, each of which stakes a claim on behalf of an idiosyncratic, eternal soul. Hence, for Western viewers, the opening sequences of the Olympics—featuring hundreds of identically clothed male drummers drumming in unison—might seem more like a nightmare, representing a total obliteration of the individual. Yet for many Chinese, to be included in such a group for such an occasion might well be hailed as the apex of a performer's career.[18]

Exactly because our notion of a unique self is so crucial, Westerners often seek for traces of it in cultures where it is not so valued. In their latest assessment of what anthropology and psychiatry can tell us about China, Arthur Kleinman and his collaborators point to the rise of what they call the "desiring self."[19] This they define as a new sense of self emerging from the new choices offered by the introduction of market capitalism. Advertising media in particular open up fantasies of what one called the "poetic lif," which, in this case, meant an apartment furnished by IKEA. The "desiring self" also takes many of its cues from Western popular culture, especially its pop music and movies. We know that the emerging Chinese middle class is traveling more to the West and aspiring to educate its precious only child abroad. Probably most of the choices of this new "desiring self" are dictated by how certain luxury goods can define a new status in a rapidly changing social scene. But can we say that such behavior is actually transforming the traditional group dynamics of the Chinese family?

Certainly when large decisions are taken, Chinese people will continue to rely on their families to guide them in how to think and what to do. In other words, choosing still remains a collective act, designed to boost a collective identity or *mianzi*. Thus in making major medical decisions, for instance, doctors tend to consult whole families rather than simply with the individuals involved, whether or not patients are competent to make such choices on their own.[20] Even in the most intimate decisions, such as whom to marry, the individual "desiring self" is less a counter than what the spouse will bring to the collective unit, whether in terms of money, prestige, family connections, or other resources. From a marriage one also expects a child—of course, not alone for personal reasons but to prolong the family in time. Such decisions are regarded as too crucial to be left merely to the individual's desire. After all, the family's reputation (or *mianzi*) as well as its entire future is at stake.

GIVING FACE

As this and other examples illustrate, significant decisions in China always involve *mianzi*: in terms of whether it will be gained or lost and even, in certain circumstances, loaned or borrowed. Of these transactions, to *give face* is the most valued. In giving face, one promotes another person's standing in the eyes of others. As everyone depends on being accorded a recognized place in this world, it is natural that all people hope to enhance their standing. Boosting someone else adds to their *mianzi* and can add to one's own as well. One gives *mianzi* through protocols of *xiao*, that is, through obvious displays of deference or respect. But in such an exchange, one may *lose face* as well: by acting badly or against the norms; by humiliating someone else or losing one's emotional self-control; or simply by failing to *give face* to others when it is expected.

Who then controls the giving and losing of face? Not everyone. Only those in relation to you are involved; these make up your *guanxi* network.[21] In turn, as you grow more influential within your *guanxi* network, you too will assume more power to enhance or diminish face. The protocols involved may be heavily strategic, as in our host's lavish restaurant meal. But the effect is never one way. Precisely because *mianzi* involves exchange, one gives *mianzi* to get *mianzi* in turn. Never an end in oneself, in this world one is almost always a means to some other end. This is a hard lesson for Westerners, who are taught to assume that, in human relations, the moral route involves treating others as ends in themselves and not as means.

There are, however, limits to the giving and getting of face, even within such a central concern as *mianzi*. For instance, one can only acquire as much *mianzi* as is appropriate to one's place in the social order. It is part of the Chinese virtue of modesty to recognize this, while at the same time focusing great energy on refining and maintaining rank ordering within any given hierarchy. Indeed, as one commentator noted, "so much energy is expended in the interplay of relations between superiors and subordinates that at times there is little left over for anything else."[22] Part of that energy is spent in calculating how much *mianzi* you can actually give—or get. The way compliments are handled reflects this reality. Compliments might, on the surface, seem easy ways of giving face. But usually in China someone receiving a compliment is likely to respond by a polite denial. Although disconcerting to foreigners, this habit persists among Chinese people—because modesty remains an important virtue. Modesty is a way of saying, "I know my place, and it is not as elevated as you are making out." Thus the foreigner should be wary of compliments, as they may often mean the opposite of what is said. If a Chinese person starts complimenting you on your command of Mandarin, alarm bells should go off. Probably it means you are murdering the language. The best response is to laugh and say that your host is very kind, but you know that your Mandarin is poor. Then everyone can relax, because the compliment is acknowledged to be the polite gesture it was meant to be—and no one can be offended.

The real danger to *mianzi* occurs during a confrontation between two individuals who appear to be equals. One friend of ours gains an evening's entertainment watching the dramas unfolding in a narrow lane outside his Beijing apartment. Bordering government offices, it is a place where two official cars would often meet where there is room for only one to pass. The situation usually remains unresolved for some time, until one driver is willing to back up—thereby giving *mianzi* to the one who prevailed while very publicly losing it for himself. Even though such contests between putative equals are unusual in China, the results may, for a Chinese person, appear drastic.

LOSING FACE

While the exchanges of giving and getting face are the social currency of the Chinese world, losing face is the social equivalent of bankruptcy. To lose *mianzi* means not only humiliation but also the end of the relationship involved and, in terms of self-respect, the equivalent of social suicide.

But for a Westerner who has little or no notion of the care involved in maintaining *mianzi*, these issues are virtually invisible. The danger can be greatest when one begins to feel at home in China, perhaps allowing one to relax into Western default systems. This happened at a conference when one of us was giving a paper. When it concluded, a world-renowned Chinese professor rose to give a response, which seemed implicitly hostile to what had been said. Unthinkingly, one went into Western, confrontational mode, to the effect that "I must disagree with Professor X's analysis, as I think it begins from the wrong premises about the case in point." A silence settled over the room—not any silence but a dire silence. The famous professor rose again, reiterated his point flatly, and then left. We were not invited back.

Later, realizing the error, we asked a Chinese colleague how we should have handled the situation. We did not understand how, in what was clearly a university

situation, we could have offended by simply following the usual professional protocols of scholarly disagreement familiar in Western circles.

"You should not have disagreed with Professor X," our colleague said darkly. "You
hurt his *mianzi.*"

"Just because he is world famous does not mean he is right," one of us countered.

"No. Not because he is famous but because you so openly disagreed with him, it
seemed to put him in the wrong. And even with other professors, you should never
publicly disagree with them. In fact, even with students you have to be very careful
not to injure them this way. The correct way to disagree—if you feel you must—is
simply to say, 'I have heard what Professor X has to say and find it very interesting.
But I would like to take a little time to supplement his remarks with some of my
own.' Then you can go on (carefully) to disagree with him, as you have not put yourself up as openly challenging him. Everyone—that is, every Chinese person—will
get the point."

His words came back to us in another situation—predictably, perhaps, when trying to teach Chinese graduate students how to debate. As they were clearly reluctant
to engage in such a confrontational exercise, we hit on the idea of showing them a
video grab from British parliamentary debates. In the one chosen, Tony Blair (then
a cultural hero to the Chinese) was caught up in a particularly contentious Prime
Minister's Question Time: jumping up and down to the red dispatch box, batting
back questions in a vigorous but edgy way, mopping sweat from his brow, and clearly
wearing thin. Watching him, the students were simply appalled. "This is very pain-
ful," one remarked. "What are they doing to him? You can't rule a country this way!
He is losing *mianzi!*"

This response echoes back centuries. When the Jesuits first introduced Christianity into China, several of their fiercest critics were Chinese intellectuals. Many of
their objections to Christian doctrine were so acute that they might be heard in
the West today. But one was singularly Chinese, that voiced by the Confucianist
writer and astronomer Yang Guangxian (1597–1659), who focused on what was
presented as Jesus' greatest claim to universality: that through him, the Most High
was, through the crucifixion, brought to the lowliest human level. Although having
a strong appeal in the West, in China, Jesus' fate worked against any credibility as
to his divinity. What offended Yang most was the humiliation of Jesus through his
mode of death. Or, as he argued,

> One might just speak of honoring the Sovereign on high without honoring Heaven and
> Earth. But one cannot speak of honoring Yesu as Sovereign on High. One might just
> speak of honoring an ordinary man as a Saint or as the Sovereign on High. But one
> cannot speak of honoring as a Saint or the Sovereign on High a criminal who has trans-
> gressed the laws. . . . The one whom they call Master of Heaven is the one who directs
> the universe. And, according to them, it is by virtue of the fact that he could direct the
> universe but was not able to direct his own life until he died a natural death that he can
> be recognized as the Master of Heaven! In their books of doctrine, they mention Yesu's
> correct laws. Why do they say nothing of the way he died nailed down?[23]

One is reminded of St. Paul's reaction to his preaching of the crucified Christ as being "a stumbling-block to Jews and foolishness to Gentiles" (1 Corinthians 23). But here the logic is purely Chinese, being that the failure of Jesus to maintain a proper place in a status hierarchy is enough to undermine all of the serious claims of Christian doctrine. One cannot worship a criminal; after all, by dying so degrading a death, Yesu lost *mianzi*!

MIANZI AS IDENTITY PERFORMANCE

Such are the risks as spelled out by the phrase "to lose face." A direct translation from the Mandarin, it stands in vivid contrast to the phrase in English "to save face." Interestingly, this latter phrase did not originate in Mandarin. It was coined late in the nineteenth century among the British community in Hong Kong as a reference to the habitual devices used among the Chinese to avoid incurring or inflicting humiliation.[24]

This neologism, as it turns out, helps us to understand a larger aspect of *mianzi*: as in today's China, the politics of "humiliation" and relations with Great Britain are inexorably linked. Seen as the instigators of what the Chinese now regard as "the Century of National Humiliation"[25] (marked by the start of the First Opium War in 1839), the British are held accountable, along with other colonizing powers, for what was perhaps the greatest loss of *mianzi* by the Chinese within their modern history. Over their time as colonizers and traders, the English had clearly become aware of the importance of "face"—not merely as a personal but also as a political issue. They too had learned that, in China, the personal is always political—and that there is a seamless transition from one to the other, just as there is a seamless transition from one's most intimate to one's most public *guanxi* relations.

In inventing the English phrase "to save face" as a counter to the native Mandarin phrase "to lose *mianzi*," the British community also recognized something else, something inherently Chinese. That is, that the two phrases, seemingly opposites, function as complementary: one always implying the other and one always in danger of morphing into the other. That creative tension itself defines what William A. Callahan has identified as the dynamic of the Chinese "sovereignty performance": as one balanced precariously between pride and humiliation, aspiration and anxiety—each perpetually feeding off the other, on a personal as well as a national and international plane.[26]

Callahan detects in this dynamic the key to how the Chinese today identify themselves to the wider world. The important question is not, he argues, *What is China?* but *Who is China?* For China's presentation of itself to that world is not one implemented simply by means of abstractly formulated policies. Rather, in China one's sense of self-worth is defined according to feeling responses (*xin* 心), ones that blend reasoning and emotion inextricably.[27] As such, this "identity performance" is inherently unstable, not least because, as *mianzi*, such a performance (by definition)

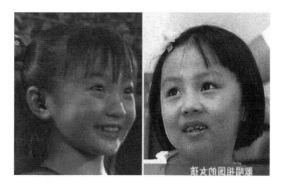

places its own sense of worth in the hands of others and how *they* respond to what China does. Although Callahan's analysis takes place within the framework of international and national security issues, what it underlines is basically how *insecure* the process of self-definition by means of *mianzi* may prove to be.

That insecurity operates on all levels. Most foreigners become aware early that what Americans might call "constructive criticism" is not welcome in this world. In China, any criticism or even *implied* criticism may lead to drastic loss of *mianzi*. Ironically, critiques by the Chinese of themselves are acceptable, although they need to be handled very carefully. But this is not true of criticism from anyone defined as an "outsider," whether, say, from a minority culture or from a non-Chinese national—or even from a Chinese national living abroad. At times, China may appear almost pathologically sensitive to Western criticism. The feeling—popular as well as official—is that China has been "humiliated" enough by foreigners in the past. So it grounds its pride on extravagant displays of what it projects as "China at its best," as in the spectacular opening ceremonies of the 2008 Beijing Olympics. The motive, as defined in popular parlance, was "to earn some *mianzi* for the motherland." To this end, no exercise of ingenuity was spared, to the extent that the voice of one little girl singing the national anthem was in fact mimed by another (much cuter—see above) little girl—fakery widely deplored in the West, despite the precedents common in Hollywood.[28] In China, however, it was regarded as simply another example of *mianzi gongcheng*: literally, of "face engineering." For this global occasion, stellar performance was deemed to override all other considerations.

MIANZI PRACTICES: CHINA AND THE WEST

Such a concept is no longer foreign to the West; at least since the publication of *The Presentation of Self in Everyday Life* (1959) by the sociologist Erving Goffman. In this groundbreaking work, Goffman focuses on what he perceives to be the theatrical performance of employees at a local hotel, as they take on the roles of servants working in an upper-class English house: "The maid . . . and the two waitresses were behaving like people acting in a play. They would sweep into the kitchen as if coming off stage into the wings, with trays held high and a tense expression of *hauteur* still on their faces; relax for a moment in the frenzy of getting new dishes loaded, and glide off with faces prepared for their next entrance."[29] From such beginnings, adapting the Chinese concept of *mianzi* has helped Western social scientists move beyond naive interpretations of selfhood as essence.[30] From this movement emerged whole industries devoted to the self-conscious manipulation of *image* as a manufactured substitute for selfhood. The rules of this game were spelled out with remarkable foresight in Daniel Boorstin's classic 1960s book under the title of *The Image: A Guide to Pseudo-Events in America*. Today no event enters public space in the West without having passed through the hands of one or more "spin doctors" who specialize in shaping public perceptions of what has happened.

As such, "face-engineering" has come to the West with a vengeance. Although it is not identified as traditionally "Chinese," many of the same practices apply. Try, for instance, applying to American politics the following Chinese wisdom: once one has "lost *mianzi*," it is hard to regain it, since one must always work through others. Keeping up *mianzi* also relies—in both cultures—on a certain flexibility in regard to "fact" and "truth-telling." In China, "truth-telling" has never had great traction, particularly in situations in which *mianzi* might be at stake. As one of our informants described the process of moving from a well-paid but junior position with Microsoft. cn to work in a senior position for a Chinese nongovernmental organization (NGO),

> My [new] boss often proudly introduced me to others by "She was a senior manager at Microsoft" or "She worked a dozen years at Microsoft before becoming our Program Director." At first, he may have known he exaggerated so that people would respect me—and him—and our organization. Later he really believed it. If I were to correct him, he would lose face. So I have to admit it. Later I have to repeat it. After a while, I myself began to believe it.

As her experience illustrates, to the extent the requirements of *mianzi* or "image" begins to dominate actual practice, the status of "truth" will, inevitably, be called into question.

TRUTH-TELLING PRACTICES: CHINA AND THE WEST

In other words, "truths" in China, like the notion of self, tend to be socially constructed. One says what is politic at the time, whether it is "apples" or "pears." Anyone who wants to work with Chinese people must take this factor into account. Words cannot be counted on to correspond to something called "reality" or "fact"; what is said must first of all serve instrumental purposes. One common goal is to smooth over a transaction, to give the interlocutors *mianzi*. In China, openness or frankness to others is *not* a virtue.

Usually, concerning inner thoughts, Westerners aim to be transparent; the Chinese, guarded. But clearly such a statement oversimplifies the situation. Even in our own culture, a certain bleak honesty is often regarded as destructive to personal relations—and potentially fatal in broader social or political contexts. In a carefully comparative book titled *Lies that Bind: Chinese Truth, Other Truths* (2007), anthropologist Susan Blum offers a balanced study of the role of *truth* in both China and the West. Of course, there is great variation not only in standards of truth-telling between civilizations but also within China and the West itself. As Blum points out, within China "honesty" is often regarded as naive and thus belonging to people of lower status—ethnic minorities, peasants, or children. How direct you are in speech is also often regarded as a class marker, with those more educated being more "polite" in speech and therefore more careful of issues surrounding *mianzi*.[31]

From her experience in China, Blum concludes that some long-standing maxims apply to truth-telling in China.[32] There, these maxims emphasize the importance of one's role. Deploy the usual lines, guard information, and avoid transparency. Stay with the script. As one must always consider consequences, it is safer to stick to saying what is expected. Any impulse to seem original or to express one's personal opinions should be rigorously avoided. To indulge in these would be unforgivably "Western"—in the worst sense. Westerners, on the other hand, might feel stupefied by the Chinese ritual exchanges of clichés, standard inquiries, and compliments. Many indirect or allusive references would also be lost. Outsiders might even wonder to themselves, *do people in China ever speak spontaneously and openly with each other?*

What the Westerner might miss is the ritual value of such exchanges, as a means of creating harmony among the group.[33] They would also perhaps discount the regulated body language that accompanies these: calibrated bows, attention to where one is seated at the table, and courteous offering of food or tea. What counts in such a scenario is the reassuring emotional atmosphere created by these gestures that say, in effect, you are safe here, you are respected, and we will not intrude on the boundaries that you count on to define your place in the world.

As an example of Western/Chinese miscommunication, Blum cites her own mystification when Chinese guests repeatedly refused her offer of tea—although she had invited them into her home precisely *to have tea*. What she did not perceive, as a newcomer, was that this was a gesture of Chinese ritual politeness: just as it was the role of the guest to refuse food and drink, it was the role of the host to *insist* on providing them. Blum soon realizes that she should persist with the performance—and simply serve the tea despite her guests' repeated polite refusals.[34] But what the scenario makes clear is that her guests were exhibiting more than merely polite behavior; it was a set performance, depending entirely on *knowing the required script*. For a social self in China is a performing self; it has to know what to do and say on each occasion.

In conclusion, after lengthy and scrupulous examination of the evidence, Blum judges that neither the West nor China is more "truthful" or "honest"—but that

these values tend to be differently displayed in either culture.[35] Her overriding conclusion rests in the title of her book: *Lies that Bind: Chinese Truth, Other Truths*. All
of us, she demonstrates, whether in China or the West, are caught up in larger, consensual conspiracies to conceal or otherwise distort "the truth" in many situations.
And our motivation for doing so is not generally destructive but in fact exemplifies
that kind of benign hypocrisy that makes civilization, in the sense of living together,
possible.

This comparative perspective helps make sense of other Chinese habits of mind.
These surface most persistently in attempts by State leaders to avoid any public admission of error or weakness, present or past, that might be attributed to the Party.
Active censorship of the media and the Internet ensures that Chinese people (most
visibly, journalists and bloggers) constantly run a risk of suppression if their observations cross a line of acceptability that is both invisible and shifting. As a public
extension of concern for *mianzi*, this present-day Chinese reality makes sense: strict
regulation helps maintain face both domestically and abroad. How long such protective measures will endure is not knowable; but at least Westerners can understand
where they come from and how they work—and perhaps that they are not so deeply
foreign to us after all.

Finally, in a fast-changing society, traditional implementation of *mianzi* is also
changing, if only by importing some of the least admirable of Western practices.
Celebrity culture is influencing urban China, perhaps starting some time ago in
Hong Kong and now reinforced by exposure to Western media hype. One Western
psychotherapist observed about Hong Kong some years ago that "name dropping,
eagerness to associate with the rich and famous, the use of external status symbols,
sensitivity to insult, lavish gift-giving, the use of titles, the sedulous avoidance of
criticism, all abound, and require considerable readjustment for someone [from the
West] used to organizing social life by impersonal rules, frankness, and greater equality."[36] This trend is now palpable on the mainland as well, suggesting that *mianzi* as
a social value is in no way being diminished by the increasing wealth among Chinese. Whereas *xiao* is being brought under pressure by the greater latitude accorded
Chinese young people, increasing wealth reinforces aspirations for *mianzi* by giving
access to much broadened means for asserting claims to social importance. The upsurge of demand on the market for Chinese antiques is only one example. Previously
obscure specialties such as carved rhinoceros horns have exploded in price. Any scarcity can translate into a chance to show off wealth. All sorts of luxury goods from the
West serve to promote *mianzi* among upwardly mobile Chinese, to the extent that
the makers of such goods now target sales in China to ensure their future viability.[37]

A few examples must suffice. In November 2012, the Party Congress in Beijing
brought together a remarkable collection of officials' cars that were parked in reserved lots. Uniformly they showed how Audi A6 models now mark accession to
power within the system.[38] But in the meantime, the new regime under Xi Jinping
says it is trying to limit the number (and certainly the visibility) of such conspicuous
status symbols within the Party elite. The model may be the richest man in China,

Zong Qinghou, remarkable for keeping a low profile, who usually dresses as an ordinary person except for one sign of status: a Swiss watch, a Vacheron Constantin, for which he paid forty-eight thousand dollars, to replace an older Rolex model. He is quoted as explaining, with a smile: "Other people say Rolex is for the newly rich."[39] His remark is a reminder that those with the highest status may gain still more status by avoiding blatant displays of wealth.

In short, *mianzi* is more visibly important as Chinese elites gain the means to implement their hierarchical aspirations. Are motivations so very different in Western countries?[40]

NOTES

1. For a comparable show of over-the-top spending ("conspicuous consumption") in order to boost one's social standing in late nineteenth-century America, see Thorstein Veblen's classic study, *The Theory of the Leisure Class* (1899; New York: Penguin, 1979).

2. For a memorable analysis of these issues in regard to Western ideas of self-presentation, see Lionel Trilling, *Sincerity and Authenticity* (New York: Harcourt Brace Jovanovich, 1971).

3. From T. S. Eliot, "The Love Song of J. Alfred Prufrock," in *The Complete Poems and Plays, 1910–1950*, 3–7 (New York: Harcourt, Brace, 1952).

4. For further elaborations on the protocols of "face" in intercultural situations, see Hu Wenzhong and Cornelius Grove, "The Concept of 'Face' in Chinese-American Interaction," in *Encountering the Chinese: A Guide for Americans*, 117–32 (Boston: Nicholas Brealey Publishing, 1999).

5. Austin Coates, *Myself a Mandarin: Memoirs of a Special Magistrate* (London: Heinemann, 1977), 243. Coates, recounting his experiences as a magistrate serving the British administration in Hong Kong from 1949 to 1956, recalls the "curious" habit of his Chinese contacts actually laughing when announcing a dire tragedy, in this case, the death of a young girl in childbirth.

6. It is not accidental that this expression echoes a crucial factor about Willy Loman in Arthur Miller's *Death of a Salesman*, a play that has enjoyed a singular success among Chinese audiences.

7. These terms were first coined to describe Asian as opposed to Western notions of selfhood by Hazel Marcus and Shinobu Kitayama in 1991. For further discussion of their relevance, especially to literary narration, see Gish Jen, *Tiger Writing: Art, Culture, and the Interdependent Self* (Cambridge, MA: Harvard University Press, 2013), 6–7.

8. *CCCW*, 438.

9. This particular affirmation has a loaded history in Western discourse from Justinian's late Roman law code of the sixth century to Thomas Hobbes's launching of social contract thinking about politics in *Leviathan; or, The Matter, Form, and Power of a Commonwealth, Ecclesiastical and Civil* (London: A. Crooke, 1651). The currency of "freedom" as a Western ideological marker follows directly from such antecedents. *CCCW*, 397, 431.

10. There are, of course, exceptions to the Western paradigm of finding oneself on one's own. One noteworthy example comes from George Herbert Mead's analysis of the construction of the self in his book *Mind, Self, and Society*, ed. Charles W. Morris (1934; Chicago: University of Chicago Press, 1963). The self, Mead argues, is not an entity that is there from

birth. It is something that comes into existence insofar as the subject becomes an object for itself. But how does this come about? How can the subject see itself as an object? The answer Mead gives is that the subject can only see itself as an object insofar as it assumes the vantage point of another toward itself, as only the other can initially see the subject as an object. For the self to exist, I must stand outside myself and take the attitude of another toward myself, which is why, for Mead, the construction of the self is necessarily a social construction and, therefore, must incorporate the attitudes of others toward oneself. Wording here is indebted to Karsten J. Struhl, "No (More) Philosophy without Cross-Cultural Philosophy," *Philosophy Compass* 5, no. 4 (2010): 289.

11. This character is so resonant that we will return to it more than once. Victorian translators with their penchant for moral abstractions launched the standard English translation as "benevolence." This translation fails to respect the root emphasis on relations between humans. Perhaps a more precise rendering would be the Latin *humanitas*, the qualities that make one human. For a fuller analysis of the implications of this character, see chapter 12, "Question Two: Human Rights?"

12. Of course, there are several variants on how this moral model is expressed. See *CCCW*, 473–78.

13. The echo of Yahweh in the Old Testament, "I AM who I AM," is deliberate, as both Jews and Christians regard themselves as made in the divine image. For excerpts from Exodus 3, with variant translations, see *CCCW*, CD, 878.

14. The pianist in question is Finghin Collins, resident artist at Ireland's RTE Symphony Orchestra for 2010–2013.

15. See, for instance, Gish Jen's reflections on the nature of Asian versus American construction of selves and the consequent narrative modalities in her latest book, *Tiger Writing* (2013). Further discussion of her meditations on Asian selfhood can be found in lecture 2, "Art, Culture, and Self," in *Tiger Writing*, 57–102.

16. For a further elaboration of this hypothesis, albeit in a radically different context, see Jean Baker Miller, *Towards a New Psychology of Women*, 2nd ed. (Boston: Beacon, 1986); *CCCW*, 166–69.

17. Richard E. Nisbett, *The Geography of Thought: How Asians and Westerners Think Differently—and Why* (London: Nicholas Brealey, 2003), 77.

18. The aesthetics implicit in this image are common in China. The performers seem to extend beyond the edge of the image, implicitly suggesting a limitless group of individuals acting in solidarity. This visual affirmation of "we-awareness" confirms the collective will to realize national aspirations.

19. The term is ascribed initially to Lisa Rofel, *Desiring China: Experiments in Neoliberalism, Sexuality, and Public Culture* (Durham, NC: Duke University Press, 2007), as cited in Arthur Kleinman, "Introduction: Remaking the Moral Person in a New China," in *Deep China: The Moral Life of the Person; What Anthropology and Psychiatry Tell Us about China Today*, by Arthur Kleinman et al. (Berkeley: University of California Press, 2011), 4, 47. It is used generally throughout various chapters in this book to assert an emerging ethical shift the authors perceive in China from a collective system of responsibility and self-sacrifice to one to a more individualistic system of rights and self-development.

20. Xiaoyang Chen and Ruiping Fan, "The Family and Harmonious Medical Decision Making: Cherishing an Appropriate Confucian Moral Balance," *Journal of Medicine and Philosophy* 35 (2010): 573–86.

21. See chapter 3, "The People Network: *Guānxi*."

22. Lucian W. Pye, *Asian Power and Politics: The Cultural Dimensions of Authority* (Cambridge, MA: Belknap, 1985), 209.

23. *CCCW*, 479.

24. *Oxford English Dictionary*, 2nd ed. (Oxford, UK: Clarendon, 1989).

25. The contemporary exploitation of this narrative is a major emphasis throughout William A. Callahan's *China: The Pessoptimist Nation* (Oxford: Oxford University Press, 2010). For an extended study see Zheng Wang, *Never Forget National Humiliation: Historical Memory in Chinese Politics and Foreign Relations* (New York: Columbia University Press, 2012). Orville Schell and John Delury give a well-balanced overview of the last century and more in *Wealth and Power: China's Long March to the Twenty-First Century* (New York: Random House, 2013), emphasizing the importance of China seeking "respect."

26. Callahan, *China*, 1.

27. Because the Chinese have no categories that separate "reason" from "emotion," this "feeling" mixture of reason and emotion defies abstract or intellectual definition. See chapter 4, "Where Is My Mind? *Xin*."

28. Image titled "Not Cute Enough?" accessed August 10, 2014, at http://imagemanage ment.in/.

29. Monica Dickens, *One Pair of Hands* (1951), as quoted in Erving Goffman, *The Presentation of Self in Everyday Life* (1959; Harmondsworth, UK: Penguin, 1971), 124.

30. Goffman's book was especially shocking to its American readers. Traditional European cultures have long acknowledged the kind of values inherent in *mianzi*: for instance, "honor killings" in Italy, which take place when a young woman is thought to have disgraced her family by dating or marrying a man whom the family regards as unacceptable.

31. Susan Blum, *Lies that Bind: Chinese Truth, Other Truths* (Lanham, MD: Rowman & Littlefield, 2007), 55.

32. Adapted from Blum, *Lies that Bind*, 18–19.

33. This is a major concern in China; see chapter 8, "Thinking in Harmony: *Hé*."

34. Blum, *Lies that Bind*, 51–52.

35. Blum, *Lies that Bind*, 156–57.

36. Michael Harris Bond, *Beyond the Chinese Face: Insights from Psychology* (Oxford: Oxford University Press, 1991), 59.

37. An interesting side effect of the pressing need to promote *mianzi* comes from Switzerland, where the sales of expensive Rolex and similar watches has boomed among Chinese tourists who may buy ten or more at a time. The reason is that these watches, purchased in Switzerland as gifts, are sure to be authentic—unlike those on sale in the PRC.

38. Michael Wines, "In China, 'Audi' Means 'Big Shot,'" *New York Times*, November 16, 2012.

39. "How China's Richest Man Made It," *Washington Post*, November 3, 2012.

40. Here again we find many echoes of the United States in the late nineteenth century as dissected, for example, by Veblen in *The Theory of the Leisure Class* (1899) with its focus on conspicuous consumption.

Guānxi

3

The People Network

Guānxi 关系

One October evening in 2010 as she was Rollerblading with a friend on a campus road at Hebei University, Chen Xiaofeng was struck down by a speeding car. The car was driven by twenty-two-year-old Li Qiming. He was drunk. She was killed; her friend, badly injured. The car drove on, stopped to let out a passenger—and only when the driver attempted to flee was he at last intercepted by security guards. Undeterred he yelled out to them, "Go ahead—sue me if you dare. My father is Li Gang!" (Li Gang was then the deputy director of the Public Security Bureau in the Beishi district of Baoding in Hebei Province.)[1]

Officials moved swiftly to ensure that this story never gained traction. It was, after all, a nightmare scenario for the Party: a commoner killed by one of the privileged elite, who now threatened to pull strings in order to escape punishment. But over the Internet, the story went viral. The father apologized in public (losing *mianzi*). Compensation was paid to the family of the dead girl. Ultimately the son was sent to trial and sentenced to six years in jail. Since then, "My father is Li Gang" has become a bitter insider joke, a catchphrase for evading any responsibility—large or small—with impunity.

   Could events such as these happen in the West as well? Certainly. What was distinctively Chinese was the bland confidence of the drunk driver. What he was really boasting was, I have *guanxi* connections to protect me—from any and all consequences of my actions. It is significant that the connection was to his father, not only the head of the family but also a powerful local official. Family connections, the perpetrator assumed, would be more powerful than the law, more powerful than any "justice." It is a routine assumption about the nature of power deeply embedded in Chinese culture, where "rule of law" remains more rhetorical than actual. Even where such "rule of law" does apply, in China implementing it often depends on the vagaries of personal relationships.

Thus, as with many Chinese practices, *guanxi* is a two-edged sword. On the one hand, it sounds benign, even noble. *Guanxi* begins with family. From there its connections are extended metaphorically as far as one is able, transforming part of the world from "outside" to "inside." While drawing outsiders into family values of *xiao* loyalty, *guanxi* is primarily based on expectations of exchange. As in family relations, these are lifelong, unless something uncontrollable intervenes or someone fails to contribute as expected. But whereas family relations are normally governed by *xiao* deference, *guanxi* relations differ insofar as they tend to be mutual and reciprocal.

GUANXI: DIVIDING "INSIDE" FROM "OUTSIDE"

How *guanxi* works may be divined from its etymology. *Guan* (关) as a isolated noun means a (mountain) pass, a critical juncture, a barrier, or a turning point, originally depicting gates with threads being woven inside. By implication this weaving together helps one *over* a barrier or *through* a gate or a difficult situation. *Xi* (系), taken by itself, implies "tying together," as with silk threads, now extended to associations assumed to be tied closely together, such as a family or a system. Together these characters redouble the associations with woven threads by signifying those

Entrance gate to Xidi village, Anhui Province. *Source:* John G. Blair.

relationships that help one overcome obstacles, including, by implication, "backdoor connections."

Not surprisingly, gates and entranceways are important in this world. In old China, rural villages were usually formed around extended families or clans. Prosperous villages typically had at least one elaborately carved gate, usually dedicated to an honored ancestor, to mark that symbolic point where *guanxi* starts—and ends.

The image on the previous page shows the only surviving entrance gate to the ancient village of Xidi in Yi County of Anhui Province, a settlement dating from the Huangyou era (1049–1053) of the Song dynasty. Raised during the Ming dynasty (1368–1644) in honor of a "virtuous widow," this gate's symbolism is central to the way Chinese people see their society: as radically divided between "insiders" and "outsiders." One of the oldest self-distinctions made by Chinese society, it still persists today—predetermining mindsets that operate not only domestically and nationally but also, as we shall see, internationally.[2]

The village of Xidi, for instance, is still dominated by the Hu clan; for centuries most of its inhabitants were born or married into that family. In the middle of the village, accordingly, stands a structure called "The Hall of Respect." Centered around Ming dynasty portraits of the "original" Hu ancestors, dressed in Tang dynasty robes, this is the place one comes to on ritual occasions (such as the Spring Festival) to honor one's family, the dead as well as the living. Prominent on the wall just inside is the Chinese character for *xiao*. Interpreted in two different ways, even today it is used to instruct young children on their obligations to elders. The children are told,

Giant Ming calligraphy of *xiao* in Hu Clan "Hall of Respect" in Xidi (Anhui). *Source:* John G. Blair.

"Look: if you see a howling monkey's face turned to the top left, that is the image of the child lacking in *xiao*. If you see the figure of a young person on the upper right, looking up with hands clasped respectfully, that means you understand your obligations to your elders. Which do you want to be? A howling monkey—or a respectful (hence respected) person?"

There is a Chinese saying: "At home one relies on one's parents and outside on one's friends."[3] In practice, *guanxi* is, in effect, an extended family. A Chinese parent will often encourage a young child, for instance, to address a neighbor or colleague as "uncle" or "aunt," implicitly drawing them into an enlarged family circle. Once Chinese students move from home into a college dorm, they may call their fellow residents "Eldest" or "Second Eldest"—observing the same deferential rituals of *xiao* as would apply to an extended family. Sometimes years after graduation, they may still use this way of addressing each other. Why do college friends maintain such loyalty to each other? Certainly this loyalty remains because they recognize that *guanxi* is, in all but name, an implicit equivalent of their own family ties.

On a recent trip with a former student, now a professor at a leading Chinese university, we were taken up the Minjiang Valley in northwestern Sichuan, through the 2008 earthquake zone, toward his place of origin. During the eight-hour drive up the valley, we stopped in two villages, for lunch and then tea. In the first, we met the second brother. In the second, we met the eldest brother. When we finally arrived, we were introduced to the cousin who owned the hotel in which we were to stay. Over the next few days, there followed introductions to what seemed to be swarms of relatives, cousins all. Trying to sort out the complexity of the blood bonds, we asked our guide, "How is your cousin who owns the hotel related to you?" He seemed taken aback at the question. "She is not really a blood relation at all," he replied. "She is a fictive cousin. We are very close. In fact, all the relations you have met, except my brothers, are fictive relations." We laughed, saying, "With so many relations, you must wish that your job was closer to home." "Not at all," he shot back. "I couldn't cope. Too much *guanxi*. Too many required visits. Too many requests to fill. I am comfortable coming here now and then. Otherwise I would have no time for my own [academic] work."

They may require visits, and they may require gifts; but as this story illustrates, your *guanxi* relations will look after you when you have plans. In a huge, indifferent world, they will protect you—are thus in themselves a precious resource, both practical and social. Just as the extended Chinese family may pool its finances to send a talented son or daughter to university, so one's *guanxi* network will provide resources (services) on which one can draw. Just as the Chinese family sees its role as advising and guiding its children, so older (often more prestigious) people, brought into a *guanxi* relation, may also be counted on to provide all kinds of counsel and support as well as exerting discreet pressure in cases where such influence is needed.

Your *guanxi* relations are thus critically important. These are the people who give—and protect—your *mianzi*. But, unlike *mianzi*, *guanxi* can be created. Even if no prior connections exist on which to begin building a *guanxi* relationship, there are always ways to generate that possibility. One might begin by claiming some distant family or other ties to someone in a related *guanxi* network. Or one might offer some exceptional help. If simply giving face does not suffice, then arriving with suitable gifts or arranging access to significant others may do the trick. Of course the superior who is solicited must decide whether or not to agree to enter into the proffered relationship. But the net result of all this befriending pressure is wide proliferation of *guanxi* ties among all Chinese people—and among those who arrive for any length of time in China.[4]

NETWORKING: CHINA AND THE WEST

Networks and the way they operate are thus qualitatively different in China and the West. Clarifying the difference is a telling graphic by Yang Liu, below.

Note that, while no dot on the Western side is completely isolated, ties remain limited in number and the small groups are cut off from each other—so that reaching out from one to the other requires conscious effort to bridge the gap. Unlike the Chinese world, one cannot move from one person to another without crossing an unstructured space. The Chinese side, however, offers multiple paths for reaching virtually anyone within its boundaries. On the other hand, once one reaches the limits of one's *guanxi* network, one discovers that it's a harsh, cold, and very big

Yang Liu, "Contacts: Comparative Networking." *Source:* Yang Liu, *Ost trifft West* [East meets West], 10th ed. (Mainz, Germany: Hermann Schmidt Verlag, 2014). Used by permission.

world out there—all the more reason to seek to move inside the protecting walls of a familiar *guanxi*.

When Chinese audiences first see these images, they laugh in recognition—whereas those from the West often seem puzzled. Perhaps Westerners don't recognize what is so different about networks at home. Networks in the West are often merely instrumental, fostered by a kind of informal *bonhomie*. In China, *guanxi* means not merely helping out someone in a friendly fashion. On the contrary, *guanxi* connections involve a reciprocal, often lifelong, commitment. This difference in quality builds on the model of those *xiao* commitments to the family, as extended outward to others. Contrast such grounding with that of our associations in the West, which tend to be defined mostly in terms of small, disparate primary groups. Here we would distinguish each group by a quite different quality of relationship. For family, we would speak of lifelong ties; for friends, of mutual loyalty; for colleagues, of quasi-contractual relationships based on mutual assistance; and for acquaintances, of a casual on-and-off relationship often based on coincidence. Moreover, each group would normally remain separate from the other, with only occasional overlaps. On the Chinese side, by contrast, everyone seems connected to just about everyone else in a multiplicity of relationships. Furthermore, they tend to relate to each other in much the same way: by being *obligated* through bonds of mutual trust. Perhaps for some Westerners this Chinese image may seem like a nightmare: too many entanglements, too many obligations, and too much like an anthill. And of course it does come with a price.

GUANXI INTERDEPENDENCE

One price of being involved in a *guanxi* network is that decisions cannot easily be made alone; important choices must fit in with the interests of the group and must be made *with* the group. In China, it seems, one does not *make up one's own mind*—precisely because one's mind does not, strictly speaking, belong to oneself, but belongs to the sum total of others with whom one is connected. What may be invisible to those from the West is the way a Chinese person would normally make critical decisions: not alone but in active consultation with one or more of one's *guanxi* networks. In particular, the immediate family will often have a decisive say about a young person's career choices, whom to marry or when, and where to live (if a choice is available). This attentiveness to the opinions and wishes of others often results in what one, as a Westerner, might well see as a startling degree of social consensus.

For instance, a great deal of pressure is exerted on young men approaching the age of thirty to marry. If one presses for a reason, usually the response traces back to Kongzi, who said, "At thirty, I was established."[5] He did not actually say he was married, but that is the common interpretation of his saying. Equally, once young people are married, they are put under considerable pressure to have their only child. Very often, young people concede to their elders' opinions on how and when and even with whom they should undertake these things—which they see not altogether as personal choices but as something closer to duty. If having a child is the way to prolong the family, it is not a personal choice.

Not having a *mind of one's own* might, in the West, seem a high price to pay, but in China there is a higher price for being alienated from one's *guanxi* network. For this reason, Chinese people are often quite taken aback when a Western person insists on "doing for himself." In their world, independence is not only not valued but also seen as a little foolish—precisely because in a Chinese world, one actively *needs* to depend on others.

GUANXI PROTECTION

In fact, for foreigners especially, *guanxi* is indispensible. Unless one can speak, read, and write Mandarin with some fluency, one is effectively deaf, dumb, and blind from the first moment in China—as dependent on others as a child. But even as one becomes more competent in this world, the dependencies only multiply—for many reasons. Although China is governed by a vast bureaucracy that infiltrates almost every aspect of life, people cannot count on these systems to work. When they fail, then one calls on the underlying Chinese default system, that is, one asks someone from one's *guanxi* network to intervene, someone well placed enough in the relevant hierarchy to advance one's cause.

In short, *guanxi* is about protection. As an example, gateways are almost always protected in China. At both entrances to our university, young guards stand at attention, vetting all cars and other traffic in and out. At many doors into temples or other public institutions are placed symbolic *fu* or "lion dogs," said to protect against evil spirits.

At temples, tombs, and gardens, these lion dogs, usually benign, have a particularly menacing snarl. Outside key entrances to buildings within the Forbidden City in Beijing, they are larger and sternly fierce (see below). These figures represent the necessity in China of protecting "inside" from "outside," just as *mianzi* protects oneself from those intrusions that may threaten or humiliate one's standing in society.

There are many reasons that such protections are important. China is still a world in which resources can be scarce. Such occasions tend to be unpredictable, but with a population of more than 1.3 billion, many things may suddenly turn out to be in short supply. When official systems for distribution yield only shortages, in case of need one calls on one's *guanxi* to help out, whether you need train tickets or good-quality cooking oil. Further, the item often in shortest supply is information. In China, the official news is heavily filtered so that reliable information may also be very hard to obtain. When the media are silent or in denial (as was long the case with the SARS epidemic[6]), one's *guanxi* networks will likely yield the most reliable reports on any given situation.

Fu entrance guardians in the Forbidden City.

COOPETITION AND CHINESE HIERARCHIES

Guanxi values, however, may pose difficulties for the outsider. While we in the West are heavily invested in systems based on a contest of "equals," the concept is quite alien to the Chinese. In fact, Chinese culture itself might be seen as a vast construct designed to mitigate the most destructive effects of competition. Perhaps the Chinese approach is best summarized by a neologism, *coopetition*, a portmanteau word combining cooperation with competition. Although devised within the context of game theory,[7] it is a concept useful for fusing the cooperative features of *guanxi* with the aggressive tactics of open competition.[8]

The way it functions might be sketched out in relation to the present Standing Committee of the Politburo within the Chinese Communist Party (CCP). Each of its members is a "top leader" with a large *guanxi* hierarchy at his command. At the top table, from all the evidence available, there is ruthless competition as to whose opinion or influence will prevail. At the same time, between the hierarchies, particularly when a top-level Party order is made, there will be significant cooperation in implementing such an order at ground level. And finally, when the Standing Committee needs to present a unified front for the sake of *mianzi*, the signifiers of cooperation are everywhere, from the coordinated public speeches even down to the choice of suit and tie.

Perhaps it is significant that someone has to coin, for the West, a new word to encompass what are seen there as the contradictory values of the Chinese world. They are, of course, not contradictory to the Chinese but complementary (like *yin* and *yang*), and have been seen so for centuries, their protocols of competitive cooperation inscribed in the words of Kongzi himself.[9] The key is the use of hierarchies, dependent on the protocols of *xiao*, to act as a brake to the socially corrosive forces of "win or lose" strategies.

Thus the sages, with few exceptions, recommend that people act to maintain the hierarchies into which they are born. Kongzi, calling for moral self-cultivation of individuals, does not approve of rebellions. Mengzi, writing a few centuries later, agrees with the Master except that he finds rebellion justified in extreme cases of bad leadership at the top. What is relevant here is what one scholar calls the "peculiar" Chinese concept of revolution—not as overturning or eliminating hierarchies but "as a call for a stronger, more omnipotent, more competent authority rather than the abolition of authority."[10] The importance of hierarchy is in defining—and maintaining—leaders and their followers. Without such a system of defined priorities, it is argued, there will be no system for distributing scarce resources: hence open competition and, along with it, the risk of chaos (*luan*).[11] Thus, in China, vertical authority is valued as the brake on the chaos threatened by unbridled competition.

Xunzi, one of the pivotal sages in the Chinese tradition, theorized it well over two thousand years ago. There will never be enough goods to go around if everyone can claim an *equal* share. Worse, *two men of equal eminence* will always be squabbling because neither one is designated to command or to follow; thus "two men of equal eminence cannot govern each other; two men of equally humble station cannot employ each other. This is the rule of Heaven. If men are of equal power and station and have the same likes and dislikes, then there will not be enough goods to supply their wants and they will inevitably quarrel. Quarreling must lead to disorder, and disorder to exhaustion."[12]

Xunzi was writing in the third century BCE, praising the still older Book of Documents for affirming that "equality is based on inequality." However paradoxical this reasoning may seem to a Westerner, it still applies today in China. *Unequal* distribution, as long as it is agreed to as necessary by all concerned, results in everyone feeling "equal" in the sense of having a recognized place within the hierarchy. Those who object to a place low on the totem pole will be encouraged to find a way to rise, one that will bring prosperity and honor to their family—if not for themselves, then for their child. Similarly, while ambitious individuals may seek strategic advantage even against the odds, they are always encouraged to work within the system, not to challenge it.

As it happens, sooner or later, everyone in Chinese life, foreign or not, has to learn these lessons. A few years ago a Carrefour (a French-owned supermarket) in Shanghai announced that it would celebrate its anniversary by offering retirees a free breakfast (minimal, Chinese) at opening on a Monday morning. Shortly after the doors had opened, the crowds inside were so dense that the store was obliged to withdraw the offer. Only then could the store be closed, emptied, and returned to normal functioning. From that episode, a Carrefour executive learned a cardinal unwritten rule of Chinese life: *anything perceived as advantageous will be pursued in short order by a large number of people.* Thus one must always guard the entrances, not open them indiscriminately. This is one reason too that information about what appears advantageous is so closely held, reserved for members of the family or one's *guanxi* networks. The threat of one's plans being overwhelmed by competitors is a daily fact of life in an overcrowded society. Restricting valuable resources to one's *guanxi* ensures the floodgates are not left ajar.

GUANXI RECIPROCITY: PAYBACK TIME

As these examples show, the necessity of always working through a *guanxi* network ensures access to scarce resources as well as a way of actually getting things done. But it also makes for complications. It means a very roundabout way of doing business. Worse, for every favor done, one is owed back. Hence it is easy to build up a considerable backlog of obligations. Chinese people are accustomed to keeping track of who owes what to whom and on approximately what scale over long periods of time. And some kind of reciprocity is always called for, even years later.

Although this invisible accounting system appears to be looser in China than in Japan, it is a mistake for Westerners to respond to a favor with a simple "thank you" and a smile. If you are given a service above and beyond that required, then you have incurred an obligation. It is true that, when you do thank someone, you may be met with the common expression *mei guanxi.* Translated as "you're welcome" in response to a "thank you," it literally asserts "no relationship." But, as a formulaic response to a favor, the assertion of *no relationship* is merely polite. While intended to reassure you that you have not incurred an obligation, *in China there is always an obligation.* More than a question of etiquette, this becomes a way of life.

In short, *guanxi*, like *mianzi*, works as a system of exchange. By returning one favor with another—such as a gift or an invitation to eat together—one inevitably becomes woven into the fabric of *guanxi* relationships. But this is not merely personal; it is the way the whole place works. In both hiring and promotions procedures, for example, *guanxi* will probably be invoked—and without shame. This may extend routinely to nepotism; in fact, the Chinese tend to be mystified as to why hiring someone from one's family is considered as a questionable practice (if not explicitly outlawed) in such places as the United States. They will ask, But who else would you *trust*—if not your family? Even the "incorruptible" British administrator of the late Qing dynasty Imperial Customs Service, Robert Hart, justified such a practice, declaring that "I have never advanced a worse man over a better; yet, if promotion is due to one of two men of equal deserts, and one of them is my own flesh and blood, it would simply be unnatural to pass him over."[13]

If, in the *guanxi* world, it's not *what* you know but *whom* you know, we must also acknowledge that this principle applies outside the Chinese world as well. In the West, despite aspirations to meritocracy, everyone knows about promoting the "ol' boy system" (in England commonly known as "the old school tie"). In America, more so than in Europe, these ties are often mentioned in a tone of contempt, as if to dismiss the idea that one might be hired or promoted because one has the "right" connections, rather than purely on the basis of one's merit. Insisting on such Western-style abstractions as "merit" in a Chinese world, however, would be naive (some might argue that it is naive outside China as well). In China, as elsewhere, one may well be advanced in a career precisely *because* of the contacts one brings along. Once again, one is judged partly by the company one keeps, not just on what one can do on one's own. Moreover, in the Chinese world, trying to get along without the help of others can make one very vulnerable in a place that depends so heavily on such relationships, both for survival and for advancement.

How *guanxi* works may be illustrated by a simple example. You are faced with an obstacle you cannot shift—perhaps do not even fully comprehend. Normally, the way around obstacles in China is to call on the person with the highest possible status to lend *mianzi* or *face* to one's request to resolve the problem; that status makes it harder for someone else to say no. Thus are issues of *mianzi* and *guanxi* inextricably linked. In fact, one might define *mianzi* as that sense of your own self-value as granted to you by your *guanxi*.[14] So imbricated are the two that one foreign observer describes *mianzi* in much the same terms as *guanxi*, saying, "*Face* . . . is the currency of advancement. It's like a social bank account. You spend it and you save it and you invest. And when you take away somebody's *face* you take away someone's fundamental sense of security."[15]

As in managing a bank account, one must always weigh consequences when invoking *guanxi*. To decide whether or not (and to what degree) to give *mianzi* to other people by helping them out through your own *guanxi* networks can be a real form of power. The people appealing to you do so through trust. But they also make themselves vulnerable to a possible refusal. Thus a request to someone in one's *guanxi* network implicitly tests the degree of commitment within the relationship. Minimally, one may choose to maintain *mianzi* in responding to an appeal for help. Or one might seek to enhance relations by pursuing a win-win interaction (for example, earning praise for modesty by promoting the other's *mianzi*). Or one may choose to distance or even close off the relationship by pursuing a zero-sum game (triumph over the other party, who thereby loses *mianzi*, or vice versa).

Thus, by definition, your own sense of worth is dependent on others within your *guanxi*. Again, one is always in China at the mercy of one's relations with others. Yet it is through such relations that one's worth may literally be translated into social—as well as actual—capital through the Chinese way of doing business.

BUSINESS PRACTICES

As the incident at Carrefour illustrates, the ways of *guanxi* are not always cognate to business management's "best practice" formulas. Let's say a top Western executive has been dispatched to China because his company plans to globalize. If he has not done his research, what is likely to happen? Flying in from abroad, our Western executive has plans to attend (pretty well immediately) a series of focused meetings in which, from his point of view, everything is directed toward the single goal of "signing the deal."[16] If his company is "going global," he will readily assume his deal-making will also proceed upon "global" (that is, Western) patterns. If so, what he will encounter may well baffle him: a series of lengthy introductions to various Chinese stakeholders (whose hierarchy eludes him, as he has not informed himself of their status in advance). A seemingly endless series of meetings—many over meals—will involve conversations in which his Chinese coequals, amidst some general remarks about how business is doing, inquire apparently at random about his flight, his family, his health, what he has seen of China, and so forth.

As lunches and dinners pile up, our stereotypical Western businessman finds himself in a lather of impatience. The deal has been mentioned, discussed in general terms, and then shied away from. He has introduced his agenda several times, to be met by pointed silence followed by deflection. He has also explained, in detail, how dealing with his company will improve on what he sees as weaknesses on the Chinese side—to even more pointed silence. From his perspective, little or nothing has been accomplished, and his flight home leaves in only a few days.[17]

From the Chinese point of view, however, much has been learned. After a time, the Chinese managers implicitly agree among themselves that they are facing an all-too-typical Western businessperson: impatient and blunt to the point of being impolite about what he or she sees as the Chinese company's weaknesses—and now, in complaining about apparently unnecessary delays in getting down to "the deal." They are understandably less than impressed with those who have not gone to the trouble of instructing themselves sufficiently about their own hierarchies or otherwise about Chinese ways. Such people have not been responsive to their polite deflections or, worse, their silences. While they may decide, for reasons of *mianzi*, to continue the meetings, they may already have concluded that they cannot trust someone so culturally arrogant. After all, China has already suffered what its history books depict as a century and more of foreign humiliations. Now that China is rising, they have no intention of allowing a Westerner to dictate the ways they do business.

Things would have gone more smoothly had our Western businessperson understood that, given the crucial role of *guanxi*, his first job would be to establish trust. Trust is intangible but also indispensable. It cannot be established by Western virtual "networking" but on personal presence. Establishing trust begins with observing the traditional protocols: an exchange of gifts and personal information, many meals together, and (unfortunately for our jet-lagged businessman) many ceremonial drinking sessions. Building *guanxi* takes time. Wise Westerners allow for this contingency—keeping their return flights open, so as to allocate days or even weeks for the necessary negotiations. During their visits, they would try to remain receptive to all the occasions, especially ceremonial meals, that would allow them to establish a personal connection with the most important people in the organization—even if it required drinking inordinate amounts of alcohol and stumbling through a few karaoke sessions. In the end, even such visitors might have to admit that *establishing trust* through such Chinese measures could, after all, contribute substantially to doing good business in the West as well.

THE DARK SIDE OF *GUANXI*

What is significant about such trust in China, however, is that it is strictly limited to one's family and its extension into a *guanxi* network. Outside this magic circle it can be a callous and fiercely competitive world. Inside, unwavering loyalty applies, sometimes at the expense of what Westerners might regard as "higher principles."

Precedent for such practice is venerable, having been legitimized centuries ago by none other than Kongzi himself. This is how his implicit endorsement is reported in the *Analects*: "The Governor of She in conversation with Confucius said, 'In our village there is someone called "True Person." When his father took a sheep on the sly, he reported him to the authorities.' Confucius replied, 'Those who are true in my village conduct themselves differently. A father covers for his son, and a son covers for his father. And being true lies in this.'"[18] Clearly in the West, a son "covering" for a crime committed by his father is problematic. In the West, one would typically invoke the "higher principle" of justice in urging a son to turn his father in. As a careful reading of this saying of Kongzi suggests, however, the nature of official justice remains a divisive issue in China, where an abstract notion of "higher principles" is largely absent. The basic question is where should one's loyalty be focused: within the family and *guanxi* network?[19] Or should one's loyalty be higher up, toward the Party and the nation—or toward the uniform application of regulations as embodied in "the rule of law"? Clearly Western ideals about what is "right" and "just" are going to make little headway against centuries of Chinese thinking, particularly given that the latter is grounded in the wisdom of one of its leading sages.

Western ideals in any case have little place in today's China. Though Mao Zedong's regime worked hard to promote enthusiasm for the Revolution and the rebirth of the nation, today's "reformed" China places much more emphasis on money, for better and for worse. That emphasis tends to make one even more dependent on one's family and *guanxi* networks. Its result today is a great deal of what the Chinese call *fu bai* (腐败). The usual English translation is "corruption," though this general label is too crude to bring into focus the many ways that *guanxi* affects or even controls everyday life. Nepotism is so widespread as to be considered "normal"; elaborate "gifts" are routine in sealing business deals; and political decisions are all subject to intense competition among interested *guanxi* groups, each structured as a pyramid headed by one highly placed individual who may well require some gesture of loyalty to influence decisions. The courts are explicitly structured to be responsive in the first instance to the Party and its policies. Political "interference" in such courts would be part of normal procedure in a country where there is no "independent" judiciary or trial by jury.[20] Even so, these structures may leave room for some changes. The Administrative Procedure Law (1990), which allows citizens to file lawsuits against local governments and public agencies, now results in one hundred thousand cases per year, with the plaintiffs winning more than one-third.[21]

But despite such initiatives, little is *impartial* in China; everything seems to operate on the level of the personal, at least when it operates effectively. Reconciling this mode of operating with Western assumptions about the necessity of impersonal and impartial decision making is often a difficult task for those from the West living in or working with China today. What many conclude is that working with China necessarily involves recognizing that Chinese ways of getting things done—even when clearly opposed to Western standards—may prove, in the long run, no more or less "corrupt" than the various deformations of systems, both judicial and political, in the West.[22] In any case, to try to change ways of thinking that, despite radical social and political disruption, have persisted for millennia in China is as useless as trying to check the flow of the Yangtze. Better to recognize that this world, at least in these aspects, has its own logic and its own justifications, as legitimized by centuries of practice.

What the necessity for *guanxi* does make clear is that this is a very different and complex world compared to that of the West. Not only are its values radically different, but also so is its history. As a media specialist who has been in China for twenty years, Eric Olander observes the following in an interview:

> The Chinese have more experience with suffering than they do with prosperity. In the past 50 years, they've gone through war and famine and drought and dislocation and economic revolution. They do not have the confidence as a society that tomorrow will be better than today. . . . *Guanxi* is this idea that relationships will protect you and insulate you from the variability of life, of a very difficult life in China. . . . So I tie *guanxi* relationships to that innate sense of survival.[23]

Survival is still an issue in China, where the world is perceived to be unpredictable and coldly competitive, if not brutally hostile. In China, it is your *guanxi* or group that saves you from this overwhelming indifference. In today's China, with its vast population and radically enhanced mobility, *guanxi* is more important than ever. Without *guanxi*, you have no *mianzi*, making you literally nobody and nothing. As every Chinese knows, without *guanxi*, you might just as well be in outer space.

NOTES

1. Michael Wines, "China's Censors Misfire in Abuse-of-Power Case," *New York Times*, November 17, 2010. The incident was widely reported in the Western press.
2. For its application in international policies, see chapter 14, "Question Four: Ruling the World."
3. Li Gang, *The Way We Think: Chinese View of Life Philosophy* (Beijing: Sinolingua, 2009), 13.

4. Such promotional activities are known in Chinese as *la guan xi* (拉关系), meaning "to pull" a *guanxi* relationship. The expression carries a negative connotation, but the phenomenon is widely practiced.

5. Roger T. Ames and Henry Rosemont Jr., trans., *The Analects of Confucius: A Philosophical Translation* (New York: Ballantine, 1998), 2.4, in *CCCW*, 40.

6. Thomas Crampton, "Chasing the Rumors to Chase Down SARS," *International Herald Tribune*, June 4, 2003.

7. Basic principles of coopetition emerged in game theory, notably with *Theory of Games and Economic Behavior* by John von Neumann and Oskar Morgenstern (Princeton, NJ: Princeton University Press, 1944), as furthered by John Forbes Nash (*A Beautiful Mind*—book and film) working on noncooperative games. Coopetition implies cooperation as a means of gaining competitive advantage for one or more players.

8. Compare the unwritten code of Western corporate conduct, spelled out by Robert Jackall in *Moral Mazes: The World of Corporate Managers* (New York: Oxford University Press, 2009): "(1) You never go around your boss. (2) You tell your boss what he wants to hear, even when your boss claims that he wants dissenting views. (3) If your boss wants something dropped, you drop it. (4) You are sensitive to your boss's wishes so that you anticipate what he wants; you don't force him, in other words, to act as a boss. (5) Your job is not to report something that your boss does not want reported, but rather to cover it up. You do your job and you keep your mouth shut." As quoted by Peter Ludlow, "The Banality of Systemic Evil," *New York Times*, September 15, 2013. The only distinctively un-Chinese factor here is the idea that the Western boss might claim he wants dissenting views (though Mao Zedong did just that in 1957, trapping many unwary opponents). In the West, whistleblowers, despite official attempts to protect them, are commonly subjected to punishment.

9. The Master said, "Exemplary persons (*junzi* 君子) are not competitive, except when they have to be in the archery ceremony. Greeting and making way for each other, the archers ascend the hall, and returning they drink a salute. Even in contesting, they are exemplary persons." Ames and Rosemont, *Analects*, 3.7.

10. Lucian W. Pye, *The Mandarin and the Cadre: China's Political Cultures* (Ann Arbor: University of Michigan Center for Chinese Studies, 1988), 138–39. He continues, "Filial piety appears to be at the base of the explosive anger Chinese seem to manifest when they feel that authority has not lived up to their belief in its omnipotence."

11. See discussion of Xunzi next, and *CCCW*, 406–8.

12. From Xunzi, "The Regulations of a King" (section 9), in *Hsün Tzu* [Xunzi]: *Basic Writings*, ed. and trans. Burton Watson (New York: Columbia University Press, 1963). *CCCW*, 407.

13. See Richard O'Leary, "An Irish Mandarin: Sir Robert Hart in China, 1854–1908," in *China and the Irish*, ed. Jerusha McCormack, 26–39 (Dublin: New Island, 2009), 37. It is notable that Hart's receptivity to *guanxi* practices in China is related here to his upbringing in Ireland, where such practices were and might still be thought of as customary.

14. See chapter 2, "Locating a Self through Others: *Miànzi*."

15. Tom Doctoroff of the J. Walter Thompson advertising agency, quoted in "Saving Face in China," *International Herald Tribune*, December 13, 2010.

16. A "deal" in the form of a contract will itself be subject to specifically Chinese reopening clauses; hence no deal can be definitive. See chapter 6, "Chameleon Reality: *Yi*."

17. Although this example is based on common elements in many case studies, the most telling one may be from Carolyn Blackman, "Coming Out of China Crying: A Case of Failed

Negotiations," in *Negotiating China: Case Studies and Strategies*, 106–21 (Crow's Nest, Australia: Allen & Unwin, 1997).

18. Ames and Rosemont, *Analects*, 13.18, in *CCCW*, 131. If you suspect that such valuing of loyalty over legality may be outdated, ponder the following recent remark by a twenty-four-year-old Chinese man in the UK who deplored British lack of loyalty among friends by affirming that "if my friends were criminals, I would still protect them, because Chinese people are loyal." Vanessa L. Fong, *Paradise Redefined: Transnational Chinese Students and the Quest for Flexible Citizenship in the Developed World* (Stanford, CA: Stanford University Press, 2011), 182.

19. In traditional China the virtue known as *zhong* (忠) signified loyalty to the center, specifically to the emperor, but was assumed to be in accord with, and in extension of, *xiao*. *CCCW*, 447.

20. See the PRC's Dual System of Governance, in *CCCW*, 444–53, esp. 449 in relation to the judiciary.

21. "China's Slow but Sure Democratization," *South China Morning Post*, March 20, 2013, accessed March 20, 2013, http://www.scmp.com/.

22. The complex comparative issues concerning "corruption" are treated in more detail later. For the moment, suffice it to say that practices widely condemned around the world as "corruption" may be perfectly legal in a country such as the United States, where the Supreme Court decision known as "Citizens United" authorizes unlimited and untraceable contributions that attempt to influence election outcomes. The fact that such donations had little impact on the 2012 elections does not change the functioning of what is clearly a dubious practice for a system called "democratic."

In relation to "corruption," the shifting complexities of U.S. definitions and practices is summarized in Zephyr Teachout, *Corruption in America: From Benjamin Franklin's Snuff Box to Citizens United* (Cambridge, MA: Harvard University Press, 2014).

23. "Business Etiquette for Hong Kong and the Mainland," *International Herald Tribune*, December 7, 2010.

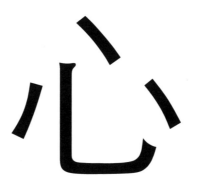

Xīn

4

Where Is My Mind?

Xīn 心

Temple Grandin is known as one of the world's most accomplished and articulate adults with autism. In her latest book, The Autistic Brain: Thinking across the Spectrum, she seeks a deeper assessment of what current science does and does not explain about the characteristics of autism. In particular, Grandin is skeptical about functional MRI scanning as offering no more than a narrow window into the dynamic nature of the autistic brain. She writes,

> Even when researchers do think they've found a match between an autistic person's behavior and an anomaly in the brain, they can't assume that if a patient is exhibiting abnormal behavior and the scientists find a lesion, they've found the source of the behavior. I remember sitting in a neurology lecture in graduate school and suspecting that linking a specific behavior with a specific lesion in the brain was wrong. I imagined myself opening the back of an old-fashioned television and starting to cut wires. If the picture went out, could I safely say I had found the "picture center"? No, because there are a lot of wires back there that I could cut that would make the TV screen go blank. I could cut the connection to the antenna, and the picture would disappear. Or I could cut the power supply, and the picture would disappear. Or I could simply pull the plug out of the wall. But would any parts of the television actually be the picture center? No, because the picture depends not on one specific cause but on a collection of causes, all interdependent. And this is precisely the conclusion that researchers in recent years have begun to reach about the brain—that a lot of functions depend on not just one specific source but large-scale networks.[1]

Through such accessible metaphors, Temple Grandin tries to explain her frustration with the fixation of Western medical science on finding the "location" and thus the "cause" of that complex behavioral dysfunction called autism, with which she was diagnosed as a child. It is true that, even in her latest book, Grandin does tend to collude with the Western paradigm of locating behavior in a specific organ: here, the brain. But she also emphasizes, for autistic people, the importance of sound and touch, that is, their embodied responses as part of their distinctive intelligence. Overall, her frustration reflects the limitations of modern neuroscience, particularly in regard to current models of the mind and how it functions. For Temple Grandin, other models—such as that offered by the radically alien mentalities of animals, into which she feels she has special insight—seem more appropriate.[2]

Many of the same frustrations arise when explaining to a Western audience the Chinese concept of *xin* or "heart-mind." Because it is so radically alien to normal Western models, *xin* best explains itself through what can be actually observed. During one sequence of the opening ceremonies of the 2008 Beijing Olympics, for instance, a series of performers were made to move across a scroll, marking their path with ink from brushes fixed to hands or feet. For the Western audience this might seem only a clever trope. But for the Chinese audience this was a way of producing not merely a graphic trail but a dance—moreover a dance that mimes the larger energies that move the world. Further, they would have understood it as analogous to those movements that guide the calligrapher's brush in a sequence of strokes that, as surely as those of a dancer's choreography, would manifest meaning through making explicit what can only be translated as "body thinking."[3]

Dance sequence choreographed by Shen Wei, opening ceremony, Beijing Olympic Games (28). *Source:* Photo from David Massio Studio. Shen Wei Dance Arts, New York City.

Even in writing the character for *xin* 心, the calligrapher must inscribe the sign for "heart" (including three dots symbolizing drops of blood), thus literally conscripting the body itself as the source for what we in the West call "mind." By means of such compact complexity, *xin* marks perhaps the most profound of divides between Chinese and Western modes of thinking.

Western translation dictionaries, however, tend to blur this divide, often dictating its meaning as *either* "heart" *or* "mind." Clearly such a "definition" grossly misleads Westerners by encouraging them to believe that Chinese people think about thinking in much the same way we do. For in our world, we distinguish sharply between thinking and feeling. Even more drastically, we in the West also tend to locate their functions in discrete parts of the body. *Where is my mind?* we ask ourselves. The usual response to this question locates "thinking" in the brain and "feeling" in the heart (or, occasionally, the gut). Furthermore, we in the West can readily imagine the two as being at odds with each other, engaged in a kind of war between heart and head (as in, "I love him, but I know he's not suitable for me"). Thus it is surprising to learn that a Chinese person would not normally make such a distinction, as in China *there can be no thinking without feeling, no feeling without thinking.* So the most accurate translation of *xin* into English would be the made-up compound noun *heart-mind.*

A WORLD WITHOUT REASON?

What would Plato have made of such a word? His entire approach depends on discerning "the Truth" by discovering "ideal forms" through the use of reason. For Plato, emotions were dangerous impulses, relegated to the lowest functions of the human being. "Passion" was so named because it reduced the reason to a passive rather than an active agent. Passion was so dangerous to his Republic that Plato banned its most blatant expositors, the poets, on the basis that they were "daemonic," hence subject to forces they themselves could not regulate or control. For all else in the Republic, the regulation of emotion by reason—through education and physical exercise, carefully chosen music and readings—was the desired norm.

If all philosophy in the West is deemed to be a "series of footnotes to Plato," as Alfred North Whitehead famously asserted,[4] then the Platonic version of how we think is still relevant in the West. According to this venerable view, humans ordinarily perceive mere appearances; to grasp *reality* requires reaching beyond them. To do so, one must learn to reason; passion is not only misleading but dangerous. Despite Martin Heidegger's polemics against metaphysics—that is, the whole European philosophical tradition from Parmenides on—which believes itself capable of grasping the ultimate foundation of reality in the form of an objective structure such as an "essence" or mathematical "truth," most people in the West still implicitly hold to that tradition in the way they think. Even Freud's dissection of the psyche (into superego, ego, and id) replays, once again, this scenario of conflict between "higher" and "lower" impulses, which must be modulated in order to achieve some kind of balance.[5]

In common with other Western science, Western-style psychology has also been recently imported to China—where, inevitably, it undergoes a sea change. What happens to psychology in China? Given *xin* or heart-mind as characteristic of ideas about human nature in China, there is no basis for isolating something called *psyche* or *soul*. Therefore maladies of the psyche, such as depression, are often somatized, that is, interpreted as being bodily responses to a certain situation.[6] Or given that there is little credence extended to the belief in an individually as opposed to a socially defined self, there are sometimes startling applications of psychological explanations for unwelcome behavior, as reported in the *People's Daily*:

> Some psychologists believe that many Chinese individuals have never been quite so bothered by psychological crises. Recent media reports have recounted the case of a college student who became a murderer after a minor confrontation with peers, ignorant workers committing suicide after failing to obtain overdue wages, members of the social elite falling into hypochondria and government officials ruining their careers by succumbing to greed and taking bribes.[7]

The idea that corruption could be treated as a psychological failing is surprising to Westerners, as is the suggestion that failing to obtain overdue wages may be classified among causes of mental problems. As here, "psychology" is often used in China as yet another means of controlling behavior defined as antisocial. The dominant focus, as is habitual in China, remains on the social sphere and on restraining any actions that threaten to disturb it.[8] Science in this sense has come to be used not as a source of knowledge but as an instrument of social management.

Because (as in this instance) Chinese thinking does not follow Western philosophical or scientific models, there tends to be a misconception in the West that the Chinese do not know how to think. As we will show, they know very well how to think—but they think of thinking quite differently.[9] Chinese habits of mind are simply nearer to what we might call "intuitive intelligence." Chinese people judge people and situations not merely from the stated issues in front of them but within broader contexts and on the basis of more subtle cues. In conversation, for instance, attention is only partly given to what someone is saying. Instead, a Chinese audience would be remarkably receptive to body language, listening for hidden issues and interpreting silences. In responding, questions might well be directed toward framing a context for the discourse, not necessarily to the subject of the discourse itself. What is said might, to a Westerner, seem quite roundabout or even starkly deflective. Responses might come qualified by such words as "perhaps" or "maybe"—baffling any Westerner who expects clarity, if not certainty. Gradually one begins to understand that such a response is in fact a refusal in a culture where it is almost impossible to say no. After a time someone from the West may even learn to read the signs—to translate the body language and to interpret deflections or silences. By that time, the Westerner will have, in effect, learned to respond in the mode of *xin* or heart-mind.

THINKING THROUGH THE BODY

Thinking through the body is not thinking *of* the body nor is it thinking *about* the body. Rather it presumes that thinking begins with the body, operates through the body, and has consequences for the body; it is, in other words, implacably specific and concrete.[10]

The divergence from what we call "thinking" in the West, therefore, could not be more drastic. Whereas in the West, we invoke the use of reason to link everyday experience to abstract (and reified) categories, in China, one experience relates to another in a sequence of episodes best expressed by stories. Take the category, for instance, that we have already examined as *xiao* or "family reverence." In an early dialogue of Plato, Socrates encounters Euthyphro, about to accuse his father of murder. Rather than directly engaging with this specific action, Socrates uses it as a springboard to question exactly what makes *any* action pious.[11] By way of comparison, we turn once again to the anecdote about Kongzi contending with the Governor of She, who praises the moral integrity of a young man from his own province who reported his father for sheep stealing. Kongzi's response, as we have already seen, is, "Those who are true in my village conduct themselves differently. A father covers for his son, and a son covers for his father. And being true lies in this."[12] Apart from its obvious shock value as a defense of *xiao*, what is remarkable about this conversation is that, fully translated, Kongzi's definition of the "True Person" is, in the original, literally that of a "Mr. Straight Body (直躬)." Thus the moral uprightness of the person (similar to the expression in the West) is inscribed in his very posture.

As it stands, this anecdote from the *Analects* might be used as a kind of touchstone for Chinese thinking, illustrating many of its most salient features. It is, first of all, a story—a very short story. Its outcome is unexpected, even paradoxical, thus provoking (like the parables of Jesus of Nazareth) multiple interpretations. Because it refuses to be resolved into any general maxim beyond its own situation, it has the qualities of a small gem. Turning it around in the light of one situation or another, it reveals different facets. Unlike the goal of Socratic interrogation, this situation is not to be resolved into a universal, abstract moral principle, other than, this is what is appropriate in this situation now; think of it as you may, thus provoking the listeners to review their own entire moral perspective.

That quality of being concretely embedded in a situation is true of many of the sayings attributed to Kongzi. As a result, they can be wildly inconsistent with each other. Take, for instance, Kongzi's habit of giving radically different advice to different disciples:

> Zilu asked, "Upon learning something, should one immediately put it into practice?"
> The Master replied, "As long as one's father and older brothers are still alive, how could one possibly put what one has learned immediately into practice?"
> [On a later occasion] Ranyou asked, "Upon learning something, should one immediately put it into practice?"

The Master replied, "Upon learning something, you should immediately put it into practice."

Zihua [having observed both exchanges] inquired, "When Zilu asked you whether or not one should immediately put into practice what one has learned, you told him one should not, as long as one's father and elder brother were still alive. When Ranyou asked the same question, however, you said that one should immediately put into practice what one has learned. I am confused, and humbly ask to have this explained to me."

The Master said, "Ranyou is overly cautious, and so I wished to urge him on. Zilu, on the other hand, is reckless, and so I sought to make him more cautious."[13]

Kongzi thus advises each according to his personality and situation (in this case, in relation to family members to whom *xiao* is owed). This is true teaching, Chinese style: not from abstract principle but to the specific pupil as he comes to you, with a view to shaping not merely the mind but also the character. Because this is the implicit goal of much Chinese teaching, it often defines the teacher's position toward pupils as that of a parent giving guidance to a growing child.

How can such practice be defined, then, as "body thinking"? Like the body, it is a mode of thinking anchored in specific time and place. Like the body, it constantly changes. It responds to different people and situations differentially. Being grounded in the concrete experiences of our bodies, which are not abstract, and therefore not having the same relevance at all times and in all places, such thinking does not seek to generate the "universal truths" posited by the Western world.

And, finally, "body thinking" is performance based. It is important to remember that all of Kongzi's sayings were initially oral, delivered to disciples at a certain time and place. Like the sayings of Jesus of Nazareth, they were memorized and passed down through generations before being actually congealed into script. In accordance with their origin, they are usually invoked to shed new light on, or to change one's perceptions of, a certain defined situation.[14] Finally, they present themselves as obstinately opaque to those who seek to rephrase them as universal moral laws, that is, to force them into a Western mode of thinking.

To say this another way, if we consider Western thinking as vertical—insofar as it insists on referring concrete experience to "higher" abstract (and invisible) categories—then Chinese thinking might be considered radically lateral. That is, it does not seek to define experience in terms of "higher" abstract categories. Nor does it reify experience (via such methods) into "facts" or information to be acquired. What it seeks to do is to seek out, ceaselessly, the relations between things and people.[15] In so doing, the things or "facts" would not be considered as important as those interactions between them—and how these interactions change the way we view them.

Such a mode of thinking is well illustrated by the opening calligraphy dance of the Beijing Olympics, as in China, calligraphy is not merely writing in the Western sense; it is a performance. Although based on years of discipline, one gets only one chance to get it right. Once the brush inscribes the stroke, it cannot be corrected or changed. Thus every performance differs from the last. And, crucially, every performance depends on preparation, not only of the brush and ink, but also (for most calligraphers) of the heart-mind itself, often after hours of meditation. It is an exercise that requires nothing less than total focus.

And what do calligraphers actually do? They connect things. Inscribing the character itself, they are involved in a series of intricate strokes, each of which must be precisely delineated. But this exercise is not as simple as calligraphy in the West. Here one has to learn to write only the twenty-six letters of the alphabet. In China, the calligrapher has to memorize thousands of characters (say two thousand at a minimum), many of which may differ only in the smallest detail. And for each character, the very act of writing may often become a visible recollection of its etymology, as that character would have evolved over many centuries—from its ancient form in Seal script to classical Chinese and the modern simplified version.

Out of such an unfolding over time, each character or ideogram carries its own particular energy—just as each dance posture within a dance sequence reveals its own expressive force. Like a dancer, the calligrapher connects one apparently static moment with another, implicitly connecting one force field to another, through the rhythm of studied choreography (see image below).

Within the script such a sequence is inscribed as movement and rest, and then movement and rest: the characters registering as discrete chords within the flow of the greater music, moving, like music, through time out of time.[16]

Within Chinese thinking, moments of stasis or rest might be thought of as anecdotes or episodes, often compressed into aphorism or metaphor. For many Westerners, these seem to be protean collections of "random" analects, journals, story bits, and argument bits that seem to typify "Chinese thinking." Narratives, in particular, tend to congeal around disparate episodes, tenuously connected and often without clear beginnings or endings.[17] Clearly, it is difficult for people with Western educations, accustomed to the systematic logic of an Aristotle or a Kant, to think of this as "thinking"—or to relate to novels that seem to go on and on endlessly (as in the

Early still photographs of motion by Eadweard Muybridge. *Source:* **Special Collections, Fine Arts Library, Harvard University. Used by permission.**

great classics, such as *The Story of the Stone*)[18] without an apparently clear narrative structure. If these are frustrating, it is even more difficult for those from the West to attune themselves to the flow of body thinking as it engages with an ever emerging, merging, and submerging series of notions and forces (such as *yin/yang*) and in what one Chinese philosopher calls the "opalescent layers of implications in simple facts and descriptions (compact affirmations, negations, metaphors and ironies) sinuously following things, letting them grow, and thereby growing with them."[19]

At the furthest reach of incomprehension, Westerners may get very tired of Chinese interlocutors answering questions with old stories, rather than facts or category statements (based on their own comfortable distinctions that "this" is not "that"—as in "the 'body' really is very separate from the 'mind'"). At other times, Westerners may be deflected or bemused, until there comes a Zen-like moment of enlightenment, when they recognize the implications of the recounted story as it applies to their own questioning. Yet, however oblique or strange this may seem, "body thinking" is the true mode of thinking for most Chinese people, who regard Western philosophy as overabstract, desiccated, imperious, and at bottom, inhuman—insofar as it insists on distancing itself from all that is human, contradictory, and grounded in actual experience in order to formulate abstract, formal, and universal "laws" for its assessments of the world.

THE GREAT DIVERGENCE

Yet notions of "heart-mind" are not totally foreign to the West—although when they appear, they are often dismissed as off center or even as dissenting forces within the dominant paradigms inspired by Greek models.[20] In contemporary life, for instance, dancers, actors, sports stars, and craftsmen must, by definition, seek to work through embodied thinking. Artists, even ones engaged in language, have often sought to explain its modalities. One such, T. S. Eliot, even imagined there was a time when poets could "feel their thought as immediately as the odor of a rose."[21] He saw such "direct sensuous apprehension of thought" as characteristic, in particular, of the poetry of the early seventeenth-century English poet John Donne. But then, Eliot asserts, "something happened."

What happened, in fact, can be exemplified by René Descartes. His project, which has set an agenda for philosophy since the mid-seventeenth century, was to separate out the rational from the emotive processes. He did so in order to find grounding for "certainty" other than that of an immaterial, transcendent God. That grounding Descartes located in what we might call consciousness. While all else might be open to doubt, he argues, the one principle that cannot be separated from me is my own thinking, as summarized in his famous formula: *Cogito, ergo sum* ("I think, therefore I am").[22]

In reaching this conclusion, Descartes separated out the physical body, regarding it merely as a system of mechanical parts, animated by a "mind" or "soul" located in the pineal gland.

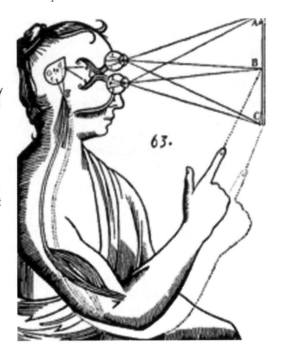

René Descartes's illustration of mind/body dualism. Descartes believed inputs are passed on by the sensory organs to the pineal gland in the brain and from there to the immaterial spirit. What is important here is not the obviously outdated model but the implied metaphor of the act of perception as being a purely mechanical process. That notion of the body as machine is still routinely invoked in the West—where brain research attempts with varying success to locate where in the brain "reality" is perceived (or created).

By Descartes's time, the dissecting of dead bodies was rapidly becoming the norm for Western medicine.[23] Even today, medical students begin their training with a dead body, only belatedly getting to examine in detail the actual bodily processes of a living patient. Is it surprising then that they tend to consider the body itself more as an object, with definable parts, rather than as an intricate, shifting, radically interconnected conscious organism? But this emerging model of the modern, inert, and mechanical body inhabited by an enlivening mind has led to even more drastic presumptions: as Descartes's spectacular alienation of "thinking" from all other bodily processes was to provide the model for what was to become modern science, radiant with the belief that rationally devised experiments could now discover what is objectively *true*.

For the Chinese, such "objectivity" is placed firmly in quotation marks. Although modern Western science is practiced in China, it has come (in the words of one acute Chinese observer) "ready-made, and so the broader quest for certainty that had originally helped give rise to science in the West did not have to come with it."[24] Thus, while science as a mode of knowledge developed in the early modern West does in fact flourish in certain educated circles in China, it is practiced more as a "technique than as spirit," resulting in it being "confined to the domain of science itself."[25] Even inside this domain, it is notoriously difficult to elicit "objective" peer reviews, although awareness of their utility is growing. Outside of this specialized domain, the Western meaning of "objectivity" is alien to a Chinese sense of how one normally interacts with the world.

Thus, from the point of view of heart-mind, the whole Western Enlightenment project collapses. China never had an Enlightenment and, not having ever entered its mindset, tends to consider that nothing can be "objective," if only because it is always apprehended through bodily experience. In such a world, all the precision of science—which has as its premise the existence of a disembodied, abstract world of "facts" and "things" governed by "universal rules" or "first principles"—implodes.

Of course, such a worldview would still be supported by those Chinese scientists who do Western science. But they would do so only as scientists, not necessarily as everyday participants in their own cultural world. For most Chinese people (as for some sophisticated Westerners), "objective facts" are regarded as themselves constructions.[26] And, in regard to quantification, they suspect that claims to precision tend to be arbitrary and artifactual.

What is the difference? In the West, we are told to use "reason." Reason works by distancing the world. It sees the world in terms of things, from which it abstracts qualities, taking them out of context to pin them down. From the time of Plato, but particularly since the rise of science from the seventeenth century onward, the role of reason is to reduce the world to one of "dead" matter subject to "unchanging" rules, as in "the laws of nature." To be more precise, the process of interpreting the world in terms of "fact" renders it as "dead"—as part of a world of things (Wordsworth: "We murder to dissect"). In China, however, one does not think in this disembodied way: one thinks *through the body*, calling upon it to understand the world as a whole, absorbing it through a living sensibility. As one historical example, consider that up until the twentieth century, Chinese units of measure commonly varied according to experiential factors. Before "rational" quantitative measures began to be introduced in nineteenth-century treaties at the insistence of Britain and then other Western powers, the standard Chinese measure of land for cultivation, *mu* 畝, varied in area depending on how fertile the soil was.[27] Similarly the standard Chinese measure of distance, *li* 里, varied according to how difficult the terrain made travel: uphill being counted as further than the distance downhill. James C. Scott, in an apt phrase, refers to this phenomenon as the "friction of terrain."[28] What moves these categories outside of the "rational" is the fact that they were subject to idiosyncratic variation, based on a context-based assessment of their felt value—rather than the "universal" and thus constant values imported from the West.

WESTERN REVOLTS IN THE NAME OF "HEART-MIND"

Artists and writers in the modernizing West have often sought to evoke such an experiential world—as an alternate to the one usually presented to them. In an older Western tradition, such understanding would not have been seen as so deeply estranged from our bodies as our current "scientific" or "rational" understanding of it. Without knowing anything about China, a poet such as John Donne, writing at the moment of emerging modern Europe, exemplifies a stance nearer to the Chinese reliance on heart-mind. In one poem praising a beautiful woman, for instance, he ditches the blazon or conventional dissection of body parts (rosy lips, pale skin, etc., so beloved of Petrarchan sonneteers) to explain how

> we understood
> Her by her sight, her pure and eloquent blood
> Spoke in her cheeks, and so distinctly wrought,
> That one might almost say, her body thought.[29]

Here, the subject's integrity is exemplified by the way her body itself articulates the purity of her mind.

In England, the first concerted revolt against Enlightenment thinking began with the Romantic poets, most explicitly in William Blake's lifelong war on Isaac Newton. But one of their greatest difficulties lay in the language itself. As English is a language that often works by freezing verbs into nouns, and elevating particular nouns to general abstractions, any attempt to explain how body and mind relate to each other—not as separate entities but as interpenetrating energy systems—becomes something of a feat. Blake resorted to inventing his own language and, eventually, his own poetic system. For his part, William Wordsworth often worked by actually contorting the language to convey a radically new sense of being in the world, as in describing how

> The sounding cataract
> Haunted me like a passion: the tall rock,
> The mountain, and the deep and gloomy wood,
> Their colours and their forms, were then to me
> An appetite: a feeling and a love.[30]

Within these lines, the distinction between "self" and "world," inner and outer, and the realm of spirit and that of things, by a process of systematic dislocation, dissolve into the flow of the poet's sensibility.

In such heroic attempts to heal the divide between subject and object, and self and world, Wordsworth could have been paraphrased by Cezanne, when he remarked how, through his painting, "the landscape thinks itself in me and I am its consciousness." Thus (writes the philosopher Merleau-Ponty), "the painter recaptures and converts into visible objects what would, without him, remain walled up in the separate life of each consciousness: the vibration of appearances which is the cradle of things."[31] How does one capture "the vibration of appearances"? One enters this world, as was said of the American writer James Agee, not through "fact" or through the use of mere reason but by an "earthly, earthy sense and sensibility . . . [that] would have been lost were it not seined and seen through our bodily sensibility."[32] To "seine" is to catch fish with a net. For Agee, as for many artists, the body is seen as a net collecting the world within itself—and not merely collecting but also consuming and transforming the world around him even as it itself is consumed and transformed by it. In this way, he re-creates the world and is in turn re-created by it, using his body as the root of its apprehending.

Despite the rise of modern science, such a mode of thinking has persisted in the modern West, often in defiance of it. One might locate this revolt, in the name of reunifying and reclaiming one's humanity, among the Romantics. In more recent times, writers such as D. H. Lawrence have celebrated the body as a central way of knowing the world, one displaced, however, by the modern preoccupation with soul or mind. In philosophy, too, thinkers have tried to heal its own self-inflicted wound. Such schools as the pragmatists (William James, John Dewey, and Richard Rorty) or the process philosopher Alfred North Whitehead (among others) as well as the antimetaphysics of Martin Heidegger all represent ways of moving beyond what they saw as the philosophical complexities posed by relating mind to body as if it were "the ghost in the machine."

By contrast, Chinese thinking never entertained such a theoretical division. It escapes such dichotomies by following a mode of thinking that emerges through *xin* as from a whole bodily sensibility, reaching out to connect with the ambient *qi* or vital energy in a gesture as natural as breathing in and breathing out. Just as we do not consciously select what part of the air we breathe, so *xin* itself opens to the world with no conscious discrimination or division and, through its action, binds the body into the world and the world into the body as a whole and indissoluble one.

THE THINKING HAND

Although we Westerners abandoned Aristotle's physics many centuries ago, most of us still tend to follow his (and his teacher Plato's) paradigm when it comes to human nature. Routinely separating out body and mind, "matter" from "spirit," we impoverish each by mutual alienation. Even so, in recent times Western thinkers are slowly moving away from this model to one nearer to the Chinese concept of heart-mind, in interpreting "body" and "mind" as arbitrary locations within an interpenetrating energy system.

If, for instance, we gesture as we talk, do we think of the brain as ordering up such gestures from the body for the purposes of rhetorical emphasis? Or is something more complicated and instinctive going on? *Where is the mind operating from?*[33] *Does it have a headquarters in the brain? Or can the body actually think in other ways?* Psychologists and linguists such as Susan Goldin-Meadow and David McNeill have tried to answer these questions by devising experiments in which very obvious use of gesture is inhibited (as, for instance, tying one arm behind the speaker).[34] Surprisingly, from such a situation, they discovered a *decreased* ability to perform various kinds of mental tasks. Now, obviously, if such is the case, then the body is obscurely but deeply implicated in thinking processes. Perhaps "hand waving" itself is part of actively thinking a problem through. Can the hand itself have a mind?

Zhuangzi certainly thought so. As early as the fourth century BCE, Zhuangzi was developing the insights of that great master of the *Dao* known to us only as Laozi, the "venerable old guy," through a series of parables. Whereas Laozi's masterpiece, the *Daodejing*, tends to explore how that great unity of *qi*, the *Dao*, manifests itself in the universe, Zhuangzi is more concerned with how *Dao* reveals itself in ordinary life. For him, one way that one's *xin* or heart-mind reaches the *Dao* is through the hands. His heroes are not thinkers or scholars or even mystics but ordinary artisans who have so mastered their craft to the extent that the hand works without consulting the conscious self at all. One of Zhuangzi's exemplars is the wheelwright, who risked his life by arguing for *xin*:

> Duke Huan of Qi was reading books in his hall, when Bian the Wheelwright was cutting a wheel in the court. Laying down his mallet and chisel, Bian the Wheelwright came into the hall and said, "May I ask whose words you are reading now?"
>
> Duke Huan said, "The words of the Sages."
>
> Bian the Wheelwright asked, "Are the Sages still alive?"
>
> Duke Huan said, "They are all dead."
>
> Bian the Wheelwright said, "Then what you are reading now is all rubbish left over by the ancients."
>
> Duke Huan said, "How can you, a wheelwright, make wild comments when I am reading? If you give a good explanation, you will be all right. Otherwise, you shall die."
>
> Bian the Wheelwright said, "I look at things from the point of view of my own work. In cutting the wheel, if I cut slowly, the spokes will be loose and the wheel is not solid. If I work quickly, the spokes will be tight and will not fit. If I cut neither too slowly nor too quickly, I do well with my hands and feel it in my heart-mind [*xin*].
>
> "I cannot put it into words, but there is indeed some know-how in it. I cannot tell my own son what it is, and my son has not been able to learn it from me. That's why I am still working at the age of seventy. The ancients are dead and gone with what they cannot hand down in words. It follows that what you are reading now is all rubbish left over by the ancients."[35]

If the intelligence that informs the wheelwright's hands cannot be transmitted through books or words or even by demonstration, why would we insist that it exists only in our brains? And, if it is not located in our brains, in what other locations (beside the hands) can it reside?

HEART-MIND AS COLLECTIVITY

One response is, it resides within the individual's own bodily performance. But such performance cannot be (paradoxically) individual, if only because it lives within a certain performance protocol.[36] Those protocols have been handed down by wheelwrights over generations. Just because this wheelwright cannot (literally) hand it down by teaching his skills to his son does not mean that the tradition itself dies out. It will continue in the protocols of other wheelwrights as long as wheels continue to be made by hand. For the thinking hand can learn, though it cannot be taught.

The exercise of *xin* or heart-mind is thus always within an actual tradition—and always for an implied or actual audience. How the calligrapher's or wheelwright's hand performs is tested by its outcome, which will, in turn, be judged by how it conforms to or deviates from the larger tradition. While Daoists such as Zhuangzi have always focused on the individual's self-cultivation within a given tradition, the Confucian emphasizes the necessity of conforming to the tradition. Yet for both, the notion of *xin* is central and collective; one's heart-mind is channeled through others, whether living or dead.

In other words, one's heart-mind or *xin* doesn't belong to oneself. Rather *xin* defines the way one connects to others and, through connecting with others, helps define oneself. Memorably, Kongzi's concept of *humanity* invokes a character for "person" combined with the character for "two."[37] In other words, as we have seen earlier, one cannot be a "person" on one's own. Thus one's heart-mind or *xin* is always shared, as an intuitive sense of how to act. Performance is its testing ground.

What does this say, then, about the collective self? Looking at how people tend to act, Kongzi's chief exponent, Mengzi, argued for the innate goodness of all people, observing,

> No man is devoid of a *heart-mind* sensitive to the suffering of others. . . . The reason why I say all men have a *heart-mind* sensitive to the suffering of others is that, even today, if one chances to see a little child about to fall into a well, he would certainly be moved by his *heart-mind* to compassion, not because he wanted to get in the good graces of the parents, nor because he wished to win the praise of his fellow villagers or friends, nor yet because he disliked the cry of the child.
>
> From this it can be seen that whoever is devoid of the *heart-mind* of compassion is not human, whoever is devoid of the *heart-mind* of shame is not human, whoever is devoid of the *heart-mind* of courtesy and modesty is not human, and whoever is devoid of the *heart-mind* of right and wrong is not human. [For] the *heart-mind* of compassion is the beginning of benevolence; the *heart-mind* of shame, the beginning of righteousness; the *heart-mind* of courtesy and modesty, the beginning of decorum; the *heart-mind* of right and wrong, of wisdom.[38]

Mengzi continues, "Man possesses these four beginnings, just as he possesses four limbs." Thus *xin*—or, more precisely, the four heart-thinkings emanating from *xin*—form the basis for all morality: the heart-mind that Westerners might name as "conscience." In the good person, these four heart-thinkings, once developed, will gush from him as out of a spring. Once they are so developed, Mengzi states, "such a person can protect the whole world; if not, he will not be able even to serve his parents."[39] For Mengzi believes mankind to be basically good. This goodness can either be cultivated through education and self-discipline or corrupted through neglect and negative influences. Cases where it is lost altogether were expected to be rare.[40]

Clearly Mengzi's vision of human nature differs sharply from that of Plato and Aristotle, who believed that each individual soul was divided by the competing forces of reason and appetite. Ideally, these could be brought into harmony, with reason (mind) controlling the lower-appetitive bodily emotions (heart). In this schema, the basis for traditional Western concepts about human nature, the body is seen as both degraded and relatively trivial, to be held in check by the individual and rational mind. Mengzi, on the other hand, refines what was to become the great Chinese tradition of locating moral feelings at the center of a bodily sensibility: if one feels rightly, one can then act righteously. To act admirably, one thinks from the heart— not just from one's individual heart-mind but also that which is shared by others within your intimate circle, in other words, out of a collective and humane sensibility.[41] Once again, thinking from heart-mind emphasizes how one becomes human through others, while the body-mind split in the West alienates ourselves even from our own self, in the sense of our own most basic intuitions.

BODY THINKING IN THE WEST

Such alienation arises, at least from the time of Descartes and Newton, from a division of ourselves into bodies and minds. From the perspective of Chinese bodily thinking, and specifically from such categories as *xin*, thinkers in the West are now exploring another way of encountering the world: one that would at last release us from such an impoverished view. Recently, some of its more exciting scientific work has emerged from at least two distinct fields: those of cognitive linguistics and cognitive psychology. The first seeks to overturn our standard notion of words and how they relate to "reality." It challenges the so-called correspondence theory of truth, as one that grows directly out of Christian faith,[42] sometimes dismissed as "logocentrism." Under its aegis, words are presumed to give us reliable insights into "reality," the world around and inside us.

This naive faith in words has already been widely attacked in the later decades of the twentieth century under the banner of "postmodernism," for example, in Jacques Derrida's deconstruction of Western logocentrism. Although his *Of Grammatology* represents a serious misreading of the nature of the Chinese language, it also provides a vivid example of how China, even in stereotype, can be singularly useful in rethinking the West.[43] In this case, the chief use of Chinese for Derrida was to promote his own radical decentering of Western confidence in the order of language as a key to the order of the world—a cornerstone of Western belief starting millennia ago but culminating in the Enlightenment's confidence in rationality as conveyed by language logic. From the entire deconstructionist movement, a whole new skepticism has emerged (particularly among Western intellectuals) about how words relate to—or even serve to construct—so-called realities. But showing the tricks that language can play still does not supply a credible alternative to traditional views. How this occurs is sketched out in the field of cognitive linguistics, as exemplified by George Lakoff and Mark Johnson in their *Philosophy in the Flesh* (1999).

What Lakoff and Johnson argue is that our ideas of things come not from direct connection with something outside us, as naive realism would like to believe. Nor are they grounded in something a priori in our minds, as Immanuel Kant once posited. Instead, Lakoff and Johnson claim that all our more complex ideas are composed bodily, emerging from our basic experiences of the physical world. These are extended or combined by *metaphorical extension*, that is, by projecting or mapping familiar characteristics onto unfamiliar domains in order to make sense of them. For example, all children experience what it feels like to stand straight and tall. Later on, this bodily experience will allow them to think of what it might mean to be "morally upstanding."[44]

The larger significance of this view of language is spelled out by Mark Johnson in a more recent book titled *The Meaning of the Body: Aesthetics of Human Understanding*.[45] In this view, *truth* is a largely irrelevant notion in human terms, because it can only apply to a limited range of propositions of a type that have been overprivileged in Western thought, especially in Anglo-American analytical philosophy. What is more important, says Johnson, is *meaning*: a much larger and messier concept that refers to what results from extrapolating bodily experience into ever new domains. To make something *meaningful*, in Johnson's terms, is to connect it with one's past experiences and one's ongoing concerns. In that way, things will make sense because one will have established connections between different aspects of one's life experience. *Meaning*, then, is always individual and personal, though everyone will share many meanings with other members of one's home culture (and some meanings with all other humans).

From Lakoff and Johnson's reformulation of *meaning*, radical implications have emerged. In the introduction to *Philosophy in the Flesh*, they respond to the question, Who are we? with three propositions that will likely seem radical to most Westerners:

The mind is inherently embodied.
Thought is mostly unconscious.
Abstract concepts are largely metaphorical.

"In these three major findings of cognitive science," they continue, "more than two millennia of *a priori* philosophical speculation about these aspects of reason are over." Western philosophy can never be the same again, because the way we understand reason has changed. Those changes in understanding they list as follows:

Reason is not disembodied, as the tradition has largely held, but arises from the nature of our brains, bodies, and bodily experience.

Reason is evolutionary, in that abstract reason builds on and makes use of forms of perceptual and motor inference present in "lower" animals.

Reason is not "universal" in the transcendent sense; that is, it is not part of the structure of the universe. It is universal, however, in that it is a capacity shared universally by all human beings. *What allows it to be shared are the commonalities that exist in the way our minds are embodied.*

Reason is not purely literal, but largely metaphorical and imaginative.

Reason is not dispassionate, but emotionally engaged.[46]

In the last proposition, as well as in the italicized passages above, these statements closely approach a Chinese understanding of the concept of *xin*: as embodied mind that operates often on an unconscious or preconscious intuitive level—and one that engages both reasoning and emotion in one gesture.

Such ideas are not altogether new, even to the West. Versions of them can be found in the work of Martin Heidegger, William James, and Maurice Merleau-Ponty, among others. Philosophically, as we have seen, among its most recent exponents are the cognitive linguists who work to explain mind/body relations in terms of "embodied cognition" or "extended mind." In everyday life, actors and dancers have long known that the body thinks, expressed through actual performance. How much of a musician's performance, for instance, can be said to be embodied in his hands—or his heart?

Giving evidence to these theories is new scientific research on what is called cellular or tissue memory; this research is helping to establish, if so far only anecdotally, that transplanted hearts, for instance, may carry with them memories that enter into the body of the new recipient.[47] In another related field, the work of Professor Andrew Schwartz on how artificial limbs and other nonbiological circuits come to function as parts of the material underpinnings of our minds is also widening our Western conceptions of where we locate our minds.[48] Yet Westerners still resist the notion that intelligence can infuse all parts of our body in a diffused consciousness that resembles the energies of heart-mind or *xin*, even though they seem to have few qualms about seeing the mind extended into the artificial intelligences of computers and other such machines. Because of this resistance, radical changes in the understanding of the ways we think will continue to remain controversial. But insofar as they are accepted, they move Western thinking closer—if still distinct in many ways—to the Chinese concept of heart-mind. For to change the way we Westerners understand reason is nothing less than to change something fundamental to the way we understand ourselves. Research continues to accumulate to suggest how weak the role of rationality is in the actual way people think and reach decisions.[49]

Other experiments demonstrate the impact on thinking on what one wears. Using a doctor's white coat, experimenters found our minds are literally invested in what we wear. Apparently, clothes invade the body and brain, putting the wearer into a different psychological state. But the effect occurs only if you *actually* wear the doctor's coat and recognize its symbolic meaning; in this case, the implication is that physicians tend to be careful, rigorous, and good at paying attention. Conceived as part of a growing scientific specialization called *embodied cognition*, there is, according to the authors of this study, a huge body of work in this field, demonstrating such varied correlations as how the experience of washing your hands is associated with moral purity; how people are rated personally warmer if they hold a hot drink in their hand, and colder if they hold an iced drink; or how carrying a heavy clipboard will make you feel more important. In other words, our thought processes are based on physical experiences as affected by associated abstract concepts.[50]

In short, as the West is beginning to find out, we do not think just with our *brains but with our bodies and through our social stereotypes as well.* What is also important in these experiments is the new emphasis on not merely *what we think* but *how we think.*[51] Such an emphasis would come as no surprise in a Chinese context; *xin* has long described the human heart-mind as unitary and rooted in intuitive, social responses. Insofar as such new perspectives, as confirmed by such research, gain credibility among Westerners, Chinese understandings of the way we think will not only become more comprehensible but also broaden our own grasp of the nature of being human.

NOTES

1. Temple Grandin and Richard Panek, *The Autistic Brain: Thinking across the Spectrum* (Boston: Houghton Mifflin Harcourt, 2013), 37, 49.

2. Currently professor of animal science at Colorado State University, Grandin is also the author of several books, in particular (with Catherine Johnson), *Animals in Translation: Using the Mysteries of Autism to Decode Animal Behavior* (2005) and *Animals Make Us Human: Creating the Best Life for Animals* (2009).

3. Kuang-Ming Wu, *On Chinese Body Thinking: A Cultural Hermeneutic* (Leiden, Netherlands: Brill, 1996).

4. Alfred North Whitehead, *Process and Reality* (New York: Macmillan, 1929), 7.

5. Plato's metaphor of the charioteer struggling to manage two horses pulling in a contrary direction prefigures remarkably well Freud's ego striving to regulate the competing claims of id and superego. See *CCCW*, 203, 259.

6. For instances of such somatization of an illness now usually regarded as psychological in the West, see Arthur and Joan Kleinman, "Comparative Diagnoses of Depression," in *CCCW*, CD, 1427–30.

7. Xinhua, "Seems Money Can't Buy Happiness, as Saying Goes," *People's Daily Online*, August 31, 2004, accessed June 1, 2007, http://en.people.cn/.

8. See chapter 8, "Thinking in Harmony: *Hé*."

9. In the West, too, there are claims that groups defined as "other" (such as children, women, Native Americans, African Americans, etc.) also think in ways quite distinctive, if not actually quite divergent, from what is regarded as the Anglo-European tradition. However, none of these groups are as consistently divergent in their thinking as is the general majority of Chinese people.

10. This passage relies on Kuang-Ming Wu's "A Preliminary Remark" in his seminal book, *On Chinese Body Thinking*, 7.

11. This passage is indebted to Wu, *On Chinese Body Thinking*, 7–8. In the *Euthyphro*, although the interpretation remains ambiguous, Socrates seems to be denying Euthyphro's all-too-concrete definition of piety by enumerating its examples. Unless Euthyphro knows what piety is, how can he accuse his father of impiety? And, it is implied, wouldn't Euthyphro's accusation of his own father itself constitute an act of impiety? It is of course a further irony of this discourse that Socrates himself is ultimately to be condemned to death for "impiety" to the gods.

12. Roger T. Ames and Henry Rosemont Jr., trans., *The Analects of Confucius: A Philosophical Translation* (New York: Ballantine, 1998), 13.18. The translation of the "True Person" as "Mr. Straight Body" is by Wu, *On Chinese Body Thinking*, 8.

13. *Analects* 11.22, in *Readings in Classical Chinese Philosophy*, trans. Philip J. Ivanhoe and Bryan W. Van Norden (Indianapolis: Hackett, 2001), 30.

14. Michael LaFargue, "The Semantic Structure of Aphorisms: The Proverb as a Special Genre of Speech," in *Tao and Method: A Reasoned Approach to the Tao Te Ching*, 133–44 (Albany: State University of New York Press, 1994).

15. Again, this exposition of Chinese modes of thinking is indebted to Wu, *On Chinese Body Thinking*, 9–10.

16. To see these stills in motion, see a feature on National Public Radio: Neda Ulaby, "Muybridge: The Man Who Made Pictures Move," April 13, 2010, accessed September 5, 2014, http://www.npr.org/.

17. Qi Wang, "Are Asians Forgetful? Perception, Retention, and Recall in Episodic Remembering," *Cognition* 111 (2009): 123–31. For further elaboration on this point, see Gish Jen, *Tiger Writing: Art, Culture, and the Interdependent Self* (Cambridge, MA: Harvard University Press, 2013); and the section "From Language to Mentalities" in "Introduction: Entering a Chinese World" in this text.

18. This classic eighteenth-century text by Cao Xueqin has also been translated into English as *A Dream of Red Mansions* or *The Dream of the Red Chamber*.

19. Wu, *On Chinese Body Thinking*, 13–14, n1.

20. There are precedents for such body thinking in the West, drawn more from the Hebraic traditions than the Greek, for instance, in the famous phrase from the Gospel according to St. Luke 2:19, where it is said that, following the Annunciation, "Mary pondered these things in her heart" (King James Version). Writing in Greek, Luke obscures the Hebrew tradition of thinking. As in the Chinese notion of *xin*, the composers of the books of the Old Testament had only one word for *heart-mind*, the Hebrew word *lev*, which "taken literally, refers to the physical organ we call the heart. . . . [But] Classical Hebrew has no parallel to the later Western dichotomy between the 'heart' as the seat of the emotions and the 'mind' as the seat of thought. For the biblical authors, sentiments are a part of the process of human thought and of reason, and not something separate from it. And when human beings are thinking, or reasoning, or believing, they do so with their *lev*, which is most directly translated as *mind*." Yoram Hazony, *The Philosophy of Hebrew Scripture* (New York: Cambridge University Press, 2012), 171.

21. T. S. Eliot, "The Metaphysical Poets," in *Selected Essays, 1917–1932* (1934; New York: Harcourt, Brace, 1964), 241–50.

22. See his *Discourse on the Method* (1637).

23. See page 98 for an image of Vesalius's skinless, muscular human body dating from 1543. *CCCW*, 198, 254.

24. The full text, including the following quotation, reads as follows: "As it happened, modern science came to China largely ready-made, and so the broader quest for certainty that had originally helped give rise to science in the West did not have to come with it. While science as a mode of knowledge has since flourished in China, little of the quest for certainty—the spirit of science, as it were—has come to inform fields of intellectual inquiry other than science. Since the quest for certainty started life in China in a reified form, more as technique than as spirit, it is not surprising that it has been confined to the domain of science itself." Jiwei Ci, "What Is in the Cloud? A Critical Engagement with Thomas Metzger on *The Clash between Chinese and Western Political Theories*," *Boundary 2*, no. 34 (2007): 74.

25. As an example of how science is resisted when it seeks to influence culture, there is the case of the genealogy of Kongzi. Now in its eighty-third generation, the Kong family pedigree is the longest recorded in the world today, numbering between two and three million descendants. But when the Chinese government offered claimants DNA testing in 2006, the idea met with such resistance that it was withdrawn three years later, the grounds being that the Kongzi family tree has such enormous cultural significance, it could not "just" be a question of science. (Interpretation: the scientific route to establishing the Kong genealogy would exclude too many people from claims that may have persisted for centuries.) See "Confucius: Descendants," *Wikipedia*, accessed January 31, 2013, http://en.wikipedia.org/.

26. For an investigation into the Western invention of "fact," see Mary Poovey, *A History of the Modern Fact: Problems of Knowledge in the Sciences of Wealth and Society* (Chicago: University of Chicago Press, 1998).

27. See Shen Fu, *Six Records of a Floating Life*, trans. with notes by Leonard Pratt and Chiang Su-hui (London: Penguin, 1983), 19–20.

28. James C. Scott, *The Art of Not Being Governed: An Anarchist History of Upland Southeast Asia* (New Haven, CT: Yale University Press, 2009), 47.

29. John Donne, "The Second Anniversary of the Progress of the Soul," in *The Complete Poetry of John Donne*, ed. John T. Shawcross (New York: Doubleday, 1967), 299.

30. William Wordsworth, "Lines: Written a Few Miles above Tintern Abbey," in *Wordsworth: Poetry and Prose*, ed. W. M. Merchant (Cambridge, MA: Harvard University Press, 1967), 154.

31. Maurice Merleau-Ponty, *Sense and Non-sense*, trans. Hubert L. Dreyfus and Patricia Allen Dreyfus (Evanston, IL: Northwestern University Press, 1964), 17–18, as quoted in Wu, *On Chinese Body Thinking*, 268.

32. Here the insight referred to is that of James Agee in Agee and Walker Evans, *Let Us Now Praise Famous Men: Three Tenant Families* (1941; Boston: Houghton Mifflin, 1960), as quoted in Wu, *On Chinese Body Thinking*, 267.

33. The following examples are drawn from a provocative article by Andy Clark, "Out of Our Brains," Opinionator, *New York Times*, December 12, 2010.

34. Also from Clark, "Out of Our Brains." For more information on these frontier studies in the role of gesture in language, see Susan Goldin-Meadow, *Hearing Gesture: How Our Hands Help Us Think* (Cambridge, MA: Harvard University Press, 2003); and David McNeill, ed., *Language and Gesture*, Language, Culture and Cognition (Cambridge: Cambridge University Press, 2000).

35. Wang Rongpei, trans., *Zhuangzi*, 2 vols., Library of Chinese Classics (Changsha, China: Hunan People's Publishing House, 1999), 1:13, 219–21; *CCCW*, 59.

36. In his magisterial *Chinese Art of Writing* (Geneva: Skira, 1990), Jean-François Billeter identified Henri Matisse as the Western painter whose understanding of his work as perfor-

mance came closest to the Chinese tradition. Matisse, commenting on his line drawings, said, "The page is written, no correction can be made. If it is inadequate, all I can do is to give it another try, as if it were a matter of acrobatics" (223).

37. The key concept here is once again *ren* 仁. For a fuller discussion see chapter 12, "Question Two: Human Rights?"

38. Mengzi, 3.6, from *Mencius* (bilingual ed.), trans. Zhao Zhentao, Zhang Wenting, and Zhou Dingzhi, Library of Chinese Classics (Changsha, China: Hunan People's Publishing House, 1999), 70–73. A less felicitous translation, which does not give *xin* due weight, appears in *CCCW*, CD, 1236.

39. Also from Mengzi, 3.6.

40. About three generations later, the philosopher Xunzi—at the opposite end of the spectrum from Mengzi, insofar as he believed that human beings without education and monitoring would naturally tend to become evil—recommended the death penalty for those who steadfastly refuse reformation and were therefore considered irredeemable.

41. These insights are echoed in the work of Pierre Teilhard de Chardin (1881–1955), a French philosopher and Jesuit priest trained as a paleontologist and geologist who took part in the discovery of Peking Man and Piltdown Man. From 1926 to 1935, he made five prolonged research expeditions in China. While there is little doubt that his signature work, *The Phenomenon of Man*, represents Teilhard de Chardin's attempt at reconciling his religious faith with his academic interests as a paleontologist, it is also, in some of its thinking, remarkably Chinese, especially in its insistence that human evolution requires a unification of consciousness. This is particularly evident when he argues that "no evolutionary future awaits anyone except in association with everyone else," reasoning that "evolution is an ascent toward consciousness," and embodying a continuous upsurge toward the Omega Point, which for all intents and purposes, for Teilhard de Chardin, is God. *The Phenomenon of Man* (New York: Harper & Row, 1959), 250–75.

42. See analysis in chapter 7, "Realizing a Way: *Dào*."

43. Through an extended series of readings (following Western thinkers such as René Descartes, Gottfried Leibniz, Ernest Fenollosa, and Ezra Pound), Derrida's *Of Grammatology* replicates the age-old idea of Chinese as a language that "remained structurally dominated by the ideogram" and, as such, "the testimony of a powerful movement of civilization developing outside of all logocentrism." Jacques Derrida, *Of Grammatology*, trans. Gayatri Chakravorty Spivak (Baltimore: Johns Hopkins University Press, 1998), 90. Derrida's analysis of Chinese as a language has long been rejected by sinologists, condemned as "hallucination," because more Chinese characters function phonetically than ideographically. Yet this stereotype inspired a radical and liberating critique of a prevailing Western shibboleth: that language allows us, literally, to access in some direct way what is termed "reality" or "truth." Thus, in the words of one scholar, during the process of globalization, Derrida's reading of Chinese writing might be taken as an example of those "stereotypes that, rather than simply being false or incorrect (and thus dismissible), have the potential of changing entire intellectual climates." See Rey Chow, "How (the) Inscrutable Chinese Led to Globalized Theory," Special Topic: Globalizing Literary Studies, *PMLA* 116, no. 1 (January 2001): 71.

44. As a phrase, note the similarity to the invocation of the upright man as "Mr. Straight Body" in the Chinese language; see the section "Thinking through the Body" in this chapter. Because Lakoff and Johnson work so exclusively on the basis of English as a language, their assertions are open to challenge on the basis of cultures tied to other languages. Hungarian scholar Zoltan Kövecses, for instance, devotes an entire book to sorting out the kinds of meta-

phors that can credibly claim universality and those better understood to be culture specific: *Metaphor in Culture* (New York: Cambridge University Press, 2005). Some Chinese correctives are available in the work of Lan Chun, *A Cognitive Approach to Spatial Metaphors in English and Chinese* (Beijing: Foreign Language Teaching and Research Press, 2003), 94.

45. Mark Johnson, *The Meaning of the Body: Aesthetics of Human Understanding* (Chicago: University of Chicago Press, 2007).

46. George Lakoff and Mark Johnson, "Introduction: Who Are We?" in *Philosophy in the Flesh: The Embodied Mind and Its Challenge to Western Thought* (New York: Basic, 1999), 3–4 (italics added).

47. One notable report by Paul Pearsall and collaborators involved questioning of 150 heart transplant patients: "Changes in Heart Transplant Recipients That Parallel the Personalities of Their Donors," *Near-Death Studies* 20, no. 3 (Spring 2002): 191–206.

48. John Tozzi, "Andrew Schwartz: Brain Control for Artificial Limbs," Innovator, *Bloomberg Business*, January 10, 2013.

49. A recent book probing the "psychophysics" of thought is Daniel Kahneman, *Thinking, Fast and Slow* (New York: Farrar, Straus and Giroux, 2011). It shows how often and how diversely humans make decisions that are *not* based on the evidence available to them.

50. Originally published by Hajo Adams and Adam J. Galinsky, "Enclothed Cognition," *Journal of Experimental Social Psychology* 48 (July 2012): 918–25, this summary of its conclusions is indebted to Sandra Blakeslee, "Mind Games: Sometimes a White Coat Isn't Just a White Coat," *New York Times*, April 2, 2012.

51. "Our results open new directions within the growing research on embodied cognition. First, research on embodied cognition has mostly focused on *what* we think (i.e., judgments of morality, importance, or power), but the current research broadens the scope of outcome variables by examining *how* we think (i.e., attentional processes)." Adams and Galinsky, "Enclothed Cognition," 922 (italics added).

Qì

5

The Energy Unifying the World

Qi 气

My job was to teach Chinese graduate students in American studies a course based on ideas—Big Ideas. To begin with the biggest, I settled on a text by an American who, more than a century and a half ago, set out to discover Reality.

I explained how Henry David Thoreau decided to leave his job, his town, his family, and his friends to take himself off to a pond called Walden because (in his own words) he wanted to wedge his feet "downward through the mud and slush of opinion, and prejudice, and tradition, and delusion, and appearance, . . . through Paris and London, through New York and Boston and Concord, through church and state, through poetry and philosophy and religion, till we come to a hard bottom and rocks in place."[1]

"Rocks in place," I emphasized. "That's what Westerners think of as reality." I paused for effect. "We say in the West, you should build your house on rock but not on sand, so it can remain a stable foundation for your life."

Perhaps it was the sudden silence—or simply jet lag—but my mind began to play tricks, suddenly throwing up images of earthquakes and volcanoes and the shifting tectonic plates that keep the earth's rocky crust moving. Then a student raised his hand.

"This is not what Chinese call reality."

A little taken aback by this challenge, I asked, "And what do the Chinese call reality?"

"Chinese . . . ," he faded and then looked to his classmates for help and evidently found it. "For Chinese, reality is qi."

"And what is qi?" I asked, pronouncing it carefully (as "chee") but feeling suddenly exposed.

"Qi. Qi is qi," he said, as if it were self-evident. Then raising his hands, he began to make long undulating movements. "Qi is everywhere—in air, in rocks, in people, in things—everywhere. Qi never stays in one place. Qi moves all the time everywhere and through everything. Not possible to stand on qi."[2]

Meditating on this exchange, I had to concede that my student had a point—not only one point but several. Over the year as I had tried to explain my world to these very bright graduate students, Western civilization began to seem increasingly weird.[3] "In the West," I would begin a talk, "most people divide the world into matter and mind," a division, I would explain, mandated by the earliest thinkers in the West. Both Plato and his disciple Aristotle argued that the universe is divided into "substance" or matter (which was in some sense "dead" or inert) and "spirit" (which in some sense enlivened matter). In this world, rocks are things, and things have no life of their own; they are inanimate. Humans, on the other hand, have, beside their material bodies, immaterial "minds" or "souls"—the latter deemed by many to be eternal.

The implication is that most of the world in which we live and move and have our being is "dead matter" (mere "stuff"). In the West, little account was traditionally taken of the life of rocks. Only a couple of centuries ago did geologists start pointing out that rocks and mountains have a life too but live that life out on a far grander scale than ours. And not everyone living in the West automatically shares the assumption that we move in a "dead" world. Exceptions can be found in Native American views of landscape, for instance. Or in those revolts against Western Enlightenment thinking, exemplified by poets such as William Wordsworth, who, in "Tintern Abbey," worked hard to articulate how

> I have felt
> A presence that disturbs me with the joy
> Of elevated thoughts; a sense sublime
> Of something far more deeply interfused
> Whose dwelling is the light of setting suns,
> And the round ocean, and the living air,
> And the blue sky, and in the mind of man,
> A motion and a spirit, that impels
> All thinking things, all objects of all thought,
> And rolls through all things.[4]

Chinese students of English literature are attracted above all to the English Romantic poets and for good reason. They understand that Wordsworth is struggling to articulate what is, from a Chinese point of view, an intuition of *qi*: an energy circling restlessly through all things, objective and subjective—including the human mind. In this poem, as in the Chinese world, a "thing" is no longer a thing; it vibrates as a force within a larger energy system.

For instance, in China, rocks are often collected by connoisseurs. Their value lies in their unique energy, as evident in shape, coloration, and grain. These "scholar rocks" are not merely ornaments for the collector's desk or garden; this is not about merely collecting "stuff." They are also objects eliciting meditation, through which one seeks to enter into the rock's unique *qi*.

Guo Xu, *Mi Fu Honoring a Rock* (1503). *Source*: Shanghai Museum. Used by permission.

Sometimes this ascription of life to what we would regard as inanimate matter goes to extremes. In the painting above, for instance, the scholar-artist Mi Fu, a famous eleventh-century calligrapher, pays homage to a rock—not any rock but a rock from the sacred Lake Tai, which he adopted as his older brother, regularly paying to it his respects.[5] Of course, in adopting a rock as a member of the family, Mi Fu was regarded as eccentric—but not so eccentric that he would be dismissed as merely crazy. In fact, many cultivated people in China acquire a scholar-rock as a way of initiating a kind of exchange, channeling the rock's energy by allowing it to flow *through* one's heart-mind (*xin*) into the larger flow of the universe. The rock, in turn, is no longer a thing to be collected but an organism registering the vibrations of those invisible energies that shape the greater world.[6]

For many Westerners, this may sound like pantheism: the belief that everything composes an all-encompassing, immanent God or that the universe is identical in some sense with divinity.[7] Derived from the Greek roots *pan* ("all") and *theos* ("god"), pantheism has many definitions and has historically flourished in many varieties. But what differentiates Western pantheism sharply from beliefs in the underlying unity of *qi* is its invocation of a personal God who is both within as well as outside nature. Only if pantheism is understood as the extreme and utter identity of all things in the world—as an immanent presence neither anthropomorphic nor personal—does one then approach the quality of *qi* as manifest through *Dao*: that "motion and a spirit" celebrated by Wordsworth and other Romantic writers.

The differences remain radical. Although Daoists speak of *Dao* with similar reverence, *Dao*, unlike God, cannot be named—but only implied—as the mysterious and numinous ground of becoming from which all things of the world emerge.[8] The Daoist sage Zhuangzi becomes its best exponent when he says, "The heaven and the earth and I came into existence at the same time; all things in the world and I are one uniformity."[9] When someone asked Zhuangzi where *Dao* was, he replied that it was in the ant, the grass, the clay tile, and even in excrement: "You don't have to search for *Dao* in any particular place, as nothing in the world can stay away from it."[10] As the unity of all *qi*, its source and circumference, these qualities of *Dao* write large the qualities of *qi*: it is in all places and everywhere, always moving, never resting, emerging and submerging as it transforms itself from one thing into another. In such a context, it makes as little sense to ask, Where is my mind? as to ask, Where is the wind? or, Where is the world?

QI AS TRANSFORMING ENERGY

In providing a locus for such meanings, the character for *qi* is particularly rich semantically. As a character, *qi* 气 refers in a physical sense to *air* or *vapor*. But in the present context its more important signification is *vital energy*, understood as animating everything that exists. In its older full form, *qi* 氣 adds (in the lower left) the icon for *rice*, so that the whole signifies, literally, the "vapor given off by cooking rice." This older complex form of the word stresses its root in the *processes of transformation*: as a hard raw grain (rice) being cooked becoming soft and edible, just as water becomes steam and then air. Thus the philosophical usage of *qi* as *vital energy*[11] is, through its etymology, rooted in everyday experience of a constantly shifting, mutating world.

As so often in the Chinese world, such a discourse is derived from the act of eating, for eating is, par excellence, our most intimate process of transformation, by which raw plants and animals are converted into living tissue.[12] As such, *qi* might be defined as a noun that operates as a verb. Always moving, never stable, *qi* is never identifiable as simply "one thing"—but as the force continually transforming the world through its enabling energy. As the prime mover of Chinese reality, *qi* thus ensures a world in which *everything changes*.

When defined in its more concrete form as "breath" (rather than "energy"), *qi* discloses another of its qualities. Breathing brings air in and out of the body. One cannot "own" or hold on to air. As such, breathing constitutes an exchange with the universe, in which we take in oxygen and breathe out carbon dioxide; carbon dioxide is then taken in by plants, which in turn give back oxygen. Everything works in a cycle and through an exchange in which all benefit. It is a small model of the way that Chinese people commonly understand how their world works. In a world so organized—on a principle of continuous, symbiotic exchange—*everything is connected*.

In these two aspects, *qi* might be taken as revealing the central principle governing the Chinese world, one in which *everything changes and everything is connected* or, more simply, *everything is connected as it changes*.

MARKING ENERGY EXCHANGES AS *YIN* AND *YANG*

In the way it operates, *qi* is marked as oscillating between two modes: *yin* and *yang*. Over the last two thousand years and more, these two aspects of *qi* have evolved into hundreds of apparently dualistic correlates: *yin* 阴 characterizing *water, women,* and the *moon,* for instance, while *yang* 阳 characterizes *fire, men,* and the *sun*.

Although some might at first tend to identify *yin* with the weak and *yang* with strong forces, such easy categorizing can mislead; *yin*, for instance, may overcome *yang*, as water may put out fire. It would be more precise to say that, as their relationship is complementary rather than oppositional, *yin* and *yang* always exist together in a shifting balance in which the very qualities attaching to one can (at any time) transform into the other, just as a stream (*yin*) can carry away part of the rock face (*yang*) as silt.

Eventually Chinese thinking came to identify these forces through the *taiji* symbol. Usually given as a static image, *yin* is here represented by the color black, *yang* by white. But unlike their symbolism in the West, black and white are not opposed but interact as two interreliant forces, ceaselessly shifting between each other. Nor are they exclusive. As the *taiji* symbol indicates, each embraces a small part of the other: the black having a spot of white; the white, a spot of black, thus signaling mutual interdependence and inherent tendency to transmute, one into the other.

This diagram, however, is severely limited by depicting their relationship in terms of stasis, as at any given moment, their exchanges of energy guarantee that one aspect will always overcome the other, by means of a dynamic both relentless and without pause.[13] As such, the *taiji* is a key image for how the Chinese perceive the world as it keeps transforming itself, endlessly and unpredictably.

Given the Western tendency to separate categories into stable binary opposites, few images in the Western world echo the *taiji*. Exceptionally, one striking correlative was created by William Blake—whose outsider views seem eccentric even today. What distinguishes Blake is his stubborn sense that the way we interpret the world is itself destructive. For Blake too perceived the world in terms not of things but of

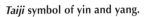
Taiji symbol of yin and yang.

energy. "Energy," he wrote, "is eternal delight." Resisting what he saw as the emerging scientific paradigm (as exemplified by Isaac Newton), Blake declared that it was a case of either someone else's system or his own. So he created his own, within which the forces of good and evil, black and white, coexist and exchange energies.

In *The Angel Michael Binding Satan*, that energy exchange is made visible. It is probably the closest that any Western thinker has come to the Chinese sense of the interpenetrating, complementary qualities of the *taiji*. Yet, by playing on its ambiguities, Blake manages to create an image that might be read in more than one way. One view would observe how Michael, in binding Satan, also binds himself into what may be read as eternal conflict. Another, more Asian reading, would see Michael and

William Blake, *The Angel Michael Binding Satan* (1805). *Source:* Fogg Museum, © President and Fellows of Harvard College.

Satan as forever bound together into the eternal fluctuations of good and evil.[14] Here is the "fearful symmetry" of Blake's famous poem "The Tyger," which itself revolves around his question about the potential duality of God himself, asking, "Did he who made the Lamb, make thee?"

"THING" THINKING VERSUS "ENERGY" THINKING

Writing at the pitch of Enlightenment thinking, Blake was one of the few who instinctively saw that, as he phrased it, "Without Contraries is no progression. . . . From these contraries spring what the religious call Good & Evil." He feared his world was being deadened by the new thinking, as exemplified, for example, by Descartes. In this world, Blake discerned the following errors: first, "that Man has two real existing principles: Viz: a Body & a Soul." And secondly, that "Energy, call'd Evil, is alone from the Body; & that Reason, call'd Good, is alone from the Soul." Exactly because we divide the world between "Good" and "Evil," "Soul" and "Body," we divide ourselves against ourselves, and the wholeness of the world is thereby violated.

Within Blake's vision, the whole Enlightenment project of progress through reasoning collapses. For, as he understood, it is in the name of reason that we divide the world into *component parts*. To divide is to play down connections—except the analytic connections we make ourselves (and often argue about endlessly), usually in terms of high abstractions. The long-term result is that the *connection* of an eternal unchanging world to the one we live in every day remains as problematic as the connection between body and spirit or between one thing and another.[15]

Blake saw the inevitable outcome of such a way of thinking, seeking to counter it through his great manifesto "The Marriage of Heaven and Hell":

1. Man has no Body distinct from his Soul.
2. Energy is the only life, and is from the Body; and Reason is the bound or outward circumference of Energy.
3. Energy is Eternal Delight.

Because he imagined the world in terms of energy, Blake declared himself at war with the world of proliferating dead things. Of these things, the greatest evil, as he saw it, was our habit of seeking to "abstract the mental deities from their objects," pronouncing that "the Gods had order'd such things." In other words, through this habit of mind we invest invisible categories with a life of their own, as if they were actual entities; thus granting to such entities a sense that they are more "real" than the actual things they are taken to represent. Plato, for instance, believed that these categories must have a permanent (and therefore superior) life to the actual phenomena that they organized.[16] He called them "the Forms."

As a modern philosopher observed, this tendency to "reify" abstractions is inherent in the English language.[17] As already noted, in its privileging nouns over verbs,

English allows us to promote something quite mundane to a higher category by granting it a capital letter and a singular article. Thus "a mind" becomes "the mind" and "a good" can become "the Good." Once promoted, we believe that, as a thing, it should have a clear boundary or definition. Thus defined, we believe, it will remain stable: black, for instance, will always be black and can never become white; white will remain pure, untainted by any bit of black. In the West, in short, assigning a name is a way of imputing stability to the world at large.[18]

As a consequence, many if not most of our Western arguments turn out to be boundary disputes incurred while trying to "define" or "clarify" the categories to which we are assigning particular phenomena. Where, for instance, does the "body" end and the "mind" begin? How does the brain (as opposed to the larger nervous system) define their relationship? Is it "mind" and "body," or is it "mind" or "body"? And by what coordinates are the "self"—or the "soul"—to be located? If these questions seem absurd by their very nature, their absurdity results directly from our Western habit of defining the qualities of things by analyzing them according to abstract categories.

In the Chinese world, no such questions arise. In that world, as defined by *qi*, a thing is not a "thing" but a manifestation of energy—in greater or lesser concentrations. Thus, in the Chinese world, categories tend to be permeable and overlapping, vague and shifting. If defined, they are defined in terms of the energy that is constantly in exchange with the world around it—and thus endlessly crossing all such borders.

Take, for instance, once again, the image of the "self." In the West, defining ego boundaries is often seen as the work, in particular, of adolescents as they grow away from the dependencies of childhood into the independence of young adults. In China, the ego is imagined not as a thing to be defined but as a nexus of *qi*. By analogy, one can imagine such a self as neither a defined body-mind but as an energy center made visible, below, as a kind of force field.

What the image implies is a self composed by a concentration of *qi*, thus having no definitive boundaries between itself, other selves, or those forces that govern the wider world. Contrast this to the self as defined in the West as the unique source of its own energies, by which it organizes those beyond it. Such a self insists on its difference—therefore its boundaries—in response to others and the world at large.

These two kinds of selfhood have been described by cross-cultural psychologists as "independent" as opposed to "interdependent" selves.[19] The first—the "independent" self—stresses qualities of uniqueness, defining itself through inherent traits, abilities, values, and preferences. It tends to see things in isolation. The second—the "interdependent" self—stressing commonality, sees itself as defined by place, roles, loyalties, and duties. It tends to see things in context. In terms of culture, it is too simple to assign one to the Chinese sense of self, the other to the Western. Like all cultural phenomena, the way one constructs oneself lies along a spectrum. Selves are not stable; one might move along this spectrum from one end toward the other during a lifetime—or from moment to moment, as the situation dictates. Yet as a working generalization, the isolated, independent sense of self more clearly belongs

This image, familiar from science classes, depicts a black magnet under a glass plate with iron filings on it. The magnetic field, itself invisible, shows up in the way it orients the filings. In the Chinese tradition, the magnet is itself seen as made up of *qi* energy in a more concentrated form. Hence what the bar and its surroundings share seems more fundamental than what distinguishes them.

to Euro-American ideas of self-construction, just as the contextual, interdependent self tends to belong to the Chinese.

In this context, exciting new studies in cognitive psychology are emerging that demonstrate the ways that cultures and selves shape each other. One such study examines the kind of stories that people growing up in each culture tell about themselves. In this analysis, Qi Wang contrasts the kinds of self-narration created by Asians and Asian Americans as opposed to European Americans. What her experiments indicate is that Euro-Americans tend to tell stories that explain what is special about themselves, whereas Asian American newcomers typically do not. Each group tends to structure their stories differently, with Euro-Americans telling their stories in terms of more and more disparate episodes whereas Asian Americans prefer fewer segments and larger continuities in their narratives.[20]

The key word here is "continuity." To comprehend the body-mind in terms of a concentrated force field, as above, also implies understanding oneself as existing in continuity with ambient energies. Chinese culture expects people to attend to contexts, always. In fact, a distinctive Chinese sensitivity to energy fields may help us understand why the Chinese demonstrated such an early grasp of magnetism (resulting in the development of the navigational compass). A second implication involves acoustic resonances: ramifying energies that surface in Chinese as a phonic language. Chinese words may be perceived to have a potential to impact events far beyond their literal meanings. We have already seen in the introduction how homophones can affect events simply through being uttered, like the *si* sound of the number *four* and *death*, which was regarded as so potent that, in two provinces, car license numbers were changed to avoid potential hazard. Chinese has many such instances where words that sound nearly alike carry implications for what may happen. In another such instance, there is a kind of locust tree known in English as a "scholar tree"; the Chinese call it *huái* 槐.[21] But for them this word sounds all too much like *huài* 坏, meaning something bad. Implication: one should not make dwellings or furnishings from the wood of this tree, especially not for a young couple getting married. For Chinese people, such homophones risk activating an energy field with potential for wider (in this case, dire) consequences. So what initially appears to outsiders as a linguistic feature actually reflects a far wider cultural orientation: a Chinese alertness to the way *qi* energies radiate out far beyond what we can actually perceive.

Such wider implications of self as a force field impact on every aspect of Chinese civilization, including one's sense of control. Because this world is not seen as composed of dead *matter*—stuff just waiting for human actors to do something about or with it—all things in the Chinese view are understood not as stable but as constantly in the process of unfolding; in François Jullien's apt choice of words, for the Chinese things have *propensity*.[22] Those who work *with* the propensity of things will find their path smooth, like Zhuangzi's butcher who never has to sharpen his knife.[23] Anyone who fails to respect the present tendency of things will encounter endless obstacles. One pavilion in the Forbidden City carries the inscription *wuwei* 无为, to remind rulers that, however great their power, they would be well advised to respect the greater powers of these all-pervasive forces.[24]

From such radical differences in thinking, it is clear that China and the West diverge in the way they perceive the world—and themselves. To the casual visitor, each world may at first appear superficially similar, especially in today's large modern cities. But one learns quickly that things are understood as happening quite differently in each world because the *assumptions* that shape each worldview are different—and at times in terms not only incompatible but also sometimes simply incommensurate.

WHY THE CHINESE DO NOT HAVE BODIES: MODERN WESTERN MEDICINE VERSUS TRADITIONAL CHINESE MEDICINE

Take, for instance, the question of bodies. Everywhere across the world, with only superficial differences (such as skin color), we assume that human bodies are basically similar. But the bodies (see the next page) do not seem at all the same. While

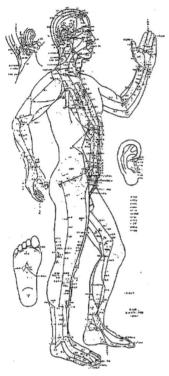

"Acupuncture Man." *Source:* John
G. Blair and Jerusha McCormack,
*Western Civilization with Chinese
Comparisons*, 3rd ed. (Shanghai:
Fudan University Press, 2010),
206.

Vesalius's "Muscle Man," 1543. *Source:* U.S.
National Library of Medicine.

the Western body is depicted as very muscular, the Chinese body seems almost immaterial. In fact, according to traditional Chinese views, they might not have (in our
Western terms) bodies at all.

Our Western medicine, by comparison, is relatively modern. It may be said to
have developed from the time of Vesalius (Andries Van Wesel, 1514–1564), whose
Seven Books on the Structure of the Human Body (1545) were based on the dissection
of actual corpses. When we contrast Vesalius's image of the body with the body map
normally used by traditional Chinese medicine (TCM), the difference between the
two conceptions is literally worlds apart.

While the Chinese body chart marks the flow of *qi* energy through the different meridians with their distinctive acupuncture points, the Western one (like classical Greek sculpture) emphasizes the integrity of the body as articulated by its muscles, each carefully individuated for labeling. While the Chinese body is one whole, the Western body—shown as it would appear in actual dissection—is divided into distinct parts or functions. In depicting the body as primarily muscular (and male), Vesalius also *underlines the importance of individual agency or energy*. Placed against the ruins of a great but now derelict civilization, this image reinforces Vesalius's implicit message that this Renaissance "new man" will, through sheer personal force, create a world to surpass even the glories of ancient Greece and Rome.

The Chinese body image is, by way of contrast, almost insubstantial. No muscles appear at all. None of the sites pinpointed on the acupuncture diagram would be visible by means of dissection. Instead, the chart indicates paths along which energy flows. And that flow is *through* the body, implicitly extending outward into the surrounding world. Vesalius's body, however, is depicted as quite separate from his surroundings; it is assumed that this body will act upon, do something, to them. It is also quite self-contained. There is no implication (as in the Chinese chart) that its energy would draw on—and then flow back into—its ambient environment. Finally, it should be noted that Vesalius's body is clearly articulated as merely the sum of its different parts; whereas the Chinese body is, as clearly, part of a greater unity: a particular concentration of energy within a force field of surrounding energies.

For these reasons, Chinese people have been said in a Western sense to not have material *bodies* at all. That is, all the words in Chinese usually translated as "body" carry implications that go far beyond mere Western "matter."[25]

"WELL-BEING": CHINA AND THE WEST

Given these assumptions about the body, what does it mean to "be well" in China? Within traditional medical practice, health, for the Chinese, consists in the free flow of *qi* into and through the person in continuous exchange with its surroundings. Blockage or insufficiency of vital energy does not signal ill health; it *is* ill health.

TCM consists of a series of techniques, honed over centuries, for restoring the flow of *qi*. There is not space here to explore the full range of these techniques, only to acknowledge that they include herbal extracts, *qigong* exercises, acupuncture with needles, or moxibustion for pinpointed heat. The most striking diagnostic tool developed in TCM might be called "taking the pulse"; but we may use this term only if we sharply distinguish that practice from what Western doctors do under the same label.

What is the difference between the pictures below? For two thousand years and more, Western doctors have been trained to read the pulse by feeling the surge of

Traditional Chinese *qièmài* (切脉).
Source: HUG China.

Michiel van Musscher (1645–1705), *Doctor
Taking a Young Woman's Pulse* (ca. 1675).
Source: Private collection/Bridgeman Im-
ages. Used by permission.

blood, usually at the wrist. Doing this gives doctors a way to read the patient's car-
diovascular functioning as a gauge of overall vitality. Once again, note the Western
investment in focusing on a particular bodily part—significantly, a muscle: the
heart, as it pushes blood through the arteries.

In the accompanying picture, the traditional Chinese doctor appears to be doing
something similar. In fact, he has something completely different on his mind: reading a whole variety of pulses to gauge the state of a patient's well-being. Following
this method, the TCM practitioner uses three fingers on each wrist, attending to
one finger at a time at two different depths of pressure. Such a method gives a total
of twelve routes of access to different *meridians*—channels through which *qi* is presumed to flow through the body. If he senses blockage at any one location, he will
respond by trying to free up the flow of *qi*. If he uses acupuncture needles to do this,
they may be placed far from where a patient reports pain or other symptoms. The
vocabulary used to express diagnoses may strike Westerners as hopelessly poetic,[26]
but much of the time this kind of medicine works, most noticeably when Western
alternatives do not produce cures.[27]

The point here is not to claim that one medical tradition is automatically better
than the other (though some differentiated judgments are possible) but to emphasize
the radically different approaches. Today's West has committed medicine to intensely
analytical and quantitative procedures. When you go to Western doctors, they want
to know what part is troubling you. Where does it hurt? How long has it been this

way? Does it involve symptoms elsewhere in the body? The doctor would then focus on that bodily part as a way of trying to restore health, perhaps after a general overall physical examination. They would do so because, in this world, disease means that something is keeping some part of the body from functioning properly. The Western doctor's view of the body is, in other words, similar to that of a machine. The body is seen as a thing that is an assembly of its component parts; if a part is disabled, that part should be fixed or, in extreme cases, even replaced. Sometimes the Western doctor might decide that one particular part would be affected by another part; thus a stroke in the brain might disable a hand or an arm. But the Western diagnostic procedure would remain unchanged: focus on the specific part that is seen to "cause" the illness with a view to fixing it.

A doctor practicing traditional Chinese medicine, on the other hand, would see your body as part of an overall energy system. Hence if you are ill, what needs to be fixed is not a specific part but the entire energy flow within—and through—your body, even as it extends to the world outside. His or her aim would be not to heal the part but to restore flow—illness being understood as a blockage of *qi* within the body as it connects to its ambient energy field. To restore health, a TCM practitioner may prescribe traditional medications (usually herb based) to *keep you well* by increasing your resistance to the predictable strains of your life—or even to those associated with a certain time of year. Another body-mind practice involves *qigong* exercises. Although they may seem to resemble yoga, *qigong* has a different objective, which is to enhance the energy flow between your body and its surroundings.

If one world regards the body as a machine, the other as an energy field, what differences in practice arise from such divergent assumptions? First of all, the TCM practitioner would always consider the body within its context. He might ask patients what they have been eating, what their everyday life has been like, and whether there were any particular stresses at the present time. Only then would there be questions about what seemed wrong—and where pain or discomfort might seem to be located. In short, a TCM practitioner would consider the person as a whole, within a certain context, just as the body is itself merely a matrix for the energy that flows through it. Thus an earache, for instance, might be treated not by examining the ear but by an acupuncture needle in the ankle. Within TCM there can be no sense that one part is isolated from the other; pain in one place is always seen as implicated within its larger energy system.

Finally, the TCM practitioner would make no distinction between "body" and "mind." These would be regarded as merely different aspects of the same energy flow. As explained in our introduction to *xin* or "heart-mind," the body-mind is regarded as a single concentration of energy—and therefore would be treated as being at one. Consequently, what Western medicine might regard as a psychological problem would tend to be somatized (expressed through bodily manifestations) while bodily illness would always be considered within a context of the experiential state of the patient.[28]

FUSION (OR CONFUSION?) MEDICINE

Although evolving from radically different assumptions about the nature of illness, over recent years the two practices have each begun to recognize the efficacy of the other. Thus Western medicine has made some moves in the direction of Chinese holism, for example, in recognizing psychosomatic interactions between mind and body. Nonetheless, Western approaches to mental health remain deeply divided between psyche-only treatments (like psychoanalysis) and that kind of body-oriented psychiatry that focuses on modifying brain chemistry.[29] In the other direction, within China itself, TCM has been slowly declining, as, over the last century, many Western medical practices have been imported. During that time, despite or even because of various campaigns for and against TCM (the latter under Mao's new PRC and the Cultural Revolution in particular),[30] Chinese doctors trained in Western medicine have tended to dominate. By some recent estimates, as many as 85 percent of the medical procedures performed in China these days are inspired by Western medical practice. At the same time, impressive numbers of Westerners are coming to China to learn TCM; it is the second most popular reason for foreigners to study in China (after language study). They do so because traditional Chinese medicine is gaining credibility in Western countries, often as "preventive medicine," a concern that has long been ignored in the West.

Perhaps the greatest limitation of TCM is that it takes many years to become skillful.[31] As it relies heavily on the accumulated practical experience of a single dedicated practitioner, there is no easy way to parcel out medical responsibility to individuals with lower levels of paramedical training, as in the West. Because Western medical practice follows the way the body/mind is conceptualized, it is divided up potentially into as many specializations as there are bodily parts. Contrast China, where one TCM doctor will dedicate him- or herself to healing the whole person.

Today China operates two kinds of quite separate medical establishments (from training colleges to practicing hospitals and clinics): one following modern Western medicine (MWM), the other TCM. A clear majority of such places apply modern Western medicine; and certainly world-class medical care of that type is available in major cities such as Beijing and Shanghai. But TCM persists and will continue to do so, because it can ease human suffering in areas beyond the reach of modern Western medicine. In fact, collaborative treatment under both MWM and TCM has already been practiced for some time in China. In a Chinese hospital, for instance, modern Western equipment may be used for diagnosis, but medications may be prescribed according to TCM. As for our Chinese university colleagues, they say that in every case of illness they will choose which type of doctor to consult. For infections, fractures, or any acute condition, they seek out doctors trained in MWM. Yet, for chronic conditions that cannot be cured but must be lived with, say arthritis, they count on TCM for better ways of coping. Each time they do so, they reaffirm the utility of thinking of the world in terms of *qi*. When human suffering can be reduced, who are we to say they are wrong? In fact, in the sense that China provides for both kinds of medicine, its medical system might be said to be more complete than those in most Western countries.

QI AND WESTERN REALITY: THE CONFIRMATION OF THE HIGGS BOSON/FIELD

Those energy-based notions of reality that underlie TCM may at first seem quite alien to Western minds, as many in the West still assume a mechanical model for *matter*, traceable to Aristotle by way of Isaac Newton. The physicists, however, have moved on. As of the late nineteenth century, the importance of *energy* began to be recognized. A century ago Einstein's Theory of General Relativity explored how energy and matter could be converted into each other. Thereafter, and even more fundamentally, the development of quantum physics began to suggest the primacy of energy. Through recent decades, successive theories have given more and more importance to quantum field concepts that support a general view of particle/field duality as attributable to "quasi-particles" (that is, those particles that arise as excitations of an underlying field).

While Western writers such as Fritjof Capra in *The Tao of Physics* (1977) or Gary Zukav in *The Dancing Wu Li Masters* (1979) have tried to popularize what they see as cognate Chinese-inspired concepts, these books have had little long-term popular impact. But now stunning new experiments, culminating in actual evidence of what has been named the *Higgs Boson/Field*, seem to confirm ancient Chinese presumptions about the primacy of energy.

Appropriating its (rather awkward) name in the 1960s from a British physicist named Peter Higgs, the theory aimed to explain how things acquired *mass* in a physical sense by postulating an *energy field* permeating the whole universe, filled with particles he called *bosons*. Within the omnipresent Higgs Field, it was theorized that things acquire mass by displacing bosons with greater or lesser resistance. The field itself has been described by CERN (Centre Européen pour la Recherche Nucléaire)[32] as "something like an electromagnetic field."[33] In 2012 CERN researchers established beyond reasonable doubt the correctness of Higgs's intuition. What is called the "standard model" thus stands confirmed: the foundation of physical reality is not *matter*—it is *energy* based.

Confirmation of the Higgs Boson/Field may in the long run sponsor a new paradigm for Western thinking. If so, it implies an unprecedented convergence of Western with Chinese ideas of reality.[34] As we have seen in terms of *qi* energy, long fundamental to the Chinese worldview, energy fields are nothing new to Chinese thinking. Though the Greeks investigated magnetism, they saw it only as an isolated phenomenon. Even back then, the Chinese saw magnetism as a visible manifestation of the *qi* energy fundamental to all that exists, leading them to develop, among other things, the maritime compass. Insofar as it is understood as so elemental that it exists everywhere, the Higgs Field is easily compatible with such long-standing

Chinese ideas about cosmic unity. Indeed, if we understand the Higgs Boson/Field as all encompassing, then it can be held up as a metaphor that allows us to envision a kind of total unity as expressed through even the smallest-scale manifestation within the universe.[35] Here is a fresh way of understanding William Blake's "world in a grain of sand."

In Chinese the final name for this ultimate unity is *Dao*, that which binds the whole while manifesting itself even within its smallest parts. As a name, the word *Dao* is to be understood as arbitrary and inadequate. Yet certainly for traditional Chinese thinkers, *Dao* is everywhere as constitutive of *reality* as is the Higgs Boson/Field.[36] It is possible that, in time, the confirmation of the Higgs Boson/Field may signal a transformation not only in the standard models of physics but also in other Western paradigms of longer standing, such as that of scientific "certainty." It is already the case that physicists speak not in absolute but in probabilistic terms, thereby accommodating indirectly Chinese emphases on the indeterminate and changing nature of "reality." In comparative terms, this convergence is encouraging for those who consider that the civilizations of China and the West are not destined to remain as alien to each other, or even as far apart, as they might once have seemed.

NOTES

1. Henry David Thoreau, "What I Lived For," in *Walden* (1854; Boston: Houghton Mifflin, 1960), 67.

2. There was one final episode in this story, rich in implications for understanding a Chinese worldview. After a long pause, the student erupted again, with a tone of urgency: "Professor, please explain. This man leave his family, he leaves his village to stand in a lake where he found this reality, yes?" In response, I tried to be as clear as words would allow: "Yes. You must understand. The rocks at the bottom of the lake are a figure of speech; they represent the ground of stability amid changing things, such as lakes and trees, villages, and people. Thoreau left his family, his friends, his village, because he believed he could find true reality beneath all these things if he went looking for it hard enough." "Professor," the student said, rising slowly. "This man Thoreau." There was a considered pause, as all looked at him in some alarm. "This man Thoreau," he continued, "I think he has wasted his life."

3. This word, in the hands of recent comparative researchers, has become an acronym, WEIRD, that defines our civilization as idiosyncratically Western, Educated, Industrial, Rich, and Democratic. See discussion in Part III, "Rethinking the West."

4. William Wordsworth, "Lines: Written a Few Miles above Tintern Abbey," in *Wordsworth: Poetry and Prose*, ed. W. M. Merchant (Cambridge, MA: Harvard University Press, 1967), lines 93–102 (italics added).

5. Such deference due from a younger brother to an older is one of the "five relationships" dear to the Confucian tradition. See explanation in chapter 1, "Binding Families: *Xiào*."

6. It is perhaps significant that two literary classics of the traditional Chinese world—*The Story of the Stone* (also known as *A Dream of Red Mansions*) and *Journey to the West*—feature heroes who began their mortal life as stones but stones infused by a sacred magic that allows them to enter the world as humans.

7. In this sense, "pantheism" may be distinguished from "panentheism" (from Greek πᾶν [pân] "all"; ἐν [en] "in"; and θεός [theós] "god"; "all-in-god"), which explicitly entails a transcendent God, existing above and beyond the world as we know it.

8. There have been correlatives in the Western hermeneutic tradition, such as in the thinking of the Irish scholar John Scotus Eriugena (ca. 815–ca. 877). For further explorations of those similarities, see Joseph Grange, "An Irish Tao," *Journal of Chinese Philosophy* 29, no. 1 (March 2002): 21–34.

9. Wang Rongpei, trans., *Zhuangzi*, 2 vols., Library of Chinese Classics (Changsha, China: Hunan People's Publishing House, 1999), 1:2, 28–29.

10. Wang Rongpei, *Zhuangzi*, 2:22, 372–73 (italics added).

11. The echo of Henri Bergson's "élan vitale" in this translation is not accidental.

12. Eating as transformation, a central concern in China, is further developed in the section "Food for Thought," in chapter 6, "Chameleon Reality: *Yi*."

13. For moving images of these two interacting energies, see David Forbus, "Yin Yang in 3D," YouTube, February 25, 2007, accessed September 8, 2014, https://www.youtube.com/.

14. Blake, knowing his Old Testament, here recalls the origin of Satan as Lucifer, the archangel who revolts against God, thus initiating war in heaven. As such, he represents the mirror image of the Archangel Michael who binds him, throwing him into hell. Blake works from a long tradition, which he explicitly traces to Milton, of seeing these two opposing forces of angel and devil, good and evil, as two parts of the same whole. Thus, Blake wrote that Milton, in depicting his Satan, was "true Poet and of the Devil's party without knowing it." William Blake, "The Marriage of Heaven and Hell" (1790), from the original plates, number 3, William Blake Archive, Bodleian Library, accessed March 31, 2015, http://www.blakearchive .org/. All following quotations from Blake are taken from this source. For further exploration of Blake's debt to the Far East and specifically to Indian mythology, see David Weir, *Brahma in the West: William Blake and the Oriental Renaissance* (Albany: State University of New York Press, 2003).

15. In relation to the body-soul conundrum, for instance, ancient Greek concepts of the soul varied considerably according to the particular era and philosophical school. Plato believed that the soul was incorporeal and immortal; Aristotle's conception of it remains obscure (and a matter of controversy); and the Epicureans, considering that both body and soul were made up of atoms, believed that they perished together. Christian concepts of a body-soul dichotomy, adapted from Plato, were introduced into Christian theology at an early date by St. Augustine among others. St. Thomas Aquinas returned to the Greek philosophers' concept of the soul as a motivating principle of the body, independent but requiring the substance of the body to make it individual. The debate about the nature of the relationship of body and soul in both Christian theology and Western philosophy (although phrased more often in terms of body/mind dichotomies) continues to this day (as summarized in "Soul," *Encylopaedia Britannica*, accessed June 13, 2013, http://www.britannica.com/).

16. Here is Plato in the *Cratylus*, as translated by Benjamin Jowett: "Nor can we reasonably say, Cratylus, that there is knowledge at all, if everything is in a state of transition and there is nothing abiding; for knowledge too cannot continue to be knowledge unless continuing always to abide and exist. But if the very nature of knowledge changes, at the time when the change occurs there will be no knowledge; and if the transition is always going on, there will always be no knowledge, and, according to this view, there will be no one to know and nothing to be known: but if that which knows and that which is known exists ever, and the beautiful and the good and every other thing also exist, then I do not think

that they can resemble a process or flux, as we were just now supposing." Plato, *Cratylus*, trans. Benjamin Jowett, Project Gutenburg, January 1, 1999, accessed November 23, 2012, http://www.gutenberg.org/.

17. In the process philosophy of Alfred North Whitehead, this is identified as a "fallacy of misplaced concreteness," that is, of mistaking an abstract belief, concept, or opinion about the way things are for a physical or "concrete" reality. See his *Science and the Modern World* (1925; New York: Simon and Schuster, 1997), 51.

18. Thus Western thinking habitually proceeds by multiplying distinctions in order to define with ever greater precision the characteristics of each new subcategory. For an example involving microbes, see *CCCW*, CD, 649. One might also cite the proliferating categories concerning sexual identity: the modern term "homosexual" (only emerging about a century ago) now augmented by "lesbian," "bisexual," and most recently, "transgendered."

19. These terms were first coined as applying to Asian versus Euro-American self-conceptions by Hazel Rose Markus and Shinobu Kitayama in "Culture and the Self: Implications for Cognition, Motivation, and Emotion," *Psychological Review* 98, no. 2 (April 1991): 224–53.

20. Qi Wang, "Are Asians Forgetful? Perception, Retention, and Recall in Episodic Remembering," *Cognition* 111 (2009): 123–31.

21. In the case of this character, the etymology reinforces the phonic implications: the left side is the sign for *wood*, and the right side signifies *demon*. Chinese culture, naturally, provides a story to explain why one should stay away from this tree for building things.

22. See François Jullien, *A Treatise on Efficacy: Between Western and Chinese Thinking*, trans. Janet Lloyd (Honolulu: University of Hawaii Press, 2004), esp. chap. 2, "Relying on the Propensity of Things."

23. See chapter 7, "Realizing a Way: *Dào*."

24. It was presumably Zhu Di as the Yongle emperor, the third emperor of the Ming dynasty, who built the Forbidden City early in the fifteenth century and chose this inscription. He was in no way identifiable as a Daoist, but his choice of this governing principle serves to remind us that it reflects Chinese wisdom about attentive inaction.

25. In the sense that none of the Chinese terms are clearly defined and bounded (as definitions of the material body in the West tend to be), all of them involve considerations not only of body but also of wider implications of personality or the way one lives. See Nathan Sivin, in *CCCW*, CD, 1234–35.

26. For examples, see *CCCW*, 222.

27. See *CCCW*, CD, 735–36, treating comparatively a test case of tinnitus.

28. As mentioned in chapter 4, "Where Is My Mind? *Xīn*," such somatization of an illness now usually regarded as psychological in the West would often be routine in China. For instances, see Arthur and Joan Kleinman, "Comparative Diagnoses of Depression," in *CCCW*, CD, 1427–30.

29. The distinction is professionalized by the division of mental health practitioners into psychoanalysts (who can administer therapy but not prescribe psychotropic drugs) and psychiatrists (qualified medical doctors who can so prescribe).

30. TCM survived multiple attacks in China during the twentieth century. Around 1930, under the Republic of China, Chinese doctors returning from study in the West even tried vainly to have TCM outlawed. Under Mao Zedong, TCM was yet another "feudal" practice based on superstitions worthy only to be cast aside. Once again, under the Cultural Revolution of 1966–1976, hostility toward TCM crested. But during these same decades, as skilled

exiles carried TCM to the West, it gained increasing credibility there as "alternative" or even as something wholly new to Western insurance companies, "preventive" medicine.

31. A similar difference in procedural explicitness shows up in cookbooks. U.S. recipes spell out in great detail how much of each ingredient to include and how long to cook under precise conditions. The cook is presumed to be inexperienced and unskilled, like the factory workers who work on assembly lines. Chinese cookbooks by contrast suggest adding or leaving out ingredients at will and cooking "until done." The cook needs to draw on considerable experience to perform well, and each occasion is likely to produce different results. Standardization cannot result, any more than in TCM, whereas that is a goal in American cookery. Interestingly enough, French cookbooks fall somewhere in between these extremes.

32. CERN uses the Large Hadron Collider housed in a circular tunnel twenty-seven kilometers around under Geneva, Switzerland.

33. See "The Higgs Boson," Origins, CERN, accessed January 2, 2012, http://www .exploratorium.edu/.

34. One may reasonably ask why the Chinese physicists working at CERN have not called attention to this unprecedented convergence of Western science with ancient Chinese ideas of reality. It could be that the Chinese physicists selected for appointment to CERN are so deeply engaged in Western science and its procedures that they either ignore or do not care about traditional Chinese perspectives. In the end, it takes a comparative perspective to draw out these implications.

35. As CERN director Rolf Heuer said in his lecture at Trinity College, Dublin, on July 13, 2012, "Telescopes can look into the history of the universe; but that history can also be found in the smallest thing." In the case of *Dao* and the Higgs Boson/Field, this perspective reinforces the idea that the Higgs Field is *scalar*, that is, like the primal *qi* energies of *Dao*, it has no predetermined direction or size.

36. Why does the West invoke two names for this phenomenon ("Boson" and "Field"), even though in this new discourse the two are so intimate that it is the *field* that allows the *particle* to become expressed? One can only surmise that Westerners are still so habituated to thinking in terms of particles as components that go to make up *matter* that they remain more likely to refer to the phenomenon as involving *bosons* (or more fancifully as the "God particle") rather than as a *field*. If one were to invent a more efficient binomial it would be *energy-matter*. But then Westerners might all too easily take this expression as an oxymoron, because energy and matter have so long been understood to be mutually exclusive.

易

Yì

6

Chameleon Reality

Yi 易

"*The Chinese mind, as I see it at work in the* I Ching *[Yijing 易经], seems to be exclusively preoccupied with the chance aspect of events. What we call coincidence seems to be the chief concern of this peculiar mind, and what we worship as causality passes almost unnoticed. . . .*

"*The manner in which the* I Ching *tends to look upon reality seems to disfavor our causalistic procedures. . . . In other words, whoever invented the* I Ching *was convinced that the hexagram worked out in a certain moment coincided with the latter in quality no less than in time. To him the hexagram was the exponent of the moment in which it was cast—even more so than the hours of the clock or the divisions of the calendar could be—inasmuch as the hexagram was understood to be an indicator of the essential situation prevailing in the moment of its origin.*

"*This assumption involves a certain curious principle that I have termed synchronicity, a concept that formulates a point of view diametrically opposed to that of causality. . . . Synchronicity takes the coincidence of events in space and time as meaning something more than mere chance, namely, a peculiar interdependence of objective events among themselves as well as with the subjective (psychic) states of the observer or observers.*"

—*Carl Gustav Jung*[1]

Sometimes we come up against situations that challenge our most basic beliefs about *reality*. Most of the time, we do not even broach the questions they raise, either because we are too busy just coping or because this is the sea in which we swim. "Fish," as the saying goes, "do not know water." As long as one stays within one's own civilization, there is a dominant consensus as to what, in general, *reality* means. But if, like Carl Gustav Jung, you leave that cultural consensus behind, you are bound to encounter critical divergences.

So, finally, what is really *real*? Is Jung right to say we in the West "worship" causality? In a formal sense, no, because few Westerners would list "causality" among their religious concerns. But on the other hand, educated Westerners have had a strong indoctrination in identifying causes. Modern Western science is a formalization of this concern. But in addition we count on causation to identify what—or whom—to blame when things go wrong. Our sense of moral responsibility derives ultimately from the process of pinning down what we see as the agents behind specific effects. In the end, we count on finding the "one true cause" as a clear and unambiguous explanation of what should then be done to control events.

How does this Western reliance on causation make it so difficult to grasp a Chinese sense of *reality*? Normally, in Western thinking, identifying a cause implies a stable substratum underlying changing appearances.[2] But—in the Chinese tradition—*reality* consists of the changing appearances themselves. Theirs is a fleeting world in which things fluctuate—all the time and everywhere—endlessly and unpredictably. The Chinese character *yi* 易, signifying *change* or *transformation*, is central to this understanding.

For at least the last two thousand years, this character has been read as related to the chameleon (see below), a lizard famous for its ability to transform itself. Taking a cue from its surroundings, it alters its color in order to blend into the immediate environment. Thus *change*, as exemplified by the chameleon, leads to a process of transforming and adapting as embodied in a living organism. For Westerners, it is important to note that *change* here is initiated not by the chameleon but by its situation. It is the shifting circumstances that dictate not only a change of color but also what particular coloration is appropriate. Such color changes are advantageous: the chameleon's best strategy for catching prey and protecting itself in turn against predators.

In these aspects, the chameleon offers an appropriate emblem for *yi* or *change* as understood by the Chinese. However, a Chinese person attuned to *yi* would not view the change in color as *caused* by its immediate environment—any more than understanding that change as being *caused* by the chameleon's peculiar chemistry. Rather, it would be understood as a reciprocal reaction best captured in the old Chinese saying "If you are close to red, you will turn red; if you are near black, you will turn

(±700 BC)   Great seal script   Regular
                          (±300 BC)   (1700)

Evolution of the *yi* character from the Zhou dynasty to the present. *Source:* Harmen Mesker, Netherlands Yi Jing Centre.

black" (*jìn zhū zhě chì / jìn mò zhě hēi* 近朱者赤近墨者黑). Thus recognizing the reciprocity of the event within a larger energy field, a Chinese view would see the chameleon's color change in terms of what Jung calls *synchronicity*.

Here is a Westernized sketch of the logic implied. If what binds all things together is *qi* energy, then within such a world, *yi* can be taken as affirming two basic principles: first of all, that everything is connected; second, that everything changes. Given that the larger forces of the world are always more powerful than any creature within it, all must be alert to the direction of changing circumstances. If you can adapt in time, you can protect yourself—and also perhaps close in on something good (dinner!) that might otherwise elude you.

Although it often appears as a concept in traditional Chinese culture, *yi* is not often invoked explicitly today. However, that in itself may be taken as the hallmark of a fundamental principle within a culture—invisible until brought out, as if in an X-ray, by the very act of comparing with a culture that is quite distinct from it. Other terms for "change," such as *bian* and *hua*, more current today, are less ancient, originally derived from the introduction of Buddhism from India about two thousand years ago. *Yi*, however, has been traditionally accepted as a primary premise within that Chinese world in which change is seen as natural, inevitable, and without beginning or end. There, it is a force known to humans only through *the way things happen*. As such, *yi* defines the humanly perceptible face of *Dao*, the ultimate Chinese concept for the total order of things.[3] The multiple function of *yi* 易 as a way of accessing *Dao* may be judged from its polysemy; as one Chinese scholar points out, *yi* could mean equally "conciseness" or "change" or "constancy."[4] Thus the *Yijing* (or *I Ching*) may as readily be translated as the "Concise Book of Constancy" instead of as its better-known title, *The Book of Changes*, as "it is essentially a book about changeless presence in a world of always changing configuration." As the "changing changeless," the *Dao* may be understood as simply the largest concept for framing the ultimate reality of the world around us.

Thus *to be in the Dao* is to be able to read and fit in with the larger tendency of things. If one anticipates forces that might affect one's life in a negative way, one moves to protect oneself. If one anticipates that these might bring advantage, one must seize the opportunity or else someone else will get there first. Thus timing is everything. While a Chinese person would concede that one cannot ever know *why* things change, one must, on pain of losing out, sense *how* they are changing. Taking control of things ultimately uncontrollable is out of the question, but responding strategically is not.[5]

Contrast this to Western ideas of *change* as implying an agent. In the West it is common for a young idealist to speak of going into action "to change the world." He or she would regard change as something initiated by individuals themselves, guided by the goals they have in mind. Such thinking is already implicit in the model of a transcendent, eternal Judeo-Christian God who created humans deliberately, from nothing, and in his own image. Thus any Westerner initiating an action has, implicitly, a divine mandate for instituting change, almost as if they see themselves as working in cooperation with Providence and therefore as its appointed agent—perhaps even its sole agent.

Ideally, those changes Westerners wish to effect will be seen to occur (as in the divine model) as the direct result of one's actions, without undue interference from circumstance. If circumstance defies them, Westerners may then go into heroic mode: defying the forces that oppose them. Western Romantics thought of this as noble. In China, such heroism might be thought of as foolhardy; there the chameleon model, being humbler, is regarded as more effective. For, as a small part of an immense cosmos, even an emperor knows he is not in control. External forces will always win; there is no point in dying, however nobly, unless one consciously seeks martyrdom for a reason.[6] Therefore one aims to change in line with the changing circumstances—in order to survive—and with luck, to thrive.

THE ESSENTIAL TEXT: *YIJING*

If the chameleon's tactics seem obscure to the West, we have useful access to chameleon thinking through one of China's earliest classic texts. Under the title of the *Change Classic* or, more conventionally, *The Book of Changes*, 易经, *Yijing* (in the West, still widely known in Wade-Giles romanization as the *I Ching*[7]) has been already active in Chinese culture for about three thousand years. Traditionally used as a way of divination—that is, for discerning where things are heading in the world—the *Yijing* is useful to us in the present context as revealing a system built around the most basic Chinese presumptions about *reality*.[8] And in these terms, the *Yijing* speaks volumes. Its two simple premises—that everything is changing and everything is connected—underpin the essential orientations of Chinese civilization over the thousands of years that the *Yijing* has been put to use.

The basic presumptions of this worldview are by now familiar. The energy of the world we perceive as *qi* expresses itself in the interaction and exchange of *yin* and *yang*.[9] It is through the *Yijing* that the connection between these cosmic forces and the human world can be read. As in all reading, this process involves interpreting. Tracking present movements of forces behind events, the *Yijing* defines sixty-four way stations through which this *qi* energy flows, phrased in terms of images interpreted as metaphors. As should now be clear, consulting this book is not a case of a "subject" observing an "object"; it is a consultation. And because everything is connected, the act of consultation itself will also affect the forces active in the larger world (long before Heisenberg, the *Yijing* was on to an indeterminacy principle). By this means it is believed that each consultation can offer an insight into the way things are tending—situating the human within the larger forces of the universe at just the moment it is consulted. But there is a difference between Jung's Western reading and one from within that Chinese world; where Jung (in our opening quotation) interprets the interaction of *Dao* with the human as chance, the Chinese person using the *Yijing* sees a conjunction of simultaneous forces: a revealing *synchronicity* rather than a *cause*; in life's progression, a chord rather than a melody line.

HOW A CONSULTATION WORKS

To open a consultation with the *Yijing*, one begins by focusing on a situation with which one is trying to cope. The kind of question that is most likely to provide a useful response is focused on *how* or *what*, not on *why*. Explaining how things got to where they are now is not important in this world; facing up to it is. So one may ask, for example, How should I respond to my present situation?

Ideally, according to the tradition, any question should be asked in two ways: first positively and then negatively. Asking the question in this double fashion reflects a peculiarly Chinese mindset.[10] In the West, one expects questions such as, What must I do now? and, How should I act in this situation? Those queries presume that I myself, as the primary agent in question, will seek to initiate change. But the Chinese way of asking the question negatively presumes an additional possibility. Perhaps you should do nothing at all! Doing nothing at all and letting the situation run its course would respect the principle of *wuwei*—or "acting by nonaction," as espoused by the great Daoists. Most Chinese, unlike their counterparts in the West, assume that *things of themselves have a propensity*, which will continue to evolve without human intervention, as *Dao*, visible only as *change*, remains always in force no matter what we as humans do.

The actual consultation ritual is simple enough. Using coins or sticks of wood, the user allows the *Yijing* to identify, six times over, a line as either dominantly *yin* (broken line) or *yang* (solid line). These six lines, from bottom to top, form a "hexagram." Mathematically, these two types of lines (*yin* or *yang*), taken six at a time, generate sixty-four (2^6) possible combinations and permutations. These sixty-four "hexagrams" are deemed to be sufficient to glimpse the movement of vital energy (*qi*) along the paths of change.[11]

As markers for *yi*, the hexagrams indicate not its outcome but the direction of its flow. But how does it work? How can we say that the *Yijing* connects the larger forces of the world with a user's question? The Chinese response would begin in terms of *qi* as channeled through one's *xin*. Whoever is consulting must thus first concentrate intently on the question to be clarified. Such concentrating initiates the ritual of consultation, and the consultation may not be reliable without it.[12] Yes-or-no answers are excluded: the consultation is not a demand. It is a petition on the part of properly humble questioners seeking some clarity on how they might best situate themselves in relation to larger prevailing forces.

During the process of consultation, a "hexagram" is delivered. But its specific relevance to the question asked remains in the hands of the questioner (or a professional diviner), who is likely to turn to one or more of the many commentaries that have accumulated over the centuries. Although some of these may seem more congenial or relevant than others, direct advice is never available. Like the Delphic oracle, the "hexagrams" always need to be interpreted. Their statements are offered in images often transmuted into obscure metaphors; these are the sole source of whatever situational "advice" emerges. Unlike the Delphic oracle, however, the process does not depend on a person (such as the priestess who prophesizes) but invokes an impersonal system of sixty-four hexagrams that may be used to decipher the moving matrices of the *Dao*.

Does the *Yijing* "work"? Experiences with consulting it vary a great deal. Coming into such a consultation with an open mind usually proves more fruitful than looking for concrete recommendations. At the very least, the "hexagram" and its commentaries invite the questioner to rethink whatever situation led to the consultation in the first place—and to rethink it in a more creative, if not transformative, way. For this reason the *Yijing*, almost alone among the Chinese classics, has gained a considerable Western following over the last half century or so.[13]

OPENING THE *YIJING* TO THE WEST

A key to opening the *Yijing* to the West was first forged by the Swiss psychologist Carl Gustav Jung (1875–1961), whose observations opened this chapter. Intriguingly, the *Yijing* itself was crucial in convincing him to accept this role. In 1949, when Jung was asked by Princeton University Press to write an introduction to the Baynes-Wilhelm translation of the *Yijing* (under the title of *The Book of Changes*), he at first declined, pleading lack of sinological knowledge. Having second thoughts, he decided to consult the *Yijing* itself.

The consultation gave him hexagram 50 (see below), named *Ding*: taken from an ancient food vessel used during and since the Western Zhou dynasty (twelfth to eighth century BCE) in rituals offering food to the ancestors who, in turn, were expected to nourish and care for their people.

As Jung interpreted hexagram 50, following the traditional commentaries assembled by his friend, Richard Wilhelm, the *Yijing* seemed to be speaking for itself. Its message was that this wisdom is no longer available because, as a ritual food dish, it has been turned upside down and has lost its handles. Jung read this as a plea that his introduction should offer "new handles" so that Westerners, too, could now be nurtured through its traditional Chinese wisdom.

Zhou dynasty *Ding*.

Jung succeeded, not only well but brilliantly. A new and astonishing Western attention to *The Book of Changes* can be attested to by the hundreds of thousands of copies sold in the last half century.[14] Since 1990, half a dozen other translations into English have also appeared, seeking ever more "authentic" versions. How did Jung succeed in making available a text as obscure as the *Yijing*? A clue emerges in his own reflections on his experience of consulting it, observing how "while the Western mind carefully sifts, weighs, selects, classifies, isolates, the Chinese picture of the moment encompasses everything down to the minutest nonsensical detail, because all of the ingredients make up the observed moment."

> Thus it happens that [in consulting the *Yijing*] when one throws the three coins, or counts through the forty-nine yarrow stalks, these chance details[15] enter into the picture of the moment of observation and form a part of it—a part that is insignificant to us, yet most meaningful to the Chinese mind. . . .[16]
>
> In other words, whoever invented the *Yijing* was convinced that the hexagram worked out in a certain moment coincided with the latter (i.e., that moment) in *quality* no less than in time. To him the hexagram was . . . understood to be an indicator of the essential situation prevailing in the moment of its origin.

From this observation, Jung concludes that

> the ancient Chinese mind contemplates the cosmos in a way comparable to that of the modern physicist, who cannot deny that his model of the world is a decidedly psychophysical structure. The microphysical event includes the observer just as much as the reality underlying the *I Ching* comprises subjective, i.e., psychic conditions in the totality of the momentary situation. Just as causality describes the sequence of events, so synchronicity to the Chinese mind deals with the coincidence of events.

What Jung presents here is no less than a radical alternative to Western mentalities fixated on *causation*.[17] His term for the Chinese alternative was *synchronicity*: implying that two events could be related to each other in time without one necessarily "causing" the other.[18] According to Jung, consultation through the *Yijing* allows one to glimpse, for a moment, that process correlated with those larger *qi* energies that make all things happen as they do. Further, the act of consulting itself allows a small person in a huge universe to intuit, within his or her own situation, the workings of its vast energy system. Thus the goal is not to define the "cause" of any one event—but to enter into the flow that directs the present propensity of everything.

Jung was quite conscious that his explanations might never occur to a Chinese person. This was not his goal. His aim was to make this ancient Chinese artifact intelligible—and hence useful—for people who start from Western and not from Chinese premises, just as he himself made it a part of his own psychotherapeutic practice. As authors we similarly risk, from time to time, describing Chinese views of the world in terms that would not necessarily occur to most Chinese people as "Chinese." In this sense, our goals and methods are similar to those of Jung.

YIJING IN CHINESE CIVILIZATION

During its three millennia of existence, the *Yijing* has proved remarkably resilient, consistently retaining the esteem of the most powerful people within its own civilization. Perhaps its greatest danger came in 213 BCE when the first emperor, Qin Shihuang, decreed the burning of all tradition-oriented books. For this ruthless modernizer, it was a move to eliminate opposition to the new uniform standards he imposed on everything—from weights and measures to writing styles. Very few categories of books were to be preserved: only those on practical subjects such as agriculture. Significantly, this category also included books on divination. These were deemed "practical," for if, as emperor, he was perceived as being out of touch with the larger forces shaping the world, his legitimacy would surely be questioned. Thus the *Zhouyi* (the then current version of the *Yijing*) was considered not merely useful but also indispensable for governing successfully.

The *Yijing* retained that kind of prominence throughout the centuries of imperial China. It was so important to the great seventeenth-century Emperor Kangxi, for instance, that when he suspected his divination experts of falsifying results—telling him only what they thought he wanted to hear—he insisted on double-checking their consultations with his own.[19] Such reliance on *Yijing* did not, of course, guarantee that wise decisions would always be taken. But it did confirm one important aspect of what it meant to be Chinese; that is, even if one is emperor, one must live with a reality implicitly defined in terms of change and connectedness, one that, as it cannot be controlled, must therefore be *read*.

Such continuity of esteem is confirmed in other ways. For instance, from the Tang dynasty of the seventh century to the end of the imperial exam system in 1905, the

Yijing was one of the classic texts memorized by every candidate for high public office, thus assuring that this central text was transmitted from generation to generation among those who governed China.[20]

What about the fate of the *Yijing* in more recent times? Even before the People's Republic of China (PRC) launched its several campaigns against all outdated "feudal" beliefs, the *Yijing* was under pressure from Chinese modernizers. Hu Shi, who completed his PhD dissertation in 1917 at Columbia Teacher's College under John Dewey, told Carl Gustav Jung in the 1930s that it was "nothing but an old collection of magic spells, without significance."[21] During the Mao years, use of the *Yijing* was forced underground. But soon after his death, books on it began proliferating once again in Chinese bookstores. Today, not all Chinese know the *Yijing* directly, but all live in a civilization that has been profoundly shaped by its premises. In much the same way, not all Westerners believe in God—but all live in a civilization that has been profoundly conditioned by this presumption.[22]

THE WORLD AS PRESUMED BY THE *YIJING*

The world presumed by the *Yijing* is so radically alien to the world as presumed by the West that it is worth translating some of its unspoken premises into Western mode, if only to gauge the distance between them. They might be listed as follows:

Understanding Is Instinctive, Not "Rational"

The chameleon does not seek to understand life; he seeks to survive in it, if possible to thrive within it. To do so, he needs to sense what is happening around him, not just with his mind but also with his whole body—and it is his whole body that changes in response to his changing world. He lives, as most Chinese people do, by exercising *xin*, the heart-mind that he registers viscerally, as a kind of instinct.[23] This manifests a kind of *embodied thinking* that is not widely recognized in the West, except perhaps for situations where thinking takes too much time (as in a situation of acute danger) or when one suspects that rational thinking may not be adequate to the actual situation (one speaks of a "gut feeling" that something is not quite right).[24]

Thus the way our human chameleon sees *reality* is not the way most Westerners usually understand it, particularly when matters of predicting the future arise. Whereas the chameleon's body instinctively registers the reality around it, the Western intellectual tradition encourages people to locate *reality* in an invisible zone that can best be reached by using one's head, that is, through reason. In that case, one should feel justified in ignoring or putting aside visceral feelings or instincts. Indeed, the Western tradition recommends distancing oneself sufficiently from any situation in order to analyze it. The point of such analysis is to break up the situation into component parts to isolate what they might call the One True Cause, presuming that to find the cause will then tell one how to cure or deflect or otherwise control the situation in question. This is the kind of thinking that sustains modern Western science, as well as the calculation of risk and probability that underlies most prudential initiatives in the West (for instance, of the actuarial premises of its insurance industry).[25]

In contrast to Western linear thinking, which tends to regard the cause as leading in a straight line to an analyzable effect, Chinese people acknowledge that the relations of cause and effect are so complex that, even if one could isolate a cause, its outcomes may be unpredictable. The Chinese tendency therefore over many centuries has been to have recourse to the idea of "luck"; although, on inspection, this is less about things happening randomly than things happening in accordance with the larger, diffuse energies of *Dao*, which may lead to not one but several outcomes.[26] Or as one sinologist is fond of remarking, "Not all acorns become oaks; many become squirrels."[27]

Isolating "Causes" versus Registering Effects

Why would a typical Westerner assume that acorns would logically become oaks? It has to do with the amalgamation of classical and Christian traditions that teach that every being has an "essence." Believed to have been originated in a creator-god, essences are defined as that core being destined to be fulfilled, as potential becoming actual. For such thinkers as Thomas Aquinas, this God is presented as the one original cause who causes all change to take place in accordance with his divine plan. In China, in a world with no such God[28] but only large, inhuman forces moving around unpredictably, one cannot attribute anything that happens to a divine plan (or even, except for persistent Marxists, to a plan based on scientific predictability). Thus "causes" as such cannot readily be discerned; the forces that constitute the *Dao* are multiple and finally unknowable.[29] They register, like the wind, only through their effects.[30]

Transgression versus Transformation

From such a context, one can apprehend these forces only through "the ten thousand things" of this world, in all their buzzing booming confusion—including one's own self as a locus of such energies. These must also be understood as things constantly in the process of being transformed from their present manifestation into something quite different, as acorns about to become—perhaps oaks—or perhaps squirrels.

Due to the presumption that such transformations are normal and inescapable, the Chinese world may often cross what the West might consider inviolate boundaries. As already pointed out in regard to categories, the Western tradition prefers clear and defined boundaries, ignoring anything that does not belong to a carefully delineated intellectual territory. On the other hand, to live in a world composed of one category—that of *qi*—is to live in a world of no categories at all. Thus Chinese categories (in the Western sense) are constantly overlapping, interwoven, and permeable to a degree unknown in the West.

Because Chinese thinking through *xin* does not tend to exclude in order to keep clear distinctions, these boundary crossings often puzzle or even distress Westerners. We have already observed how a Chinese person seeking help in difficulties would find little contradiction in going to Daoist, Buddhist, and Confucian temples—and then attending Roman Catholic mass.[31] In doing this, his or her view would be thoroughly pragmatic: the more higher powers invoked, the better chance of finding help. Furthermore, if after much petitioning, one or the other of these powers did not provide succor, why should one persist in making further appeals? For Western Christians, saturated with the doctrinal exclusions that define not only their faith but also even sects within that faith, such an attitude might well seem puzzling or even downright unacceptable.

FOOD FOR THOUGHT

Perhaps the most telling example of such boundary transgressions may be found in the Chinese attitude toward that which can be assimilated in a literal sense: food. What the Chinese eat is often a subject of fascination to Westerners, who sometimes regard it with dismay (Eating *rat*? Eating *insects*? Eating *dog*!). Although some Westerners might try to rationalize such transgressions as a kind of barbarity sustained by memories of famine in a country that has long been poor, few would stop to consider how it extends to other habits of Chinese thinking. As instanced, in China one can be Buddhist and Christian and Daoist and Marxist—by turns or all at the same time—without any alarm bells going off.

To widen the metaphor, an enduring Chinese capacity is to ingest all kinds of unfamiliar entities into their ways of life—without ever ceasing to be Chinese. One useful way of approaching the cultural history of China is to view it simply as a giant digestive system. Over its long history, this cultural capacity to assimilate foreign elements has applied to Buddhism, Marxism, and Capitalism, not to mention modern Western science and pop culture.[32] Yet, despite periodic anxieties as to whether China is becoming "too Western," Chinese modalities of thinking have proved, over many millennia, to be admirably suited to processing the foreign in such a way as to make it, ultimately, Chinese.

ORGANIZING *YI*: HISTORY IN CHINA AND THE WEST

This capacity to ingest other modalities of thinking while still remaining Chinese might be exemplified admirably by its multiple practices of historiography. Traditionally, China has looked to its own deep past for models. Kongzi said, "He can be a teacher who finds what is new in reviewing what is old."[33] More than two thousand

M. C. Escher, *Metamorphosis II* (1939–1940). The strips are
made to be seen as continuous, illustrating how a linear view
of history can become cyclical, through the agency of metamorphosis or transformation. Here Escher uses a scroll format
that envisions a Chinese modality. *Source:* M. C. Escher's
"Metamorphosis II" © 2014 The M.C. Escher Company-The
Netherlands. All rights reserved. http://www.mcescher.com/.
Used by permission.

years later, near the end of the Qing dynasty and on the brink of another transformation of the traditional Chinese world order, this injunction was echoed by the reformer-historian Kang Youwei (1858–1927): "Rely upon the precedents of the past in order to reform the [present] political system."[34] But how can this tendency to *look to the old* to *make it new* square with the basic Chinese premise of the world as relentlessly changing? Broadly speaking, this can be done because events are commonly seen there as always recurring, albeit unpredictably, in long-term cycles rather than in a linear, teleological narrative. Chinese premises presume that the basic situations humans face do not change all that much. The best summary of enduring Chinese views may well accord with Daniel Lord Smail's assertion: "The deep history of humanity has no particular beginning and is certainly driving to no particular end."[35] Despite intensive modernization, we think most Chinese have not abandoned this understanding of history for one nearer the Western model.[36]

To be sure, the Chinese tradition is not single-minded in its ideas about the shape of time. There is evidence that *both* linear and cyclical models are used by Chinese thinkers (category blurring again!). But the consensus is that cyclical thinking has been considerably more widespread and influential than Chinese linear thinking, despite the recent Marxist sponsorship of the latter. And traditionally, it has been typical of the cyclical model, in cosmological as well as calendrical time, to be seen as governed by the fluctuation of *yin* and *yang*: those ceaseless natural processes as tracked by the hexagrams of the *Yijing*.

Cyclical thinking is also reflected in the tendency in Chinese history for each dynastic change to restart the counting of years from year one each time a new emperor took over. In such ways the Chinese tradition encouraged "a built-in 'return to square one,' symbolized by a frequent willingness to tear down palaces built by the preceding dynasty and/or the construction of a new capital."[37] Perhaps Westerners visiting Beijing might accept more easily its successive destructions and reconstructions if they understood the deeper mindset behind such actions. Then they could make better sense of Mao's demolishing the city wall to build what is now the Second Ring Road with the subway under it—as well as of today's leaders, who are in the process of demolishing the old, single-story houses of most of its traditional *hutong* neighborhoods.

Of course, in making these changes, State leaders are apt to invoke the Western idea of "progress" through a pervasive rhetoric of five-year plans. From such official pronouncements, one might derive the idea that China is a planned and orderly place—a misleading perception. Following the original Soviet model, these plans serve the basic purpose of identifying the rhetoric bureaucrats will find useful in seeking approval and funding for their projects.[38] In actual fact, enforcement of such plans is likely to be only sporadic, as in the old Chinese proverb observing that the mountains are high and the emperor far away. Hence, in ordinary as in official Chinese life, many things are left to the last minute, whether or not they have been announced in a master plan.[39] Moreover, a healthy skepticism about the extent of implementation usually prevails; there will always be contingent circumstances waiting to intervene along the way. *Yi*, as ever, prevails.

Making the opposite assumption, one that counts on stability, Westerners today tend to regard "change" simply as *making it new*. A related discourse of innovation, creativity, or even revolution is currently privileged in a world that affirms (at least since the Enlightenment) a rhetoric of "progress." To believe in progress is to believe in a linear, not a cyclical, model. Presuming a beginning and an ending, such a model is buttressed in the West by a master narrative of origins (as in Genesis) that lead to a clear ending (as in the Apocalypse announced in Revelations). A cognate, although secular, science-based alternative starts with the Big Bang and ends with the Heat Death of the universe. No such master narrative constrains the dominant Chinese worldview, which imagines neither origin nor eschaton.[40] While orthodox Marxists—aided by the *mianzi*-inspired practice of suppressing mention of any failures whatsoever—still try to read Chinese history in accordance with the approved narrative of "progress," it never fits comfortably into the stages derived by Marx from Western history.[41]

So much for the rhetoric of "progress" in either world. Today, with the current economic crisis—not to mention the looming ecological one—the West's model is increasingly under stress. In China, the enduring progress narrative is still constantly at work shaping the public face of governance, dished out with statistics that inevitably show "improvement."[42] Yet single-minded pursuit of "progress" has led—almost everywhere in the world—to boom-and-bust economies along with an increasingly degraded physical environment. Given these circumstances, the bankruptcy of this model, for both China and the West, is now becoming increasingly evident.

PRAGMATIC IMPLICATIONS

As always, the truth of any premise in the Chinese world is validated by what actually happens in practice: some acorns become oaks; quite a few, squirrels; others just rot away. Looking at things this way is one good reason China has sustained a civilization with the longest continuous existence on earth. Although it may seem a contradiction, the *Yijing* affirmation of constant change orients humans to valuing continuities above all else. Changes have to be lived with because they happen all the time; continuities have to be striven for if they are to be protected. From this point of view, *reality* resides in *this* world, not some other. For most Chinese, lacking an orientation to transcendent otherworldly realities, the primary goal of a family is to prolong itself in time, generation after generation (whence the central importance of *xiao*). What "civilization" means in a Chinese world is maintaining a human community in the face of vast and dangerous forces that never stop moving. No wonder that Chinese business contracts routinely list a "reopening" clause in case conditions alter so radically that the original provisions are simply no longer viable.

While the premise of uncontainable change persists through all of China's history, the rate of actual change over the last hundred years has been extreme, testing again and again the ability of families and individuals to cope. If you anticipate that many things in your life may suddenly alter, then it will seem logical to fall back on the tried and true—which often means the wisdom of elders (as in traditional sayings, still deployed with authority in the Chinese world). It might even be argued that the innate conservatism of Chinese life owes itself to the pervasive presumption of *yi*. Even so, events have often galloped ahead of conventional wisdom. In such circumstances, life may seem to depend on taking it as a gamble, with luck playing a large role in the way one views experience. Some are inclined to take large risks, but many try to maintain a safer and more familiar way of life, to the extent humanly possible.

That may be true too of many in the West as well. But given our premise that reality is essentially stable, we in the modern West stake our hopes for the future not on stability but on innovation (as in the early Obama election rhetoric of "Change!"). In our own history over recent centuries, revolutions (such as the French, the American, the industrial, and the scientific) are usually applauded as good things, despite the obvious violence they may entail. On the other hand, a "revolution" for today's Chinese (who have seen perhaps too many of them over the past century) entails *luan* or chaos: one of the most feared side effects of change. In Chinese life, where underlying reality is conceived in terms of *yi*, the most widespread response (as we will see) is to acknowledge its pervasive force by acting the chameleon—and responding, in all situations, adaptively, and with that relentless pragmatism that deals only with the here and now.

NOTES

1. Carl Gustav Jung, preface, in *The Book of Changes*, trans. Richard Wilhelm and Cary Baynes (Princeton, NJ: Princeton University Press, 1950). The full text of Jung's preface is available online at http://www.iging.com/. Pertinent excerpts appear in *CCCW*, 531–35.

2. As described by Henry David Thoreau in the chapter "What I Lived For," in *Walden; or, Life in the Woods* (1854; Boston: Houghton Mifflin, 1960), 67. See opening passage in chapter 5, "The Energy Unifying the World: *Qi*."

3. See chapter 7, "Realizing a Way: *Dào*."

4. Zhang Longxi, "The 'Tao' and the 'Logos': Notes on Derrida's Critique of Logocentrism," *Critical Inquiry* 11, no. 3 (March 1985): 386. The following quotation is from this source.

5. See chapter 10, "Strategizing Life: *Cèlüè*."

6. See "Comparative Martyrdoms," in *CCCW*, CD, 755–58.

7. This usage follows the earlier Wade-Giles romanization system, now supplanted by *pinyin* as, for the first time, a worldwide system for writing Chinese sounds in Western letters.

8. Among Chinese readers, *Yijing* has the reputation of impenetrable obscurity. This is because the grounding of its metaphorical explanations was lost centuries ago; thus those who try to read its advice about the future often feel frustrated. But this problem does not affect

our reading of the significance of the text. We are trying here not to use the *Yijing* but to understand how it embodies fundamental premises about the nature of *reality* according to the Chinese tradition. One does not have to practice divination in order to grasp its implications.

9. See chapter 5, "The Energy Unifying the World: *Qi*."

10. This double-take evaluation of a situation is characteristic of Chinese divination from its earliest origins in consulting oracle bones. It has penetrated so profoundly in Chinese thought patterns that even Mao Zedong (who dismissed the *Yijing* as feudal nonsense) nonetheless employed its dual procedures. When he was reassuring Zhou Enlai about the decision to commit Chinese troops to the Korean Conflict, here is how Mao expressed his dual evaluation (telegram to Zhou Enlai, October 13, 1950): "Entering the war is greatly to our advantage; conversely, it is greatly to our disadvantage if we do not enter the war." See John Lewis Gaddis, *We Now Know: Rethinking Cold War History* (Oxford, UK: Clarendon, 1997), 80.

11. Arresting parallels can be found between the mathematical structures of the *Yijing* and those of the DNA genome sequence. While the parallelism embedded in these two cultural constructs is remarkable, each of these conceptual schemes interprets its sixty-four elements differently, in accordance with the presumptions of its civilization of origin. How then can we understand such striking coincidence? It might be dismissed as mere happenstance. Or it might be interpreted as reflecting a fundamental numerical orderliness to existence, a possibility that was first articulated in the Western world by the followers of the Greek philosopher Pythagoras (died about 497 BCE). For further information, see *CCCW*, CD, 765–67. Such visions of large-scale world unity are typically seen as mystical by most Westerners today. Chinese theories of the world, however, might encourage seeing such parallels as proceeding from the larger nature of things. Each remains free to interpret this and other phenomena as seems best, but the parallels invite speculation about how they might be brought closer together in our understanding of cultures and worldviews. See a website pursuing DNA/*Yijing* parallels: M. Alan Kazlev and Christián Begué, "The I Ching and Genetic Code," last updated November 19, 2005, accessed February 9, 2013, http://www.kheper.net/.

12. A lack of ritual would presume that the person asking the question would in some way have primacy over these forces, whereas they should be approached humbly. Thus respecting the ritual procedures itself honors the primacy of the forces being consulted.

13. Richard J. Smith, *The "I Ching": A Biography*, Lives of Great Religious Books (Princeton, NJ: Princeton University Press, 2012) follows its long career in China as well as the West. Among those influenced in the West by the *I Ching*, Smith identifies the architect I. M. Pei; choreographers Merce Cunningham and Carolyn Carlson; composers Joseph Hauer, John Cage, Udo Kasemets, and James Tenny; the artwork of William Littlefield, Eric Morris, Arnaldo Coen, Arturo Rivera, Augusto Ramírez, and Felipe Erenberg; and the writings of a wide range of Western authors, including Philip K. Dick, Allen Ginsberg, Octavio Paz, Herman Hesse, Raymond Queneau, and Jorge Luis Borges.

14. The Baynes-Wilhelm translation originally published in 1950 is confirmed by the Princeton University Press as its all-time best-selling title, with sales peaking in the 1960s and 1970s. Most Western readers of *Yijing* have university educations; many are oriented to alternative or "New Age" lifestyles inspired by diverse non-Western practices. The use of the *Yijing* for randomizing by composer John Cage is a classic example. See Richard Kostelanetz's collection of remarks by John Cage, in *Conversing with Cage*, 2nd ed. (New York: Routledge, 2002), 12.

15. Of course, to a Chinese practitioner these details are not at all a matter of "chance."

16. Obviously the details only seem nonsensical to many Western minds. Jung, preface (as noted earlier, the full text of Jung's preface is available online at http://www.iging.com/); pertinent excerpts appear in *CCCW*, 531–35.

17. Determining what caused something to happen is a matter of not only modern science but also the West's long-standing morality. Only when one can determine who or what caused an event can responsibility for it be assessed. For more analysis, see *CCCW*, 473–74.

18. A Westerner might say, in the interests of preserving the universality of causation, that whatever happens now is "caused" by larger invisible forces.

19. As Kangxi wrote himself, "My diviners have often been tempted to pass over bad auguries, but I have double-checked their calculations and warned them not to distort the truth." For more of the emperor's reflection on the worth of the *Yijing*, see Jonathan Spence, *Emperor of China: Self-Portrait of K'ang-hsi* [Kangxi] (New York: Vintage, 1988), 58–59; *CCCW*, CD, 1354–55.

20. During the Tang dynasty, the Gaozong emperor (628–683) added the Daodejing to the list of classics (*jing* 經) to be studied for the imperial examinations. See Isabelle Robinet, *Taoism: Growth of a Religion* (Stanford, CA: Stanford University Press, 1997 [French original, 1992]), 185.

21. As reported in Jung's autobiographical *Memories, Dreams, Reflections* (New York: Vintage, 1989, reprinting final revised edition, 1973), 374. See *CCCW*, 531.

22. How seamlessly Western sacred history can be transmuted into more recent secular revisions is shown by Daniel Lord Smail in *On Deep History and the Brain* (Berkeley: University of California Press, 2008), esp. chap. 1, "The Grip of Sacred History."

23. See chapter 4, "Where Is My Mind? *Xīn*."

24. One widely publicized book promoting this emphasis is *Blink: The Power of Thinking without Thinking* by Malcolm Gladwell (Boston: Back Bay Books, 2007). As already noted, in recent years "embodied" thinking has gained considerable recognition in the West, largely through developments in cognitive psychology, linguistics, and philosophy. See chapter 4, "Where Is My Mind? *Xīn*."

25. See discussion of how Western science enters China in chapter 4, "Where Is My Mind? *Xīn*."

26. Mark Elvin in particular shows how, despite a succession of games involving gambling, premodern China did not develop explanations by "probability." Mark Elvin, "Personal Luck: Why Premodern China—Probably—Did Not Develop Probabilistic Thinking," in *Concepts of Nature: A Chinese-European Cross-Cultural Perspective*, ed. Hans Ulrich Vogel et al., 400–68 (Leiden, Netherlands: Brill, 2010). Similarly the Romans depended on a notion of Fortuna to offer sufficient explanations for wildly varied outcomes. Only when the West turned to quantification for scientific purposes, especially in the seventeenth century, did it begin to develop the mathematical concepts necessary for probabilistic thinking.

27. This remark was made by Roger Ames, distinguished philosopher and sinologist at the University of Hawaii.

28. See chapter 11, "Question One: Christianity?"

29. See chapter 7, "Realizing a Way: *Dào*."

30. The reference to *wind* is not accidental. In ancient China a few hundred years before *yin* and *yang* became the dominant concepts for the ways that *qi* expresses itself, the classic *Zuozhuan* (Duke Zhao 昭公, first year [645 BCE]) identifies "six *qi*": *yin* and *yang*, wind and rain, dark and light. *CCCW*, CD, 1197–98.

31. There do exist in China individuals who reserve their loyalty to one or another orthodoxy: Christian (labeled separately as either Protestant or Catholic), Buddhist, or Daoist, among whom we also place those loyal to Marxist-Leninist-Mao Zedong Thought. But these constitute a small minority of the Chinese population as a whole.

32. For an extended study of the Chinese talent for eclecticism, particularly in regard to its absorption of foreign influences, see Odd Arne Westad, *Restless Empire: China and the World since 1750* (London: Bodley Head, 2012).

33. Roger T. Ames and Henry Rosemont Jr., trans., *The Analects of Confucius: A Philosophical Translation* (New York: Ballantine, 1998), 2.11, in *CCCW*, 41.

34. As quoted in Achim Mittag, "Historical Consciousness in China: Some Notes on Six Theses on Chinese Historiography and Historical Thought," in *New Developments in Asian Studies: An Introduction*, ed. Paul van der Velde and Alex McKay, 47–76 (London: Kegan Paul, 1999), 49. Our remarks on historiography follow this insightful essay.

35. Smail, *On Deep History*, 80. Ironically Smail has to work hard to reach this formulation focused on "deep history" by clearing away the pervasive fixation of Western historians on teleological narratives.

36. The best evidence for this assertion surfaces in the extraordinarily high savings rate in China. The materialist explanation is that the lack of social security guarantees by the government pushes individuals to save. But modest improvements in social guarantees are accompanied by still further increases in savings rates. The cultural explanation is that most Chinese continue to act on the expectation that what goes up must one day come down. The materialist explanation does little better in relation to the United States. The savings rate, after declining to near zero in the boom times, has now risen, despite the fact that Obamacare offers much more protection against medical catastrophes. In short, confidence factors carry much more weight—in both worlds—than rational calculations.

37. Mittag, "Historical Consciousness," 60.

38. As a sample of how such plans work out bureaucratically, consider how, a few years ago, when boosting auto production was announced as a priority, developers found that the best way of securing local approval for lucrative land deals was to build a factory for assembling cars. That assured local officials of promotions for furthering Party priorities and helped justify the national boast of surpassing the United States in annual automobile production. The result was perhaps as many as one hundred small auto-assembly factories scattered around the country; they were never assessed for economic viability because their reason for coming into existence lay elsewhere. Then in 2013 it all turned sour when automobiles were held largely to blame for unprecedented air pollution in Beijing and some other cities. Keith Bradsher, "Chinese Titan Takes Aim at Hollywood," *New York Times*, September 22, 2013.

39. Indeed anyone involved in planning public events in China, such as a conference, knows by experience how hard it is to induce those responsible to plan ahead. If everything is seen as changing all the time, they may see no point in making large-scale advance plans; one would only have to change them at the last minute (as often in fact happens). Therefore it seems more efficient to postpone planning until the event is almost about to happen. The primary goal then is to cope with emerging circumstances—each of which may appear as an emergency—and therefore eliciting intensive cooperation and accelerated work, which may then call forth the best qualities of those involved.

40. See, for example, the indicative story of the old frontiersman who lost his horse (*Sai weng shi ma*) in Part III, "Rethinking the West." *CCCW*, 509.

41. For example, the "slavery" stage had to be located in the Shang dynasty, a source of unresolved debates. The next phase, "feudalism," expanded implausibly to characterize China from the Zhou dynasty to the fall of the Qing in 1911, some three thousand years or so. Overriding many important changes during this long period, orthodox readings, for example, ignored the market economy that flourished during the Song dynasty a thousand years ago. Mao Zedong, in order to fit the narrative somewhat less awkwardly, introduced neologisms such as "semifeudal." *CCCW*, 543–47. In the 1990s when officials felt the need to justify the introduction of some features of the market economy, they informed the Chinese that they had not after all been living and working in the "Communist phase" but would only arrive at that stage in some ill-defined future.

42. It is not clear to what extent this charade is convincing to Chinese people themselves, but it obviously still has potency in what remains a developing country, as well as aiming to comfort the residual loyalists who still back Marxist-Leninist-Mao Zedong Thought.

道

Dào

7

Realizing a Way

Dào 道

Confucius was touring Lüliang, where the water falls from a height of thirty fathoms and churns for forty li in rapids that no fish or water creature can swim. He saw a man dive into the water and, taking him for one whom despair had driven to suicide, he ordered his disciples to line the bank and pull the man out. But after the man had swum a few hundred paces, he emerged from the water with his hair streaming down and strolled beneath the cliffs singing. Confucius rushed to question him. "I took you for a ghost, but now I see you're a man. May I ask if you have some special dao *of staying afloat in the water?"*

"No," replied the swimmer. "I have no dao. *I began with my original endowment, grew up with my nature, and let things come to completion with fate. I go under with the whirlpools and emerge where the water spouts up, following the* Dao *of the water and never thinking about myself. That's how I go my way."*[1]

As a character created by Zhuangzi—for his own mischievous purposes—this "Confucius" is stunned by what he sees: a man diving into rapids where "no fish or water creature can swim." He wonders whether the diver has a "special *dao*" allowing him to stay afloat in the water—that *dao* (with a lowercased *d*) that might correspond to a learned skill. But Zhuangzi's swimmer has come to learn something bigger, the *Dao* with a capital *D*: one that corresponds to the flow of forces into which he submerges and emerges, embodying the way that one engages with the cosmos, not through one's own skill but by submitting oneself completely to its propensities.

What this *Dao* (道) implies may be construed by examining its two graphic elements one at a time: on the right a sign for *head*, with a prominent place for the eyes. From this first element, we might at first think that *Dao* signifies using one's head by using one's eyes: something like Ralph Waldo Emerson's "I become a transparent eyeball."[2] But interpreting it this way simply translates *Dao* into Western terms: *seeing as a form of knowing*. To move out of that world, one must turn to the left and lower sides of the character, which signal *walking* or *moving about*. Together, the two evoke *moving around using one's head*—or, perhaps more precisely, *of using one's head by moving about*. Now we are engaging with a Chinese world, one where one gains perspective on the world by actively participating in it.

In such a world, the nature of knowing changes: one knows the world not by thinking *about* things (as if they were entities distinct from oneself) but by *becoming part* of the processes by which things change. As Zhuangzi's swimmer confesses, "I go under with the whirlpools and emerge where the water spouts up, following the *Dao* of the water and never thinking about myself. . . . I'm not aware what I do but I do it." In the West, conscious awareness is all. We aim to think *about* things or people as distinct from us—and believe we can do so because we assume that they remain stable entities, therefore able to be isolated for "objective" analysis. But in the Chinese world, where everything changes and everything is connected, as a person one is always swept into the larger, shifting forces shaping the world.

How can such shifting forces constitute anything as stable as a cosmos? The secret lies in its driving force, or *yi*, interpreted (as we have seen) as a "changeless presence in a world of always changing configuration."[3] In other words, *yi* is the way that *Dao* becomes manifest, as in the varying colors of the seasons. That "changeless change" best summarizes the resonances of *Dao*, rich in complexities that may seem paradoxical to most Western mentalities.

If elusive, such a formulation at least has the advantage of evading the more common and misleading translation of *Dao* as *way*. According to Professor Chad Hansen (the Westerner who has studied the word most seriously), *Dao* may be understood as *way* only if it is purged of associations of any material kind, such as those with roads or paths that a person might physically walk on.[4] Instead, *Dao* entails paying attention to the *way things happen*, implying the natural course of events, free from human interference.

As such, *Dao* may be used to designate the totality of all that occurs, manifest at any moment in even the most trivial events. When William Blake saw a world in a grain of sand, his vision would have been approved by the two great philosophical Daoists, Laozi and Zhuangzi, who understood the cosmos to be implicit in even the smallest concrete event, beyond the reach of mere reason. For in the Daoist world, knowing things with one's head is of no great use; what one knows, one knows with one's whole being, one's heart-mind or *xin*.[5] "A way is made in the walking of it," as Zhuangzi observes.[6] One finds one's way by intuition, not by mapping it out rationally. Partly for this reason neither Zhuangzi nor Laozi generated a systematic, reasoned philosophy. Both speak aphoristically, through paradox and parable, and thus outside the realm of Western formal logic.

GETTING IN TOUCH WITH *DAO*

As *Dao* cannot be captured by the rational mind, how does one approach it? To illustrate that process, Zhuangzi tells one of his most famous stories: that of a butcher whose work was so perfectly attuned to *Dao* that he never needed, over many years, to sharpen his knife. Watching his rhythmic slicing up of a carcass, his master asks the butcher how he learned such consummate skill. The butcher explains:

> When I first began to carve a bullock, I saw nothing but the whole bullock. Three years later, I no longer saw the bullock as a whole but in parts. Now I work on it by intuition and do not look at it with my eyes. My visual organs stop functioning while my intuition goes its own way. In accordance with the natural grain, I cleave along the main seams and thrust the knife into the big cavities. Following the natural structure of the bullock, I never touch veins or tendons, much less the big bones!
>
> A good butcher changes his knife once a year because he cuts the flesh; an ordinary butcher changes his knife once a month because he hacks the bones. Using this knife for nineteen years, I have carved thousands of bullocks, but the edge of my knife is still as sharp as if it had just come from the whetstone. There are crevices between the joints, but the edge of my knife is very thin. When I insert the thin edge of my knife into these crevices, there is plenty of room for it to pass through. That is why, after nineteen years, the edge of my knife is still as sharp as if it had just come from the whetstone.[7]

This butcher has no claim to formal education. On the contrary, he has learned *not* to use even his eyes, suspending the workings of his conscious mind in favor of intuitive spontaneity. Thus his intimacy with *Dao* expresses itself solely through the way he proceeds. His method might be taken as one of the purest examples of Chinese body thinking, to which theory—or conscious thinking at all—is quite peripheral.[8]

Indeed, all theories are useless in Zhuangzi's philosophy precisely because they depend on words—which lead only to more words. Words alone cannot put one in touch with the ultimate. Philosophical Daoism is particularly strong on this point. As the opening verse of its core text, the *Daodejing*, asserts,

> The Dao that can be expressed in words
> Is not the true and eternal Dao;
> The name that can be uttered in words
> Is not the true and eternal name.[9]

As a result of its allergy to words or to systematic philosophizing, *Dao* remains elusive to many human beings, who often require something more tangible on which to focus their beliefs.[10]

Rather than words, getting in touch with *Dao* has to come through felt experience, as Zhuangzi's parable illustrates—and not just any experience but one gained by working in the right spirit. Ralph Waldo Emerson expressed a similar insight when he contrasted a mere farmer to the "Man on the farm." A farmer, he writes, is a man "metamorphosed into a *thing*, into many things. . . . He sees his bushel and his cart, and nothing beyond, and sinks into the farmer, instead of [becoming] Man on the farm." While "Man on the farm" may perform the same actions as the mere farmer, he does so in a completely different spirit, conscious of how his activities fit into a vast cosmic scheme of planting, growing, maturing, harvesting, and dying.

Guo Xi, *Early Spring, Zaochuntu* 早春图 (1072). *Source:* The Collection of the National Palace Museum, Taipei. Used by permission.

Through cultivating this consciousness, Emerson explains, "Man on the farm" falls back not on the things of the farm but "on this elemental force of living them"—a force in China best recognized as *Dao*.[11]

Even though he resisted the notion of a farmer as being one thing among others, it is highly probable that Emerson would not have understood, even intuitively, this painting (on the preceding page) by Guo Xi.[12] Emerson remained still Western enough in his thinking to believe in the efficacy of words; Daoists see words as misleading. Precisely because it resists words, *Dao* seems more accessible in painting than in writing. Hence, over many centuries, a formidable school of painters have called on Daoism for inspiration, their practice dedicated to manifesting the flow of *qi* through their hands by means of brush and ink.[13]

What these painters try to achieve is not (as in the long-standing Western art tradition) a recognizable representation of things; rather, they try to capture the living rhythms that flow through one thing to another. Emerson, for all his investment in the life of the spirit, might well have objected to this painting as not being "realistic." Indeed, it is not of any particular mountain but of the forces that constitute "Early Spring": mists and water flows and nascently sprouting trees. Nor would he have understood the focus on the forces of nature at the expense of the man perceiving them. For Emerson's "Man on the farm" is above all an individual and as such constitutes the center of his own very Western world. But here, in a Chinese world, humans are depicted as strictly peripheral—tiny figures in the lower left and right dwarfed by the "elemental forces" through which *Dao* becomes manifest. Such forces are represented by earth, trees, water, and clouds (themselves speaking of the shifting aspects of *yin* and *yang*) that seem to dissolve the massive mountain into a rhythmic, shifting presence.

Emerson also believed in the efficacy of seeing (again, his famous remark being, "I become a transparent eyeball").[14] "To see" here implies focusing at a given distance from a single fixed standpoint, in this case from the ego or "I" of this passage. To move the viewer out of ego, from seeing into sensing (or *xin*), Guo Xi developed a strategy of depicting multiple perspectives from what one of his contemporaries called an "angle of totality."[15] As Guo Xi himself observed,

A mountain nearby has one aspect. Several miles away it has another aspect, and some tens of miles away yet another. Each distance has its particularity. This is called "the form of the mountain changing with each step." The front face of a mountain has one appearance. The side face has another appearance, and the rear face yet another. Each angle has its particularity. This is called "the form of the mountain viewed on every face." Thus can one mountain combine in itself the forms of several thousand mountains. Should you not explore this? Mountains look different in the spring and summer, the autumn and winter. This is called "the scenery of the four seasons is not the same." A mountain in the morning has a different appearance from in the evening. Bright and dull days give further mutations. This is called "the changing aspects of different times are not the same." Thus can one mountain combine in itself the significant aspects of several thousand mountains. Should you not investigate this?[16]

By exploring these diverse aspects of his subject, the painter consciously seeks not to cultivate one single, static perspective but to incorporate as many changing, multiple viewpoints as possible within one seeing (as opposed to one "scene"): a lively illustration of how the "walking head" of Dao actually engages with the larger world—in this case, of mountains, "as though," in the words of Guo Xi, "you were really on the point of going there." Surely no one can look at this painting without becoming absorbed into the mutable energies of *Dao*, which means, in actual experience, that no one can see the same painting twice.

TWO CHINESE USES OF *DAO*

As the opening story amply illustrates, *Dao* itself generates shifting meanings. Part of its humor arises from this parodic Confucius's amazement at the ability of the swimmer—which he sees as the kind of *dao* he himself values, that is, of a kind of personal, self-cultivated skill. But Zhuangzi's story exposes such assumptions as small minded. Here, even an uneducated swimmer knows that *Dao* is bigger than this and that his own skill consists only in attuning himself to the powerful flow of the water's force.

As such, the story graphically illustrates a basic confrontation in Chinese understandings of *Dao*. From the time it first emerged as a primary way of thinking about the world (during the centuries leading up to the unification of China in 221 BCE), *Dao* has been evoked in two quite distinct and even hostile orientations. The philosophical Daoists, led by Laozi and Zhuangzi, turned their attention upstream, back toward the origins of their world. They typically saw human intervention as destroying the natural purity of life in primitive circumstances. In the West, the discourse of Jean-Jacques Rousseau responds to similar preoccupations. But unlike Rousseau, the philosophical Daoists tended to withdraw from the larger world in order to cultivate a kind of creative spontaneity, inspired by wine if not by meditation. Like Henry David Thoreau, perhaps our nearest equivalent in the West, philosophical Daoists also tended to see civilization as a mistake.[17] They opposed all except the most minimal of governmental organizations and idealized the life of the hermit as one of contemplative solitude. In that sense, philosophical Daoists might be understood to be the world's first anarchists.

The other, competing lineage also took the concept of *Dao* as touchstone. Concentrating on that practical world spurned by Laozi and Zhuangzi, the teachings of Kongzi focused on social and political affairs. One might say that the Confucianists, later exemplified by Mengzi and Xunzi, turned their attention downstream. To them, *dao* was a word for *the right way* for humans to act. For Kongzi, the goal was to live up to one's given role within the hierarchy as well as humanly possible—as such embodying to perfection the central Chinese (and Confucianist) virtue of *xiao*.[18] Since everything is open to change and change cannot be counted on to be positive, the most urgent project was to maintain a human community strong enough to withstand the multiple disruptions that by the very nature of things threaten it: natural disasters, external enemies, bad leaders, disobedient children, and self-seeking individuals of any age.

Distinguished in this way, these two fundamentally different ways of engaging with *Dao* might be compared to the differing interpretation by Christians on the doctrine of salvation: is one saved by means of "faith" or "works"? As in that controversy, the distinction between the philosophical Daoists and Confucianists has given rise to a very different emphasis on how one finds the "way." Those Christians who rely on salvation by faith might, like the Daoists, concentrate on the solitary life of prayer.[19] On the other hand, those Christians who rely on salvation by works would, like Confucians, emphasize the necessity of participating in the larger social world, as exemplified by acts of benevolence. In short, the Daoists focused directly on the elusive nature of things; the Confucianists, on its consequences: the fragility of the human community and the need to strengthen it.

Starting more than two thousand years ago, under the active promotion of the Emperor Han Wudi, the Confucian tradition came under official sponsorship and, ever since, has tended to dominate Chinese discourse on how to live. Within that worldview, the Daoist tended to be increasingly marginalized: the one who seeks solitude being regarded as inimical to the ultimate Confucianist project of becoming human by becoming encultured as a social creature.[20]

A COMMON CORE

Despite these two very distinct approaches to finding the "way," both schools of thinking attribute the same two basic presumptions to *Dao*: that everything changes and that everything is connected.[21] For in this world, Dao's pervasive presence means that everything manifests itself through a continual process of transformation (*yi* 易).[22] In response, Chinese life seeks to accommodate to whatever happens with as much equanimity as possible. The philosophical Daoist would withdraw from the turbulent outer world to find inner peace by communing with the forces that govern it. A follower of Kongzi would, on the other hand, seek to fulfill his given family role to the best of one's ability, in the process ensuring that the larger community could survive the traumas threatening it. In this way the negative implications of change can be contained and continuities can endure. But to think of these two worldviews as inimical to each other would be a Western mistake. As is true of so many aspects of Chinese life, Daoist and Confucianist beliefs overlap and amalgamate in actual practice, so that Confucianist artifacts/sayings are often found in Daoist temples, and Daoist beliefs infuse many Confucianist teachings.[23]

Moreover, presuming a world as continually transforming itself also allowed Chinese thinking to absorb readily other cognate schools of thought. One might even argue that Daoism acted as a powerful receptor for Buddhism, coming to China early in the Common Era. Although originally taking Daoism as its chief rival, Buddhism was eventually assimilated in terms compatible with *Dao* thinking. Advocating an eightfold *path* toward spiritual growth, aiming ultimately at liberation from all worldly desires, Buddhism too centers on process—not as self-realization or even self-preservation but ultimately as moving beyond selfhood itself. And again, like Daoism and Confucianism, Buddhism also emphasizes practice over principles, as doing over saying, and orthopraxis over orthodoxy. Like its predecessors in China, Buddhism also tends to teach its disciples orally or through example rather than through any systematic philosophy.

In so doing, Buddhism has cultivated a style similar to that of philosophical Daoism. Each seeks to liberate itself from words by teaching through paradox, parable, and other modes that systematically subvert what Westerners privilege as rational thinking. For all these reasons, Buddhism, rather than Islam or Christianity (both word-based religions), has been the imported religion most readily absorbed into mainstream Chinese thinking.[24]

DAO AS A PRIMARY PRESUMPTION OF CHINESE CULTURE

Even though someone in the West may not subscribe to Christian tenets, he or she lives in a world profoundly influenced by the way those beliefs have shaped the ambient culture. In the same way, Chinese people who may never have read the *Daodejing* are acculturated to its way of thinking. Not every Chinese person consciously seeks to be in touch with *Dao*; indeed, many today do not even use the term. But the way the vast majority of Chinese focus their lives every day has been profoundly conditioned by beliefs associated with *Dao*. As one instance, *Dao* may be taken as the name for that primal unity that gives rise to *qi*, itself expressed in the shifting forces of *yin* and *yang*. As such, in daily life, *Dao* provides the frame of reference for practices as diverse as diet, traditional Chinese medicine (TCM), and multiple Chinese arts and sciences, from calligraphy to *qigong* to meditation. As its principal enabling concept, *Dao* points to energies that shape a world in which everything is connected—and everything changes.

A sense of the complexities of a worldview based on *Dao* thinking may be offered by the *Daodejing*, one of the fundamental classic texts memorized—from the seventh century into the twentieth century—by all who aspired to leading positions in China.[25] While remaining elusive, it offers a shifting perspective on the totality of existence, as

The *Dao* produces the One
The One turns into the Two
The Two give rise to the Three
The Three bring forth the myriad of things.
The myriad things contain *Yin* and *Yang* as vital forces,
Which achieve harmony through their interactions.[26]

While most Chinese people focus their lives on the myriad things that fill the world, the *way* they think about those things reflects an implicit understanding that everything originates from—and is animated by—the impersonal forces known as *Dao*. In other words, any particular focus will evoke in a Chinese person an implicit reference to its larger field (as in William Blake's finding a world in a grain of sand). To respond in this spirit is thus to attune oneself to the way everything changes—and in changing, becomes changed by what it changes, thus reaffirming, once again, the connecting force of *Dao*.

Is it possible to organize a whole culture around *linking together* as opposed to the Western propensity for *taking apart* through the analytic distinctions we call "knowledge"? Absolutely. But clearly the resulting culture will differ greatly from its counterpart in the West.

UNTHINKING THROUGH THE DAO

In fact, trying to understand such pervasive *Dao*-thinking can be for Westerners a head-wrecking process. Mostly this is because it entails *un*thinking a large number of long-standing Western presumptions. Several of them might be enumerated as follows:

1. We need to *un*think that classic Daoist texts may be made "to mean" in any literal sense. In fact, the classic texts—the *Daodejing* and the *Zhuangzi*—work very hard to elude translation into any single meaning. Not only do they proceed by parable and paradox, but also they have elevated the art of ambiguity—of multiple possible meanings—into high art. One of the reasons these remain classic texts is that readers must themselves construe their sayings line by line; as a creative use of intelligence fully cognate with *Dao* thinking, this method relies on multiple interpretations that may shift with every reading.

2. We need to *un*think the mentality that considers *parts as merely pieces of the whole—and the whole as merely a sum of its parts*. Daoist sages concentrate on every specific instance as exemplary of the widest possible significance. The *part* is a gateway to the *whole*; the *whole* gives meaning to the *part*. All are connected in an unending transaction that confers weight to every event, every gesture, every perception. In Zhuangzi's words, "We are one with all things."[27]

3. We need to *un*think that *things exist* in some absolute sense. To these Daoists *everything is always becoming*, absorbed in a ceaseless and cadenced flow of experience. In other words (to paraphrase John Dewey), there are absolutely no absolutes: no God and no reliable sense in which any one of us "exists" apart from our immediate lives in the here and now. In fact, the Chinese language has no usage of "to be" as meaning "to exist."[28] Nor is there any presumption that the world has had a beginning—or will come to an end. *Dao* is infinite, without beginning or boundary.[29] It operates not as an external, eternal force

(like the Judeo-Christian Creator-God) but as endless transformative change identified here as *yi*.

4. We need to *un*think that we can, as Westerners have long hoped, *know the world as it is.* No matter how long or strenuously one searches, it is not possible to find eternal, "universal" principles or laws that point to external, "objective" causes or an overarching design to the world. Among Western thinkers, Heraclitus comes nearest to stating the difficulties of "knowing" the world according to *Dao.* If, as he argues, everything is in flux—and we can never stand in the same river twice—then we can never find the "eternal forms" sought by Plato or the worldly categories posited by Aristotle and all the Western thinkers who have followed their lead.[30]

In the postmodern West, many of these exercises of *un*thinking prevailing Enlightenment assumptions are already underway. As pointed out at the close of the chapter on *xin*, traditional Chinese thinking may even be interpreted as reinforcing new challenges to the West's own understanding of the language-logic of its world or of thinking itself as a purely "rational" process.[31]

WHAT THE DAOIST MODE HAS TO OFFER

The philosophical Daoists, then, would make us into far humbler humans. Western ways of knowing the world readily presume we can permanently or easily draw boundaries between "this" and "that." The Chinese world sees no such possibility. Chinese mental categories do not work like black and white. Opposites cannot be said to exclude each other, precisely because, in the world of *yin* and *yang*, each one both entails and enables the other. Thus, according to the *Daodejing*,

> When the people of the world know the beautiful as beauty;
> There arises the recognition of the ugly.
> When they know the good as good,
> There arises the recognition of the evil.

Thus,

> Difficult and easy complete each other;
> Long and short contrast with each other;
> High and low are distinguished from each other;
> Sound and voice harmonize with each other;
> Front and back follow each other. [32]

These lines exemplify the *Daodejing*'s conviction that concepts are not stable entities; each pair is brought forth and made manifest through mutually enabling what might seem its opposite. In this world, in other words, contradictions are not to be regarded as obstructing goals, for the very way the world proceeds is by means of opposition, as one term transmutes into the other.[33]

The classical Daoist line of thinking does not stop there. Given these assumptions, it is not plausible to think/act following the Western habit of gathering clear information, setting goals, and proceeding toward one's destination as if it were an unchanging and unambiguous target. Instead, in Daoism the wise practice of *wuwei* enjoins staying alert to the larger propensity of things as they evolve, acting minimally, and following one's instinct as to how best to intervene (if at all) in the changing situation to hand. Things will be changing anyway, so pursuing goals of necessity tends to give way simply to the effort of coping.

Finally, as must become evident from the Chinese reasoning sketched above, one *cannot control—or seek to possess—whether by knowing or actually holding on to stuff— as a means of control.*[34] In this fleeting world, one cannot hold onto anything. For, just as one is about to make one's entrance, the scene may shift; and suddenly one may need to know the lines for a whole different part in a different drama. Consequently, to hold clear and unchanging views, in the sense of set principles, is to fail to engage with this world as it is.

As a guide to Chinese modalities of thinking—and the way they can overturn conventional habits of Western thought—the sayings of the *Daodejing* offer an invaluable resource. While it is not difficult for Westerners to identify features of their own worldview that they think the Chinese could profit from adopting—such as less reliance on luck, more on planning, less on authoritarian leadership, and more on personal liberties—it may be harder for people from the West to discern what *they* might have to gain by glancing at the world through Chinese eyes. Yet what China has to teach are valuable correctives to many of our own habits of mind, if we can suspend judgment long enough to consider them.

ASSESSING CHINESE HABITS OF MIND

In observing Chinese habits of mind, what stands out most to someone from the West is a Chinese readiness to assimilate and engage with broader perspectives—rather than the Western instinct to draw back and exclude by emphasizing distinctions.

Perhaps this tendency is most readily demonstrated by the difficulties of teaching even elite Chinese graduate students of English how to write a Western-style essay.[35] As anyone who has tried this knows, the typical Chinese student will seek to undertake an assignment first by downloading everything that can be found on the topic from the Internet and then by avalanching the reader with the results. Usually the essay takes a meandering form: beginning from some unexpected tangent and then gathering in more and more "information" (status not calibrated) and, finally, by summarizing the sum total in terms of a practical application or moral. This approach does not stem from lack of discipline; in fact, it is the way that high school students are taught to write an academic essay in Chinese.[36]

For the Westerner, what is lacking in such an exercise are characteristics already noted in wider Chinese thinking: no plain statement of thesis to be argued; lack of clear definitions of key concepts; an impulse to collect rather than select information; an apparent inability to calibrate information by mustering it to support a central thesis; and, finally, in lieu of a clear conclusion, an assumption that "facts" are presented only to provide a moral, that is, to be offered as guidance from and to the larger community. By writing in this manner, the Chinese graduate student is simply exemplifying the way most Chinese people think: relating all particular instances to the whole rather than taking them apart (thereby synthesizing rather than analyzing), all the while blurring any distinctions that might interfere with the sense of an overriding unity.[37] The result is that Chinese discourse rarely seems to be direct or straightforward. To take in the whole, one must circle around it, reaching one's conclusion, in the words of François Jullien, "by indirection."[38] For a Westerner, this approach may seem merely baffling. If you want to be convincing, why not get straight to the point? Why not say what you mean right away? Why all this apparent deviousness?

Here is one of the great divides, as exemplified in the graphic by Yang Liu below that wittily exaggerates the contrasts between Western and Chinese ways of thinking—and thus writing and speaking. She places it under the rubric of "opinion"; we read it more readily in terms of "meaning." If one wishes to discern *meanings* in Chinese discourse, one must often look to the silences, the hesitations, the circumlocutions, diversions, and euphemisms.

Note that the Western way is different but not automatically superior. To get from A to B in such a determined fashion requires pushing aside a host of factors that remain relevant to the situation. Such directness, in other words, comes at a price. While the Chinese way of writing risks never reaching the goal, it has the advantage of bringing into the discourse a variety of related (if relatively peripheral) factors

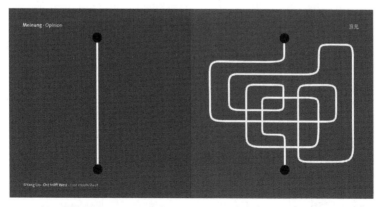

Yang Liu, "Opinion": How Minds Are Taught to Work. *Source:* Yang Liu, *Ost trifft West* [East meets West], 10th ed. (Mainz, Germany: Hermann Schmidt Verlag, 2014). Used by permission.

routinely sacrificed to Western logic. Even so, Chinese students certainly can learn how to write in a Western-style academic essay. Why are they so reluctant to do so? There may be many interlocking reasons, each inseparable from the others. The first might be social: that to state something directly might contradict or offend the opinions of the person spoken to or about, who would then lose face. As all social relations are hierarchical, to criticize a superior in a direct manner might risk disrupting good relations, which depend on a perceptible demonstration of deference. Another reason, also social, is that a high degree of attention to implicit meanings is both necessary and expected. Almost all of the time one cannot say what one means (or at least one hesitates to do so). Given the millennia of social control exerted by central authorities in China over what is written or said publicly, these reasons have carried and continue to carry significant weight. One always has an audience but one from which one's clear meaning may need to be routinely shielded.[39]

Or on a larger scale, one might say simply that such indirection has become habitual because that is how Chinese people tend to think. From the onset Chinese people have been acculturated to consider the focus of a discussion in terms of a larger context or field. That field perception usually dominates thinking—and ensures that someone from China routinely considers wider implications as significant factors in any situation. That habit reinforces the perception that one is part of a much larger, impersonal system that takes no heed of one's own desires. Thus setting clear goals is difficult, as a Chinese person is acutely conscious that "reality" is always shifting, in a continuous process without apparent cause, beginning or end. This is *Dao* going on its way.

In short, Chinese people tend to be acutely aware that *they are not in control.*[40] Thus, in speaking as in acting, rather than set artificial goals that will be, inevitably, thwarted to some degree or other, the sensible thing is to adapt pragmatically, by staying alert to the implicit potential of any situation as it develops. To proceed by indirection implicitly acknowledges the centrality of the forces of *Dao* within one's own life. One copes with them not by seeking to affront or override them but through devising strategies attentive to the larger Powers That Be.

NOTES

1. A more formal translation may be found in the bilingual Wang Rongpei, trans., *Zhuangzi*, 2 vols., Library of Chinese Classics (Changsha, China: Hunan People's Publishing House, 1999), 2:19, 308–11.
2. "Standing on the bare ground—my head bathed by the blithe air, and uplifted into infinite spaces—all mean egotism vanishes. I become a transparent eyeball; I am nothing; I see all; the currents of the Universal Being circulate through me; I am part or particle of God." From Ralph Waldo Emerson, *Nature* (Boston: James Munroe, 1849), 8.
3. Zhang Longxi, "The 'Tao' and the 'Logos': Notes on Derrida's Critique of Logocentrism," *Critical Inquiry* 11, no. 3 (March 1985): 386. For further elaboration, see the previous chapter (chapter 6, "Chameleon Reality: *Yi*").

4. See Chad Hansen's website: "Daoist-Oriented Interpretations," Chad Hansen's Chinese Philosophy Pages, accessed November 25, 2012, http://www.hku.hk/philodep/ch.

5. See chapter 4, "Where Is My Mind? *Xīn*."

6. Wang Rongpei, *Zhuangzi*, 1:2, 22–23.

7. Wang Rongpei, *Zhuangzi*, 1:3, 43–45 (italics added); *CCCW*, CD, 1254–55.

8. The great theorist in English of Chinese body thinking is Wu Kuang-Ming, as in his book by that name from 1996, *On Chinese Body Thinking: A Cultural Hermeneutic* (Leiden, Netherlands: Brill). See chapter 4, "Where Is My Mind? *Xīn*."

9. Lao Tzu [Laozi], *The Book of Tao and Teh* [*Daodejing*], trans. Gu Zhengkun, 2nd ed. (Beijing: Peking University Press, 2006). Here, Professor Gu uses the older Wade-Giles romanization for "Tao" (instead of "Dao," the pinyin used in this book) and Lao Tzu (instead of "Laozi").

10. On the other hand, religious Daoism, emerging centuries later (early in the Common Era), provided what had been lacking: statues and temples and established rituals. This is often regarded as a kind of degraded "folk" Daoism by the philosophical Daoists; but like doctrinal and popular Christianity, in Daoist temples they tend to exist side by side: with the *Daodejing* being chanted in shrines centered around statues and other paraphernalia of popular Daoism.

11. Ralph Waldo Emerson, "The American Scholar," in *Selections from Ralph Waldo Emerson*, ed. Stephen E. Whicher (Boston: Houghton Mifflin, 1957), 64–65, 72 (italics added).

12. To view details of the Guo Xi painting, consult Patricia Buckley Ebrey, "Northern Song Landscape Painting," Visual Sourcebook of Chinese Civilization, accessed December 27, 2011, http://depts.washington.edu/.

13. To get some idea of its range, see Stephen Little and Shawn Eichman, eds., *Taoism and the Arts of China* (Chicago: Art Institute of Chicago, 2000).

14. "I become a transparent eyeball; I am nothing; I see all; the currents of the Universal Being circulate through me; I am part or particle of God." Emerson, *Nature*, 8. Note how the Western emphasis on "I" as the center of this experience, as well as the diction specifying the ego as a "part" or "particle" of God, reinforces the indissoluble nature of the ego even while being nominally absorbed into a greater whole (in this case, the deity).

15. The phrase is that of the Song dynasty critic Shen Gua, as quoted in Michael Sullivan, *The Arts of China* (Berkeley: University of California Press, 1999), 168.

16. Guo Xi [Kuo Hsi], "Advice on Landscape Painting," in *Early Chinese Texts on Painting*, ed. Susan Bush and Hsio-yen Shih (Cambridge, MA: Harvard University Press, 1985), 153–54. The following quotation is from this source.

17. Zhuangzi, for example, describes in chapter 29 how an early paradisiacal (and matrilineal) world of humans was lost forever when the Yellow Emperor began his endless wars. Rongpei, *Zhuangzi*, 2:29, 516–19; *CCCW*, 310–11.

18. See chapter 1, "Binding Families: *Xiào*"; *CCCW*, 113–16.

19. The theological debate over the question of whether salvation is by faith or by works has caused Christian denominations to disagree for centuries. Differences of conviction are still common among Christians today. To get around the apparent dichotomy, some Christians (e.g., Roman Catholic contemplative orders) define "prayer" as "work."

20. See our analysis of the character *ren* 仁 in chapter 12, "Question Two: Human Rights?" in the section titled "*Ren* (仁): What Is 'Human'?"

21. The degree to which Daoism and Confucianism have long shared a core Chinese orientation is confirmed by a report from an early 1940s report of how monks were trained at Baiyunguan, the national center of the Quanzhen sect of Daoists. Morning lectures focused not

only on some specifically Daoist classics but also on the *Four Books* and *Five Classics*, which were dominantly Confucian in origin and orientation. Yoshitoyo Yoshioka, "Taoist Monastic Life," in *Facets of Taoism*, ed. Holmes Welch and Anna Seidel, 229–51 (New Haven, CT: Yale University Press, 1979), 245. Western reluctance to recognize this Chinese interpenetration of belief systems should not all be blamed on Arthur Waley's 1939 classic *Three Ways of Thought in Ancient China*. That work simply presumed and prolonged the ethnocentric Western habit of presuming that individuals should be loyal exclusively to one or another set of beliefs.

22. See chapter 6, "Chameleon Reality: *Yi*."

23. See note 19 above. Another sign of the closeness of Confucian and Daoist beliefs surfaces in the two fictions written in English by Ding Wangdao (1924–2010), influential teacher and translator of classic Chinese texts at Beijing Foreign Studies University. His first novel, *A Continuing Climb*, published in 2000 by the Foreign Languages Teaching and Research Press, he described as Confucian. A few years later, in 2007, he published with the same press *A Turning Point*, which he characterized as Daoist. What intervened was not a change of heart but a shift in focus.

24. See chapter 11, "Question One: Christianity?"

25. See chapter 6, "Chameleon Reality: *Yi*," and note 20 above.

26. Wang Keping, trans., *The Classic of the Dao [Daodejing]: A New Investigation* (Beijing: Foreign Languages Press, 1998), 239.

27. Roger T. Ames and David L. Hall, trans., *Daodejing: Making This Life Significant; A Philosophical Translation* (New York: Ballantine, 2003), 17.

28. Ames and Hall, *Daodejing*, 51.

29. Zhuangzi's way of putting it in chapter 25 is as follows: "When we try to find out the source of the world, we trace back into infinity; when we try to find out the end, we look into infinity. Infinity into the past and into the future implies that it is beyond description." *CCCW*, 502.

30. "All things flow" is the way Plato described Heraclitus's doctrine in order to oppose it. See Plato, *Cratylus*, trans. Benjamin Jowett, Project Gutenberg, January 1, 1999, accessed November 23, 2012, http://www.gutenberg.org/, 402a. It should be noted that Heraclitus also subscribed to the Daoist teaching of the underlying identity of opposites, in affirming "the way up is the way down." Similarly, the opposites in their simultaneous and instantaneous interactions can result in "hidden harmony."

31. For further elaboration, see chapter 4, "Where Is My Mind? *Xin*."

32. Wang Keping, *Classic of the Dao*, 104.

33. This aspect of traditional Chinese thought suggests how Marxist emphasis on dialectics could link this cultural importation with preexisting Chinese presumptions.

34. The fundamental impossibility of control does not discourage today's rulers of China from trying, but everyone knows that their mastery is fragile and temporary.

35. For a comparative perspective on this topic, see Jerusha McCormack, "Framing Academic Discourse: East and West," in *English Education and Liberal Education*, ed. Sun Youzhong et al., 307–20 (Beijing: Foreign Language Teaching and Research Press, 2008). It should be emphasized that our experience is in teaching graduate students how to write an academic essay in *English*. In the experience of another teacher whose native language is English but who teaches in Chinese, letting his students discuss issues in Chinese allows them to express their points more freely.

36. See *CCCW*, CD, 575.

37. In social or political contexts, as we will see shortly, this impulse is expressed in terms of "social harmony."

38. See Jullien's brilliant dissertation on this modality of thinking in poetry and other forms of discourse in *Detour and Access: Strategies of Meaning in China and Greece*, trans. Sophie Hawkes (New York: Zone Books, 2000).

39. However, our experience confirms that, in teaching at the PRC, speaking in English gives one far greater freedom for direct expression of views than is available to our Chinese colleagues teaching in Chinese.

40. When asked if they attribute what happens to them to their own doing, Chinese respondents said "yes" 39% of the time, among the world's lowest. Americans said "yes" 82% of the time, among the world's highest. Responses from other Western nations covered a considerable range from lows of 49% in Russia and 62% in Portugal to highs of 76% in the UK and 86% in Norway. Fons Trompenaars and Charles Hampden-Turner, *Riding the Waves of Culture: Understanding Cultural Diversity in Business*, 2nd ed. (London: Nicholas Brealey, 1997), 144.

和

Hé

8

Thinking in Harmony

Hé 和

*The Marquis of Qi had returned from the hunt and was being attended by Master Yan at the Chuan Pavilion when Ju of Liangqiu galloped up to them. The Marquis said, "Only Ju is in harmony (*he* 和) with me!*

"All that Ju does is agree with you," said Master Yan. "Wherein is the harmony?"

"Is there a difference between harmony and agreement?" asked the Marquis.

"There is," replied Master Yan. "Harmony is like making congee. One uses water, fire, vinegar, sauce, salt and plum to cook fish and meat, and burns firewood and stalks as fuel for the cooking process. The cook blends these ingredients harmoniously to achieve the appropriate flavor. Where it is too bland, he adds flavoring, and where it is too concentrated, he dilutes it with water. When you partake of this congee, sir, it lifts your spirits.

*"The relationship between ruler and minister is another case in point. Where the ruler considers something right and yet there is something wrong about it, the minister should point out what is wrong as a way of achieving what is right. When the ruler considers something wrong and yet there is something right about it, the minister should point out what is right as a way of setting aside what is wrong. In such a way governing will be equitable without violating ritual propriety (*li* 礼) and the common people will not be contentious. . . .*

"Now Ju is not acting in this way. Whatever you say is right, Ju also says is right; whatever you say is wrong, Ju also says is wrong. If you season water with water, who is going to eat it? If you keep playing the same note on your lute, who is going to listen to it? The inadequacy of agreement lies in this."

—Zuozhuan[1]

The character for harmony, *he* 和, combines the sign for grain on the left with that for mouth on the right. Thus its etymology resonates with a culinary metaphor, having to do with the "art of combining and blending two or more foodstuffs so that they come together with mutual benefit and enhancement without losing their separate and particular identities."[2] There is no hint of negativity here. As the etymology of this character suggests, harmony originates as a social virtue, tied to the protocols of decorum (*li* 礼) and thus positive in every aspect. It should come as no surprise, then, that eating together remains China's primary social activity, part of that civilization's amazing longevity.

The West, for its part, also has the concept of harmony deep in its roots but in terms of cosmic, rather than social, harmony. In the late sixth century BCE, Pythagoras invoked the metaphor of harmony in terms of mathematical ratios used to express the orderly movements of planets in what he called "the music of the spheres." With this phrase, Pythagoras offered a mystical vision of the harmonic interactions between humans and nature, one that has now largely disappeared from the West—even though, in today's ecological crisis, valiant efforts have been made to revive this sense of *the world's interconnectedness*.[3]

Around for an equally long time in China, the concept of harmony is still very potent, though focused less on cosmic than on communal concerns. Although the history of this word goes back far before his lifetime, its greatest proponent is Kongzi. In the *Analects*—the surviving record of his oral teachings—Kongzi recommends *he* harmony as the highest cultural achievement available to his civilization. In particular, Kongzi emphasizes that harmony arises from the right practice of social rituals, especially those that reinforce the primal order as expressed within families.

Knowing something about the historical Kongzi (ca. 551–479 BCE) makes sense of this preoccupation with social order. A contemporary of Pythagoras, Kongzi was born in the ancient state of Lu (now Shandong Province) during one of China's intensely turbulent eras known as Spring and Autumn period; like its successor, this was a time of warring states. Growing up orphaned and poor, Kongzi realized, as did many others during this time, that grave social disorder endangered civilization itself. With multiple small statelets contending for hegemony, generation after generation had sacrificed its young men to war. From the ferocity of these internecine conflicts emerged new thinkers, also contending as how best to reach some kind of basic social order. "In times of chaos," the Chinese saying goes, "great leaders arise."

The greatest of these became, eventually, Kongzi. His teaching was innovative in that it did not seek anything new. "Following the proper way," he explained, "I do not forge new paths."[4] In fact, to counter the anarchy of his own times, Kongzi looked back to the early Zhou dynasty of the twelfth century BCE. For him, the Duke of Zhou proved a touchstone model because he served faithfully as regent for his young nephew and then turned over the throne to him when the latter came of age. In living up to his role as regent, the Duke of Zhou performed all the pertinent rituals at the prescribed times. Though he was slandered, he did not try to usurp power. When his brother the king fell deathly ill, he even proposed to the ancestors that he should die instead.[5] For Kongzi, the Duke of Zhou exemplified an ambition not to climb the hierarchical ladder to power but to live up to his role within the given hierarchy as well as humanly possible, embodying to perfection the central Chinese virtue of *xiao*.

Thus the teachings of Kongzi concentrate on that social and political world around him. Under the rubric of Confucianism, "harmony" springs from the right actions of individuals as defined by their positions. To act rightly each person must follow the right *way*. According to the Confucian classic *Zhongyong* (*The Doctrine of the Mean*), "When moderation and harmony are attained, heaven and earth are in the right position and material things are bounteous."[6] For centuries, candidates for the imperial exam had to memorize its tenets: that personal harmony—defined as that state of equilibrium in which pleasure, anger, sorrow, and joy became restrained and moderated—in turn allowed "all things in the universe to attain the Way."[7] From the time of Xunzi, the third-century BCE thinker who was one of Kongzi's most influential interpreters, that connection became a commonplace facet of Chinese thinking. Harmony, it was said, led to unity, unity to strength, strength to power, and power to prosperity. In this way, *he* harmony exemplifies the connecting and correlating energies of the world as channeled through orderly relations between self and society, society and the larger world, as implicit in its basic musical metaphor.

Why should *he* harmony remain for China such a persistent core value? In a world in which everything is open to change and change cannot be counted on to be positive, no modern Western belief in *progress* makes enduring sense. Therefore, as the Confucians believe, the most urgent project is to maintain a human community strong enough to withstand the multiple disruptions that by the very nature of things threaten it: natural disasters, external enemies, bad leaders, peasant revolts, corrupt officials, and disobedient children. The conviction that community alone provides a bulwark against chaos endures into the present day, both publicly and privately.

CORE VALUES: KONGZI AND SHAKESPEARE

Often the West follows a traditional Chinese habit of referring all conventional wisdom to a purported "Confucius"—even though many of these sayings cannot be found in the teachings of the historical Kongzi.

All that this demonstrates is that, much as the West is shaped by Christian ideology, so Chinese thinking is shaped from an early age by the conventions of Confucianist thought. As already rehearsed in the chapters on *xiao* and *mianzi*, these influences shape one's sense of self as constructed through relations with others. Rather than being born (as in the West) with an implicit entitlement to individual rights, a Chinese person is born into roles. These roles are defined at birth by gender, by his or her place in the family, and later by that person's place in the larger hierarchies defined by work and communal status.[8] According to Confucianist teaching, social order consists of fulfilling one's role within that hierarchy in an exemplary fashion. If one fulfills one's role in such a fashion, then social order will follow. In the words of Kongzi, for governance to be effective, "the ruler must rule, the minister minister, the father [be a] father, and the son [a] son."[9]

In the West, at the turning point of the late medieval to the early modern era, Shakespeare worked with a similar conceit. It occurs in a famous speech on the nature of "order"—delivered at a key point in his play, *Troilus and Cressida*, loosely based on that founding chaos of Western civilization, the Trojan War. The speech is delivered by its hero, Ulysses, who foresees in the destruction of "degree" (hierarchy) a future defined by not merely social but also cosmic chaos:

> The heavens themselves, the planets, and this centre
> Observe degree, priority, and place,
> Insisture, course, proportion, season, form,
> Office, and custom, in all line of order;
> And therefore is the glorious planet sol
> In noble eminence enthron'd and spher'd
> Amidst the other. . . . But when the planets
> In evil mixture to disorder wander,
> What plagues and what portents, what mutiny!
> What raging of the sea, shaking of earth!
> Commotion in the winds! frights, changes, horrors
> Divert and crack, rend and deracinate
> The unity and married calm of states
> Quite from their fixure! *O, when degree is shak'd,*
> *Which is the ladder of all high designs,*
> *The enterprise is sick.*

Sounding consummately Confucian, Ulysses employs the same kind of musical metaphors for social harmony when he asks, rhetorically,

> How could communities,
> Degrees in schools, and brotherhoods in cities,
> Peaceful commerce from dividable shores,
> The primogenity and due of birth,
> Prerogative of age, crowns, sceptres, laurels,
> But by degree stand in authentic place?
> *Take but degree away, untune that string,*
> *And hark what discord follows.*

Confucian too is Ulysses's focus on social discord as infecting everything from the cosmos to the intimate ordering of the family, resulting in a life that is brutish and wolflike—in short, no longer human. Out of such discord, he foresees a world in which

> Strength should be lord of imbecility,
> And the rude son should strike his father dead;
> Force should be right, or rather, right and wrong

(Between whose endless jar justice resides)
Should lose their names, and so should justice too!
Then every thing include itself in power,
Power into will, will into appetite,
And appetite, an universal wolf
(So doubly seconded with will and power),
Must make per force an universal prey,
And last eat up himself.[10]

Devised at a time when modernity was beginning to undermine the structures of a venerable feudal world, Ulysses's speech appeals to those values under attack from the ferocity of a new venture capitalism that was to result, some centuries later, in the British Empire. It is safe to say that today the values that Ulysses advocates—in an inclusive summary of the worldview of his time—have been swept away in the West. Yet they still endure as core values within Chinese culture and the larger sphere of its historical influence. Is it part of its persistence that, of all traditional values in the Chinese world, "harmony" is perhaps the one most easily manipulated for social and political control, both informal and formal?

KONGZI AND CONFUCIANISM

During his own lifetime, the influence of Kongzi was virtually nil. Ironically, in later centuries, thanks to such interpreters as Mengzi and Xunzi, the teacher Kongzi became the sage "Confucius," repeatedly cited as the wisest of all Chinese thinkers. When, more than two thousand years ago, under the long reign of Emperor Han Wudi (ruled 141 to 87 BCE), the Confucian tradition came under official sponsorship, it had an effect similar to the institution of Christianity as a state religion by the Emperor Constantine.[11] Henceforward, as the disparate teachings of Kongzi were systematized into official ideology, the principles of duty to family were extended vigorously to the State and its bureaucracy, disseminated for the first time through an official school and then deployed to unify the many newly conquered territories of the empire. This empire, at its largest, stretched from Korea in the northeast, into Vietnam in the south, and far into Central Asia to the west. Arguably, it was these Confucianist doctrines of *xiao* that enabled Han Wudi to control effectively such a vast and otherwise diverse territory.[12] Even today, Confucianism, as a self-consciously ideological formation, still retains much influence within that larger cultural zone.

By such means the historical Kongzi became transformed into the great "Confucius," the reputed font of all civilizational wisdom in China. Although "Confucius" is constantly evoked, it is less for his own teachings—which can be ambiguous—than for his status as a sage whose name guarantees the honorable ancestry of any newly proclaimed ideology. His actual teachings (insofar as they can be reconstructed) had a similar fate. In fact, the *Analects* did not even appear among the initial designations of official classic texts. Since Kongzi, like Socrates, taught only orally, what was actually said could be altered or disputed. Most scholars believe that, over roughly three centuries, disciples of Kongzi and their descendants compiled numerous short books that purported to represent his thinking. After the notorious burning of traditional books under Qin Shihuang starting in 213 BCE, Kongzi's reputed teachings survived only through various written fragments and recovered memorizations. To further his own ideological project, these were assembled under the Emperor Han Wudi into the composite text we have today—filtered through many centuries of controversy over newer and older versions.

As a result, for many Chinese today, returning to the text of the *Analects* has about the same effect as Christians turning to the Bible: it can often prove a disconcerting experience. Just as a biblical scholar has to distinguish between texts, translators, redactors, and differing doctrinal and editorial agendas, so a Confucianist has to distinguish between what Kongzi (the historical figure, insofar as he can be reconstructed) may be said to have taught and the social doctrines attributed later to figure we identify as "Confucius."[13]

CONFUCIANISM AS A STATE TOOL

That seamless movement of Ulysses's speech tracing the collapse of order from the heavenly planets to government, and from government to the family, is almost flawlessly Chinese. But the way Ulysses evokes the cosmos is not properly "Confucian." Kongzi, unlike the Daoists, had little to say about larger cosmic forces. Instead, Kongzi concentrates on how maintaining the basic hierarchies of roles within the family will act to support the larger hierarchies of community and government through periods of disorder. Kongzi's other preoccupation (given the times he was born into) is the way in which rulers may achieve, and retain, legitimacy in the face of larger social mayhem.

This rethinking sometimes leads to startling insights. For instance, in responding to a question from one of his disciples, Zigong, about "governing effectively," Kongzi set out the following conditions:

"Make sure there is sufficient food to eat, sufficient arms for defense, and that the common people have confidence in their leaders."

"If you have to give up one of these three things," [Zigong] said, "which should be given up first?"

"Give up the arms," [Kongzi] replied.

"If you had to give up one of the remaining two," he said, "which one should be given up first?"

"Give up food," [Kongzi] replied. "Death has been with us from ancient times, but if the common people do not have confidence in their leaders, community will not endure."[14]

The situation here is obviously artificial. As a favored disciple, Zigong can launch a set-up question that allows the sage to make an arresting point. Arms may be given up if necessary, but how can one ask the people to give up food? The answer is that although one may die without food, nothing is possible for a community without confidence in leaders. A Western rephrasing might identify the crucial third element as "trust." Or as Franklin Roosevelt put it in response to the Great Depression, the most urgent need is for that confidence that alone can counter the fear of fear itself.[15]

Although fear is used routinely to maintain social order within the People's Republic of China (PRC), the promise of hope for the future is one of the Party's most powerful legitimizing tools. In fact, one expert observes that, in "their grand ideological visions" Chinese leaders "have made the Chinese exploit the human potential of hope more than any of the other Asian political cultures."[16] Such a promise takes as its premise good social order—as defined not so much by Kongzi as by the current exploitation of his teachings. Indeed, some aspects of Kongzi's own teachings might even be seen as inimical to the Party's version of Confucianism. For instance, in the *Analects*, Kongzi emphasizes the notion of "harmony" as loyal opposition, saying, "The gentleman is harmonious although he does not assent," while "the small man assents, but is not harmonious."[17] As this chapter's opening story illustrates, harmony is not the same as agreement. A loyal minister will point out what is wrong in the policies of his ruler. Kongzi's observation also lays bare the ambiguity of the metaphor. He needs to protest that "harmony" does not mean homogenization but can only be achieved through degrees of difference. Who makes a meal out of one dish? Or a dish out of one flavor? Who makes a melody from a single note played on a single instrument?

In making these remarks, could Kongzi have foreseen the fate of his teaching? When asked by a ruling official if there were a saying that could destroy a territory, Kongzi remarked, "What about the saying: 'The only joy of being a prince is that no one opposes what one says.' If what the ruler says is good, then it is a good thing that it will not be opposed. But if the ruler is wrong, he cannot be opposed. Is this not, then, close to a saying that could lead a territory to destruction?"[18] Yet, in its promotion of *he* as harmony, the Party has itself harmonized the ancient concept into one that is both superficial and selective. Among the tensions between legitimate opposition, negotiation, and assent, the Party (perhaps predictably) comes out on the side of assent, although this is often modulated into a rhetoric of "consensus." In terms of official pronouncements, it tends to produce an amalgam of Kongzi, Mozi, Mengzi, and other sages, ancient and modern, Eastern and Western, in order to reach the overwhelmingly bland conclusion that everyone should get along together and that following the Party line is the obvious way of doing so.[19]

The ensuing script has, in other words, all the subtlety and authenticity of the Ming dynasty vases sold in the local flea markets. But as a script it has great potency, invoking the most honored wisdom of the most honored Chinese sage. Although temporarily replaced during the Mao years—in particular during the Cultural Revolution—by quotations from *The Little Red Book* and flagrantly dismissed as "feudal," the teachings of "Confucius" are now invoked to counter all the ill effects of China's sudden wealth and vertiginous plunge into modernity. As a mantra, the ideal of *he* harmony can be applied to any situation: whether conflicts between local and central government; the growing gap between the new rich and the poor, the urban and the rural; or the growing culture of protest and the felt necessity for strong central control. Without harmony, they are all advised, prosperity and stability cannot be achieved. So who would want to be seen as opposing harmony?

Significantly, the new "harmony" script made its newly reinforced public appearance in October 1989, a few months after the most notorious incident of disorder in recent Chinese history: the Tiananmen Square events of 1989. As John Delury points out, the occasion was a government-sponsored celebration of the 2,540th birthday of Kongzi.[20] It was then that the new official catchword first caught the attention of close observers. These analysts know that the Party pays close attention to linguistic nuance. After all, its leaders are guilty of no spontaneous speech acts. Their lines are all rehearsed in a preapproved script. What is scripted can then be deciphered by interested parties deploying all the finesse of hermeneutic scholars. In this way, departures from former scripts can be readily detected and, in turn, new directions intuited. For those who pay close attention, this method makes it easier to identify shifts in policy positions than is usually the case in the more anarchic linguistic environments of the West with less constricted media, more readily articulated public opinion, and more open political competition.[21]

But there is a further, significant difference. In China, words themselves are deemed to have agency. Those attuned to the new rhetoric repeated it, until "harmony" ascended, in the words of John Delury, from keyword to buzzword to paradigm.[22] Under his presidency, Hu Jintao as head of the PRC, General Secretary of the Party, and Chairman of the Military Commission, made harmony into a clarion call but this time with the explicit focus on achieving a "harmonious society" or *hexie shehui* (和谐 谐社会).

The result, especially under Hu Jintao's leadership, was an ongoing series of public campaigns designed as positive motivators for good citizenship. Within the context of such thinking, to disrupt the *harmonious society* implies calling undue attention to one's personal concerns at the price of undermining the larger national effort. Instead, in the name of a *harmonious society*, citizens are expected to contribute with obvious goodwill to all sorts of efforts said to be for the welfare of the larger polity. In a world where "being volunteered" is synonymous with "volunteering," such efforts represent a triumph of subordinating one's own desires to those of the larger society.[23]

To understand how such slogans work, one must appreciate that governing the world's largest nation works by a habitual carrot-and-stick strategy. In this scheme, a *harmonious society* emphasizes the carrot or positive side. Its main aim is to motivate the citizenry to feel they must contribute to the national effort, however defined from one moment to the next. Slogans work well in China because everyone credits words with having an energy that can actively influence events. So the resonance of *harmony* may actually be seen as energizing a mass audience to undertake large projects for the sake of the nation's welfare. Or conversely, since every educated Chinese person knows the difference between harmony and uniformity (or conformity), the political aim of invoking harmony might even be seen as an effort to "deenergize" a mass audience if it strays from Party mandates. While the government recognizes there are many social conflicts, such a watchword encourages these to be resolved by peaceful means and not by violent conflict, as in the revolutionary past. By the same token, anyone who undermines these collective efforts will be regarded as guilty of disrupting or blocking this positive injunction. In either case, such bland, top-down slogans could not work unless they were greeted with a positive response on the part of most of the people. However, where the slogan is too obviously manipulative, that response may be corroded by popular skepticism and other forms of resistance, such as satire.

RESISTANCE TO SOCIAL HARMONY

As a mantra, *social harmony* is routinely used by governing officials to explain to Chinese people why they should defer to what many perceive as impositions from above. Only a few resist more or less openly, ignoring all the inducements associated with promises of prosperity and a return to national greatness. These are often sought out by Western journalists as evidence that the Chinese would, if given a chance, organize their collective life along more Western lines. Given the momentum residing in Chinese culture, this outcome appears highly improbable. Too many people have a stake in China's rising prosperity and world reputation. Nonetheless, there are multiple signs that many Chinese are ready to respond to their situation, if not with rebellion, then with satire. With sly humor, bloggers on the Internet (now increasingly an instrument of protest) have begun to shift *harmony* from a noun to a verb in the passive voice, complaining about the ways they have been "harmonized."

THE RESONANCES OF RIVER CRABS: *HÉXIÈ* (河蟹)

In fact, Chinese people are quite aware of the artificial attempts to motivate the masses by such campaign slogans as *social harmony*. As one Chinese scholar lamented to us, "As students, we never read Kongzi. We were told that he was feudal, a relic of the old days, whose works should be razed to the ground. The Cultural Revolution cut people off from the sources of their civilization. Now the authorities are remaking it to suit themselves."

Since open resistance is usually counterproductive, those who take exception to the system often turn to mischief. Slogans are easy marks for satire. Often turning these on their heads, dissidents exploit the homophonic resources of the Chinese language to articulate publicly their shared skepticism. As we have seen, in China language has a unique energy that may leak into the surrounding world (as instanced by the implications of *luck language* for the price of mobile phone numbers[24]). In the case of *harmony*, the connection with river crabs offers another set of phonetic echoes. Though the characters in the written language have nothing to do with each other (和谐 *social harmony* versus 河蟹 *river crabs*), the pronunciations are remarkably close: *héxié* (rising intonation on the second syllable) versus *héxiè* (falling intonation on the second syllable).

Once the homophonic pun connection is made, even the written characters for river crab can be generally understood as implying a politically sensitive meaning. It is probable that official censorship targeting certain words—such as the hypersensitive three T's: Tibet, Taiwan, and Tiananmen—will miss the implicit satire, at least for a certain time. And by the time the censors learn to block out "river crab," further circumlocutions will always be possible, as in references to an "aquatic product."[25]

While such tactics do not change the fact of censorship, it ensures that the most articulate and educated segment of the population, those with Internet access, can wink their way through a shared awareness of their situation and thus demonstrate their resistance to it. A vivid recent example is dissident artist Ai Weiwei's use of the metaphor for his 2012 exhibit at the Hirshhorn Museum in Washington, D.C.[26]

The installation spills over with river crabs, exporting to the outside world Ai's satire on the Shanghai authorities who first built—and then ordered destroyed—his elaborate studio in that city. Shortly before the studio was razed, Ai Weiwei arranged and paid for a dinner there serving river crabs for friends and supporters, though he himself was not allowed to attend. Sending an installation of ceramic river crabs to the United States calls worldwide attention to a deeply Chinese kind of satire,

River Crabs, He-Xie (2010), *AI WEIWEI: According to What?* October 7, 2012–February 24, 2013. *Source:* Courtesy Hirshhorn Museum and Sculpture Garden, Smithsonian Institution. Photography by Cathy Carver. Used by permission of Ai Weiwei in Beijing.

no longer merely local but now international. Through such strategies, Ai Weiwei engages in a kind of psychic jujitsu, undermining the authorities by implicitly turning their own rhetoric against them—and then creating a spectacle out of the whole process. For many, he has become an icon of how strategical resistance can put pressure on what some regard as overweening—if not overtly paranoid—authority.[27]

SOCIAL HARMONY VERSUS LOCAL PROTESTS

Despite the availability of such tactics, it is clear that the ongoing rhetoric of social harmony tends to encourage Chinese citizens to mute any overt criticisms of officialdom. And it works, most of the time, except where local frustrations override caution, resulting in open protests. Any such manifestation of social unrest calls forth swift policing in the interests of keeping the unrest local, disconnected from any possibility of wider contagion. In 2010 alone, China saw 180,000 protests, riots, and mass demonstrations—on average about five hundred every day—a number that has likely since increased.[28] So far, the Powers That Be have succeeded in heading off any momentum that might threaten their control. Why this may be so is demonstrated in one exemplary case. In Wukan, a village in southeastern China, protesters held up a sign reading, "We are not a revolt. We support the Communist Party. We love our country." As the issues involved were largely local, the villagers saw themselves as appealing to the central Party authorities to take corrupt local officials in hand.[29] In this case, the protest was apparently settled by deft action on the part of provincial officials—thus turning a threat to the system into public proof that the system can actually work.[30]

Most protests, however, are treated as potential revolts. In these cases, the central officials take control (rather than negotiate). Police action is swift and often drastic. Cell phones are confiscated. Internet and cell phone networks are cut off. Sometimes the local site will be surrounded by police or even the army. Ringleaders are arrested, since they are the ones that dared to step out of line. Then they may or may not be tried in courts whose official duty is to protect the national interest. The courts routinely draw on vaguely worded statutes condemning "crimes against state security," the laws under which Liu Xiaobo was condemned to prison for eleven years.[31]

The seriousness with which these statutes are applied matches their vagueness, reminiscent of the Soviet models for this type of legislation.[32] Basically the State will decide on the spot what activities it feels threatening to its security and through its courts will punish offenders severely.

The courts, then, play a crucial role in enforcing a "rule of law"—frequently evoked in official statements justifying clampdowns on anyone who disturbs public harmony. What is the current status of the "rule of law" in China? An authoritative statement of the relation between the courts and the Party affirms, "The Party committees guarantee judicial bodies the independent power to fulfill their legitimate roles by coordinating their relationship with other departments."[33] This is a wonderful example of the doublespeak that a Western (but not necessarily a Chinese observer) would pinpoint in such regulations. Obviously, if the "independence" of the judicial body is to be enhanced by "coordinating" its activities with other departments of the State, the result may be greater governing coherence—but at the expense of judicial independence. However, in a world where the values of "coordination" underline the prime value of *interdependence*, few Chinese leaders would advocate "independent" courts that might after all reveal, if not result in, unambiguous instances of social *disharmony*.

SOCIAL HARMONY WESTERN STYLE

As an expression, "social harmony" ordinarily has no great leverage in the West because there the emphasis is on its opposite: how to limit "social disorder." Western democracies presume a certain degree of unruliness. Although citizens will often disagree, it is assumed that democratic political systems will allow differences to be ultimately reconciled. Hence riots are rapidly suppressed, but peaceful demonstrations are tolerated within limits, as long as they do not prove overly disruptive. As we have had to explain to Chinese visitors, amazed at "Occupy" sit-ins, demonstrations themselves are seen as expressions of individual citizens' rights. At its most extreme, in the early days of theorizing democracy for the modern West, Jean-Jacques Rousseau imagined that there would be no political parties at all to interfere with the independent thinking of citizens.[34] But this ultimate vision of individual liberty has never (at least so far) been implemented in any Western state.

Historically, contentiousness among citizens has been justified in the West by referring back to the Athens of the fifth and fourth centuries BCE as a prototypical democratic state. The key Greek concept was *agon*, meaning "contest," as applied to Olympic sports and to oral debates in the assembly. Out of this venerable ancestry, the modern West derived, as of Adam Smith's time in the late eighteenth century, a faith that *competition itself* provided a guarantee that, in any contest, whoever managed to "better" the opposition was automatically superior (at least until the next contest). Although the credibility of this affirmation is clearer in sports contests than elsewhere, even in sports, rules and umpires had to be introduced to ensure at least minimal fairness in the contest. Still, the ideal of ensuring a "level playing field" continues to haunt debates surrounding such contests today, whether in economic or political contexts.

In short, there is no direct equivalent in Western life for social harmony in its Chinese applications. Rather than social harmony, the West promotes a rhetoric of "fairness" in competitions and a balancing of opposing powers, as in the constitution of its governing bodies and through the relation of its judiciary to its legislative and executive powers. It is worth noting too that even in today's PRC, the status of the Confucianist sponsorship of a rhetoric of social harmony appears problematic—as dependent on political factors that may change at any moment. To illustrate, one might consider the recent career of "Confucius" in today's China.

THE UPS AND DOWNS OF AN OFFICIAL "CONFUCIUS"

During our stay in China in 2011, we encountered a bizarre story concerning the public presence of its greatest exemplar, Confucius himself. We had noted how, for half a decade or more, the Hu Jintao administration encouraged a return of Confucian influence. The phrase "social harmony" rose from rhetorical keyword to what seemed an almost coercive paradigm. Classic texts were reintroduced into schools; "Confucian" classrooms were set up within China (sometimes with teachers in traditional robes); while around the world hundreds of Confucius Institutes and spin-off Confucius Classrooms have been established in nearly a hundred countries.[35] At the same time, hundreds if not thousands of academic articles explored—and thereby justified the use of—the term as central to Chinese civilization. And even up to recently, political campaigns featuring slogans echoing new versions of Confucian thought continued to be generated.

Their climax was perhaps marked by a large bronze statue of the sage installed in January 2011 outside the north entrance to the newly refurbished National History Museum (at the northeast corner of Tiananmen Square). There are few more symbolically prestigious sites in all of China. But this statue, some twelve feet high, quickly drew criticisms, dominantly from two factions within leadership circles. The residual Maoists complained about rehabilitating a "feudal" mentality that had been thoroughly rejected during the early decades of the PRC. A rival group of modernizers complained that Kongzi stood, above all, for respecting tradition, whereas they see China's priorities as challenging anything that stands in the way of reforms and thus of ever greater prosperity. Then, in early 2011, after two months of ferment, the top leadership, deciding that discretion was the better part of valor, one night had the statue bundled up and taken away.[36] In time it was discovered inside the museum, where it can still be found today at the back of a discreet courtyard—out of sight, unless one knows where to look.

Today's message: the new top leadership of seven, that is, the Standing Committee of the Politburo, is less likely to pursue Confucian models of exhortation over its next phase of governing, although sporadic public tribute will be paid. Just as one can only speculate about the selection processes that operate behind closed doors, one can only guess what slogans will dominate in the new orientation.[37] Certainly Xi Jinping's catchphrase of the "China Dream" does not automatically invoke Confucian dictums. His visit in November 2013 to the Confucius Temple in Qufu, Shandong Province, has been heavily interpreted as a new gesture of approval, although it was only one among such visits to strategic interest groups.[38]

This short history demonstrates how social harmony, a millennial influence in the forming of a Chinese mentality, has in recent years acquired a new political

New positioning for Kongzi, a side courtyard at the National History Museum in Beijing. *Source:* John G. Blair.

dimension associated specifically with the presidency of Hu Jintao. Yet, no matter how its political emphasis evolves in the future, "social harmony" as a slogan will still remain a formative influence on people growing up in China. In the end, as fundamentally Confucian—and thus a basis for much traditional Chinese thinking—social harmony may be read as a rhetorical tool for containing threats to public order.[39] Whenever such positive motivators do not suffice, the carrot can readily be supplemented by the stick; both are necessary in limiting what is seen as perhaps the most powerful threat to Chinese life: the ever-present dangers of *luan* (乱) or chaos.

NOTES

1. *Zuo Commentary to the Spring and Autumn Annals (Zhao 20)*, "Introduction: The Chinese Lexicon," in *The Analects of Confucius: A Philosophical Translation*, trans. Roger T. Ames and Henry Rosemont Jr., 254–58 (New York: Ballantine, 1998), note 216.

2. Ames and Rosemont, "Introduction," 256.

3. One thinks of the work of environmentalists such as James Lovelock and Lynn Margulis, as in Lovelock's *Gaia: A New Look at Life on Earth* (Oxford: Oxford University Press, 1989). These ecologists turn for inspiration to an ancient metaphor: that of a mythical Greek goddess, Gaia, once seen as the presiding deity of all creation. The fact that they need to go so far back into Western civilization to find such a paradigm, however, might be taken as a sign of how archaic such cosmic concerns appear today to most Westerners.

4. Ames and Rosemont, *Analects*, 7.1, 111.

5. The story is retold in *CCCW*, 402.

6. As quoted in John Delury, "'Harmonious' in China," *Policy Review* (Hoover Institution) (April–May 2008): 42.

7. Delury, "'Harmonious' in China," 42.

8. In terms of gender, for instance, Ban Zhao, in her first-century CE *Lessons for Young Women*, made explicit the basic pattern: girl babies, in order to teach them humility, were to be placed below the bed and given potsherds to play with. *CCCW*, 143.

9. Ames and Rosemont, *Analects*, 12.11, 156.

10. William Shakespeare, *Troilus and Cressida*, act 1, scene 3, lines 538–77 (italics added).

11. One result was an institutionalized church, replacing the communitarian emphasis of early Christianity. As Rodney Stark suggests, institutionalization came with high costs as grassroots piety was swallowed up in jockeying for imperial preferment. *For the Glory of God: How Monotheism Led to Reformations, Science, Witch-Hunts and the End of Slavery* (Princeton, NJ: Princeton University Press, 2003), 33.

12. His rule also, of course, included a great deal of raw brutality, as in his castration of Sima Qian, one of the world's greatest historians in any tradition. *CCCW*, 409–11.

13. Thus distinguishing between the historical Kongzi and the fabricated Confucius continues to be useful, as explained in chapter 1, "Binding Families: *Xiào*," note 22.

14. Ames and Rosemont, *Analects*, 12.7, 154–55.

15. Franklin Delano Roosevelt's first inaugural address in 1932 articulated this memorable point. Fear is indeed a crucial opposite in this context, one we will examine in detail in chapter 9, "The Lurking Threat of Chaos: *Luàn*."

16. Lucian W. Pye, *Asian Power and Politics: The Cultural Dimensions of Authority* (Cambridge, MA: Belknap, 1985), 207.

17. *Analects*, 13.23. The translation is taken from Delury, "'Harmonious' in China," 42, as are the ensuing observations. Ames and Rosemont translate the opposition as between "harmony" and "sameness," 169. Citing this passage from the *Analects*, one Chinese colleague remarked, "The government is advocating not harmony but conformity."

18. *Analects*, 13.15. Translation is taken from Delury, "'Harmonious' in China," 42.

19. The contrast in thinking styles is dramatized graphically by Yang Liu in chapter 7, "Realizing a Way: *Dào*." John Delury writes a deliciously satirical account of Hu Jintao's logic-defying speech launching his new campaign for harmony (on which this analysis draws); but at the same time Delury shows no signs of appreciating the Chinese rhetorical situation that calls for blending together mention of *all* prestigious presences. In other words, Western "logic" has simply no place here. Delury, "'Harmonious' in China," 39.

20. The following passage is derived from Delury, "'Harmonious' in China," 36.

21. For a consummate analysis of how Chinese rhetoric works, see François Jullien, *Detour and Access: Strategies of Meaning in China and Greece*, trans. Sophie Hawkes (New York: Zone Books, 2000), especially his analysis of Party discourse following the death of Mao, 21–34.

22. Delury, "'Harmonious' in China," 38.

23. During the preparations in the months leading up to the Beijing Olympics, for instance, these professors were startled to find large percentages of their classes of graduate students in English disappearing because they were "volunteered" by their university for work in the national interest, hardly something one would encounter in a similar situation in the West.

24. See "Entering a Chinese World," our introduction to this book.

25. The detailed options are spelled out in "River Crab (Internet Slang)," *Wikipedia*, accessed November 24, 2012, http://en.wikipedia.org/.

26. Ai Weiwei is an extraordinary figure, surviving tenuously as an internationally celebrated artist-gadfly. His direct challenges to authority are recorded in the 2012 documentary film directed by Alison Klayman, *Never Sorry* (accessed March 13, 2013, http://aiweiweinev ersorry.com/). Viewing the film should be supplemented by his telephone interview published in the *New York Times* under the title "He May Have Nothing to Hide, but He's Always Under Watch," February 24, 2013. His core comment on the Powers That Be is as follows: "So the film becomes important, to reveal power. They are so powerful, but sometimes they are extremely fragile; they cannot really take any kind of resistant attitude or questioning."

27. In late 2014, the Powers That Be instituted new regulations designed to punish those who exploit publicly the punning so characteristic of Chinese as a language. This move suggests that paranoia may be rising, since such regulations are bound to fail, except as a potential tool for silencing selected individuals who might otherwise escape "rule by law." "China Media Watchdog Bans Wordplay Puns," *Guardian*, November 28, 2014, accessed December 8, 2014, http://www.theguardian.com/.

28. Max Fisher, "How China Stays Stable Despite 500 Protests Every Day," *Atlantic*, January 5, 2012. Even the official Chinese press quantifies such protests as rising sharply in recent years: Feng Shu gives the figure of 180,000 "mass incidents" for 2010, three times the number in 2003. Feng Shu, "A National Conundrum," *People's Daily Online* (English ed.), February 10, 2012, accessed July 8, 2012, http://en.people.cn/.

29. In fact, most protests involve appeals to central authority in hopes of outflanking local corruption, as in the case of Wukan village in Guangdong Province.

30. Later events confirm that there are no easy solutions to problems like these. See "Wukan Democracy Leaves Village Divided," *South China Morning Post*, February 15, 2013; and "Wukan Villagers Decry Vice-minister's Mixed Message on Free Polls," *South China Morning Post*, March 14, 2013.

31. See discussion of Liu Xiaobo in chapter 12, "Question Two: Human Rights?"

32. Such crimes, from 1979 to 1997, were called "crimes of counterrevolution." For a compact assessment of Chinese law codes since they were reinstituted in the late 1970s, see *CCCW*, 453–56.

33. Shigong Lu, *Studies on the Contemporary Chinese Party and Government Relations* [in Mandarin] (Shanghai: People's Press, 2001), 290, trans. Qin Chuan. *CCCW*, 449.

34. See Jean-Jacques Rousseau, *The Social Contract, or, Principles of Political Right*, trans. G. D. H. Cole (1762; London: J. M. Dent, 1955), accessed October 3, 2013, http://archive .org/; *CCCW*, 437–41.

35. The Ministry of Education (Han Ban) is reported to foresee sponsoring one thousand such institutes by the year 2020. Confucius Institute Headquarters (Hanban), accessed November 25, 2012, http://www.hanban.org/.

36. "Beijing Removes Controversial 'Confucius,'" *Irish Times*, April 22, 2011.

37. Xi Jinping, as an astute politician, used his early time in power to visit competing interest groups, reassuring each one of them understanding and support. Examples include the People's Liberation Army (PLA; expansive actions in the South and East China Seas), the Maoist faction (evoking Mao to revive old-style Party loyalty), and businessmen (rapid launch of duty-free zones). Given the anticorruption drive he has sponsored, support from such groups, including neo-Confucians, is indispensable.

38. "President Xi Jinping Works to Revive Confucianism in China," *Larouche PAC*, September 26, 2014, accessed October 14, 2014, http://larouchepac.com/.

39. A further possibility for this key concept is developed by Daniel A. Bell and Yingchuan Mo of Tsinghua University, who proposes an innovative "Harmony Index" as a superior approach to comparing nations and their relative ability to deliver satisfactory modes of living to their citizens. See their "Harmony in the World 2013: The Ideal and the Reality," accessed April 16, 2015, https://www.academia.edu/.

乱

Luàn

9

The Lurking Threat of Chaos

Luàn 乱

A Western professor visiting China for the first time decided to offer, in the next-to-last class for graduate students, airmail stamps that, over the course of a semester, had come off envelopes mailed from the United States, Switzerland, France, and a scattering of other Western countries. He guessed that a few, maybe three or four out of twenty-five, might have an interest in stamp collecting. Announcing at the end of class that these stamps would be left for those who might be interested on the table at the front, he stepped back. Then the room exploded. Normally well-behaved students converged madly on the table, vying to get their hands on some—any—stamps. Chaos reigned. Why?

Invisible to the Western teacher was the guanxi *value of these exotic stamps. Indeed only a handful of these students had any personal interest in the stamps themselves, but every single one of them knew someone in their* guanxi *network who would value them; the stamps were something they could offer in return for favors of one kind or another, past or future. The lesson: in a ruthlessly hierarchical society, whenever no one imposes a system of distribution, chaos will result.*[1]

Social harmony (*hexie*), as we have seen, describes the ideal order within the Chinese world. But it is an ideal reinforced by a powerful negativity—a deep-seated fear of chaos. China is not the only nation in the world to experience a deepening undercurrent of fear in recent years. But whereas others may identify that fear as a fear of "terrorism," in China the underlying threat is spoken of as *luan*.

Luan 乱, the word for *disorder*, originated, in iconographic terms, from a character showing two hands and silk thread hung on a stand. It used to mean *unraveling* before evolving to signify that idea of pervasive disorder known in the West as *chaos*.

While in the West *chaos* may carry strong metaphysical overtones—as in the lack of order said by both Hebrews and Greeks to have preceded creation—in China *luan* points to social disorder but with cosmic implications. The word itself evokes forces deeply threatening to family, clan, or to the nation as a whole. Given that everything changes and everything is connected, when *luan* strikes, all that has been accumulated can be lost in what may seem like no time at all. Even if one does not have much to lose, with *luan* even that little can be quickly swept away.

If chaos rules, Chinese thinking goes, everyone will lose. It seems wiser, therefore, except under exceptional circumstances, to avoid making waves. Thus the kind of dissent normal to Western society—along with its history of articulated protest and open debate—may be seen by many Chinese as courting *luan*. As a corollary, acknowledging the pervasive possibility of *luan* also discourages any easy belief in *progress* as anything more than temporary.

In its role in Chinese discourse, *luan* does not enjoy the same categorical status as *harmony*. Although clearly opposite to "harmony," *luan* operates as a kind of enabling concept—as the force that reinforces the necessity of firm social order. Paradoxically, therefore, recent Chinese history shows how just such a pervasive threat tends to encourage far-sighted planning. By means of their strong, centralized control, People's Republic of China (PRC) authorities have worked to create infrastructure such as highways, railroads, ports, and airports well in advance of actual demand. In many ways their record for such forward planning is superior to that of richer Western democracies. One way of understanding such planning might be as itself a way of keeping the threat of *luan* under control. After all, natural disasters (such as floods and earthquakes) will of themselves promote social disorder. Seen from this perspective, planning might be interpreted as a grand protective strategy against the higher forces that rule the world—just as the massive and still controversial Three Gorges Dam project was justified in part to control the frequent floods of the Yangtze River.

Yet in trying to evaluate the actions of China's leaders, an outsider with a Western background faces a quandary. On the one hand, to a Westerner it may seem that Chinese authorities sometimes react to apparently small-scale threats with almost paranoid intensity. On the other hand, such an observer might conclude that those in power are so well versed in their own culture that they believe they can remain on top only by suppressing immediately any and all signs of opposition, however small. As if to underline the point of such prompt action, an outsider would be startled to discover how easily chaos can, at any moment, disrupt the smooth surfaces of life in China (as in the classroom chaos, inadvertently triggered by the naive foreign teacher whose story opened this chapter).

INSPIRING FEAR

What does such a Westerner need to know that might explain such apparent overreactions on the part of Chinese authorities? First of all, those in power are fully aware that, in the words of one historian, "China has a history of bottom-up rebellion almost unrivalled anywhere else in the world."[2] Second, "China" consists of many Chinas, pulling in many directions at once and directed by officials who routinely "spin" or suppress information as to what is going on in their particular (frequently distant) locales. Finally, China itself is such a mass of inner tensions that holding it together is, as Stefan Halper observes,

> a far from happy union: keeping the conservative old guard in line with the younger, reform-minded entrepreneurs; laying claim to the mantle of a "harmonious society" while brutally suppressing ethnic groups in Tibet and Xinjiang or religious groups nationwide; keeping the military brass loyal to a government that affords them ever less emphasis in the national mythology; embracing information technology while maintaining information censorship; enforcing contract law and the legal framework for doing good business, while staving off calls for legal accountability; decentralizing Party control while clamping down on corruption; and, perhaps most of all, placating the 650 million rural Chinese, or the migrant urban underclass, many of whom have yet to see the rising quality of life they have helped to create for the new middle classes of the eastern seaboard and river cities.[3]

Given such a complex balancing act, how *do* the Chinese authorities hold it all together? Whenever pressures mount, they manage it by invoking the strongest motivator available to any government—fear. The ruling Party's greatest threat is *luan*: losing political and social control. Given the turbulent history of the last century, it is a fear shared by the vast majority of China's people. What they seek most of all is prosperity, which as they know from experience, requires stability. In order to ensure that stability, most are willing to cede to those in power the authority to control the political and social situation as best they can, and through the most effective strategies available.

"KILLING THE CHICKEN TO SCARE THE MONKEY"

The strategies employed may best be summarized in the well-worn Chinese proverb "killing the chicken to scare the monkey" (杀鸡儆猴). In other words, attacking a smaller target to frighten a larger one. Regulators commonly draw inspiration from this proverb in highly publicized prosecutions for local corruption—meant to send a message to others higher up to reform their ways. Even today the slightest critique of current policy in an Internet chat room or a quiet collective gesture of protest often leads to an immediate, and what often seems a hugely disproportionate, response. Similarly, any local demonstration calls forth prompt and heavy-handed policing. Sentences to hard labor camps are frequent.[4] Sentences for prominent dissidents— those who have caught the attention of the international media, for instance—are far longer, up to ten or even fourteen years in some cases. The harshness of the response is a good measure of just how threatening the authorities find these incidents.

If the prosecutions seem out of proportion with the crime, that is the intended effect. In China a "strike hard" policy may even be endorsed by a majority of the populace. "Strike hard" policy focuses on rounding up "criminals" or "terrorists" (that is, anyone deemed to be threatening State security)[5] often by the hundreds—and making them disappear—into jails or worse. The criminal justice system is so aligned with the political powers that usually the victims have little chance of appeal against the massive powers of State machinery.[6]

What is the thinking behind such a response? Clearly the authorities believe that threats, however small, must be quashed before the contagion can spread. The belief in contagion arises from a view of the world in which things are connected, connections not merely grounded in the virtual contagion of the mass media but also effected through a mindset oriented to a world that works by correlation and analogy. For instance, after the Nobel Peace Prize was awarded in 2010 to Liu Xiaobo, himself in prison for a long term, even a picture of a chair was deemed by the authorities to be inflammatory. As Liu's empty chair at the Nobel ceremony symbolized his absence, so *any* empty chair—within Chinese analogical thinking—could set off a chain of virtual critiques of the presiding State leaders. As a result, the censors at once blocked all empty-chair images from Internet sites where they were proliferating (including some empty beach chairs advertising a seaside resort). While empty chairs may seem insignificant to Western observers, they fail to understand how pervasively metaphorical resonances can permeate Chinese thinking.[7]

By taking such action to suppress not only well-publicized events but even incidents perceived as minor gestures of dissent, the Chinese authorities see themselves as checking incipient *luan*. While some living in China may see the reactions of the authorities as excessive, they understand the thinking behind it; for, in China, *luan* always lurks close to the surface.

How close to the surface chaos lurks, any visitor to China may testify. Because rules do not flow from general principles (as in "the rule of law"), they are regarded as mere regulations; and regulations are made to be circumvented if not actually bent or broken. Waiting in line—"queues," as the British call them—is a useful indicator of social discipline under the pressure of incipient *luan*. In China, standing in line is for Westerners. Faced with a line in China, people normally insinuate themselves somehow to the front—with different feints, such as pretending they have a query rather than a purchase—or by simply walking up to the counter to be served next. Hence a line in China is less a line than a scrum. One has to protect one's position robustly, always alert for tricksters: as in the way one Westernized Chinese artist compares the different approaches to waiting in line, West versus China (next page).

The reason this happens in China seems to be the following. In public lines, you normally would not know anyone. Without an established *guanxi*, there can be no hierarchy, thus the requirements of *xiao* (deference) are suspended. What follows is seen as a competition between equals—exactly the situation in which *luan* flourishes.

What follows from the implosion of such "line rules" follows also for other rules and regulations in China. The thinking seems to be that, if you can get around it, you should, either through connections (*guanxi*) or by stratagem (*celüe*). As one businessman said about deploying Western systems in his joint-venture company, any self-respecting Chinese employee will find loopholes in a new system within a

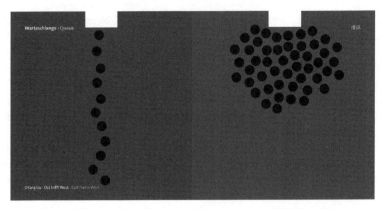

Yang Liu, "Waiting in Line." *Source:* Yang Liu, *Ost trifft West* [East meets West], 10th ed. (Mainz, Germany: Hermann Schmidt Verlag, 2014). Used by permission.

few weeks at most. This is considered not only smart but also admirable; it reflects "ability." According to one of our Chinese teaching colleagues, "When we all wait in line, or all listen to the boss quietly during a meeting, then it must be out of some unusual sense of occasion."

This lurking possibility of an outbreak of *luan* gives Chinese life its own distinctive energy. Often the chaos is sparked by natural disaster, aggravated by the huge numbers of people involved (as in the many floods and earthquakes that punctuate Chinese history). The annual migration home of millions of migrant workers for Spring Festival offers regular testimony to the potential of *luan*, as, for instance, in the winter of 2008 when heavy snowstorms disrupted transport and thousands were left camping in the open outside train stations. During the subsequent earthquake in Sichuan the following May, most Chinese people proved very resilient, if not inventive, in dealing with the subsequent mayhem. But always present is the possibility that such chaos has the capacity to disable society completely—as in, for example, the ten-day traffic jam on a major highway coming into Beijing in the summer of 2010. It is such scenarios, played out on a large public/political front, that terrify the central authorities, insofar as it puts in jeopardy their mandate to maintain control— as legitimized by *social harmony.*

In fact, the official fear of *luan* probably represents a convergence of different fears. The first would be that the Party would not seem to be fulfilling its self-appointed role, which is to maintain social order at whatever cost. For the Chinese people, the trade-off for having an authoritarian government is that social harmony that, in turn, ensures prosperity. Second, if dissent occurs, however minor, it threatens the Party with loss of face (*mianzi*). They are seen to have lost face by losing control. Thus *control* becomes a paramount virtue that must be displayed under all circumstances. Even the ancient emperors tried to demonstrate their powers of control by employing astronomers to predict such events as eclipses. If an emperor were caught unawares by an eclipse, so the thinking went, it was taken as a sure sign that he had lost the "mandate of *tian*" ("heaven"), that is, his privileged communication with higher powers. With a minimum of encouragement, chaos might easily follow.

Hence episodes that the State leaders most fear are those that are not anticipated. When something unexpected comes up, a full-scale *luan* anxiety seems to take over. The two most traumatic events of recent decades were unforeseen: *liusi* 六四 ("six four"), that is, the events leading up to June 4, 1989, on Tiananmen Square; and the 1999 Falungong demonstration outside the leadership residence compound at Zhongnanhai. The first did not evolve as predicted; the second caught the authorities by surprise. Today, although the internal surveillance and spying system ensures that such events are rare, when they do occur, they are quickly treated as catastrophic. If from a Western perspective treating them as such may be seen as a sign of weakness, to the Chinese authorities the reaction is in proportion to the threat they represent. For, in their minds, they are responding not to the actual events in themselves but to their potential for creating *luan*. What Westerners should not forget is that behind reactions to all other events of recent decades is the nightmare memory of the so-called Cultural Revolution: living proof to current State leaders of what chaos can mean for China.

CHAOS IN LIVING MEMORY:
THE CULTURAL REVOLUTION (1966–1976)

Most of China's current leaders came of age during the most traumatic experience of *luan* in living memory: the Great Cultural Revolution. Initiated by Mao Zedong in 1966, its direct effects finally ended only with his death in 1976. During this time, the young Red Guards, with initial encouragement from Mao himself, turned the Chinese world literally upside down. Students invaded university offices trying to steal the seals (or "chops") that allowed documents to be officialized, thus effectively taking over control. Anyone in authority in any of China's multiple hierarchies was open to "struggle sessions" that sought to challenge, question, humiliate, and, in extreme cases, maim and kill teachers, administrators, Party officials, or anyone accused of "rightist" or "bourgeois" views. The most common complaint was that those in authority lacked revolutionary fervor and dedication in the proper Maoist spirit.

This "revolution within the Revolution" claimed to reignite the original spark of fervor that would build another and still better New China. What actually occurred was mayhem, compounded by a significant number of deaths, many of them suicides. The lives of others were ruined by long detentions, torture, and public humiliation (particularly devastating in a world in which one's face is one's life). As most universities and many lower schools did not function for nearly a decade, education and training for a whole generation was put on hold. Instead, young people were simply let loose on the streets or ran amok under the aegis of the Red Guards.[8]

This image is part of a rare collection of photos of the Cultural Revolution taken by Li Zhensheng in Heilongjiang Province. In this image students from the University of Industry are attacking Wang Liyun, the provincial party secretary. The placard around his neck gives his name and labels him "counterrevolutionary revisionist element." *Source:* © Li Zhensheng/Contact Press Images. Used by permission.

Meanwhile, teachers and other professionals were sent off to the countryside to work beside the peasants in the name of revolutionary solidarity. It is questionable whether agricultural production actually rose as a result. The goal was in any case quite different: to purge the remnants of hierarchical loyalties of the old "feudal" China. In fact, the hierarchies *were* overturned, but overturning them did not mean eliminating them in the name of some imported idea of "equality." Once the Cultural Revolution receded, hierarchies simply turned themselves upright once again—and remain very much in evidence today within China's newly stratified class system, now including a significant and growing middle class based on new money.

It is hard in China today to find anyone who looks back on the Cultural Revolution with nostalgia. Exceptionally, one businessman praised it for showing the Chinese people the folly of adhering to political ideology rather than traditional Chinese values. He had survived by joining the only functioning social organization during that time: the People's Liberation Army—not as a fighter but as a musician in the army band. Others, less resourceful or lucky, saw that a whole generation lost out on their chance for education, limiting their options for the rest of their lives.

Looking back on that era, one woman describes her generation as having got on the "wrong bus":

> We were born during the Great Leap Forward, 1958–1962, the years of natural disasters and there was nothing to eat. When we went to school, it was the "Cultural Revolution" and education stopped. We had to work and we were sent off to the countryside. When we married and had children, they came up with the "single child" policy. My child had just started school and we lost our jobs, across the board, everyone without a diploma or qualifications was laid off. Now we're old, and there's been a reform of pensions and medical insurance, and we don't qualify. It seems as if the whole of government policy is against our generation.[9]

The children born to the present generation have gotten the message. Rather than endure another experience of *luan* in which everyone suffers loss, they prefer to work within the complex competitive hierarchies that fill Chinese life today. Most individuals can only hope to work their way up these hierarchies slowly, but at least the Party offers a clear authority. Under this system, those who play by the Party's rules have a reasonable chance to prosper. For the ambitious there are always moments when one can take an exceptional risk in hopes of becoming rich; but flip-flops in Party policies can sometimes blindside the enterprising. Thus most people respond by becoming cautious, assenting to the system in place by not sticking their necks out. That way everything works more smoothly: *social harmony* as reinforced by the lurking threat of *luan*.

One friend, born in Manchuria in the 1920s, confided his formula for surviving all the ups and downs of the twentieth century that for him started with the Japanese invasion there in 1932. His secret: he never joined anything. A gnarled old tree, he lived well into his eighties.[10]

KEEPING THE LID ON: CENSORSHIP

Dramatic confrontations on a national scale occur only intermittently. Their threat of *luan* is preempted long term by the ever-vigilant censorship of all public media in China. Most people in the West know something about the Great Firewall of China, a vast official bureaucracy dedicated to policing the Internet. Systematic blocking of sites, monitoring of e-mail, and now a move to register all bloggers under their actual names are some of the controls put in place in the name of heading off *luan*. While sophisticated users of the Internet are usually able to bypass these blockades, most netizens are constrained by them. Similar constraints apply on a larger scale to all media, radio, television, and the press. Foreign journalists must have their licenses renewed every year; all their formal press releases are subject to scrutiny.

How then does one learn what is going on? In the words of one BBC producer who managed to cover the events of Tiananmen Square, "Forget the papers, forget the media; the only reliable source was rumor." If you really want to know what is going on, learn the language or establish a relationship of trust with someone who knows good English. Then arrange to meet for a walk outdoors or stop in for a meal, unannounced, to a restaurant that can supply a private room. Only then may you both feel free to talk.

However, in China, one must always be conscious that to say what is on one's mind in public is a risky business at any and all times. While Chinese people may feel free to air their views to those they trust, for the more thoughtful the omnipresent filtering systems chafe. "You have always to be alert as to what to say or not to say," one of our university colleagues complained. "You are disabled—it's like the loss of a bodily function—you never know how to express yourself, because you are never required to express yourself. You are taught from the beginning the 'right answer': not trained to think, but to memorize." The same frustration was voiced by a student emerging from a graduate course in (of all things) "Critical Thinking." For, while even an elite university may be invested in fostering "social harmony," it also felt it had to make a gesture toward more international academic values. Hence a course was approved that contained such classic Western texts as *How to Lie with Statistics*.[11] After frog-marching the students through discourse as well as statistical analysis, the teacher introduced them to Western-style debate. This they resisted robustly, as formally contradicting the opinions of a classmate in public space would offend all the protocols directed at supporting *mianzi*. The result? Under pressure to conform to course requirements, the students fulfilled the debating requirement by rigging the whole interchange behind the professor's back. And as for the outcome of the course? As the brightest student wrote the professor months later, "You taught us how to think critically. You said that, as intelligent people, we had to apply our intelligence everywhere and to everything. But I am finding I cannot keep it up. It is simply too exhausting. The whole weight of my culture is against me."

From another world subject to *luan*, Nobel Prize–winning poet Seamus Heaney put it even more eloquently: "Whatever you say, say nothing."[12] As this student was beginning to learn, in China, saying nothing is the safest course. But if you must speak, saying anything controversial is obviously less dangerous than writing it out; and speaking in English is usually less dangerous than speaking in Mandarin, with obviously a much wider public audience. Also, the degree of risk goes up and down in China in response to the extent those in power feel threatened. The more anxious these become, the more rigid and invasive the censorship.

That said, it is important to acknowledge that the Powers That Be no longer try seriously to control what people think. If one can see through the pervasive propaganda, one can think outside the box. Among thoughtful Chinese, one can hear many of the same critiques of the system that Westerners might level at China. But formulating these critiques involves real intellectual effort—and access to a proxy Internet server. They speak discreetly and in private; their opinions do not seem to be greeted by instant threat or suppression. It should also be noted that individuals may also escape censorship to the extent that they rise within the governing hierarchies—if only because they are then presumed to have a personal stake in the system. Consequently, often those who seem to speak most freely are those in positions of power. They do so diplomatically, knowing that the few who openly criticize the system can be silenced by joblessness, imprisonment, or exile. Like most Chinese, they are aware of the vast and ongoing efforts devoted to maintaining the appearance of *social harmony* in the name of preempting the disastrous effects of *luan*.

HOW THE WEST SEEKS TO CONTROL CHAOS

In the West, as in all organized societies, chaos is also perceived as a threat. But as it is conceived so differently, strategies to neutralize it also differ greatly. Whereas in China the threat of *luan* encourages obedience to an established central authority, in the West—as vividly illustrated by the ongoing financial crisis that erupted in 2008—the threat of chaos leads to stubborn conflicts between the backers of alternative countermeasures.

These conflicts arise because politically the West tends to disperse central power among competing factions. In governmental terms, these are constituted according to a principle of the balance of powers: among executive, judicial, and legislative branches of government. Such a balancing act implicitly invokes the Western principle of *agon*: an equilibrium reached by one power contesting the legitimacy or influence of the other. Although it is slow—and messy—such operating methods do incorporate the principle of dissent itself within a system, thus allowing it to be acknowledged and eventually absorbed. But as this principle of governance is invisible to most Asian, and certainly to Chinese, people, when it does become visible, as in the video of a House of Commons debate shown to Chinese graduate students, it causes consternation. Their response ("This is no way to govern a country!") vividly illustrates the perceived dangers of any sort of public confrontation.

Used to a society in which vast efforts are deployed—on both personal and social as well as political levels—to keep appearances "smooth" and therefore "harmonious," such overt confrontation in public space seems not only dangerous but also inconceivable. For, if words can be contagious (as in Ai Weiwei's satiric puns on "river crabs"), what mayhem might be instigated by direct confrontation with equal or greater authority? Thus, when the members of the Standing Committee of the Politburo, the highest political authority of the Chinese Communist Party (CCP), disagree, they invariably do so in private. Only in retrospect, by means of adept readings of different "scripts," or by such events as the removal of the Confucius statue from its original designated position, do such disagreements become public.[13]

And, indeed, the concerned students had a point. How can a country governed by a principle of conflicting powers actually do its work? As modern democracies both in the European Union (EU) and the United States have demonstrated, the Western system of balanced conflict can of itself induce political stagnation if not actual chaos. By allowing slender majorities or even minorities to block approval of any constructive responses, this kind of system can potentially (and sometimes actually does) bring a whole country grinding to a halt. Yet the chaotic state of the United States and the EU today, where financial or ideological disagreements take a different but no less disruptive form, cannot be analyzed simply in political or economic terms. Present chaos has come about through a failure of basic conceptual tools, developed in the capitalist West since the eighteenth century.

These are the tools devised to "manage" *risk*. *Risk* may be taken as the key word for the threat that even carefully laid plans may be thwarted.[14] To "manage risk" in modern Western parlance means to attempt to assert control over what may be, in the end, uncontrollable—including events such as accidents, natural disasters, illness, and death. We think of that kind of "risk" as controllable because we in the West believe in something called *probability*. That is the word for the mathematical calculations of what are seen as predictable outcomes. In Western thinking, it is assumed such calculations can be made, because the expectation is that the future will follow the *same* patterns as the past, except—well—sometimes. So one needs a word for those exceptions. But here note a crucial contrast with habitual Chinese thinking. As the Chinese expect change and connectedness, they do not natively think in terms of *probabilities*. Instead, in a world ruled by *yi* or "endless change," they prepare themselves for adapting to whatever comes up. Thus Chinese people expect to have a plan B, in case plan A turns out to be unworkable. But regardless of plan B, in the end, the best protection against the vagaries of fortune is one's *guanxi* connections—in China, your wisest insurance investment.

Compare how the Western tradition, built on the expectation of a stable underlying *reality*, sees *change* as relatively superficial, with continuity as the default case. The resulting confidence in *probabilities* is all the more reassuring because it is commonly expressed in those quantitative terms dear to the modern West. As a forecast of failed continuity, *risk* defines the degree to which one's plans are likely to be defeated. While entrepreneurs may seek out risk, most ordinary people seek to avoid it, or at least to minimize the potential losses. For these reasons, as a means of protecting against, or at least minimizing, loss, insurance has become a major industry in the West.

But confidence based on insuring against risk can have devastating consequences, as seen in the present ongoing financial crisis within the Western world. Here is how it has, so far, failed to work. At the core of the 2008 crisis were "credit default swaps": in effect, insurance policies that purported to cover the risks for institutions to issue chancy loans, mostly mortgages of various kinds and qualities. Each major player calculated that its risks were covered by such arrangements, so loans could be pyramided "without risk." But no one was looking at the system as a whole, observing that the sum total of interlocking insurance promises was extremely fragile, thereby introducing a high risk of chaos for all players. Of course, there were other factors at work as well, such as human greed. But what matters most in the present context are the Western presumptions: that, since *reality* is essentially stable, *probability* calculations may be taken as credible. Could the ensuing disasters have been avoided if those in the West had taken a more holistic view of the economic world, as one in which everything is connected and everything changes? Could they now lead to an acknowledgment that change itself cannot always be managed by calculating what are, after all, contingent variables?

But even before the present economic/political crises in the West, the task of managing a Western life has become subject to exponentially increasing anxiety. In *American Fear*,[15] Peter Stearns sets out clearly the indices of rising angst in all aspects of life there. Citing one telling sociological survey, he notes that the public's reaction to the bombing in 1941 of Pearl Harbor was, at the time, greeted with far less anxiety than the hysteria following the 9/11 attacks in New York City. After examining classic American phobias—from the contagion of germs to that of Communism—Stearns caps his analysis with a look at today's generation of "helicopter parents," monitoring every aspect of their child's development. He concludes that the G. W. Bush "War on Terrorism" became a kind of terrorism itself, insofar as it used exaggerated fears to manipulate public opinion in regard to both foreign and domestic policies. China has learned from this example. Certainly the use of the mantra of "terrorism," for instance, to suppress public protests in the (culturally Muslim) northwestern Xinjiang Province is one example of how such rhetoric can be put to work across international domains.

Worldwide, such increased anxiety has everywhere resulted in what we all acknowledge as some of the major nuisances of everyday life: from the institution of increasingly elaborate airport security measures to the escalation of bureaucratic control over every aspect of perceived risk; from insurance policies to public health and safety schemes. Is it perhaps growing public anxiety that has led to such a muted reaction to the disclosures of June 2013 that revealed operational details of the U.S. National Security Agency (NSA) and its international partners' mass surveillance of foreign nationals and U.S. citizens, in not only America but also other prominent nations of the "free world" (such as Australia, Canada, New Zealand, the United Kingdom, and Germany). How many in the West who routinely criticize the surveillance methods of Chinese governance have protested such measures at home? How many suspect that the use of *luan* as a way of manipulating public opinion may now be identified as a new commonality between China and the West?

It is a sign of the times that currently in China the Powers That Be have more or less abandoned the rhetoric of "harmony," and along with it most of the Confucianist rhetoric, which has been sent backstage along with the statue of Kongzi. The new mantra comes, significantly, not from the top but from the bottom up, and it is not one of ancient origin but a practical contemporary slogan of "maintaining stability." Traditionally, talk about one arises inevitably and seamlessly from the thought of the other. What it signals is probably an acute consciousness of the present fragile state of affairs in the PRC. In late 2012, the "smooth" transition of power from one supreme elite to another was threatened by the exposure of Bo Xilai and his family. That an official so highly placed (having been widely considered to be a likely candidate for promotion to the elite Politburo Standing Committee in the Chinese Communist

Party's [CCP] eighteenth National Congress in 2012) could, within days, disappear into official police custody, was greeted with widespread and general alarm.[16] At the same time, the Western economic crisis has impacted on China, deflating its usual extraordinary growth figures. Worse still have been the incredible smogs that engulfed China's cities during the winters of 2012–2014, with air quality going off the official measuring scales in a scenario described simply as "crazy bad." Finally, a plethora of food scandals has damaged trust in the ability of the government to manage widespread corruption in the food processing industry—hitting the Chinese where it matters most—in the stomach. Such issues have led to grave anxieties about keeping the lid on: protests in China are continuing to increase in both number and visibility. And now, with the growth of the Internet and its social possibilities, it is becoming increasingly difficult to enforce censorship at its former level.

In any case, the anxieties in both worlds are not misplaced. In both China and the West, the old certainties are perceived to be collapsing and, along with them, the trust in orderly futures. It is therefore predictable that the public, both in China and the West, has now become almost abnormally alert to what it perceives as an increasingly dangerous—that is, "chaotic"—world.

NOTES

1. There is more to this lesson. At the final class, the visiting professor proposed a trade: a pile of stamps for each of the final exam papers written in class. Order was fully restored, because the reigning authority had decreed a clear, if hierarchical, distribution system at the moment of introducing an asset. If that system privileged some students over others, few if any would have objected. Rather than complaining, those near the bottom would have tried to figure out how they could make out better next time. Chinese people are well accustomed to being treated hierarchically, understanding it as a key to keeping order within society.

2. Will Hutton, *The Writing on the Wall: China and the West in the 21st Century* (Boston: Little, Brown, 2007), 44–45.

3. Stefan Halper, "Conclusion: China's Fear of Chaos," in *The Beijing Consensus: How China's Authoritarian Model Will Dominate the Twenty-First Century* (New York: Basic, 2010), 206.

4. These may be imposed for up to four years without trial, though there have been some recent hints that this system, which gives great leverage to local authorities, will be reformed or abolished. "*Laojiao* System to Be Phased Out," *China Daily*, January 21, 2013, accessed March 15, 2013, http://www.chinadaily.com.cn/.

5. Definitions of "criminal" or "terrorist" behavior remain vague; for instance, Liu Xiaobo, guilty of no known violent acts, was branded a criminal. See discussion in chapter 12, "Question Two: Human Rights?" For the rules governing threats to State security, see *CCCW*, 426, 428.

6. For a more detailed description of how the judicial system is tied in to the governing apparatus, see *CCCW*, 449.

7. See "The Resonances of *River Crabs*: *Héxiè* (河蟹)," in chapter 8, "Thinking in Harmony: *Hé*."

8. For a selection of these photos, tracing the Cultural Revolution in five stages, see Li Zhenshen, "Red-Color News Soldier," accessed October 14, 2014, http://www.contactpress images.com/. A fuller archive has been published as Li Zhenshen, *Red-Color News Soldier: A Chinese Photographer's Odyssey through the Cultural Revolution* (New York: Phaidon, 2003).

9. Xinran, *Witness: Voices from a Silent Generation* (London: Chatto and Windus, 2008), 365. *CCCW*, 246–47.

10. Echoing Wang Rongpei, trans., *Zhuangzi*, 2 vols., Library of Chinese Classics (Chang-sha, China: Hunan People's Publishing House, 1999), 1:2, 13.

11. Darrell Huff, *How to Lie with Statistics* (New York: Norton, 1954).

12. Seamus Heaney, "Whatever You Say Say Nothing," a poem concerning "the Troubles" in Northern Ireland, from Heaney's *North* (London: Faber and Faber, 1975), 57.

13. For the story of the "Kongzi" statue, see the section titled "The Ups and Downs of an Official 'Confucius'" in chapter 8, "Thinking in Harmony: *Hé*."

14. The major steps by which *risk* comes into prominence over recent centuries are well traced in Peter L. Bernstein's *Against the Gods: The Remarkable Story of Risk* (New York: Wiley, 1996).

15. Peter Stearns, *American Fear: The Causes and Consequences of High Anxiety* (New York: Routledge, 2006).

16. Dismantling Bo Xilai's complex *guanxi* network will no doubt take time. It was headed, significantly, by Zhou Yongkang, then a member of the Standing Committee of the Politburo. Bo Xilai, during his last days before being arrested, tried to implicate this powerful figure as having approved of all his actions. Zhou Yongkang has since become the first topmost-level politician to be officially investigated since the end of the Cultural Revolution in 1976.

策略

Cèlüè

10

Strategizing Life

Cèlüè 策略

THE AMBUSH AT MALING, 342 BCE

When the state of Wei attacked the Han state, its ruler, Zhao, called on the state of Qi for help. The two commanders of the Qi army, Sun Bin and Tian Ji, immediately led it in an attack against the Wei capital. As soon as he heard about this, the commander of the Wei troops, Pang Juan, pulled them back out of Han territory to confront the Qi army.

Sun Bin knew of General Pang Juan's arrogance and his low opinion of the Qi troops. Faced with an advancing Wei army, Sun Bin began an apparent retreat. On the first day, his troops left behind traces of one hundred thousand campfires; on the second day, fifty thousand; and on the third day, only thirty thousand. Pang Juan, eager for victory, concluded that the Qi army had been seriously weakened by mass desertions. So he left the bulk of his infantry behind and set out in pursuit with some lightly equipped troops. He covered two days' worth of ground in a single day's march. Sun Bin had calculated that Pang Juan would reach Maling at dusk.

He set an ambush there and waited. As planned, the Wei troops arrived exhausted from their forced march, and Sun Bin's army demolished them. General Pang Juan committed suicide on the battlefield.

—The Book of Stratagems[1]

Certainly this consummately strategic victory must have given Sun Bin particular satisfaction as, some years earlier, General Pang Juan, having trapped him, had his legs broken, thus reducing an honored rival to the demeaning status of a cripple.[2]

For the Chinese, Sun Bin and his ancestor Sunzi (Sun Tzu in Wade-Giles romanization) are perhaps the greatest exemplars of the military applications of strategical thinking. Sunzi probably flourished in the fourth century BCE, Sun Bin somewhat later. It is no accident that their works arose from the Warring States Period in Chinese history (fifth to third centuries BCE), during which incessant warfare reduced twenty-one Chinese statelets to one.[3] During this period, armies grew in size, finally into the hundreds of thousands. Generalship became a fine art; but Sunzi, as the most venerable of all, famously sought to win wars without having to fight battles at all. In contrast with Western traditions, he found nothing "unmanly" about relying on subterfuge.

According to Sunzi and Sun Bin, the Chinese way of war would involve direct confrontation only if it could not otherwise be avoided. Head-on battles are deemed wasteful even if won. Killing enemy soldiers deprives the winner of manpower for future projects. Spies, false informants, and subterfuges are preferable if they disguise one's own intentions while destabilizing the opponent's efforts. A few excerpts from Sunzi demonstrate this way of thinking:

> III.2 To capture the enemy's army is better than to destroy it; to take intact a battalion, a company or a five-man squad is better than to destroy them.
>
> III.3 For to win one hundred victories in one hundred battles is not the acme of skill. To subdue the enemy without fighting is the acme of skill.
>
> VI.24 The ultimate in disposing one's troops is to be without ascertainable shape. Then the most penetrating spies cannot pry in nor can the wise lay plans against you.
>
> VI.27 Now an army may be likened to water, for just as flowing water avoids the heights and hastens to the lowlands, so an army avoids strength and strikes weakness.
>
> VI.28 And as water has no constant form, there are in war no constant conditions.[4]

The underlying Chinese realities here are already familiar: as nothing is constant for long, rapid and alert adaptation is called for at every moment. Armies should move like water. Even if two armies are of equal size, their distribution will make a crucial difference. The general is a strategist, not a warrior. His job is to be ready to capitalize on the potential of every situation, without preconceptions, principles, or rules of engagement. So much for the modern Western ideal of a "fair fight"!

How do modern Western theorists of warfare compare? Despite some superficial similarities with the Chinese strategists, theorists such as Machiavelli or Clausewitz are bound as Westerners into Western ways of thinking. That is, they begin by presuming an ideal, which actualized into a plan, becomes the stated goal or rationale for action. Finally, leaders then acknowledge that the ideal will need to be modified, whether by deliberate hypocrisies or by practical realities. Thus their Western vision is dual, based on distinguishing theory from practice.

These strategies included the kind of wars inherent in Western politics. Niccolò Machiavelli (1469–1527), for example, became notorious in recommending that princes should simulate virtue instead of feeling obligated to practice it, concluding that "it is unnecessary for a prince to have all the good qualities I have enumerated, but it is very necessary to appear to have them . . . to appear merciful, faithful, humane, religious, upright, and to be so, but with a mind so framed that should you require not to be so, you may be able and know how to change to the opposite."[5] This candid advice explains why, in Shakespeare's England—more invested in affirming the virtues of honesty—a "machiavel" became simply another name for a villain. While Machiavelli did not necessarily transform the way princes behaved, he had a major impact on the discourse about how to govern. By pleading the utility of premeditated immorality, he tapped into a long-standing Western discourse of ideals versus actual practice, a duality that may be traced at least as far back as Plato. The Chinese strategists, by comparison, were *a*moralists. Western dualities had no claim on their attention, because the Chinese see the world as all of a piece, all on one this-worldly level of concern.

Some centuries after Machiavelli, Carl von Clausewitz's *On War* (1832) produced the modern classic on warfare as politics by another name. While emphasizing how changing contingencies require constant adjusting of war plans, he, like Machiavelli, begins by exhorting the general to invent an ideal procedure, which the commander must then be alert to modify in response to events. The great Chinese strategists felt no need for such a plan—because they were instantly responding to changing conditions as they evolved. They understood, as Western theorists did not, that if one works with changing conditions, every moment offers fresh perceptions of what can be done. In the Western way of war, such conditions take second place, as primary agency is invested in the ability to command. As in the muscular image of the human body publicized by Vesalius, the Western way of war emphasizes above all the exertion of force, and force, in particular, as directed to a certain already defined—and stable—goal.

THE WESTERN WAY OF WAR

The origins of the Western way of war, as vividly described by Victor Davis Hanson's book of that title, go back as far as the hoplite phalanx, the mainstay of the Greek city-states starting from the fifth century BCE.[6] The goal of phalanx warfare was direct and decisive confrontation between massed squares of men. The phalanx marched or ran as a unit, ten men or more on a side, armored as heavily as they could manage. Their success depended on unwavering courage and coordination in the face of shock attacks. Engagements were short and sharp, for the aim of Athenian and other democracies was to end hostilities quickly so that its citizen-soldiers could get back to productive (i.e., agricultural) work as soon as possible.[7]

There was no subtlety in this approach; it was brutal head-on combat. As a way of war, it still persists, as for instance, in American attempts to deploy massive firepower against guerrilla groups in Vietnam and Afghanistan. And the Western way is considered "manly." It works best against opponents who play by the same (unwritten) rules. Even then, such direct confrontation no longer guarantees that Western wars would end quickly (consider, for instance, the Thirty Years' War). Nor does it work well when taking on insurgents who do not care about the rules of a "fair fight" or prescribed modes of warfare—including the "embattled farmers" at the bridge in Concord who took on the British army in April 1775.

The fact that, despite its failure over many years, the West still favors this mode of warfare shows how deeply ingrained is the thinking along the lines of *set goal, make plan, implement in the most direct and confrontational mode possible.* The Chinese strategy (equally persistent but arguably more effective) takes water as its model. Just as water moves in conformity to the terrain without ever trying to go uphill, so, the Chinese reason, armies should move with the situation, seeking to engage with the enemy at its weakest, not its strongest point. Chinese wisdom always favors deflection over confrontation, pragmatic and flexible strategies over abstract (and therefore often inflexible) plans or goals.

FROM WAR STRATEGIES TO LIFE STRATEGIES

Sun Bin, Sunzi's descendant in the fourth century BCE, extended such strategical thinking beyond mere military settings. Famously he advised his friend, General Tian Ji of the state of Qi, on how to win a horse race against the best opposition money could buy. To avoid incidental factors deciding the contest, he advised there to be three horse races, each one on one. Sun Bin then counseled that Tian's third best horse be pitted against the king's best, expecting it to lose; then to set Tian's best horse against the king's second best; and, finally, Tian's second best horse against the king's third best. In this way Tian won two out of three races—and hence the contest overall. After this episode, the king immediately appointed Sun Bin as chief strategist for the state of Qi, which he ably defended for many years.

As evidenced by this story, Sunzi, Sun Bin, and their fellow strategists did not create merely a specialist's manual for training military personnel. Their kind of thinking permeates all of Chinese culture. Etymology gives some insight into the Chinese word *celüe* 策略. The character *ce* 策 incorporates on top the sign for "bamboo," as in the strips originally used for writing in China before it invented paper two thousand years ago. The lower component supplies only a phonetic element. The second character *lüe* 略 contains the sign for "field" at the left, originally implying marking boundaries, hence suggesting an outline or plan. In everyday life, this expression for strategizing has many applications—as in sales strategy, teaching strategy, and marriage strategy—hence, in general, tactically alert approaches to any and all situations.

In China the concept was widely disseminated through a fourteenth-century fiction by Luo Guanzhong titled *The Romance of the Three Kingdoms* (三国演义). This enduring classic tells the tale of the ups and downs of powerful generals during the breakup of the Han dynasty and the subsequent division of China into three competing kingdoms (169–284 CE). As its hero, Zhuge Liang, strives to outwit the powerful and unscrupulous Cao Cao, their strategical maneuverings move back and forth across a broad landscape. Even today, most Chinese readers know this text as one of the four masterpieces of Chinese writing. It is seen as offering models for emulation in everyday life, seconded only by a collection of historical instances, *The 36 Stratagems*.[8] All these texts recommend strategizing one's life as crucial to success, regardless of one's situation.

Classical texts such as these often tell stories. Indeed, Chinese stories such as those of Sun Bin or "Old Saiweng Lost His Horse" (*sai weng shi ma* 塞翁失马)[9] are today as familiar to Chinese schoolchildren as the biblical stories of Adam and Eve or David and Goliath are to American youngsters. As one scholar from China remarked, the story is "in our bones."[10] Yet, despite their far-reaching impact throughout the Chinese world, these remain largely unknown among Westerners, who are often mystified as to why their questions about China are often answered with an anecdote rather than a piece of analytic reasoning. Only cultural insiders can understand how, in China, stories from even the distant past can speak in meaningful ways to what is going on in the present, even though this is something that has been inculcated in Chinese people from all sectors of the population since childhood. They pay attention to such stories largely for the guidance or inspiration they may offer in the present. In retelling these, there is no sense of a conflict between story and history because "history," for most Chinese, *is* the story that they are told and that they tell themselves. Much like the parables told by Jesus of Nazareth, these traditional stories never go out of date. Becoming Chinese means ingesting a panoply of these fables along with a readiness to identify which ones apply most helpfully to whatever life circumstances emerge. They constitute, in many ways, the great reservoir of Chinese wisdom and, as such, will be offered whenever the occasion seems to call for strategical judgment.

MAKING CHOICES: PRESUMING *DAO*

But regardless of its meaning, in the end strategy has to do with choice as to how one reaches certain ends. "Choice" is a word unusually privileged in the West. Yet the logic of Chinese history, coupled with its underlying presumptions of *change* and *connectedness*, means that every Chinese person faces a plethora of strategic choices all the time. Moreover, the higher one's position in the hierarchy, the more is at stake in selecting effective tactics. In this kind of situation, choice appears less as a value than as an obligation—whereas in the modern West, choice is normally seen as a good thing, an opportunity, and even a right.

In U.S. debates about abortion, "pro-choice" ultimately won out over "pro-life," partly because fewer people wanted to identify themselves as "against" choice. "Choice" here has become a kind of touchstone for the quality of life. In the West a much-vaunted feature of democratic politics is a choice of candidates at election time. And here life is supposedly enhanced by a greater and greater "choice" of breakfast cereals on supermarket shelves (though surely a law of diminishing returns must have set in some time ago). In short, for many Westerners, "choice" is seen as an exercise of individual freedom. In talking with even thoughtful people, it is hard to convince them that meaningful "choice" occurs only at certain life moments and within certain conditions, because Westerners are tempted to think of significant choice as freely available at any time and under any existing conditions.

In China choice arises differently and under different presumptions. One reason the word *celüe* has been selected as the final concept for this book is that it involves every other value-concept so far discussed. In making any decision, a Chinese person must first consider its consequences for *xiao* (family, job, and community relations). Then people must consider *mianzi*—its impact on their immediate families—and *guanxi*, as their estimate of it will reflect on themselves, as either giving or losing face. Indeed, the sense of one's self is so implicated that most significant life decisions are taken in consultation with intimate others (in order to ensure group *he* harmony). And in the Chinese world, this is a never-ending process. As *Dao* generates ever-changing circumstances and as conditions change (*yi*), so one must choose again and again. In other words, within the Chinese world one is *always* placed in a strategical situation.

Indeed, such constant pressure to choose may seem more a burden than a privilege, if only because circumstances always seem stronger than the human ability to cope with them. As the world of *yi* or change is inherently threatened by the forces of *luan*, one must be cautious. Whatever has been accumulated can quickly be swept away. But by the same token, change is constantly opening up fresh possibilities. So, if one is alert, one may move rapidly to take advantage—before circumstances change yet again. But because one is never quite sure where things are going next, one must always be ready to work around the Powers That Be, whether political, social, or natural. All the ten thousand things of *Dao* have their own "propensity," to use once again that apt expression of François Jullien, thus every aspect asks to be read and reckoned with before taking action.[11]

Clearly, the safest course in such a world is always to avoid direct confrontation: to work around the larger forces by anticipating their tendencies—rather than, heroically, to take them head on. As Zhuangzi put it more than two thousand years ago, when you see a gnarled old tree, you know that it was smart enough to avoid attracting any attention. The reason it could live out its life span was precisely that it was seen as "useless."[12]

CONFRONTING AN OBSTACLE

Thus, as Yang Liu's graphics make explicit, there is a great difference in the way a Chinese person and a Westerner might choose to confront what they see as life's obstacles (see next page).

In the West, having set a goal, one commonly (1) confronts any obstacles head-on, and (2) proceeds in a direct, head-on assault to overcome them. In China, heading

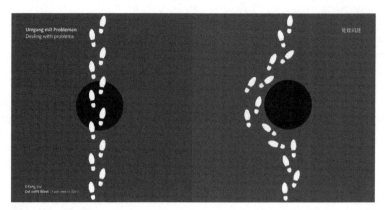

Yang Liu, "Dealing with Problems." *Source:* Yang Liu, *Ost trifft West* [East meets West], 10th ed. (Mainz, Germany: Hermann Schmidt Verlag, 2014). Used by permission.

off in a promising direction, one tends to (1) evade any obstacles by a series of clever strategies, and thus (2) circumnavigate perceived difficulties as deftly as possible.

Why is there this difference? It has to do with differing ways of thinking about the nature of the world. In the Christian West, one has a model in the divine agency of God, who sets about creating the world through his divine will (as dictated through his commands). Thus, in the West today, most of us are encouraged to grow up thinking of ourselves as small centers of autonomous agency, forging our destinies through sheer willpower. Often we do not pay much attention to surrounding circumstances—perhaps because we assume conditions will remain the same. Our goals are presumed to change rarely if at all; they are primary and must be honored at all costs. Thus, even if they fail in their intentions, our enduring heroes are defined by their ferocity of determination.

In China, however, one has no overarching model for agency. No God is known to have created the world—and willpower (like the power of words) is seen as a flimsy weapon against the larger, ineffable, and uncontrollable forces of the world. As conditions are forever changing, one has as much chance of willing oneself toward a certain goal as a boat does of getting into harbor by sailing straight into the wind. As every sailor knows, without tactical ability, the sheer dogged determination of a skipper will get one nowhere. Any such heroic defiance of natural forces would seem merely foolish in China. There one must always be aware of the force of wind and the water (if only as a metaphor for the larger forces that rule our lives). Sometimes these forces are taken quite literally into account, as in determining the very shape and orientation of a building through *fengshui* (literally, "wind/water" 风水). Finally, in China one can never simply calculate one's own goals. For one must always consider the consequences for those with whom one's life is involved: first of all family and then for all one's extended *guanxi* networks—as they will inevitably share either one's success or one's failure.

MAKING CHOICES: ATTENDING TO *MIANZI*

Though general tendencies are quite clear, these perspectives on choice are not exclusive to each world. There was, for instance, a time in the West when stratagems—in the sense of exercising cunning in the face of adverse circumstance—were also highly regarded. One thinks of "wily Odysseus" using his wits to escape the monstrous one-eyed Polyphemus, or even of the tricks employed by the Greek gods and goddesses to fool both humans and each other. And, of course, it was the same wily Odysseus whose Trojan horse finally allowed the Greeks to demolish Troy.[13] Nonetheless the most enduring Greek hero was Achilles, the confrontational warrior who became the model for the Western way of war.[14] Among Western culture heroes, there is no equivalent of China's monkey king—a trickster in every circumstance.[15]

Yet, as in other domains, it is possible to find both kinds of thinking in both worlds. In either, one must speak of prevailing tendencies, as Hamlet demonstrates when he meditates on

> Whether 'tis nobler in the mind to suffer
> The slings and arrows of outrageous fortune
> Or to take arms against a sea of troubles
> And by opposing end them? (act 3, scene 1)

In the end, Hamlet, that hero of modern Western self-questioning, turns Chinese—that is, strategical, devising a play within a play—and even (perhaps) playing at being mad himself.

What is "Chinese" about it? Hamlet pays attention to eliciting a reaction from his audience, in order (by a kind of jujitsu) to turn that reaction back against itself, thereby confirming the other's guilt. Hamlet is, in short, seeking to force the other to "lose face" by a sudden outburst of anger or fear; thus, by playing with their *mianzi*, he draws them out so that he can do them in.

If Hamlet is "Chinese" in his strategizing, then the story of the ambush at Maling (which opens this chapter) shows how General Pang Juan's stereotypically "Western" character was in turn played on by Sun Bin. General Pang is described as "arrogant." Therefore he can be counted upon to pursue his quarry in a thoughtless, straight-on, all-out effort—relying on only a single hypothesis: that his opponent's troops are "inferior." Had he acted in a more "Chinese" manner, he might have, considering the tactical acumen of his enemy, looked at the situation in terms of not one but multiple possibilities. In other words, General Pang did not consider the qualities of his rival or figure them into his strategizing. As a result, he forced his men into a two-day march that led them, exhausted, into a death trap. Sun Bin had turned the very qualities by which General Pang was best known into his own undoing; as a result, he was defeated, even before he began to fight.

Thus we say that General Pang's downfall resulted because he acted as if he were the only agent in the conflict. In the West, many decisions are made in this way. Often we in the West pay only minimal attention to the effect our actions may have on others, because we assume we are not reliant on them. We think of ourselves, in other words, as autonomous or "independent" of others. Then we talk of "unexpected outcomes" when other effects are (in due course) registered.

The limitations of that perspective become clear in a story John Cage tells about how he tried to better his game of chess while playing with the artist Marcel Duchamp. "I was using chess as a pretext to be with him," Cage explained.

> I didn't learn, unfortunately, while he was alive to play well. I play better now, although I still don't play very well. But I play well enough now that he would be pleased, if he knew that I was playing better. So that when he would instruct me in chess, rather than thinking about it in terms of chess, I thought about it in terms of Oriental thought. Also he said, for instance, don't just play your side of the game, play both sides. That's a brilliant remark and something people spend their lives trying to learn—not just in chess, but everything.[16]

To "play both sides" of the game is not merely "Oriental" but more specifically Chinese. That is because the Chinese find it very hard to understand a notion of *ego* in the Western sense: as an independent, uniquely made, and eternal entity residing in each individual (as ordained by God). Every one of those terms is alien to a Chinese sense of self, which, by its very nature, is located through relations with others, through one's *mianzi* or "face." Thus, in taking decisions, one must first of all consider the consequences for one's *guanxi* or connections, as the crucial arbiters of one's status. They can give it—or take it away; and "losing *mianzi*" is sometimes so drastic as to risk a kind of living death.

Given these considerations, one must always play both (that is, all) sides of the game. As how one conducts oneself, what one does, is always seen to reflect on others: first of all, on one's family and then on the larger hierarchies with which one is involved. One very successful Chinese businessman, the CEO of a large insurance company, told us how he "motivates" his employees. If one of his workers is not bringing in the allotted commissions, the first recourse of this boss is to call him in and say, "Now Mr. Hu, you are not performing up to standard. You have now been warned that you need to improve on your figures. If you do not, then I will be forced to call in your family and ask them what it is at home that is holding you back." Without exception, this boss reports, this kind of leverage works wonders with the employee's work performance. So, if the first rule in China is "know the script," the second is "consider the consequences"—by which is meant the consequences not merely for yourself but also for all the other people you are involved with.[17] Understanding the ripple effect of their decisions, Chinese people are quick to consult and consider the opinions of relatives, particularly parents, in all crucial matters such as where to go to university, what to study, what career to undertake, and whom to marry and when. This would be considered normal in Chinese life as it would for many of these decisions to be taken more or less independently by young people in the West.

But the overall net effect of such patterns of thinking in both worlds can be dramatic. To seek one's goals directly and to be forthright in speech are typically

Western; whereas to seek one's goals through strategic indirection and to speak, if at all, with tactful circumlocution would be natively Chinese. Here one confronts a major divergence in approaches to living between the two civilizations. It goes even further. In traditional China, for instance, only evil spirits are deemed to move in straight lines. Thus screens and deflections are carefully placed, from entrances of ceremonial buildings to the designs of gardens and hotel lobbies, to deflect their course. In China, only the reckless proceed relentlessly toward a certain set goal, as did the arrogant General Pang Juan. Their arrogance in defying the higher forces around them is usually amply repaid by defeat when more strategic opponents confront them.

THE COMPETITIVE UNDERPINNING TO STRATEGIZING

Why is strategizing so important to the Chinese as a life model? It follows inevitably from their consciousness of omnipresent and therefore intense competition imping-ing on every aspect of life in China today. For hundreds of years, China's population has been huge by comparison with all other countries around the world. Power structures within that polity have always been contested. Thus court records and histories of imperial China overflow with intrigues, deceptions, rivalries, false accu-sations, internal exiles, assassination plots (some successful), mass executions—and worse. Although there has been a single hierarchy at the top for a very long time, every position within it becomes subject to contestation whenever competition is allowed to enter. Strategical thinking aims at winning competitions, whenever and wherever they occur.

Though strategy is often conceived in the West as a game, most Chinese do not approach life situations in that spirit. There life is played as a deadly serious game, with every decision subjected to intense group scrutiny and considered from mul-tiple perspectives. In this world of *mianzi*, the stakes are, inevitably, high. Failure may mean not humiliation and death, as in the case of General Pang Juan, but rather the loss of face that results in erasure within one's own social circles.

Thus in China, competition-based pressures are felt to apply not just in periods of open warfare but always—and in just about every situation and every day. While cooperation is the rule within the gates of *guanxi* networks, outside them is under-stood as a state of virtual war. For instance, any conversation with Chinese parents about their precious only child will, sooner or later, focus on the intense pressures they are all under, especially in obtaining a place at a prestigious university. Urban parents invest much of their energy in the child's education from the prenatal months onward. Among their strategies may be selective housing—as in buying a more expensive apartment to better the chances of getting into a good school.[18] From the first, that child will be put under intense pressure to perform well, particularly in the open competition that determines college entrance (the *gaokao* exam).[19] In their own work, parents will be jockeying for the best position, with the best conditions and salary. After hours they will concentrate fiercely on their only child, whose future is seen as carrying the best life chances for the entire family.[20]

So any Westerners who come to China thinking that intense competition is a preserve of their own (capitalist) culture will come in for a shock. In general, Chinese people—Chinese students in particular—tend to be far more competitive and hardworking than their counterparts in the West.[21] As a consequence, while Chinese people may seem to have less choice than Westerners, that is only superficially the case. In fact they constantly face choices—with all the attendant complexities and anxieties that such strategical maneuvers involve.

GAMING THE SYSTEM

Given the heavy investment in strategy, *gaming the system* flourishes in China. There is even a saying that suits this situation perfectly: *shang you zheng ce, xia you dui ce* (上有政策,下有对策), roughly, "The bosses have their policies, the underlings find ways to beat the system." Westerners often think of Chinese hierarchies as top-down command systems, in which top officials should be able to enforce their will easily. On the contrary, according to one China expert, as these hierarchies are not really command structures but prestige alignments, the lower orders "will pretend to comply but in practice they will go on doing what they feel is in their best interests. The superiors know that there are limits to their capacity to command so they are usually quite prepared to play act their authoritarian roles and not press too hard for details about how their commands are being implemented."[22] As in all performances, the emphasis is on maintaining *mianzi*. As there is universal agreement that at least the appearance of social harmony is a virtue, no one has an interest in exposing how ineffectual such arrangements can turn out to be. What is important is the credibility of the performance: the bosses scold the underlings for their failings, and the underlings confess their inadequacies while praising the bosses to the skies—all the time ignoring their commands as best they can.

Strategies for such performance maintenance are best captured in this image by Huang Yongyu (1924–). Painted in Beijing near the end of the Cultural Revolution, it is known as *Owl*. In its original time in 1973 and since, this image has provoked many diverse readings.[23] Perhaps most memorably, it portrays the popular caveat to keep "one eye open and one eye closed" (睁一只眼 闭一只眼). In China, this is a way of life, one that condones what one knows is wrong or simply sloppy in order to just get on with one's life.[24] As there are many things one cannot change (such as the quality of the air—or mandates from higher authorities), one must work around them. On first seeing this image, one Chinese colleague compared it to the dilemma she faces when students use their mobile phones during class. If she stops her lecture to call attention to their behavior—thus shaming them into compliance—she herself loses *mianzi*. If she continues to lecture, ignoring their behavior, her *mianzi* (and thus prestige) is maintained. But unless she closes one eye to the students' conduct,

Huang Yongyu, *Owl* (1973–1978). *Source:* Huang Yongyu, "A Beneficial Bird," in *Huang Yongyu and His Paintings*, trans. Yang Xianyi et al., ed. Zheng Xiaojuan and Xiao Shiling (Beijing: Foreign Languages Press, 1988), 12.

her own attention is divided. Usually, this is the route she follows—but ruefully, feeling that she is now complicit in their misbehavior.

In the present context her dilemma encapsulates a duality of consciousness that, while not limited to China, is particularly functional within its cultural imperatives, where the variety of things one cannot imagine changing is larger and more diverse than in the West—and keeping up the status performance is much more crucial. Such selective or split attention might be regarded in China almost as an adaptive strategy, perhaps even a key survival skill.

But strategizing of this kind is, of course, in no way limited to China. It now flourishes everywhere in the modern West, despite major differences between civilizations. Here in the West it no longer has the burden of seeming immoral or even evil, as it did in the days of Shakespeare's Machiavellian villains. Today *gaming the system* is often regarded simply as clever and no longer needs to imply violating the law. Feigned compliance, due deference, and thinking "smart" in the office is now standard advice for those taking up desk jobs in the West. But this shift in how we in the West regard strategizing has had consequences on a larger scale. Consider, for instance, the subprime mortgage packages at the core of the 2008 financial crisis in the United States and Europe. Rating agencies apparently did nothing illegal when they were handsomely rewarded as they issued the highest ratings for bundles that included dubious loans.[25] As a result, the United States and Western Europe were brought to their knees, but almost no one has been charged with a crime.

Is the main difference between China and the West these days a matter of degree and persistence? Certainly strategic awareness has a longer life in China and, as a kind of pragmatic intelligence being exercised in a quickly changing world, is more highly valued there than the "principled" goal-directed approach of the West.

Is one way or the other automatically better in coping with life's inevitable difficulties?

NOTES

1. This text is adapted from Harro von Senger, *The Book of Stratagems* (New York: Viking, 1991), 61–64. See *CCCW*, CD, 1231–34. Mao Zedong, in his strategic writings on conducting revolutionary war in China, drew direct inspiration from stories such as these.

2. The Chinese tradition considered individuals with any visible handicap to be unworthy of respect. See, for example, how a succession in the sixth century BCE was deflected away from the first-born putative heir because he had a deformed foot. *CCCW*, 470.

3. The ultimate winner, Qin, gave us the name for China as of 221 BCE; its newly unified empire has served as the Chinese norm ever since.

4. Sunzi, *The Art of War*, trans. Samuel G. Griffith (New York: Oxford University Press, 1963), 96–101.

5. Niccolò Machiavelli, *The Prince*, 1513, trans. W. K. Marriott (London: D. Nutt, 1905), accessed January 24, 2012, http://www.gutenberg.org/; *CCCW*, 413.

6. Victor Davis Hanson, *The Western Way of War* (New York: Knopf, 1989); second edition with John Keegan (Berkeley: University of California Press, 2009).

7. Only Sparta relied on full-time professional soldiering—with the predictable result that they eventually dominated the other Greek city-states. *CCCW*, 34–37. Note that modern Chinese historians depict the ancient Greeks as primarily a maritime people, a simplification that places them in dialectical opposition to the ancient Chinese as an agricultural people.

8. Initially written down around 500 CE, this text is quite widely known among educated Chinese today.

9. See the section titled "A Chinese Paradigm?" in Part III, "Rethinking the West." *CCCW*, 509.

10. Paul A. Cohen, interview in "Coming Distractions" by *China Beat*, September 26, 2008, accessed November 11, 2012, http://thechinabeat.blogspot.ie/. The interview concentrated on Cohen's then forthcoming book *Speaking to History: The Story of King Goujian in Twentieth-Century China* (Berkeley: University of California Press, 2008). The following paragraph paraphrases this interview.

11. See François Jullien, *A Treatise on Efficacy: Between Western and Chinese Thinking*, trans. Janet Lloyd (Honolulu: University of Hawaii Press, 2004).

12. Wang Rongpei, trans., *Zhuangzi*, 2 vols., Library of Chinese Classics (Changsha, China: Hunan People's Publishing House, 1999), 1:1, 12–13.

13. See Lisa Raphals, *Knowing Words: Wisdom and Cunning in the Classical Traditions of China and Greece* (Ithaca, NY: Cornell University Press, 1992), for further comparative explorations.

14. *Mètis*, or cleverness of the Ulysses sort, was seen as a kind of pragmatic wisdom that made it possible to survive in an unpredictable world. But the Greek word *mètis*, along with the sense of its value, disappeared after attacks by Plato and Aristotle. Plato, for example, deplored the Sophists' clever rhetoric as much as he did, in his *Laws*, the ensnaring of helpless animals by traps. Jullien, in *A Treatise on Efficacy*, 7–9. Page 191 cites to this effect Marcel Detienne and Jean-Pierre Vernant, *Cunning Intelligence in Greek Culture and Society* (Atlantic Highlands, NJ: Humanities Press, 1978), 5. That Plato and Aristotle disdained the concept is confirmed by Raphals, *Knowing Words*, 228.

15. The monkey king features prominently in *Journey to the West* (西游记), another of the four classic fictions most honored in Chinese literature.

16. In conversation with Paul Cummings, 1974. As quoted in Richard Kostelanetz, *Conversing with Cage*, 2nd ed. (New York: Routledge, 2003), 12.

17. It is in line with this kind of thinking, for instance, that the emperors of ancient China punished dissidents by executing not merely them but often their whole families as well, extending to several degrees of relationship in all living generations. The classic story concerns Fang Xiaoru and the 874 persons who are said to have been executed with him by the third emperor of Ming, Zhu Di (reigned 1402–1424), the Yongle emperor. *CCCW*, CD, 701–8.

18. The model here may well be the fourth century BCE story mentioned earlier in chapter 1, "Binding Families: *Xiào*." Mengzi's widowed mother famously moved house three times in search of a positive learning environment for her son, who in time became one of the great Confucian sages. Here is another instance of how ancient stories influence current Chinese decision making.

19. For a description and some sample questions from this examination, see *CCCW*, 98–99.

20. The presumed return on this investment we have already examined as *xiao*.

21. *Two Million Minutes* (documentary), directed by Chad Heeter (Arlington, VA: Broken Pencil Productions, 2007), accessed November 24, 2012, http://www.2mminutes.com/. It turns out that two million minutes is the time taken up by a typical four-year high school career. Following the high school careers of three pairs of teenagers (one pair from China, one from India, and one from the United States), it then compares their test scores from a variety of contexts. The American pair came in highest in only one characteristic—"self-esteem." For a helpful overview, see "Two Million Minutes: A Global Examination," *Harvard Educational Review*, accessed June 29, 2013, http://hepg.org/.

22. Lucian W. Pye, *The Mandarin and the Cadre: China's Political Cultures* (Ann Arbor: University of Michigan Center for Chinese Studies, 1988), 32–33. The following sentences are derived from this passage.

23. In 1978, an inscription was added, entitling this piece *A Beneficial Bird*. An impressive range of possible interpretations of both this image and its inscription has been brought together by Eugene Y. Wang in "The Winking Owl: Visual Effect and Its Art Historical Thick Description," *Critical Inquiry* 26, no. 3 (Spring 2000): 435–73.

24. See Robert P. Weller, "The Politics of Increasing Religious Diversity in China," *Daedalus* 143, no. 2 (Spring 2014): 135–44, in which he argues that "China has seen a remarkable growth and pluralization of religious activity over the past thirty years, a development that has rapidly overtaken the incremental and sluggish changes in the relevant regulatory structures. In much of the country, the government has managed the mismatch between religious practice and official rules by governing with 'one eye open and one eye closed,' that is, by pretending not to notice violations of the regulations as long as people pretend that they are following the rules. Comparative evidence suggests that such a mode of governance can be long-lasting and effective by encouraging groups to self-censor, by allowing space for contextual experimentation, and by stressing the acceptance of nominal convention over the control of behavior. This situation is likely to continue unless China adopts a new vision of the desired relation between state and society" (135).

25. Might one even speculate that the importation of Sunzi's text into American MBA programs has encouraged this behavior?

II

WESTERN QUESTIONS, CHINESE RESPONSES

In our interactions with Westerners, both in Europe and America, whether in public or private, four questions keep coming up. While they are not the only questions, these are the ones that focus for our audiences the widest range of cultural issues in relation to China. In one sense all these questions seem to ask, Why is China not more like the West? But they also go right to the heart of each civilization. Here we repeat these Western questions, but rather than responding to them in Western terms—which only turns the whole exercise into a kind of echo chamber—we respond to each question using the key Chinese terms as analyzed in the previous section. Not surprisingly, the responses turn out to be quite different from standard Western understandings, as they are now framed from Chinese, rather than Euro-American, premises.

11

Question One

Christianity?

WHY, AFTER CENTURIES OF MISSIONARY ACTIVITY, IS CHINA NOT CHRISTIAN?

Entering China, one enters a world without God. Why does this matter? Many believing Christians consider that one cannot be moral without a grounding in the principles of their own faith-beliefs. Even for a Westerner whose belief in Christianity is only sketchy or even nonexistent, the presumptions of its world (as outlined at many junctures in this text) are still operative in shaping basic conceptions of what is real, including its fundamental values and the way they are derived. Most of the West's institutions—from its modes of governance to courts of law and even academia, not to speak of its ways of thinking—have been shaped by centuries of Christian modes of thinking and Christian values. For this reason, Christianity may be taken as a kind of cultural fault line between the West and China.

In other words, whether one subscribes to it or not, Christianity has historically supplied many of the crucial premises upon which Western civilization is based. It is therefore instructive to observe how the efforts to import Christianity into China have (comparatively speaking) failed, as its doctrines have come into conflict with key Chinese values. It is also important to note that, even though they are not predominantly Christian, the Chinese remain heavily invested in their own versions of morality and make their own peace with the inevitable end of life.

The lack of Western-style belief in China is certainly not universal. There are of course some people there who will say they believe in God: Muslims, mostly in the northwest, and tens of millions of professed Christians. Overall the total number of individuals who think of themselves as "Christian" in some sense of the word probably approximates to 5 to 6 percent of the population, that is, about the same proportion as belong to the Communist Party.[1] While the latter group is central to every aspect of life in China, Christians survive (at best) on the margins: an unexpected outcome after centuries of missionary effort.

Why should this be the case, given successive waves of missionaries who sought to bring the Christian message to China? The short answer is that Chinese culture does not offer the fundamental conceptual grounding for a creator-god who presides over an eternal heavenly realm. Historically, a fuller answer may reside in the fate of the three major waves of missionary attempts to Christianize the Chinese, each achieving only limited results as it came up against enduring priorities of Chinese civilization.

The Nestorians

The first Christians to arrive in China were Nestorians. After being declared heretics at various church councils of the fifth century, these Nestorians turned their attention to the east: to Persia, Central Asia, and by the sixth century, China, where Buddhism dominated.

Welcomed by the early Tang emperors, Nestorian churches flourished alongside Buddhist and Zoroastrian temples until the year 845. That year the Tang Emperor Wuzong condemned all three religions for sumptuous temples (which outclassed his own palaces) and for enticing too many young men away from secular duties such

Nestorian priests in a procession on Palm Sunday. In a seventh- or eighth-century wall painting from a Nestorian church built in Tang dynasty China.

as paying taxes and serving in the military.[2] Thus after several centuries of tolerance and prosperity, the secular urgencies of the Chinese empire were deemed to have priority over all religious impulses whatsoever. The Nestorians survive only as fragmentary inscriptions and archaeological remnants, a reminder that, in the long run, this-worldly needs always take priority in China.[3]

The moral? In the absence of any transcendental orientation,[4] right up to today, pragmatic this-worldly priorities continue to dominate in the thinking of State leaders.

The Jesuits

The second major missionary effort was Jesuit, led by the justly famous Matteo Ricci who arrived in China in 1582. Ricci and his fellows worked hard to enter the world of late Ming dynasty China. To fit in, they learned to dress like Confucian scholars, mastering Mandarin to such a degree of excellence that they were able to write extensively about Christianity in classical Chinese.[5] In common with many missionaries, they began by asserting a ready compatibility between existing local practices and the new faith of Christianity. As a result, in Ricci's China, Confucian-inspired rituals honoring ancestors were assimilated into the newly sinified Catholic practices.[6]

Apart from Christianity, the Jesuits brought with them the fruits of Renaissance Western culture: ranging from the new sciences—in particular, mathematics and astronomy—to clocks, musical instruments, and cartography (Ricci is himself credited with creating the first world map featuring China at its center[7]). As carriers of this new culture, the Jesuits were deemed to be particularly valuable by the Manchu rulers of China who comprised, as of 1644, the Qing dynasty. But back in Rome, Ricci's doctrinal compromises raised crucial doctrinal concerns, in particular the

Matteo Ricci in 1610, oil portrait by a Macau convert known as Pereira (1575–1633). *Source:* The Society of Jesus, Rome. Used by permission.

Jesuit accommodation of ancestor worship. The resulting confrontation (the so-called Rites Controversy) reached an unhappy climax in 1715 when Pope Clement XI ruled out such practices as heterodox. In 1721, the Emperor Kangxi retaliated by banning Christianity altogether.[8]

Although treated in Rome as a theological matter, from a Chinese point of view this controversy turned on the overriding importance of *xiao*, the family reverence manifested in honoring ancestors. In the end, the values of *xiao* endured while the teachings of Christianity faded. For the following century and more, Catholicism survived only as a fragmented underground movement. Once again, the core value of *xiao* continues (even today) to serve as the primary glue holding Chinese culture together. As such, it trumps all other loyalties or affiliations.

The Modern Missionaries

The third wave of Christian missionaries, dominantly Protestant in sponsorship, crested in the late nineteenth and early twentieth centuries. Protected by the successive treaties favoring Western powers that began with the settlement of the First Opium War in 1842, the majority were Protestants from English-speaking countries. They founded schools, orphanages, and hospitals as they set about trying to bring Western-style modernity to China along with their faith.[9]

Ironically, the surge in Protestant missions left the Chinese with the impression that the new arrivals had nothing to do with their Jesuit predecessors, an impression eagerly encouraged by the Protestants. Their legacy results in the Chinese having two separate designations for Christians. Today Roman Catholicism in China is called

Edward J. Galvin (1882–1956), bishop of Hanyang, *Baptism in the Field*, about 1940. *Source:* Columban Fathers, Ireland. Used by permission.

Tiānzhǔjiào 天主教, literally, "Religion of the Lord of Heaven," following Matteo Ricci's translation of the word for "God." The Protestants, arriving later, were called *Jīdūjiào* 基督教, literally "Jesus Religion," a name they still retain.[10] Such a division in their official Chinese designation underlines how rigorously Western Christians exported their own internal sectarian schisms to China, belying the common core of their faith.[11]

Such was the impact of this last wave of missionaries that it ultimately provoked a violent pushback from traditionalists in defense of Chinese culture. The Boxer Rebellion of 1900, among others, targeted foreign influence and specifically that of missionaries, seen as radically undermining Chinese values and practices. Although that rebellion was put down by mainly Western armies, uneasiness about foreign missionaries continues and still troubles present government policies.[12]

Under the PRC

Ultimately, all missionary efforts formally ended when, soon after 1949, the new People's Republic of China (PRC) expelled missionaries, banning all proselytizing within its territory—a prohibition still in force to this day. Although existing churches were not usually dismantled, worshipping there was never encouraged.

Thus each phase of missionary activity has come up against cultural barriers that proved, if not fatal, at least disabling to its enterprise. This third and final phase of Christian practice in China has, since the founding of the PRC, now become involved in a perennial Chinese conflict involving the location of ultimate authority (not unknown to the Western world, especially in those historical contests between the popes and presiding secular powers). In Chinese thinking, if one hierarchy is to dominate, as under the empires that endured for millennia, then alternative loyalties or power structures must always be subordinated. In the religious domain, Catholic churches—as being the most hierarchical and centrally controlled from outside China—have since 1949 suffered most obviously from such pressures.

Historically the Catholic hierarchy tends to clash with the PRC hierarchy most publicly when it comes to naming a new bishop. Despite intermittent negotiations with the PRC (and in what sometimes seems a replay of power games in medieval Europe), the Vatican insists on the pope's sole authority to appoint bishops—while the PRC State leaders persist in making their own nominations. In the fall of 2010, a "bishop" named by the Chinese Patriotic Catholic Association was promptly excommunicated by the Vatican.[13] In 2012, the PRC named Thaddeus Ma Daqin as Bishop in Shanghai. But in a dramatic turnabout, at his inauguration mass he announced that he was quitting the official Patriotic Catholic Association—and was promptly confined to quarters by the authorities.[14] In December 2012, he was reported to have been stripped of his title by the Chinese authorities.[15] Thus the standoff continues. The State is adamant that it remain fully in control, as it always seeks to be in this and every other aspect of Chinese life.

CHINESE CHRISTIANS TODAY

What then remains from this most recent missionary effort of more than a century? Chinese institutions such as universities and hospitals benefited greatly from missionary efforts, but with the arrival of the PRC, these were so thoroughly co-opted that no visible Christian ethos survives.

Today, for most Chinese people, Christian missionaries are still associated with the Republic of China (ruling nominally from approximately 1911 to 1949), which presided over the first phase of Western-style modernizing in China. Up to recently, although missionaries remain legally banned, the members of officially registered churches were still free to proselytize informally, as long as these efforts avoided public visibility. This tolerance has been periodically rescinded.

The Party has recently increased its efforts to block any evangelical activity, especially on college campuses, where, it is said, many of the most recent conversions are being made. In May 2011, the Central Committee issued strong instructions to all institutions of higher learning on how to block U.S.-led "hostile forces" that

Something rare in Western countries: a church that labels itself "Christian." The Chinese characters here, 基督教堂, Hall for Jidujiao, indicate a Protestant parish, in this case implying evangelical origins a century ago. This newly built church is located in the Haidian District of northwest Beijing. *Source:* The parish website is http://english .hdchurch.org/, accessed April 12, 2015.

try to use "religion to infiltrate China to carry out their political plot to Westernize and divide China. Foreign forces regard institutes of higher education as key targets for using religion, Christianity in particular, for infiltration."[16] The wording of this document gives some indication of how strongly State leaders have come to fear the (perhaps growing?) influence of religion, and in particular Christianity, in today's PRC.

The way the Party has reasserted its control over the years has been through its Bureau of Religious Affairs. It alone provides funding, throughout the PRC, for church buildings and their finances, managing everything to do with all the five recognized religions, including Buddhism, Daoism, and Islam. Official recognition of Christianity is restricted to named organizations: the Three-Self Patriotic Movement/China Christian Council (for Protestants) and the Chinese Patriotic Catholic Association (for Catholics), which has disavowed the pope and is considered schismatic by orthodox Roman Catholics. All these organizations are affiliated with the government and must follow whatever regulations are imposed upon them. If the numbers of professed Christians are still growing, this is probably less through overt missionary activity than through more informal co-optation—as individuals seek some form of spiritual orientation that goes beyond what is now on offer publicly in a post-Marxist, post-Mao China.

Today the most startling development involves the tens of millions of self-identified Christians who belong to unregistered "house churches." Not surprisingly, these have emerged along very Chinese lines, as essentially pragmatic efforts toward building up a new kind of *guanxi* network. Although nominally illegal and sometimes actively harassed, these members of the unofficial churches act very much like the earliest Christians. Paying little attention to doctrine, they focus on providing a sustaining community that looks after its members, offering comfort and other resources (such as food and practical help) in times of trouble as well as some limited protection from the will of the State. As long as these groups remain small, they might be allowed to operate. But if, like the Shouwang ("Lighthouse") congregation in Beijing, one of these informal churches attracts a thousand members and dares to raise funds substantial enough to try to buy its own meeting space, experience shows that such an enterprise will in time either be disrupted or suppressed.[17]

RESISTANT CONCEPTS: *DAO, YI, AND XIN*

Dao versus God

From a Chinese perspective, resistance to a Christian worldview over centuries indicates a lack of conceptual grounding for its core values. As the latest Central Committee document (see note 16) indicates, there is a fear that Christian proselytizing (forbidden but carried out informally) constitutes a plot to "Westernize and divide China." In the sense that modern Western values are shaped by—if not directly responsive to—Judeo-Christian values, there are grounds for identifying

Westernizing with Christian influence. But perhaps the Central Committee's fears that China might be Christianized are literally groundless. For instance, without a firm concept of a transcendental world, Christianity's appeal in China often seems limited to its pragmatic work: the kinds of cultural artifacts imported by the Jesuits; or the hospitals, schools, and orphanages opened a century ago by various missionary orders. Today, such practical activities show up in the work of the unofficial house churches, a haven for the old, the sick, or those who find themselves alone, in other words, an alternative *guanxi*.

Yi versus Eternal and Unchanging

Yet Christianity may fail to take hold in China if only because, in many crucial ways, China tends to operate through very different ways of thinking. As explained elsewhere, whether or not contemporary Chinese people know about Daoism, there is still a sense in which a belief in *Dao* shapes the Chinese world.[18] In this worldview, *Dao* is seen as working through the world, even though its effects are not always visible (as in the wind, for instance). Unlike the Christian God, *Dao* is impersonal; it cares for no one; and humans have no grounds for appeal against its powers. Likewise, as with *yi*, *Dao* is always moving, always shifting between *yin* and *yang*. This view, again, is completely contrary to the Christian (and generally Western) assumption that the important entities—such as God, heaven, or one's soul—are eternal and unchanging.

Xin versus Rationality

Finally, through *Dao*'s constant changes, all are connected, so that one can barely name something before it is again transformed. Contrast this with the Western confidence that concepts remain sufficiently stable for distinctions to be made between them and that on these distinctions a rational logic may be built. As a member of perhaps the most doctrinal of all religions, a Christian would be comfortable with these distinctions in a way a Chinese person, operating through *xin* (which makes no distinction between thinking and feeling), ordinarily might not. Thus, within this Chinese world, as we have seen, distinctions tend to blur and transform themselves according to situation and context. As noted, in China itself, a person might go to Christian services but also, in times of need, visit Buddhist, Daoist, or Confucian shrines—sometimes all of those within a short time. What is sought is practical help as, for instance, when a child is about to take the national *gaokao* exam, which determines which third level institution he or she will attend, if any. In other words, those doctrinal distinctions— over which Christians have fought for centuries and which serve to define (and thus exclude other) sects—are mostly a matter of indifference to Chinese people, as they tend to invest less energy in such "logical" (or theological) distinctions.

Even in those situations where Chinese do profess Christianity, therefore, it will inevitably be very different from dominant Western versions. Because of Chinese investment in *xin*, Christianity in China is often drawn to those sects that are least doctrinal and most oriented to emotional religious commitment—such as evangelical Protestant churches—as well as to those that are the most pragmatic in providing *guanxi* and other practical supports for its congregations.

A key as to how Christianity transfers into Chinese thinking may be tracked by those Chinese people who practice Christianity in the West. Here (as revealed by a survey in Ireland) they tend to follow the Chinese pattern: not too concerned with doctrinal differences but intent on receiving direct practical help with their worldly difficulties.[19]

THE BIG PICTURE: GETTING ALONG WITHOUT GOD

For some in the West, it is difficult to conceive of how one can live in a world without God. To such, it may seem like trying to live in a world without any secure orientation in basic values or clear principles. In fact, the Chinese do have such basic values and principles, as demonstrated in the preceding chapters. But they are Chinese, not Western, and, as such, grounded not in a transcendental order but in one summarized by this-worldly presences of *qi*, *yi*, and *Dao*.

In seeking to assess these differing spiritual orientations, one can learn much by comparing two classic statements of ultimate values—a verse each from the *Daodejing* and the Bible—as exemplifying the founding trajectories of each civilization. This particular comparison follows from the fact that *Dao* comes closer than any other Chinese concept to what most Westerners understand by *God*.

In an English translation of chapter 25, the *Daodejing* reads as follows:

There is a thing integratedly formed
And born earlier than heaven and earth.
Silent and empty,
It relies on nothing,
Moving around for ever.
We may regard it as the mother of all things.
I do not know its name,
So I name it as *Dao*.[20]

Here *Dao* is "born" but earlier than everything else and, in becoming itself without source, "relies on nothing." Thus *Dao* comes before even the most basic of Chinese distinctions between *tian* 天 (the *heavens* in an impersonal sense) and *di* 地 (*earth*). Having no source itself, *Dao* is seen as "the mother of all things." The motherly nature of the *Dao* is startling. But in this text being a mother to all things does not imply giving birth to them. Instead, *Dao* infuses everything as a nurturing or an enabling force—strikingly unlike the creator-father role of the Judeo-Christian God.[21]

Again, in stark contrast to the eternal God of Western heritage, *Dao* is seen as "moving around for ever." *Dao* is not even momentarily stable, much less eternally reliable. Unlike the West, which invests heavily in the stability of ultimate reality, Chinese people tend to see their world as one being driven by *yi*, or constant, relentless change. Such change manifests itself through those outward and visible signs of *qi* (the vital energies moving the universe between the eternally fluctuating, complementary forces of *yin* and *yang*). *Dao* as such is not a thing but a happening, an ongoing process.

From this aspect, *Dao* as *the way things happen* obliges humans to acknowledge that powerful forces are at work that may—at any moment—intervene to violate all reasonable expectations. When misfortune comes, there may be little mere humans can do about it except to recall that, in a world in which all things change, all things are also connected, thus other things can happen as well.[22] Under such circumstances the best one can do is pay attention to the transformations taking place in order to reorient oneself to the way things are occurring, as ordained by the greater *Dao*.

THE WORD *(LOGOS)* VERSUS *DAO*

The *Daodejing* is eloquent about the difficulties of articulating *Dao* as, being "silent and empty," its name cannot be known. The word "*Dao*" is thus offered as merely a convenient, if arbitrary, designation. By implication, words, in the Chinese tradition, cannot reliably describe what Westerners normally regard as *reality*.

In stark contrast to the Chinese tradition, Western thinking is crucially dependent on words. The connection is made explicitly in the key lines that open the Gospel according to John:

1. In the beginning was the Word, and the Word was with God, and the Word was God.
2. He was in the beginning with God.
3. All things came into being through him; and without him not one thing came into being. . . .
4. And the Word became flesh, and lived among us, and we have seen his glory, the glory as of a father's only son, full of grace and truth.[23]

Originally written in Greek, this book of the Bible plays on the word *logos* as meaning both "word" and "order." Modern derivatives include *logic*. In the Western tradition, it is assumed that the *order of the world* is echoed in *the order of words*, which is why for so many centuries the study of grammar was recommended as revealing the divinely originated *logic* of the world as a whole.[24] The same implicit confidence lies behind formidable traditions of Judeo-Christian theology. Less obviously, it also lies behind a confidence that modern Western science, in discovering and quantifying the "laws of nature," confirms a basic orderliness within the world, as both *logos* and logic—more specifically, world order as articulated through word/number order.

This world order seems, at the very least, universal and stable, and many see it also as divinely instituted.

The Chinese Union Version of the Bible, the most widely used in China among Protestants at least, translates *Word* in this passage as *Dao*.[25] This choice is understandable but misleading. Both words evoke an orderly universe, but only the Western text suggests that humans can grasp its nature.[26] The Chinese tradition affirms that words can never suffice to put humans in touch with *Dao*. The West, both in theological and scientific terms, continues to believe that we can know how to make explicit sense of things.

DAO THINKING IN CHINA

The contrast with *Dao* thinking in China could not be greater. Working through paradox—in itself a subversion of logic—the fourth-century BCE Zhuangzi, follower of Laozi and the *Daodejing*, acutely analyzes the difficulties of talking about *Dao*:

> The view that *something mysterious created the world* and the view that *nothing created the world* are based on speech; they begin and end with "things." *Dao* is formless, but it is not "nothingness." *Dao* is a term we adopt for practical purposes. Both views mentioned above are confined to "things." How can they generalize *Dao* itself? If we speak adequately, we shall be speaking about *Dao* all day long; if we do not speak adequately, we shall be speaking about things all day long. *Dao*, the perfection of things, cannot be conveyed with speech or silence. The highest form of debate is conducted without speech and without silence.[27]

This kind of paradox leaves *Dao* in a realm Westerners commonly think of as mystical, as beyond reason and logic. But nonetheless, in its cultural context, *Dao* is present as profoundly *real*, although its reality is available only through intuition (that is, as *xin*[28]) as gained by experience.[29]

For the Chinese, therefore, existence may be mysterious, but it has its own order, albeit one that pays little attention to human beings. To get in touch with *Dao*, one must set aside one's own intentions in order not to impose on the higher order merely human concerns. This is the approach favored by people who think of themselves as Daoists. Alternatively, one may concentrate on acting in the right way, thus building and maintaining a human order that can sustain us despite whatever happens—a goal shared by many Confucianists and even well-meaning members of the Communist Party.

In sum, to enter a world without God or without the secondary, transcendent world of such as St. Augustine's City of God does not mean one enters a world without spiritual or moral values. In the West, one reaches toward philosophy and religion as the domains for articulating such values. In China, one reaches toward others. For all the Christian investment in extending the work of faith communities both within and beyond their own boundaries (by ministering to those needy, sick, or poor), one can still be a professing Christian while living on one's own. Indeed there have been many honored Christian hermits. But one cannot become a Confucian by oneself.

To conclude, not only does God not exist for most Chinese people; neither does the whole Western-style transcendent world associated with such a concept. Although the Chinese have a word for "heaven" (*tian* 天), its extended metaphorical meanings simply designate the impersonal higher forces that make things happen as they do. If pressed to name them, educated Chinese people might simply say "*Dao.*" When pressed as to explain *Dao*, they might merely shrug—or gesture toward the world around them. For, as we have seen, *Dao* does not live in words, the things they designate (as unchanging "essences"), or in people (as eternal "souls"). *Dao* may be discerned only through the proclivities of things, as they emerge, take place, and then again disappear.

In other words, without being anchored in a stable, eternal entity such as the Christian God or from the perspective of an eternal heaven, "reality" for most Chinese people is exemplified by this-worldly processes as played out in everyday life. Without a creator-god acting as an ultimate First Cause with its promise of a stable *reality*, Chinese people usually tend not to speculate much about *why* things happen in life; instead, they seek to concentrate on the *how*—as in how best to get through it. Accordingly, *Dao* can be best understood, through its most modest translation, simply as "the way."[30]

NOTES

1. The exception would be Hong Kong, since the end of the First Opium War (1839–1842), a British colony, but as of 1997 designated as a "special administrative region of the PRC." Obviously its status is unique, as a highly Westernized sector of modern Chinese society. How its unique intermediate status will evolve is now the subject of much international speculation, in particular given the recent student-led demonstrations.

2. *CCCW*, CD, 1303–5; as translated by Burton Watson, in William Theodore de Bary and Irene Bloom, eds., *Sources of Chinese Tradition*, 2nd ed. (New York: Columbia University Press, 1999), 1:585–86.

3. See Philip Jenkins, *The Lost History of Christianity: The Thousand-Year Golden Age of the Church in the Middle East, Africa, and Asia—and How It Died* (New York: HarperCollins, 2008).

4. For further elaboration on this difference of perspective, see David L. Hall and Roger T. Ames, "*Tian* and *Dao* as Nontranscendent Fields," in *Thinking from the Han: Self, Truth, and Transcendence in Chinese and Western Culture*, 219–85 (Albany: State University of New York Press, 1998).

5. Ricci's portrait by Pereira (full name Emmanuele Yu Wen-Hui) was the earliest oil painting in China, marking the importation of a new medium together with new painting techniques, as well as a new message about the cultural importance of Christianity (as symbol-

ized by Ricci's Confucian robes). Macao Museum of Art, accessed March 17, 2013, http://www.mam.gov.mo/.

6. Resistance to the missionaries came mostly from Buddhists, who offered some devastating critiques of the doctrines on offer. These are detailed by Jacques Gernet, *China and the Christian Impact: A Conflict of Cultures* (Cambridge: Cambridge University Press, 1985), 221–38. Excerpts appear in *CCCW*, 510–14.

7. For a zoom-enabled image, see "Matteo Ricci, Li Zhizao, and Zhang Wentao: World Map of 1602," James Ford Bell Library, University of Minnesota Libraries, accessed October 3, 2013, https://www.lib.umn.edu/.

8. See David E. Mungello, *The Great Encounter of China and the West, 1500–1800*, 3rd ed. (Lanham, MD: Rowman & Littlefield, 2009).

9. Some were converted to Chinese culture along the way, among them their most famous offspring, Pearl S. Buck. See Lian Xi, *The Conversion of Missionaries: Liberalism in American Protestant Missions in China, 1907–1932* (University Park: State University of Pennsylvania Press, 1997).

10. See two recent Chinese books surveying these groups, treated as distinct religions, both published in English in Beijing by the China Intercontinental Press in 2004. *Catholic Church in China* by Yan Kejia and *Christianity in China* (i.e., in Western terms, Protestantism), by Luo Weihong.

11. For a small but telling example of this export into China of the doctrinal and cultural divisions between Roman Catholic and Protestant groups, see Patrick Comerford and Richard O'Leary, "'Heroism and Zeal': Pioneers of the Irish Christian Missions to China," in *China and the Irish*, ed. Jerusha McCormack, 73–78 (Dublin: New Island, 2008).

12. To be more precise, the largest number of "Western" troops was sent by Japan. On that basis, Japan laid claim in 1919 to the German zone of influence in Shandong Province, sparking the May 4th movement in China, a pivotal moment in promoting Chinese national self-consciousness.

13. See "Vatican Condemnation of New Chinese Bishop Worsens Tensions," *New York Times*, July 8, 2011, accessed March 26, 2013, http://www.nytimes.com/.

14. See, for example, "China 'Detains' Shanghai Bishop Who Quit Official Post," *BBC News*, July 10, 2012, http://www.bbc.co.uk/.

15. "China Reportedly Strips Shanghai Bishop of His Title," *New York Times*, December 12, 2012, accessed March 26, 2013, http://www.nytimes.com/.

16. Document of the General Office of the Central Committee of the Communist Party of China (Zhong Ban Fa), 2011, no. 18, 2, accessed December 20, 2012, http://www.chinaaid.org/.

17. The *New York Times*, under the title "Illicit Church, Evicted, Tries to Buck Beijing," gives an overview of this group and its travails: ministers arrested, meeting places denied, and harassment whenever the group attempts to gather at public parks. By implication, the Shouwang congregation has succeeded too well to be allowed to operate freely outside the State-controlled establishment. April 18, 2011, accessed March 26, 2013, http://www.nytimes.com/.

18. See chapter 7, "Realizing a Way: *Dào*."

19. Richard O'Leary and Lan Li, *Mainland Chinese Students and Immigrants in Ireland and Their Engagement with Christianity, Churches and Irish Society* (Dublin: Agraphon, 2008), 43–49.

20. Lao Tzu [Laozi], *The Book of Tao and Teh* [*Daodejing*], trans. Gu Zhengkun, 2nd ed. (Beijing: Peking University Press, 2006), 69.

21. However, while the superior gender status of men is still reflected in traditional Christianity, Judaism, and Islam (all related religions), in China today there seems little evidence of thinking of *Dao* as primarily either feminine or masculine.

22. See the section titled "A Chinese Paradigm?" in Part III, "Rethinking the West." *CCCW*, 509.

23. John 1:1–3, 14, New Revised Standard Version.

24. See John of Salisbury (1115–1180), in *CCCW*, 1008–9.

25. John 1:1–3 (Chinese Union Version [Simplified]), Bible Gateway, accessed April 12, 2015, https://www.biblegateway.com/.

26. In the Judeo-Christian world, only the Eastern Orthodox tradition has consistently viewed God as being so totally *other* as to be, literally, beyond words. Its practices subscribe to what is known as *apophatic* or negative theology: one that attempts to describe God by negation—that is, to speak only in terms of what may *not* be said about God. It thus stands in contrast with *cataphatic* theology, which attempts to describe God in purely positive terms as to what might be asserted about what God *is* rather than what God *is not*. In the Western tradition, *apophatic* theology is often (although not always) allied with mysticism, which focuses on an intuitive and individual experience of the divine reality beyond the realm of ordinary perception, one usually unmediated by the structures of traditional organized religion. A startling example can be found with theologian John Scotus Eriugena (ninth century): "We do not know what God is. God Himself does not know what He is because He is not anything. Literally God is not, because He transcends being." Other particularly well-known examples from the Western tradition are the writings of Meister Eckhart, the medieval text *The Cloud of Unknowing*, and *Dark Night of the Soul* by St. John of the Cross.

27. Wang Rongpei, trans., *Zhuangzi*, 2 vols., Library of Chinese Classics (Changsha, China: Hunan People's Publishing House, 1999), 2:25, 458–59 (modified, italics added).

28. See chapter 4, "Where Is My Mind? *Xīn*."

29. Given the rise of skepticism about language in the West, loosely identified as "postmodernism," followers of, say, Jacques Derrida, are likely to conclude that since words cannot "mean" in any serious sense, there can be no order we can articulate. In China, where words were never counted on as giving access to crucial truths, the credibility of *Dao* order coexists comfortably with such skepticism.

30. See chapter 7, "Realizing a Way: *Dào*." For an insightful discussion see Professor Chad Hansen's website: "Daoist-Oriented Interpretations," Chad Hansen's Chinese Philosophy Pages, accessed November 25, 2012, http://www.hku.hk/philodep/ch.

12

Question Two

Human Rights?

WHY DOES CHINA HAVE SUCH
A BAD REPUTATION FOR HUMAN RIGHTS?

Issues raised by Christianity in China are placed first because, as stated—whether one professes or not to being a practicing Christian—the way Westerners think is inevitably shaped by Christian values. One philosopher even argues that the moral and political commitments of the secular liberal democratic West can legitimately be regarded as nothing more than a secularized version of Western Christianity.[1] As the axiom of human dignity may be found in its teaching that man is made in God's image, one can appreciate the quasi-religious zeal with which Westerners seek to convert others to their version of human rights.[2] Again, its discourse exposes what is most distinctive about Western principles by means of their clear divergence from China's own distinctive core values.

A SHORT HISTORY OF "HUMAN RIGHTS"

These principles are articulated most clearly by the United Nations' Universal Declaration of Human Rights. Evolving out of the sufferings of World War II, most flagrantly out of Hitler's massacre of six million of Europe's Jews, and drafted during the acute tensions of the early Cold War, a final document was approved on December 10, 1948, by the United Nations General Assembly vote of forty-eight to zero.[3] Note that nations were not in a position either to ratify or to sign the Universal Declaration, unlike later human rights protocols or treaties.[4] The General Assembly simply *declared* this document to define *human rights*, with the support of the vast majority of nations that were members at the time. The People's Republic of China

(PRC), of course, was not involved—since China was then represented by the Republic of China, now based in Taiwan.[5]

Ironically, the UN agenda, in seeking to rally support around the world, instead has managed over time to place *human rights* at the epicenter of an ideological conflict. As the term itself is so clearly honorific, all nations seek to associate their practices with it. Nevertheless, the differences in interpreting the Declaration tend to split along what now echo long-familiar Cold War lines (perhaps not surprising given the time of its drafting). Among all the contenders today, the most relentless are the United States and the PRC. The United States began first, issuing through the State Department (as of 1990) an annual assessment of human rights around the world. Every year it sharply condemns China for human rights violations. As of 2004, the PRC began retaliating by way of its own annual reports, each censuring the United States for human rights violations while justifying its own "progress." Clearly something is badly amiss when a concept can serve such conflicting purposes—or generate fears of official repression as dramatized by the incidents of June 4, 1989, on Tiananmen Square.

On inspection, however, it becomes clear that the Declaration is itself the origin of its own difficulties. Its thirty articles do not speak with one voice, as they affirm no single-minded version of what constitutes a "human right." The Cold War split surfaces at a precise shift in the provisions of the document. In the first twenty-one articles, one locates what may be called the civic and political rights of individuals. Inspired by Western Enlightenment principles, these are implicit in a variety of democratic systems in Western countries, which regard them as "universal." Here is an example in article 21.3: "The will of the people shall be the basis of the authority of government; this will shall be expressed in periodic and genuine elections which shall be by universal and equal suffrage and shall be held by secret vote or by equivalent free voting procedures." Today this model is familiar in every Western nation. Less familiar are the economic and cultural "rights" the Universal Declaration spells out in articles 22 to 27. These are the "human rights" to which China gives the highest priority. Here is a sample from article 25.1: "Everyone has the right to a standard of living adequate for the health and wellbeing of himself and of his family, including food, clothing, housing and medical care and necessary social services, and the right to security in the event of unemployment, sickness, disability, widowhood, old age or other lack of livelihood in circumstances beyond his control." These two provisions, and the different assumptions they embody as to what is "human" and what is a "right," epitomize the conflict. As a self-appointed guardian of human rights, the United States bases its judgments strictly on the first twenty-one articles. The PRC, self-identified as a developing nation, focuses strictly on articles 22 to 27. Each, on a regular basis, finds the other severely lacking in what they separately deem to be the true "human rights." In doing so, each presumes that its own priorities suffice as a fulfillment of human rights imperatives.

Thus it is clear from studying the Universal Declaration in its entirety that neither side has an open-and-shut case. Acknowledging such complexities requires us to review exactly how human rights issues are in fact situated in each case. In the West, the United States offers an extreme instance of playing down social and economic claims in favor of civil and political rights. Most European Union (EU) nations, by way of contrast, pursue governmental policies commonly known as "social democratic." These represent an interpretation of such "rights" as drawing on both sets of articles. That is, these nations collect higher levels of tax than the United States and then devote much of that income to delivering higher levels of health care, unemployment benefits, and other elements of a social safety net. The United States, at the far end of the spectrum of "individual" rights, proportionately collects the lowest taxes of all industrialized nations—and devotes the least amount of government income to ensuring social safety nets. In other words, the United States shunts aside what other Western governments routinely see as their obligations under articles 22 to 27 in the Universal Declaration.

From such long-term orientations, the United States often takes the lead on attacks on China. Within the United States, conservative politicians exemplify this stance. Particularly scornful of any attempts to take social and economic rights seriously were Ronald Reagan's appointees in the 1980s. In a memorable phrase, Jeane Kirkpatrick, Reagan's choice to represent the United States at the United Nations, dismissed these provisions as a "letter to Santa Claus."[6] Some years later, Paula Dobriansky, assistant secretary of state for Human Rights and Human Affairs in the first Bush administration, attacked the "myth" that so-called "'economic and social rights' constitute human rights."[7] From the other end of the American ideological divide, Noam Chomsky in 2009 interpreted one analysis of Reaganite policies as "the unqualified rejection of economic, social, and cultural 'rights' as rights" as being, in fact, an "unqualified rejection of two-thirds of the *Universal Declaration*."[8] From such rhetoric it is clear that excess abounds at both ends of the spectrum and will continue to do so; that is, at least in the United States, the conservative line has dominated American policy statements for several decades now.[9]

Because these issues are strongly politicized within American discourse, politicians there tend to approach social, economic, and cultural issues as separate from human rights.[10] This (conveniently) removes them from a domestic to a foreign policy issue. Thus the dominant American rhetoric on human rights remains largely directed outside the United States, typically through condemnation of any nation that fails to implement Western models according to articles 1 to 21. Self-congratulation is presumed. Even less commendably, American conservative politicians have tried over some years to discredit the United Nations itself as an institution capable of delivering credible statements on behalf of "the international community." Americans may well deplore high unemployment or unaffordable health care, but they are not used to thinking of these as human rights concerns. The Chinese do.

On the Chinese side, human rights concerns come across very differently. The PRC has long insisted that it is making progress on human rights as it moves beyond its origins as a poor, underdeveloped country. It boasts, with considerable justification, of increased literacy and schooling, of improvements in health care, rising incomes, and virtually full employment. These are precisely the concerns of articles 22 to 27 in the Universal Declaration. Their emphasis underlines core Chinese values that, by their very nature, are resistant to those articulated by the West.

RESISTANT CONCEPTS IN CHINA

Ren (仁): What Is "Human"?

The reasons that such concerns take priority in China follow from long-held cultural orientations, as traced through the ten key concepts that are the primary focus of this book. In China, the word for *humanness* or *ren* (仁) combines two characters. One is the sign for a person; the second is literally the number two. The implication is clear: one cannot become *human* on one's own. Becoming human always involves at least one other person. Thus *human rights* must always be rights that involve another; in other words, such rights must evolve within a community.

Why aren't rights seen as inhering in a single person? Although there is a word for "I" in the Chinese language, that "I" is always defined through its relationships. As the analysis of *mianzi* makes clear, the self is a collective noun: one cannot become a person, any more than one can be human, outside of one's relationships with others. Thus rights defined as inhering in the "individual" make little sense in traditional Chinese thinking.

Xiao (孝): Roles versus "Rights"

"Human rights" evolved in the West from the secularization of Christian core values that emphasized the importance of "soul" or the "essence" of an individual person. As "rights" in China are deemed not to inhere in individuals but only to emerge through relationships, they are traditionally defined in terms of roles and duties. Within the concept of *xiao*, these duties are defined as obligations toward one's elders/superiors in what is an inexorably hierarchical world. Although one may be considered to be owed certain considerations, these do not flow automatically from simply being born. They must be achieved through one's behavior in the world and are always bound up with one's duties. Consider, by way of contrast, how in the West the rhetoric of duty (or responsibility) is often detached from that of "rights," the latter considered inherent (or "unalienable") for each and any individual from birth onward.[11]

Yi (易): Pragmatic versus Principled Rights

As such, "rights" in China are not seen to flow from first principles—but rather are constituted as a matter of cultural practice. Thus, though human rights issues are often perceived in the West as essentially political or ideological, in China they go right back to its fundamental ways of thinking about the world. Since reality, according to *yi*, is constantly changing, nothing can be stable for long. Given that everything is changing—and, through *Dao*, everything is connected—government must be, above all, pragmatic, prepared to confront challenges as they arise, and therefore not bound by inflexible first principles. In the Chinese world, in other words, nothing is "eternal" or "inevitable." Rights emerge as the situation demands and fade as the situation changes.

Mianzi (面子): Policies and Consequences

As an instructive example, one might look at the evolution of the "one-child" policy. In the early days of the PRC, Mao Zedong encouraged married couples to have many children—"to make China strong." As a result, the population nearly doubled from 1949 to 1979.[12] To counter this demographic disaster, a few years after Mao's death in 1976, Deng Xiaoping launched a process of reforms, prominent among them the one-child policy. Although this policy—and the freely available abortions that reinforce it as a backup means of contraception—are abhorrent to many in the West as a gross infringement on human rights, Chinese thinking acknowledges such policies as a necessary restriction of individual choice to achieve a greater communal good. The goal was, initially, for China to be able to feed all of its people. The secondary goal, still operative at least rhetorically, is to realize "socialist values," that is, serving the best interests of the collectivity. Later, after the loss of political capital in the Tiananmen events of June 1989, the Party moved to another discourse, committing itself publicly to delivering material prosperity to "the vast majority" of people and a return to national greatness after a century of humiliations.[13]

In defending its pragmatic emphasis, the Party tends to blame any shortcomings in human rights on the continuing emergence of China from poverty. Toward their own people, they preach patience to those low down in the socioeconomic hierarchies, with the promise that a rising tide will lift all boats. Thus the value of *he* in maintaining "social harmony" is not an optional slogan but an obligatory social practice. Rebelliousness, however expressed, threatens *luan*. Since chaos visibly undermines progress for everyone, the authorities feel justified in suppressing any signs of it, harshly if necessary.

Social criticism is also suppressed for specifically Chinese reasons. State leaders there feel they cannot govern effectively if they lose face. Thus any critiques that might undermine *mianzi* are not permitted in public. One may complain but not criticize. To act otherwise would seem to threaten *xiao* or the respect that keeps the entire hierarchical machinery functioning. Based on the model of families, *xiao* obliges inferiors to honor superiors in all domains of life. Everyone is expected to live within hierarchies, but honoring the hierarchies in one's life also brings benefits according to one's position. Thus any protests today are not conceived as revolts; almost always directed against what are seen as abuses by local officials, they represent a plea to the central government to set these injustices right. "What is not politically possible," Arthur Kleinman's analysis concludes, "is protest against the central government itself."[14]

"Tank Man" near Tiananmen Square (1989). *Source:* Photograph by Jeff Widener, used by permission of Press Association Images (UK).

If such protest occurs, it is quickly eradicated from public consciousness, as in the enforced amnesia about the events around the protests on June 4, 1989, surrounding Tiananmen Square. The photo above famously shows a single Chinese man defying the advance of People's Liberation Army (PLA) tanks on Chang'an Avenue near the Square. This image has always been banned in China.

In the West this image has become iconic. Why? Arguably, it is less a case of systematic censorship in China than a difference of values. For Chinese dissidents, this action encapsulated the singular courage of those at Tiananmen Square during the events of spring 1989. For many, it recalled the May 4th movement in 1919, the student-led demonstrations that came to define what it meant to modernize China. As such, this individual signified the greater collective movement of which he was a tiny part.

For the Chinese authorities, on the other hand, this action was a preposterous attempt of an individual to block a legitimately ordered military intervention in what those in power judged to be the national interest. Hence the image remains censored and the name and fate of this man remain uncertain.[15] Presumably he was executed soon after these events, but to confirm that publicly might risk his being honored as a martyr.

For its Western audience, this image remains well known and loaded with significance. "Tank man," as he came to be called, crystallized all the values that Henry David Thoreau, in a phrase from his classic essay on civil disobedience, called "the majority of one."[16] By this he meant the power of a single individual to transform civil society by standing against its machinery in the name of a higher law or principle. By allowing the state to use its machinery against him (in Thoreau's case, it was a matter of being thrown into jail for failing to pay a war tax), his gesture of passive resistance exposed its actual violence as well as the dubious ends that violence was designed to protect. His ultimate appeal was to a principle of "right" or "conscience" as borne out by an ideal justice. As Thoreau states in the conclusion of the essay, "The authority of government . . . to be strictly just . . . must have the sanction and consent of the governed. It can have no pure right over my person and property but what I concede to it. The progress from an absolute to a limited monarchy, from a limited monarchy to a democracy, is a progress toward a true respect for the individual."

Thoreau's version of Western democracy pushes its principles to their logical conclusion. Clearly, in China, "respect" in Thoreau's sense is reserved for the collectivity and its *mianzi*, values completely at variance with any actions of an individual that might embarrass or shame it. Hence radical modes of protest are chosen only by a very few who must know they are defying not only the full force of central government but also the dominant social values that support it.

How to Understand Chinese Dissidents

Such thinking applies as well to the most well-known case in recent years: that of Liu Xiaobo, awarded the 2010 Nobel Peace Prize while serving an eleven-year prison term for "inciting the subversion of state power." At the time, Western media leapt to praise Liu and his collaborators for composing (and then signing) Charter 08, which called for remaking China into a Western-style polity.[17] Implicit in such Western championing of his cause seems to be the hope that China would cease to be China in order to become "more like us." In taking this stance, Western commentators have overlooked what can be learned from the long history of dissidence in China. From all that we have seen about China, it should be clear that China is unlikely to follow a Western route politically. Yet Liu Xiaobo and his colleagues felt compelled to strike out in favor of just such an implausible development. As they knew well, Western democratic concepts survive in China only in the discourse of idealistic dissenters, as exemplified by Charter 08. And as they surely realized in advance, their actions would lead to suppression and, inevitably, punishment. Thus Liu Xiaobo's decision to promote this document might be seen, given these circumstances, as the ultimate strategic choice. From this perspective, Liu Xiaobo fits not into the category of principled dissenters but into a tradition of Chinese martyrs whose admirable courage is celebrated within its long history.[18]

But, as of now, his story is being told only outside China.[19] Inside China, with official encouragement, Liu Xiaobo is widely dismissed as a common criminal—thus ensuring that, even among those who have merely heard his name, Liu Xiaobo has lost *mianzi*.[20] Like many Chinese expressions of dissent, his thoughts reliably find an audience only where there is secure cultural grounding for his eloquent protest, which means today, effectively, in the Western world.

Luan (乱): Avoiding Social Chaos

Given this strongly centralized authority, a grounding force in Chinese culture since its beginnings, the Powers That Be can trust that their control will not be seriously challenged as long as it can be seen as delivering prosperity and, along with prosperity, a palpable return to national greatness.

On the other side of the equation, every State leader is aware of the many dynasties throughout China's history that have been ended by revolutions from below, including the Guomindang Republic whose demise brought the PRC into existence. Thus, in its pragmatic adaptations to changing conditions, the Party must always keep its focus on the material well-being of ordinary people. But who are the "people"? With some reason, the Party worries publicly about such questions. The protests in the Tibetan and Xinjiang regions are here a case in point. How are their rights honored? The Chinese notion of "the people" implicitly refers to the majority group—the Han—in its population. In China, as opposed to the West, there is no evolved discourse for the Western concept of "ethnicity" as legitimizing the cultural practices/beliefs of certain minority groups.[21]

As in the West such differences are deemed to have a right to be protected, from a Western point of view the policies of the PRC State leaders toward the people of Tibet and Xinjiang are not readily comprehensible. Although the policies themselves do not insist that such ethnic groups be assimilated, current practices in both regions are taken by its native inhabitants as designed to undermine their traditional spiritual beliefs, culture, and language. There is very little hope of negotiation on this issue, as the attitude of central government is that (in the words of one China expert) "any surfacing of autonomous power groupings, whether based on geography or on economic or technical achievement, has been taken as a sign of dangerous centrifugal forces. China's experiences during the decade of civil strife in the warlord era reinforced their distrust of pluralism."[22] Invested in long-held values of cohesion and stability, the Powers That Be will predictably react forcibly to what they perceive as any regional or factional resistances to their control.

Thus, when protests turn violent—or toward self-violence—there appear to be two standard responses from State leaders. One, which applies especially to the native Uighur (or Muslim) population of Xinjiang, is that such protest is really a form of terrorism, linked to international Islamic radicals. Another, as in the case of Tibet, is that protest is simply not justified, given the new benefits that such populations enjoy. In general, it seems incomprehensible to the Chinese people as a whole that a "backward" ethnic group, such as Tibetans, should resist that "modernization" imposed on them by the larger polity in terms of better housing, better sanitation, and better education. Most Han people (that is, the official identity of more than 90 percent of the Chinese population) appear to think that ethnic minorities should, in fact, be grateful for the special privileges granted them: the right to have more than one child, special schools and sports facilities, and lowered points for admission to state universities. Given such special considerations, an insistence on ethnic difference seems not only ungrateful but actually perverse.

Other crucial questions as to what defines "the people" are raised by growing income disparities between rich and poor, urban and rural dwellers. What are the rights of these people? With an aging population, there is also growing concern about the lack of social support services, such as medical care and adequate pensions. Thus, in China, those *human rights* must involve continuing attention less to issues of principle involving individual rights than to urgent social problems—if the government of the day is to survive.

THE VIEW OF WESTERN-STYLE HUMAN RIGHTS IN CHINA

In 1985, Deng Xiaoping made unusually clear the enduring concerns of the PRC. Speaking to visitors from Taiwan, he first cited recent Chinese history to justify holding back from freedoms of speech:

> In 1980, the National People's Congress adopted a special resolution to delete from Article 45 of the Constitution the provision that citizens "have the right to speak out freely, air their views fully, hold great debates and write big-character posters"—a provision that had been added during the "cultural revolution." People who worship Western "democracy" are always insisting on those rights. But having gone through the ordeals of the ten-year "cultural revolution" [1966–1976], China cannot restore them. Without ideals and a strong sense of discipline it would be impossible for China to adhere to the socialist system, to develop the socialist economy and to realize the modernization program.[23]

Nowadays, while there might be less emphasis on "socialist" ideas, the preaching of "discipline" remains undiminished. It was clever of Deng Xiaoping to imply that this one provision of the Constitution could stand for the whole panoply of Western-style *human rights*. Also it was effective of him to invoke the horror, which still shadows the older generation, of the *luan* unleashed by the Cultural Revolution. Overall, the main idea is unmistakable: building up the country overrides all lesser considerations. Here is Deng's last word, memorable because for once it acknowledges Western priorities in human rights:

> Your view of the way we dealt with these few persons is different from ours, because you think of this question in terms of human rights. I should like to ask: what are human rights? Above all, how many people are they meant for? Do those rights belong to the minority, to the majority or to all the people in a country? Our concept of human rights is, in essence, different from that of the Western world, because we see the question from a different point of view.[24]

That "different point of view" is perhaps at its most Chinese when it rejects the notion that one person can represent a "people" or even "the human." In other words, such a person could never, as in Thoreau's phrase, constitute a "majority of one."

A CHANGING CHINA?

But with a new rising middle class displaying a new sense of entitlement, is the ground shifting? Despite what Deng Xiaoping meant by asserting that "different point of view," there have been some moves afoot in the PRC to improve citizens' rights in accordance with provisions of articles 1 to 21. In particular, legal language has been put in place using human rights code words familiar in the West. In 2004, amendments to the Chinese Constitution protected (significantly) private property and did actually mention "human rights."[25] Then in 2009 the PRC published a National Human Rights Action Plan of China, which includes the following promise under the heading "Rights of the Person": "China will improve its preventative and relief measures to protect citizens' personal rights in every process of law enforcement and judicial work."[26] Chinese spokespersons often complain that American critics fail to recognize this kind of progress. True enough, Western statements habitually deny to China any congratulations on such grounds. And in fact Chinese implementation remains spotty, proceeding as if official rhetoric alone could suffice to establish credibility.

The situation in China, then, includes the coexistence of resounding promises in official documents with sporadic enforcement or even contrary actions sometimes sanctioned by different agencies within the State apparatus itself. The reason contradictory notions of "rights" coexist in the PRC today is that the new capitalism has led to new life aspirations and, with them, a newly emerging sense of the rights of the individual. Since the 1980s, there have been significant institutional changes to economic life. The market has been substantially decollectivized, encouraging new entrepreneurial enterprises. Jobs are no longer assigned by the State. State-owned enterprises have been downsized, with a consequent growth of private-sector employers. Housing, along with education and medical care, now involve privatization. All these factors encourage the individual in China to engage in more market-based competition. By encouraging personal choice, these changes above all encourage Chinese people to think of themselves as consumers—and to demand those rights that protect them as such.

Thus, with this significant economic shift, has come what appears to be a move away from a sense of collective responsibility toward a more individualistic mentality. This new desiring and consuming self tends no longer to define itself only in terms of the other, and may even be seen as moving more toward the self-definitions of its Western counterparts.[27] Yet, despite such distinct differences between the older and rising generations, the key values of Chinese *xiao*, and with it, an emphatic consciousness of the collective nature of selfhood, still persist within contemporary Chinese culture today.

RESOLVING THE PRESENT IMPASSE ON *HUMAN RIGHTS*

As exemplified by the Liu Xiaobo story as well as in differing views about ethnic clashes in Xinjiang and Tibet, China and the West remain at loggerheads over human rights. Is it conceivable that such concerns could evolve beyond the present impasse? Yes. The present impasse serves no constructive purpose, because on both sides it authorizes those in power to encourage their citizens in exercises of mere self-congratulation. What would it take to move toward constructive dialogue? As a beginning, both sides, through their political leaders, would need to acknowledge the original complexity of the Universal Declaration definitions of human rights. But such moves would require distinctive shifts of position in each case.

On the Western side, this kind of evolution would require moving away from Cold War thinking toward greater acceptance of social, economic, and cultural rights as legitimate human rights concerns. The onus of change would affect primarily the United States. Most European countries, more liberal in providing for "social democratic" benefits, accept the principle that democratic political systems maintain a significant responsibility to sustain the least fortunate members of society, even at the cost of higher levels of taxation. Yet in the United States today, conservative voices continue to condemn Europe as "socialist," thereby hoping to do away with the issue.[28] To support the more constructive approach of human rights engagement by Western Europe, the example of the Danish Institute of Human Rights (which works through a multidisciplinary approach, targeting in particular the human rights impacts of business corporations) is a particularly valuable one.[29]

On the Chinese side, the impasse could be eased to the extent that State leaders would be willing to play down the role of the Chinese Communist Party (CCP) as the sole arbiter of national decisions. To do so would involve granting measures that allow some degree of leverage against the State on the part of individual citizens. However, this kind of concession goes against the grain in a State where consultation is strictly limited—and accountability so far is required only of ordinary people and rarely of leaders.[30] As we will see, possible shifts in such a direction pose a critical challenge for Chinese leaders, the outcome of which is far from certain. Human rights is only one confrontational domain where underlying tensions within the leadership surface.

For the moment, neither of these shifts in position seems very likely, but things can change. In reaching mutual understanding—or at the very least, in avoiding systematic misunderstandings such as those over the Universal Declaration of Human Rights—we can take inspiration from a sentiment widely if obscurely attributed to the Confucian tradition: the important thing is not how slowly it goes but that it does not stop.[31]

NOTES

1. Gianni Vattimo, *After Christianity* (New York: Columbia University Press, 2002), 98.

2. For further elaboration, see Peter Dabrock, "Drawing Distinctions Responsibly and Concretely: A European Protestant Perspective on Foundational Theological Bioethics," *Christian Bioethics* 16, no. 2 (2010): 128–57.

3. There were eight abstentions: six involving the Soviet Union and its client states, plus Saudi Arabia and South Africa, each for its own reasons. The text is available on the official website: "The Universal Declaration of Human Rights," United Nations, accessed April 2, 2015, https://www.un.org/. For further discussion in a comparative context, see *CCCW*, 402–4.

4. For relevant texts and responses by individual member nations, see "International Human Rights Law," United Nations Human Rights, Office of the High Commissioner for Human Rights, accessed August 13, 2011, http://www.ohchr.org/.

5. The representative was Chang Pengcheng, of whom Eleanor Roosevelt wrote in her memoirs, "Dr. Chang was a pluralist and held forth in charming fashion on the proposition that there is more than one kind of ultimate reality. . . . At one point Dr. Chang suggested that the Secretariat might well spend a few months studying the fundamentals of Confucianism!" See "The Universal Declaration of Human Rights: History of the Document," United Nations, accessed August 16, 2011, http://www.un.org/, which draws on Eleanor Roosevelt, *The Autobiography of Eleanor Roosevelt* (New York: Harper and Brothers, 1958), 317.

6. Noam Chomsky, "The United States and the Challenge of Relativity," in *Human Rights Fifty Years On: A Reappraisal*, ed. Tony Evans, 24–57 (Manchester, UK: Manchester University Press, 1998), 32.

7. Paula Dobriansky, "U.S. Human Rights Policy: An Overview," accessed August 20, 2011, http://www.disam.dsca.mil/.

8. Noam Chomsky, "Human Rights in the 21st Century," London School of Economics and Political Science, October 29, 2009, accessed August 20, 2011, http://www.lse.ac.uk/.

9. The relevant time marker is the brief period when the Carter administration tried to make human rights a central emphasis in U.S. foreign policy. This ended in 1979 with the election of Ronald Reagan.

10. Another more general reason is that Western mentalities habitually emphasize the differences between categories; then each domain can be approached solely on the basis of its own distinct characteristics. For example, the George W. Bush administration in the United States created a new designation for prisoners interned in Afghanistan: once they were categorized as "enemy combatants," they were no longer entitled to the protections accorded "prisoners of war" under the Geneva Conventions.

11. Sometimes this is even the case before birth, depending on how much the current legal system invests in a fetus.

12. This massive growth took place despite a terrible famine that cost perhaps as many as forty million lives or more. Estimates vary considerably, reflecting the lack of authorized research into the subject, but numbers of deaths tend to rise in the most recent studies. Major recent publications include Frank Dikötter, *Mao's Great Famine: The History of China's Most Devastating Catastrophe, 1958–62* (London: Walker, 2010); Xun Zhou, ed., *The Great Famine in China, 1958–1963: A Documentary History* (New Haven, CT: Yale University Press, 2012); and Jisheng Yang, *Tombstone: The Great Chinese Famine 1958–1962*, trans. Stacey Mosher and Gui Jian (New York: Farrar, Straus and Giroux, 2012) [original Chinese edition 2008].

13. For a large-scale analysis of how this narrative dominates Chinese concerns for both domestic and foreign policy, see William A. Callahan, *China: The Pessoptimist Nation* (Oxford: Oxford University Press, 2010).

14. Arthur Kleinman, "Introduction: Remaking the Moral Person in a New China," in *Deep China: The Moral Life of the Person; What Anthropology and Psychiatry Tell Us about China Today*, by Arthur Kleinman et al., 1–35 (Berkeley: University of California Press, 2011), 25.

15. It is hard to know how many people in today's China recognize this image; that is, it remains elusive to assess what is and is not known publicly in China when censorship is involved. Louisa Lim, in *The People's Republic of Amnesia: Tiananmen Revisited* (New York: Oxford University Press, 2014), reports that when she showed this picture to a total of one hundred students at four elite Beijing campuses, only fifteen recognized what it was. Of course, being students, they were young and the events took place long before their time. On the other hand, a recent incident suggests otherwise. In August 2013, the Canadian art troupe Cirque du Soleil performed in China on its Michael Jackson Immortal World Tour, celebrating the musical legacy of the U.S. pop artist who died in 2009. On August 14, 2013, the *South China Morning Post*, under the title "Cirque du Soleil Pulls Tiananmen Image from China Shows after 'Collective Gasp,'" reported that on August 9 before an audience of fifteen thousand in Beijing, the photo of tank man appeared on three large screens "for four seconds during Jackson's track *They Don't Care About Us* 'within a montage sequence of civil-rights style protest movements, resulting in an audible collective gasp from the audience,' according to a blogpost on *That's Beijing*, which has since been deleted." That "collective gasp" indicates that a significant number of those present recognized the image despite its censorship. The troupe seems to have been admonished but not punished. Its later performances in Shanghai and Hong Kong did not contain this slide.

16. Henry David Thoreau, "Civil Disobedience," in *Walden and Civil Disobedience*, ed. Sherman Paul (Boston: Houghton Mifflin, 1960), 244. The following quotation is from this source, 256.

17. Its demands, dating back to December 10, 2008, are summarized in "Charter 08," *Wikipedia*, accessed February 13, 2012, http://en.wikipedia.org/. The name emulated Charter 77 that had helped to galvanize Czechoslovak support for independence from the Soviet Union.

18. The story of Fang Xiaoru (1357–1402), who lived and died early in the Ming dynasty, for instance, has inspired comparisons with the martyrdom of Giordano Bruno in the West; see a model comparative essay on martyrdoms by Zi Zhongyun, in *CCCW*, CD, 701–8.

19. The recent Harvard University Press collection in English of essays and other works by Liu Xiaobo shows him to be an acute observer of the Chinese scene who is deeply committed to social and political justice. At the same time, he is under no illusions as to the fate of anyone who chooses martyrdom for such causes: "The decision of one person to pay a heavy price for the ideals he or she has chosen to pursue is insufficient grounds to demand that any other person make a similar sacrifice." Liu Xiaobo, *No Enemies, No Hatred*, ed. Perry Link, Tienchi Martin-Liao, and Liu Xia (Cambridge, MA: Harvard University Press, 2012), 27.

20. Note that when the Jesuit Matteo Ricci tried to bring Christianity to Chinese intellectuals in the late sixteenth century, he encountered a similar obstacle; he was asked how someone, such as Jesus of Nazareth, executed as a common criminal, could be worthy to be worshipped. See Jacques Gernet, *China and the Christian Impact: A Conflict of Cultures* (Cambridge: Cambridge University Press, 1985), 221–38; "Ming Critiques of Christianity," in *CCCW*, 510–14, 511.

21. The discourse currently is defined in terms of "nationalities" or official bureaucratic entities. The "national majority" (90 percent plus of the population of the PRC) is deemed to be Han. All other (non-Han) groups that have a distinctive language or cultural practices (including religion) are deemed to be "minority nationalities" (currently numbered about fifty-five). But what such terminology enforces is simply their relation to the majority culture and, thus, by apparently dismissing the differences between them, consciously enforces a model of assimilation. For tentative shifts in this policy, see chapter 14, "Question Four: Ruling the World?" note 4.

22. Lucian W. Pye, *Asian Power and Politics: The Cultural Dimensions of Authority* (Cambridge, MA: Belknap, 1985), 189.

23. "Bourgeois Liberalization Means Taking the Capitalist Road," *People's Daily Online* (English ed.), May/June 1985, accessed November 3, 2012, http://en.people.cn/; *CCCW*, 456–58.

24. "Bourgeois Liberalization."

25. This document included the statement "the State respects and protects human rights," but of course Chinese understandings of "human rights" were implicit. "Constitution of the People's Republic of China," *Wikipedia*, accessed August 16, 2011, http://en.wikipedia.org/.

26. "Window of China: National Human Rights Action Plan of China (2009–2010)," *China View*, April 13, 2009, accessed August 16, 2011, http://news.xinhuanet.com/.

27. Kleinman, "Introduction," 14.

28. The United States is so politically polarized these days that governmental responsibility for the marginalized sometimes seems as far behind us as in Franklin Roosevelt's America.

29. For further information, see their website: Danish Institute of Human Rights, home page, accessed April 3, 2015, http://www.humanrights.dk/.

30. An example is the recent rule requiring bloggers to register under their own names so they can be held accountable for whatever they post on their blogs. Restrictions of this kind are rarely enforced for China's high leaders.

31. This advice comes from, among others, Xunzi; see Edward J. Shaughnessy, ed., *Confucian and Taoist Wisdom* (London: Duncan Baird, 2010), 55.

13

Question Three

Democracy?

WILL CHINA EVER EMBRACE WESTERN-STYLE DEMOCRACY?

In its own terms, China (of course) already has "democracy." According to Party orthodoxy, since 1949 China has had *democracy* in the sense that the *demos*, the people, are said to be, at least nominally, in charge. The reasoning goes that, by virtue of that very Revolution, the people confided their leadership to the Chinese Communist Party as a "people's dictatorship." This arrangement continues to be justified as necessary, if only because so many people are deemed either uneducated or too busy or self-centered to be able to attend to the greater needs of the collectivity. The Party alone is qualified to do so. If there were more than one political party, it is argued, each would claim to know how best to govern.[1] As a result, the people could only become confused and divided. As a consequence, *hexie shehui*, social harmony, would be lost and, with it, a coordinated national effort for progress. *Luan*, or chaos—the worst fear of Chinese State leaders—would then surely overtake the nation, making conditions for prosperity impossible.

Obviously if Westerners are to understand Chinese governance, they need to make a special effort to suspend judgment. With our pride in modern "democracy" as a flowering of "modernity" and "progress," we are poorly prepared to acknowledge that Chinese governance has all the weight of its tradition—and values—behind it. The crucial historical facts are two. First, China for millennia has been governed by a single centralized authority structure. Labels have changed. Sometimes the centralizing authority has ruled over large domains, sometimes smaller; sometimes more strictly in control of its territory, sometimes less. But the basic model of centralized authority has never changed. Second, despite its recent and relatively superficial modernization, respect for tradition has allowed China to maintain a cultural continuity unique in the world. Thus a rhetoric of "progress" can be misleading in China.

There it is used primarily as a means of assuring the populace that today's State leaders have totally supplanted the former "feudal" models of the past. But from an outside perspective, their insistence on a single source of power simply offers a new variation on long-established modes of governance.

In fact, for China, a centralized authority structure has served as the norm for so long that its origins have been lost to history. Even when central government has appeared to fall apart (at the end of a dynasty or during a war-lords era, for instance), the model of a centralized power has remained, only to be replicated by competing "little empires" as centers of authority. No one can say whether that model of centralized authority came first or the Chinese culture that so broadly sustains it. Note that seven of our ten keywords actively support this kind of system. In the case of importing Western democracy into China, it is important to recognize what strong cultural barriers exist—and to acknowledge how they themselves determine what modes of governance *can* work in China.

A SHORT HISTORY

Such broadly centralized governance, as anchored in Chinese cultural orientations, was once part of the West as well. For most of its history, the West has been governed by emperors and monarchies—and it has experimented even more recently with strongly centralized rule under Napoleon, Stalin, and Hitler. These last experiments have failed, if only because such governance sharply diverges from what is now acceptable under modern Western premises. How sharply becomes evident from a brief history of how Western democracy emerged from what is known as "social-contract thinking" more than 250 years ago.

Its pivotal expositor was Thomas Hobbes (1588–1679). After the beheading of Charles I of England in 1649, Hobbes took on the task of inventing a new justification for monarchy. To replace a newly outmoded idea of kings ruling by "divine right," he posited a "state of nature" into which all humans were deemed to be "born free."[2] But that state of nature, he argued, was also a state of constant war, with one man pitted against another, each one seeking power and property. Under such conditions, life was (in his famous phrase) "poor, nasty, brutish, and short."[3] But, being rational creatures, Hobbes opined, such men would surely see it in their self-interest for each to give up some share of their inborn freedom by delegating it to a king—whose primary function would be to maintain law and order. In that way, all could prosper.

The next step was provided later in the seventeenth century by John Locke; he argued that if men had at some distant time chosen to be ruled by a king, then they could still exercise that right in the present—by choosing which man should become monarch. Again, his reasoning was politically motivated, closely implicated in the so-called Glorious Revolution of 1688 that brought William and Mary to power. But it represented an important moment in the process by which voting was gradually

Hobbes's frontispiece (top half only) from *Leviathan; or, The Matter, Form, and Power of a Commonwealth, Ecclesiastical and Civil* (London: A. Crooke, 1651). The image from the title page of Hobbes's book epitomizes his whole theory. The crowned king holds a bishop's crosier in his left hand, symbolizing the Church (of England, of which the monarch was and is still the head) with its moral-spiritual authority. In his right hand, he holds a sword, symbolizing the temporal power to enforce laws. The innovative feature of the image, however, is that the king's body is made up of a myriad of individuals; these represent the citizens whose common interest he is sworn to defend. *Source:* Special Collections, Harvard University.

to emerge as a means for citizens to exercise this new central right: that of choosing their own ruler.

By the eighteenth century another thinker, Montesquieu, again sought to extend the rights of the governed. He did so by arguing for dividing the monolithic power of the state into three branches, namely, the legislative, the executive, and the judicial. These would then operate as checks and balances on each other's prerogatives. By this time, the fundamental outlines of modern Western democracy had become clear, as first institutionalized in the United States. Over the next century and a half, these provisions have been implemented to one degree or another in almost all Western nations, though practice has tended to trail behind theory to one degree or another.

Given its recent evolution, then, Western-style democracy is likely to remain an ambitious, heavily theorized, and relatively fragile experiment, largely based on Enlightenment values distant to the rest of the world.

The Chinese, by contrast, never felt any great need to theorize different modes of governance. Their implicit starting point, anchored deep within the tradition, is that humans are born not "free"—but as helpless beings into families that must care for them. Babies do not come into the world with inborn rights. Nor do they ever acquire "rights" in an absolute sense except as inhering to their social role. To take up that role, they must first be civilized, first by families and later by the larger community. It is a long and laborious task,[4] as "humanity" is something to be achieved through self-cultivation and discipline. In such a worldview, "freedom" has no obvious place, nor does "equality," that other term central to Western thinking about politics in recent centuries.

Never highly theorized as in the West, Chinese reflections on the pragmatics of governance have a long and honored history. In particular, the writings of Kongzi and his disciples Mengzi and Xunzi have formed the basis of government goals and protocols for as long as anyone can remember.[5] In world terms, the modalities of Chinese government—as pragmatic, centralized, and authoritarian—are far more common worldwide than are those of Western democracies, which are still very recent and with outcomes that yet remain uncertain.[6] How Chinese modalities of government have been sustained over the centuries becomes clear when one considers both the cultural obstacles to Western-style democracy together with the conceptual props that promote strong centralized rule in China.

CULTURAL OBSTACLES TO WESTERN-STYLE DEMOCRACY

Xin versus Rational Choice

In Western democracy, the expectation is "one man, one vote." Today citizens in the West are asked to "make up their minds" about who governs them by voting for one candidate or another. But as we have seen, in China the conception of people's "minds" is quite different. There *xin* (or heart-mind) is key, as Chinese people do not routinely make a distinction between what we in the West call "rationality" as distinct from "irrationality." In China, when thinking through *xin*, personal feelings, including expressions of self-interest, can never be suspended.

In the West, however, the new political theories of the Enlightenment presumed that men (at first it was only men and only certain men) would exercise something called *reason*, as distinct from brute visceral instinct. This is a presumption still honored in Western ideologies today.[7] They argue that, as people are—at least in theory—able to respond rationally to choice, they deserve the right to be consulted about their own concerns as well as public affairs. Historically, the opponents of democracy argued the opposite: that democracy would result in mob rule ("mobocracy"), driven by the irrational instincts of the uneducated masses. These concerns yielded only slowly, as the West restrained for a long time the number and quality of those allowed to vote (women, for instance, long being considered too "irrational" to be allowed the privilege). But despite the kind of emotive politics on view in America today, the theory of democracy continues to presume that the people can and will make reasoned choices between alternative candidates or policies.

Chinese Decision Making through *Guanxi*

In practice, of course, there is some justification for these early concerns, particularly as voters in the West have become the target of an entire industry devoted to manipulating public perceptions of events. Nonetheless, the theory, now promoted to an ideology strongly reinforced during the Cold War period, continues to focus on the ideal rather than the actual state of "democracy." In stark contrast, in China the *individual* voter is simply inconceivable as the foundation of an overall system of governance.

What then are the prospects for Western-style democracy in China? Will its distinctive practices—of multiple parties, contested elections, open franchise (with all or most adults presumed to be voters), courts of law largely free from political influence, and so forth—along with Western-style capitalism, also infiltrate "communist" China? The most realistic response is that the odds are probably nil. Impressive work has been done in documenting the reformist and democratic aspirations in local government, for instance, immediately before and after the fall of the Qing.[8] But for all their efforts, these failed because the culture favored a centralized form of power. Much the same may be said of more recent attempts at local democracy: the fate of the Guangzhou village of Wukan being another such short moral tale.[9] Indeed, if one tries to imagine a Western-style contested election on the scale of China, the mind boggles. It would require a vast and unprecedented infrastructure of education, of party development, of regional coordination, and of linguistic consolidation—not to speak of new conceptions of individual agency, including the ability to "make up one's own mind."

However, on a local level, some such experiments are now being made. A demonstration of how grassroots decision making works in China is provided by footage from a Canadian Broadcasting Company production titled *China Rises.*[10] Within a section called "Party Games," a sequence covers a village election in Sichuan Province. There are two candidates. The incumbent village head is a woman who had galvanized the local economy by shifting production away from growing grains to growing flowers. Her male challenger is a garlic merchant. On election day, a brass band plays as everyone gathers around a table of higher officials, on hand to monitor the process. Off to the side (no doubt a concession to Western cameras), there is a lone polling booth. Once the election ballots are distributed, the villagers huddle together. Ignoring the privacy implicit in the election booth, they consult each other, in groups of families or *guanxi* networks, as to how to vote—then mark the papers in each other's presence. A perfect demonstration of Chinese "group thinking."

If democracy as defined in the West depends on one's *making up one's own* mind, what happens in a culture where one's mind is not, strictly speaking, one's own?[11]

Given that decisions in China are rarely made by oneself but only in consultation with others, how could Western-style democracy possibly take hold in China?

Accordingly, except in limited and local circumstances (such as village elections), ordinary heart-minds can never be understood as capable of rising sufficiently above immediate concerns to take on responsibility for decisions affecting the community as a whole. Only exceptionally educated and experienced individuals, with decades-long training in various spheres at lower levels of government, could be counted on to rise above such self-interested concerns. Today such individuals are, by self-definition, concentrated in the Party's State leaders.

Luan: The Constant Threat of Chaos

But the most powerful determinant of the Chinese mode of governance is *luan*—or social chaos. For Thomas Hobbes, the "poor, nasty, brutish, and short" lives of those without an adequate government justified creating a new social contract to hand over power to a king. Although the West tends to see such chaos as a relic of the past, even today, when polities find themselves under even hypothetical threat, central government finds itself strengthened: consider the shifts in civil-liberties legislation in the United States since 9/11. In China, *luan* or *chaos* is not hypothetical, nor relegated to the past, but represents a vivid, ever-present danger, arising from the primary role of *yi* or change.[12] If change as such is unrelenting, unpredictable, and uncontrollable, then heading off its potentially destructive chaos must be, by definition, a great preoccupation of governors. Therefore State leaders exhibit far less tolerance for dissent or other forms of social disorder than is the case in the West's turbulent democracies. When you consider it, perhaps ruling one-fifth of the world's people in an environment of floods, droughts, earthquakes, and other routine natural disasters might itself explain, if not justify, a low tolerance threshold for disruptions of every kind.

Indeed the threat of *luan* is confirmed by any sustained study of Chinese history. Time and again, a prosperous dynasty has failed to contain its enemies, internal or external, with chaos as the destructive result. Any governing power that takes this history seriously must work hard to avoid a similar fate. In the days of the dynasties, the quality of emperors was impossible to ensure: some were able; others incompetent or distracted. Today's State leaders arrive in positions of power only after long testing in positions of lesser responsibility. Those who advance have proved their loyalty time and again. But their loyalty is less to any ideology than to the prolongation in power of the organization that promoted them, the Party itself. Their justification, again, would be the necessity of social stability in the face of an ongoing threat of *luan*.

In recent years the Party has focused on further justifying its hegemony by delivering a brace of benefits: ongoing prosperity and a return to national greatness. Any threat to displacing the Party from its privileged position is regarded as a threat to these benefits. In any case, most Chinese are too busy, too over-stretched, and too preoccupied to deal with disorder in their own world. Many resent disruptions as an obstacle to their personal success within the context of these great national goals. They live in a world where they believe the duty of government is to govern—so they can get on with what they have to do. For this reason they are willing to appear compliant to a State that promises to ensure stability. It is a relationship defined by this exchange—another kind of social contract that legitimizes what Lucian Pye calls "the politics of dependency."[13]

Conceptual Props for Centralized Governance: *Xiao, Guanxi,* and *Mianzi*

Once one admits the premise that a strong central government is necessary to stave off chaos, other Chinese values apply. Derived from the basic virtue of *xiao*, these also serve to promote stability and harmony in this world. Such values are collective—and hierarchical. Foreigners should not be misled by a fading Marxist rhetoric of "equality." *Xiao* by its nature militates against any of its forms—another reason the democratic mantra of "one man, one vote" would carry little weight in this world. For in China, relations can never prevail between equals; even in the instance of twins, one must be born before the other and is thus "superior." As the thinker Xunzi observed more than two millennia ago, "Equality depends on inequality." If (as he argues) equality prevailed, then there would be no acceptable way of distributing scarce resources.[14] In a nation now of almost a billion and a half people, this argument has even more force, as in such a context even theoretical equality would pose a nightmare scenario.

On the other hand, as entailing due obligations and benefits in proportion to one's station in life, *xiao* guarantees that hierarchies will actually function. In turn, its practice reinforces *guanxi* relationships. Not only do these provide the individual with social support; they are usually the only leverage he or she can muster in what seems a vast impersonal system of governance. But nothing is really impersonal in China. The governing apparatus itself is a vast collection of *guanxi* networks, cobbling together lesser networks in shifting coalitions. Within each one, loyalty is highly prized. In this world, no promotion will occur without contributing to the agenda determined by one's next higher superior. Breaking ranks risks isolation from all accumulated privileges.

Strategizing calculations (*celüe*) also suggest that innovation can be risky. Anyone who deviates becomes a marked person in a world that privileges, in the rhetoric of recent years, "the vast majority of the people." The safest approach is deferential, visibly not making waves. Direct confrontation is foreign—that is, Western or barbarian, the two roughly synonymous to many in China. In all transactions, *he* harmony must be seen to prevail. Dissenters risk censorship or suppression because they violate the imperative of maintaining a smooth surface, thereby disrupting the *mianzi* deemed indispensable to effective governing in China. How much more threatening would be all those institutions peculiar to Western democracy—not only in politics but also in law and academic life—that involve the starkly direct (and often therefore *mianzi*-damaging) confrontations of debate?

The payoff for reinforcing such values is the assurance of social stability that allows State leaders to engage in long-term planning; this would be hard to implement in the West, with the abrupt shifts in leadership and those flip-flops of policy endemic to elected governments.

ARE WESTERN MODES MORE SUCCESSFUL?

As many Chinese tend to note, if China has problems, in the West democracies today are not flourishing either. In the United States, the political class seems to have abandoned one of the unspoken rules of democratic politics: that the public interest ultimately depends on compromise between contending political factions. For decades up until the 1980s or so, deal makers among elected representatives assured that party loyalties would not be pushed so far as to render the country ungovernable. Now extremists seem willing to sacrifice any national vision in hopes of furthering their own partisan convictions. Under such circumstances, the ability of democracy to deliver on its promises is severely compromised. The result is not governance but paralysis—a Western form of chaos—with the implicit threat of a dictator or a mobocracy to come.

As the current economic crisis has also made clear, another kind of problem looms large in Europe, resulting from the tensions between central authorities and their local counterparts. As an experiment in supranational governance, the European Union (EU) is now itself at risk because a number of national governments failed to control greed and fiscal misbehavior among their own people. Of course, the failure to control has partly to do with the desire of such national governments to be seen as "successful" and therefore get reelected. The issues now seem to crystallize around how far national self-interest can be allowed to undermine the larger, collective public good. In other words, how can the damage be offset and ultimately contained?

Once again the outcome seems far from assured. Democracies by nature cannot react quickly to change; consultation is lengthy, exhausting, and expensive. Nor do democracies fare well when unpopular measures, such as fiscal austerity, need to be pushed through elected parliaments already riven by internal factions. Most of all, democracies no longer work well when their people are highly polarized into equally opposed ideological factions, as in the present United States. Under these conditions, the very idea of a social contract is under such pressure that the social fabric itself may well begin to unravel.

Whether and in what form Western democracies will survive the present economic crisis, not to speak of the coming ecological disasters, remains to be seen.[15] By comparison, China's response to the world financial and economic crisis of 2008 demonstrates clearly how the Party thinks and acts. Facing a decline in exports to floundering economies in the West, the People's Republic of China (PRC) launched a massive stimulus program, proportionately much larger than that approved in the United States. It provided vast amounts of money to build infrastructure. The goal was to avoid any large-scale unemployment of migrant workers, a ready source of social unrest. But in doing so, it also short-circuited environmental impact studies to facilitate new factory complexes to produce cement and other pollution-prone industries.

The PRC is now paying for this massive stimulus. Increasing inflation has become an especially sensitive issue, especially when it affects food and housing. There have also been instances of dramatic environmental degradation, particularly in terms of water and air pollution as well as food safety. Still, as a response to a major downturn, the Chinese fiscal measures have, overall, worked more effectively than either the American or the European responses. Whether it can now tackle its own almost overwhelming environmental issues effectively remains to be seen.

"DEMOCRACY WITH CHINESE CHARACTERISTICS?"

How then can one evaluate the future of Chinese governance? In response, three intertwined concepts seem indispensable, all beginning with the letter *P*: pragmatism, prosperity, and the Party. The Party is still called "Communist"—hence, uninformed outsiders may believe that Marxist-Leninist-Mao Zedong Thought still drives State leaders. The reality is that, although there remains a Maoist faction within the Party, in terms of actual decisions, pragmatism prevails. The Party will do whatever promises to deliver prosperity to large numbers of Chinese, including adopting substantial elements of a free-market economy. Early on in the history of the PRC, prosperity was not so important in Communist ideology; then it was revolutionary rigor. But this faded with the memory of the disastrous consequences of Mao's push for economic progress under the "Great Leap Forward": extreme poverty, famine, and chaos, as under the Cultural Revolution.

So why is prosperity suddenly so important? The answer is, it is not sudden. Prosperity is in fact the oldest Chinese standard for evaluating successful governance. All the major Chinese classics through 2,500 and more years, regardless of their alignment on other issues, point to prosperity as the ultimate test of how well rulers actually rule.[16] Today the Party understands that its ability to deliver prosperity is crucial to its remaining in power. Phenomenal sustained growth rates measured in gross domestic product (GDP) are not an option but now a requirement. More equitable distribution of the increased wealth may well be deemed desirable, but that still remains secondary.[17] On this reinterpretation of what it now means to be prosperous, "communism" dies a hard death.

For ordinary Chinese, this promise of increasing prosperity more than compensates for an apparently monolithic one-Party rule. It is not altogether clear that trickle-down prosperity works (at best slowly and unevenly). But it can still be held up as an aspiration, as can the hopes of a growing class of ambitious entrepreneurs. Increasing national wealth also brings international importance. As the second-largest economy in the world, China is now taken seriously by other nations, a sign of rising foreign stature in which all can feel pride.

In terms of democracy with Chinese characteristics, however, the future is more uncertain. Westerners routinely assume that importing a version of Western capitalism would automatically open the door to Western democracy as well—a dubious expectation. The Hong Kong demonstrations in autumn 2014 dramatize just how difficult it is to negotiate a middle ground between Chinese and Western concepts of "democracy." On one side, the Hong Kong protesters interpret in a Western fashion the 2007 promises by China of "free elections" in 2017 to imply not only universal suffrage but also open choice of candidates. The PRC version, however, spelled out in more detail in September 2014, involves a broadly inclusive electorate choosing among a few candidates all preapproved by a committee dominated by business and conservative interests.

Hong Kong is precious to the PRC for access to worldwide capital markets on the basis of international accounting standards. But that economic advantage would appear to be at political risk if the Party should lose control over who heads the local regime. These issues are not new: the PRC is correct to point out that Hong Kong as a British colony before 1997 was *never* governed according to Western theories of democracy. On the other hand, the Basic Law governing its transfer to the PRC allowed some hope that, over time, Western-style practices might be installed. The demonstrations reflect both impatience and a loss of trust that the future will evolve in a more liberal direction. For a long time, the situation reached a standoff, with protesters still camped in parts of the main business areas and with Beijing authorities increasingly tightening their grip. As a situation, Hong Kong is thus exemplary. Remaining both inside and outside China, it inhabits just that kind of culturally hybrid space that satisfies the ideological interests of neither side. In the meantime, the PRC government clearly feels it must assert its dominance in order to impress Hong Kong with its new status as now officially inside the central controls that have always defined national China.

AN IMAGINED FUTURE

Rather than basing perhaps naive hopes for some future "democratic" China, one may learn more about Chinese governance by working out an imaginative China-based vision of its future. Such a vision has been offered by Professor Daniel A. Bell of Qinghua University. Canadian by origin, he is the first foreigner to fill a professorship of political philosophy in the PRC. Imagining how Chinese and Western versions of government might be combined, he posits a bicameral legislature. Roughly in parallel with Western practices, the lower house would be elected proportionally to population. The upper house, however, would follow a more traditional Chinese line: made up of individuals who scored well on a new type of national examination, one that would combine mastery of traditional Chinese texts with competence in Western-style analytical reasoning. Appointments to the upper chamber would be for long terms, insulating the senators from electoral pressures. While the lower house could propose legislation, the upper house would retain a crucial decision-making mandate, so that its attention could remain focused almost exclusively on the long-term well-being of the nation.[18]

As Bell is fully aware, the PRC does not show any signs of moving in this direction. But this vision clarifies in Western terms the emphases that remain distinctively and enduringly Chinese. Regardless of the changes that may take place, they will never make China into a Western polity. Nor should they. Long before it became a nation, China founded a civilization, one that has endured with similar modes and values for millennia. As a civilization with core values very different from those of the West, China continues to proceed along its own trajectory. Whenever Chinese modes of governance come up for discussion, that distinctive trajectory must be taken into account.

NOTES

1. Despite the official existence of eight other "democratic parties," the Chinese Communist Party is the only one that counts.

2. Of course Hobbes did not originate the idea of humans being "free" at birth. This affirmation was part of Roman law, as codified by Justinian in the sixth century. But there being born "free" meant being born "not enslaved." *CCCW*, 397. Hobbes is launching a broader modern concept of "freedom" that sees humans as free to reason about their condition.

3. Thomas Hobbes in his *Leviathan; or, The Matter, Form, and Power of a Commonwealth, Ecclesiastical and Civil* (London: A. Crooke, 1651), in *CCCW*, 397.

4. One of the great exponents of this idea was Zhu Xi (1130–1200) during the Song dynasty. His writings proved influential even into the twentieth century. *CCCW*, 44–47.

5. For further elaboration, see chapter 8, "Thinking in Harmony: *Hé*."

6. See the beginning section titled "The West Is WEIRD," in Part III, "Rethinking the West."

7. See Lucian W. Pye, "The False Dichotomy of Rational-Nonrational," in *The Mandarin and the Cadre: China's Political Cultures* (Ann Arbor: University of Michigan Center for Chinese Studies, 1988), 15–20, for a devastating critique of the "myth" of rationality in Western political culture.

8. See John H. Fincher, *Chinese Democracy: The Self-Government Movement in Local, Provincial, and National Politics, 1905–1914* (New York: St. Martin's Press, 1981).

9. See "Wukan Democracy Leaves Village Divided," *South China Morning Post*, February 15, 2013; and "Wukan Villagers Decry Vice-minister's Mixed Message on Free Polls," *South China Morning Post*, March 14, 2013.

10. *China Rises*, 2 DVD set (coproduced by the Canadian Broadcasting Corporation, the *New York Times*, and Zweites Deutsches Fernsehen, 2007).

11. Earlier chapters (2 and 3) on *mianzi* and *guanxi* make this point in detail.

12. For comparative cultural perceptions of the dangers of "primitive power" or chaos as between China and the West, see Lucian W. Pye, *Asian Power and Politics: The Cultural Dimensions of Authority* (Cambridge, MA: Belknap, 1985), 32–39.

13. Pye, *Asian Power*, 86–89.

14. *CCCW*, 407.

15. Naomi Oreskes and Erik M. Conway, in their science-fictional analysis of today's world as seen from the Second People's Republic of China in the twenty-fourth century, imply that China, with its more authoritarian governance, will manage to survive the late twenty-first-century collapse of the West. *The Collapse of Western Civilization: A View from the Future* (New York: Columbia University Press, 2014).

16. For example, according to *Daodejing* 57 (offering advice on good governance as nongovernance), "the sage says, 'I disturb nobody and the people of themselves become prosperous.'" As translated by Wang Keping, trans., *The Classic of the Dao [Daodejing]: A New Investigation* (Beijing: Foreign Languages Press, 1998), 246.

17. In recent years, the Gini coefficient in China has worsened considerably, bringing it into approximate parity with the Western country with the fastest-growing income disparities, the United States (Brazil is higher; European countries, notably lower). For a graphic display of the Gini index for various countries since World War II, see "Gini since World War II," *Wikipedia*, accessed February 4, 2012, http://en.wikipedia.org/. Since the year 2010, the PRC has refused to confirm officially its Gini coefficient. Estimates for 2012 from the *South China Morning Post* suggest it may have risen as high as 0.6, the level of Brazil; if so, it has moved higher than the United States at approximately 0.5 (by far the highest among major industrialized nations). "Wealth Gap Puts China among World's Most Unequal Nations, Survey Reveals," *South China Morning Post*, December 11, 2012, accessed December 22, 2012, http://www.scmp.com/. Experts generally affirm that any readings above 0.4 indicate risks of social unrest.

18. Daniel A. Bell, "Taking Elitism Seriously: Democracy with Confucian Characteristics," in *Beyond Liberal Democracy: Political Thinking for an East Asian Context* (Princeton, NJ: Princeton University Press, 2006), 152–79. Bell has now also been named to the Zhiyuan chair, Institute of Arts and Humanities, Shanghai Jiaotong University.

14

Question Four

Ruling the World?

DOES CHINA SEEK TO RULE THE WORLD?

Why do people in the West feel this is a serious question? Largely because many here presume any powerful nation will follow Western models, that is, seeking to dominate as large a segment of the planet as possible. For several centuries now, at least in Western eyes, this is what successful nations do. Then why should a rising China act differently than a France, a Great Britain, or the United States in their most imperialist phases?

Today whole books abound (usually focused on the United States) deploring the seemingly irreversible "decline of the West" as resulting from the equally irreversible "rise of China."[1] Reinforcing such expectations, many Westerners are fixated by stereotypes of a Cold War image of the Chinese, as memorably captured by the episode of Homer Simpson's visit to the People's Republic of China (PRC).[2] Here is an updated version of the Yellow Peril: Homer is shown bound and gagged against a background of heavily armed robotic troops ready to follow fanatical leaders in a world where individual initiative is brutally suppressed. Small wonder that there is so much fear of China as an expansionist power.

Despite the stereotypes, it is almost always a mistake to read Chinese ambitions as echoes of Western-style imperatives. On the other hand, no one should swallow whole the whitewashed version of Chinese history being marketed these days by the PRC itself. Versions of the "peaceful rise of China" currently being promoted, both inside and outside of China, depict the PRC as a benign, unaggressive presence in its region. But there have been notable periods in Chinese history of aggressive expansion. The most prominent of these were the Western Han dynasty of the late second century BCE under Emperor Wudi; the early Tang dynasty (sixth and seventh centuries); the early Ming (fourteenth and fifteenth centuries); and the early Qing (seventeenth and eighteenth centuries). Note that it is only during the early years of their hegemony that these dynasties pushed out their spheres of control: a common feature of Chinese dynastic cycles—which may or may not apply to postempire China. What this history does imply is that China is much more complex than any easy simplifications about it. But for all its complexity, this history does not support an imperialist reading of China's twenty-first-century aspirations.

"INSIDE" AND "OUTSIDE" CHINA

What is crucial in assessing its future is China's determination to maintain a strategic traditional distinction between the *inside* of Chinese culture and its *outside*. In their own world, Westerners have no precedent for such views. For centuries now, the West's values and practices have been promoted as "universal" and, as such, exportable to any part of the world in which Western influence prevails. The Chinese take a different view. Despite their determination to "civilize" those ethnic minorities they deem as "inside" their own world, the Chinese have never tried to make everyone in the world over into ersatz Chinese. No one in China pretends that its core values are, or even should be, "universal," though they clearly believe that the world would be a better place if Chinese practices were applied more widely. On the contrary, China has exerted great energy over many centuries in separating out what is "inside" from what is "outside" its cultural sphere.

The outward and visible symbol of this dividing line is the Great Wall of China. Begun in segments more than two thousand years ago—then massively rebuilt five hundred years ago under the Ming dynasty—this fortification, under current Chinese rhetoric, is described to the world outside as purely defensive, that is, as an epitome of China's "peaceful rise." Of course, the situation is rather more complicated than that. But the basic point remains. Unlike powerful Western countries, China has never tried to dominate the world. On the other hand, it continues robustly to differentiate between Chinese "insiders" and foreign "outsiders."

This line is so crucial that it has never been understood as a simple division of inside from outside. As a metaphor for its complexity, the image below shows the oldest Chinese "map" of the world, dating from roughly the sixth century BCE (hence during the period when the Zhou dynasty nominally controlled China). It does not depict any actual geographical reality. Instead, what it delineates are conceptual zones detailing the different degrees to which Chinese culture is deemed to have prevailed throughout the known world.

In the center is the "imperial capital." The first outer zone (1) consists of domains where its control is direct. The second zone (2) contains those tributary feudal princes who owe allegiance to the central power. Third is the "zone of pacification" (3) where Chinese civilization is in the process of being adopted. Fourth is the zone of barbarians who maintain at least nominal alliances with the center (4). Last (5) is the zone of what Joseph Needham translates as "cultureless savagery." No "terra

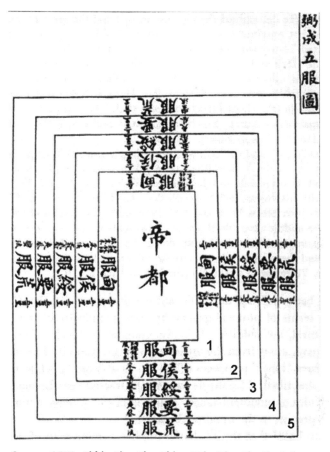

Source: SCTS: Chhin-Ting Shu Ching [Qin Ding Shu Jing], imperial illustrated edition of the Classic of Documents, 1905, as identified by Joseph Needham, in *Mathematics and the Sciences of Heavens and Earth*, Science and Civilisation in China 3 (Cambridge: Cambridge University Press, 1959), 502.

incognita" here: that would acknowledge something as actually existing outside of Chinese categories. Here the outermost zone is already labeled as lost to any possible redemption through an association with, and therefore potential future assimilation of, Chinese culture.

What makes this conceptual map of the world important even now, two and a half millennia after its initial publication, is that it still helps us understand the thinking that dominates Chinese responses to the larger world. In that sense it lays out a specifically Chinese view we can use to untangle the contradictions outsiders see in Chinese policies and practices as they unfold year by year. Clearly the key to differentiating zones is the degree of control the center is able to exercise in each case.

The Innermost Core: *Zhongguo* or the Central Kingdom

Here at the center of *Zhongguo*, the central kingdom, reside the rulers themselves: in today's terms, the 5 to 6 percent of the population who belong to the Party. Here control is axiomatic, operating through *xiao, mianzi,* and *guanxi* to maintain and perpetuate the political hierarchies by co-optation. Though corruption scandals may trouble the functioning of these hierarchies, rebellion is not a concern. Its power struggles will be resolved, when and if they are resolved, internally and under a veil of secrecy, to present an untroubled face to the rest of the world. Hope of upward mobility within the apparatus is expected to keep almost everyone in line, though strategic risk taking may on occasion disrupt the smooth surface.

Layer 1 and Layer 2: Domains Where Central Control Is Well Established

During the early decades of the People's Republic, the priority was to bring under control a variety of recalcitrant groups, variously identified as *feudal landlords, capitalist roaders,* or *bourgeois liberals.* This work was largely successful, though vigilance remains undiminished for fear of failure to foresee future pockets of opposition.

One mark of this control is the insistence that all of China, which by world standards would merit four or five time zones, is obliged to keep to a *single* time zone—Beijing time, of course. The populace within these inner zones is governed, as we have seen, by a combination of carrots and sticks. Positive encouragement, as in campaigns for public service or slogans of moral-political exhortation, promotes voluntary contributions to *he* harmony. Alternatively, the fear of *luan* chaos regularly surfaces to encourage solidarity. Outsiders regularly misread the dominant mantra of "social harmony" as passiveness on the part of most Chinese. On the contrary, it represents an actively strategic awareness that opposing the Powers That Be would gain little but risk much.

Layer 3: Pacification Zone Where Chinese Culture Is Being Adopted

Today the outer boundaries of this zone are the national frontiers of the PRC. Within those borders, the inner layers compose the Han majority, said to exceed 90 percent of the population. But the other fifty-five "minority nationalities" often prove troublesome in their resistance to conforming to Chinese cultural practices.

In relation to Tibetans and Uighurs, in particular, the contradictions in Chinese discourse are striking. On the one hand, the Party insists that these are Chinese citizens and the nation is indivisibly *one.* Thus, from inside the PRC, Chinese people often express bafflement at Tibetan resistance to Han hegemony. From their point of view, Tibet has received extraordinary benefits as a backward "feudal" world that is being "modernized," bringing in higher incomes and "development." Tibetan students receive extra admissions points on the national college entrance exam (*gaokao* 高考), and Tibetan families, like other minority nationalities, escape the one-child restrictions imposed on the Han majority. Han incomprehension is understandable, if only because all fifty-five non-Han groups are defined as "national minorities," a political designation—not a cultural one. As already noted,[3] a Western discourse concerning *ethnicity*, implying distinctions among cultural identities, is not accepted within the PRC—so attempts by any special group to maintain its own native language or spiritual beliefs in the face of an obviously superior Chinese civilization seem to many merely perverse. Instead, "national minorities" are encouraged to market their exotic status to profit from internal Han tourism.[4] In other words, they are expected to conform to the priorities of the larger, majority culture.

In cases of unrest in these regions, security forces are deployed rapidly. In relation to ongoing tensions over Tibet, the line between inside and outside is particularly sharp. The Dalai Lama is physically outside but influential inside the Tibetan culture zone. Therefore he is regularly condemned as "splittist," despite his announced willingness to abandon all claims for Tibetan independence in order to negotiate for some form of cultural autonomy that might ensure the continuity of Tibetan language, culture, and religion. In agreeing to negotiate with representatives of the Dalai Lama and the Tibetan government in exile in Dharamsala, the Chinese authorities played an *outside* card in a game that remains essentially *inside* from their point of view. Not surprisingly, nothing positive has emerged from these negotiations, because China insists on total control inside its own parameters.[5]

Though the word "negotiation" may be mentioned on these occasions, largely as a sop to Western sensibilities, the center clearly sees the pacification zone as in the process of becoming "Chinese." In the meantime, control is asserted as harshly as necessary. Westerners should note that, in general, the harshest controls apply in these regions, to enforce their conformity to what most Chinese regard as the "higher" civilization.

Layer 4: The Zone of "Allied Barbarians"

In today's terms, these are China's Asian neighbors, with whom the PRC entertains shifting relations. These relations depend on the current flow of events and on which Chinese spokespersons dominate public discourse at any given moment. There is always potential for a cultural appeal to neighbors who share Confucian heritages—such as Vietnam, the two Koreas, Singapore, and Japan. But this appeal tends to be complicated by lurking rivalry, such as those over small islands that might give access to undersea oil or mineral deposits. Specifically, flash points with Japan are those contested islands (in Chinese, the Diaoyu; in Japanese, the Senkaku) that have been the locus of several nasty incidents from 2010 onward. Similarly, on the

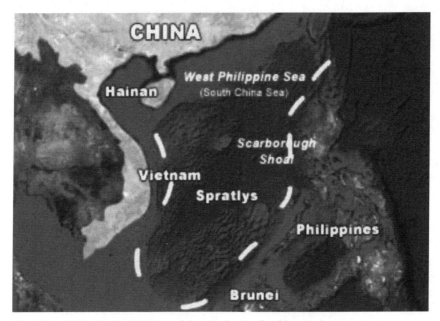

The "Nine-Dash Line" of Chinese claims in the South China Sea.

southeast side of the PRC, Vietnam, the Philippines, and even Malaysia and Brunei claim access to some of the uninhabited islands in the South China Sea—again, locations that may or may not offer access to petroleum or other mineral deposits.

Contradictions abound in Chinese statements on these issues, reflecting internal conflicts at the highest level on how to proceed. When military leaders speak, they threaten unilateral action that would, in effect, treat these islands as part of the "pacification zone" (see layer 3). When the Foreign Ministry controls the discourse, their watchword is "negotiations among equals," thereby assimilating these islands to the outermost zone (see layer 5) where negotiation is the most that China can hope for in dealing with the "cultureless."

Early in the Xi Jinping presidency, the military have clearly gained some traction, resulting in the authorities on Hainan Island issuing strong warnings to the ships of other nations to stay out of the zone claimed by the PRC. The Foreign Ministry seems to have yielded to this pressure, at least for now, by issuing new (and to outsiders, controversial) passports that include a map showing Chinese sovereignty extending far out into the South China Sea, as defined by what is known colloquially as the "Nine-Dash Line."

Since the Chinese have so far refused all moves to refer the disputes to the World Court or indeed to any international intermediaries whatsoever (deeming these issues to be "internal" to the PRC), the conflicts are bound to continue and are likely to become more intense.[6]

Layer 5: Beyond the Pale

Because to Chinese minds "cultureless" means lacking in *Chinese* culture, this outermost zone includes the rest of the world. Here China hopes to establish a mutually profitable working relationship, so the mantra of "negotiations among equals" is regularly evoked. Given that there is no relationship of "equals" among Chinese hierarchies, the rhetoric might suggest that many of these negotiations are merely gestural.

But the Chinese idea of gestural also needs to be examined. Gestures in this world (as perhaps in all diplomacy) are important. For negotiations are not, as in the West, a matter of mere abstract principles or cogent arguments; they flow strongly from *xin* or heart-mind. In terms of foreign policy, therefore, these are best understood as "a structure of feelings," according to William Callahan, adapting a phrase from Raymond Williams.[7] The issues can never be reduced to merely rational policy considerations because, in Chinese views of the world, feelings are always involved. Friends do not want to hurt each other's feelings, right? So, in the logic of heart-mind, anyone willing to offend Chinese feelings must not be a friend. Such is the nature of interchanges between "equals" as seen from a Chinese perspective.[8]

When the outside entities are powerful, such as the United States and the European Union (EU), then it is recognized by all parties that working relations must require give and take. For example, China must be willing to loan vast sums of money to the United States in order to ensure that there will be no major restrictions on American orders for goods made in China. But the very success of these policies takes Chinese manufacturing to levels that surpass the resources available within its own country. China then turns to Africa and Latin America, moving to exploit their resources in return for aid and development projects. Unlike their Western counterparts, these offers carry no strings attached concerning such "universal" principles as Western-style human rights or democratic governance.[9]

Finally, the Chinese recognize that, where control is not possible, less assertive moves to establish national credibility work best. This understanding is central to China's moves in recent years to enhance its "soft power," now visible in the several hundred Confucius Institutes in universities around the world.[10]

PARALLEL LAYERING WITHIN THE PALE

The several layers from inside to outside Chinese culture unpacked here do have other parallels within the Chinese world. Maps of the old city of Beijing, for instance, show the walled Imperial Palace at its center, with differentiated zones extending out to the old city walls. Even now, the Party leaders still hold their meetings in *Zhongnanhai* at the old Imperial Palace gardens west of the actual Palace itself. Thus central power for the whole territory is seen to be centered literally at the heart of its capital city.

On a more abstract level, in terms of power, there are always differentiated zones of access to privilege. While Westerners often criticize the "Great Chinese Firewall" for its control over the Internet, Chinese authorities manage this interface more subtly than one might think. Those in high positions of responsibility are trusted with full uncensored access. Further down the governing elites, restrictions are imposed progressively. Thus university professors typically have broad access, but undergraduate students may well be confined to computer centers with China-only access to the Internet. Censorship over chat rooms, of course, applies to everyone. But the expectation is that highly placed individuals would have no interest in upsetting the systems in place, hence no interest in expressing themselves to undifferentiated low-status audiences. Thus the nature of hierarchy as it functions in China is to distinguish between levels of "inside" and "outside" in ways that remain unfamiliar or even invisible to Westerners.

A SHORT MORAL TALE

This inside-outside line shows up as particularly divisive when Chinese students study abroad. With exponentially increasing numbers doing so, some fear that when they return to China (as most do) they may bring unsettling ideas back with them.[11] Surprisingly, the opposite may be true. Many of these students react to foreign ideas not positively but with an enhanced sense of Chinese patriotism, underlining their solidarity as insiders even when they are outside the country.[12]

Accordingly, even while abroad, anyone dissenting from Chinese homeland viewpoints may be at risk, as when, at Duke University in 2008, a small pro-Tibet demonstration by Western students was met by larger numbers of Chinese students opposing it. Grace Wang, a freshman student from Qingdao in Shandong Province, eager to try out her new lessons in Western-style diplomacy, decided to mediate between the two groups by encouraging them to talk out their differences rather than simply clashing.[13] Her attempts to promote negotiations led nowhere—and worse: a systematic trashing of her status on the Internet. A photo of her appeared on a Chinese student website branding her a traitor and including her Chinese name, identification number, and directions to her home address. She was widely vilified in the Chinese blogosphere—to the point that her parents at home in Qingdao felt so endangered that they went into hiding. They were condemned as having failed to inculcate sufficient *xiao* in their daughter, leading to national embarrassment in a foreign country, in other words, an intolerable loss of national *mianzi*. This is just one example of the extreme nationalist feeling that may flare at any moment in China today.

What can we learn from this incident—echoed on other campuses with other issues at stake—but with similar patriotic solidarity among the great majority of Chinese students?

First, none of these Chinese students overseas were acting under orders, though they had been alerted that they would be seen as representatives of their country. Most took this situation seriously. Some probably hoped to gain credit for patriotism among the monitors within the Chinese student organizations back home. Certainly the aggressive bloggers back in China were exercising highly visible patriotism. They were seizing an occasion to demonstrate their national pride as *insiders.*

Second, Grace Wang was said by the Chinese students to be backing Tibetan independence, while she herself insists she was only acting to promote discussions so that the two sides could better understand each other and thus diminish their differences. Ironically, she was using the same rhetoric that Chinese authorities habitually put forward *outside* the Chinese culture line, for example, in international disputes at the United Nations Security Council.[14]

In conclusion, Grace Wang was whipsawed because she did not grasp the complexities of the *inside-outside* line. She was outside China geographically, but the issue of Tibet made the clash on the Duke University campus an inside, pacification-zone issue as far as her fellow Chinese students were concerned. In trying to apply the negotiations line appropriate to Chinese *outside* discourse, she was overwhelmed by *inside* pressures to defend Chinese leadership positions unconditionally. As the persecution of her parents suggests, the price of behavior deemed to be unpatriotic can be steep. Chinese people, more than most, can be wildly chauvinistic at any hint of outside pressure or criticism. In part, this is a consequence of the way Chinese history has been framed in recent decades. As far as history textbooks are concerned, the rise of China serves to compensate for a "century of humiliations," stretching from the first of many "unequal treaties" resulting from the First Opium War in 1842 up to the Japanese invasion that ended only in 1945.[15]

INTERNATIONAL POLICY: THE CRUCIAL VALUE OF *MIANZI*

Western nations live under a very different conception of history, in addition to a much freer political atmosphere. They are accustomed to thinking of their nations, despite many disagreements, as sharing the management of the outside world by sponsoring what they deem to be "universal" values. Thus, although they are ill prepared for seeing themselves as required to compromise with those whose worldview differs so radically from their own, they do not feel large issues of "face" are at stake. Dissent, moreover, has a recognized, even honored, place within the Western world. Americans, for example, may well express views highly critical of their own government or nation because they feel empowered, even called upon, to do so. Criticism might even be seen as a patriotic duty. No such presumptions apply in China because, for those on the inside, the pressures to demonstrate solidarity are overwhelmingly compelling. From outside the Chinese world, dissidents may gain sympathy from abroad—as in the case of Liu Xiaobo, particularly after gaining worldwide status as recipient of the Nobel Peace Prize. But inside that world, he was widely condemned as a criminal and, as damaging China's *mianzi*, a traitor to his country's standing in the world.[16]

With those both inside and outside the Chinese world, *mianzi* is clearly crucial. Since all of Chinese culture encourages thinking in strategical terms, they are well aware of the effective difference of expectations between "inside" and "outside." Inside, everyone is expected to conform to whatever conceptions and policies that State leaders are currently promoting. Any deviation invites condemnation as unpatriotic, a near synonym for "un-Chinese." Fundamental national unity is an item not just of conviction but also of active policing. Concerning outside relations, PRC rhetoric regularly calls for negotiation to settle conflicts. Thus, in international affairs the PRC commonly votes against military actions or even sanctions designed to put pressure on states that offend the dominant nations in the world. In particular, the PRC is sensitive toward any measure they deem as interference with the "internal" affairs of a state, reflecting their own priority of control over inside affairs.

But whenever the PRC itself becomes involved in negotiations, the line between inside and outside begins to blur. As two distinguishable mindsets come into tension, contradictory impulses may often surface as one or the other momentarily dominates public actions and statements. The *inside* view presumes (and enforces) top-down control. Dissent is not welcome and certainly not tolerated within the boundaries of the State itself. The *outside* view seeks compromises that will not hurt Chinese "feelings" (*xin*). These feelings are particularly sensitive on any issue touching what is seen as national sovereignty or international image. Although there may seem to be implicit tensions between these two orientations, both inside and outside views clearly stem from a new sense of Chinese nationalist pride—manifest in efforts to maintain *mianzi* at all costs.

Within their own world, this tension between maintaining *mianzi* and losing it must always be kept in mind as the dynamic of what William Callahan calls Chinese "sovereignty performances": ones balanced precariously between pride and humiliation, aspiration and anxiety—each response feeding off the other, on a personal as well as a national and international plane.[17]

This dynamic holds the key as to how the Chinese today identify themselves to the wider world. The important question, as Callahan argues, is not *What is China?* but *Who is China?* To ask *Who is China?* gets nearer to the logic of its relations with others. For as mentioned, China's presentation of itself to that world is not one implemented by abstractly formulated policies but defined according to *xin* as a *structure of feeling* in which reason and emotion are inextricably mixed.[18] When the Beijing authorities canceled the 2008 EU-China summit because then French president Nicolas Sarkozy "hurt the feelings of the Chinese people" by planning to meet the Dalai Lama, the statement was greeted in the West with bafflement and then with satire. What does foreign policy have to do with feelings? Pity the poor translator for the Chinese Foreign Ministry who tried to honor the heart root in *xin* by speaking of the "feelings" of the Chinese people, rather than incorporating its thinking aspect. The resulting English implies a childishness on the part of a people who would respond in such an impulsive fashion. But anyone attuned to the centrality of *xin* as both a moral and imperative force in Chinese thinking would have recognized that, in fact, no stronger objection could have been made. To "hurt the feelings of the Chinese people" is to wound their entire collective sensibility, moral and vital; as such, it injures their sense of *mianzi*, inevitably seeming to diminish Chinese face before the larger world. In other words, to offend its clear and stated policy on meeting the Dalai Lama was to offer an insult to China's own sense of self-worth.

What then legitimizes such policy statements? The Chinese leaders speak through *xin*. Understood as a collective sensibility, it allows the family to decide for the individual; local leaders to speak for the village; and the Chinese government to speak on behalf of the entire Chinese nation. Without an acknowledgment of how the personal merges into the political, Western policies concerning China continue to remain seriously ineffectual. In our world, most Westerners believe "reason" should dictate distinctions between private and public, as well as those between individuals, their primary groups, and the entire citizenry of a nation. As public discourse should be rational (or, at least, appear to be so), so we hold it should also appear both impartial and impersonal—invoking a cathedral of impersonal principles that we regard as "universal." By way of contrast, one expert says, simply, that in China "there is no way even to think about power as being in the service of policies guided by rational choice."[19]

Accordingly, the phrase that best captures China's dealings with others is thus one not of "policy implementation" but of "identity performance." But as such, it is inherently unstable, not least because, as *mianzi*, such a performance (by definition) ultimately places one's sense of worth in the hands of others and how *they* respond to what China does. All this underlines is basically how *insecure* the process of self-definition by means of *mianzi* can prove to be, as in this world of identifying oneself through others must mean that international perceptions of China will inevitably play into national perceptions.

Thus a consequent, radical insecurity operates on all levels. Most foreigners become aware early on in this world that any criticism or even *implied* criticism may lead to drastic loss of *mianzi*. Following the logic of the insider/outsider divide, critiques by the Chinese of themselves are usually deemed more acceptable, although they need to be handled very carefully. But this is not true of criticism from anyone defined as an "outsider," whether, say, from a minority culture or from a non-Chinese national—or even from a Chinese national living abroad. Thus, at times, China may appear almost pathologically sensitive to Western criticism. China, it is felt, has been "humiliated" enough by foreigners in the past. So it grounds its pride on extravagant displays of what it sees as "China at its best," as in the spectacular opening ceremonies of the 2008 Beijing Olympics. The motive, as defined for its domestic audience (in the mantra repeated by one of our colleagues) was "to earn some *mianzi* for the motherland."

DOES CHINA SEEK TO RULE THE WORLD?

Given its sense of itself as the "Central Kingdom," does China now aim to use its increased economic power to rule the world? No. China has enough trouble trying to rule China.[20] The multiple challenges to its future (as outlined in chapter 9 on *luan*) are overwhelmingly internal, from adapting a new kind of economic model, to deficits in social welfare, threats to social and civil stability, and a now disastrously degraded environment.

What remains the Party's most urgent mandate is maintaining iron control over whatever is defined as inside "China." But what is inside and what is outside? This is a crucial question in understanding official policies. Several concrete instances, such as China's claims to the small offshore islands at the center of recent disputes,[21] tend to play on its insecurity as to where national boundaries begin and where they end. In William Callahan's words, "China's twentieth-century maps exemplify the simultaneous appeal of two quite different readings of space: the ambiguous frontiers of the imperial domain and the clear national boundaries of the international system."[22] The fact that these are contradictory readings does not concern Chinese policy makers, who in formulating protocols for dealing with the outside world may invoke one or the other, or if necessary both.[23]

TOWARDS THE FUTURE

Territorial claims aside, China's overriding preoccupation now is in maintaining the stability of its own internal affairs, however defined. The three enduring elements, pragmatism, prosperity, and the Party, taken together, allow us to track what is likely in the future. That implies assessing the degree to which the Party has shown itself able to learn from its experience pragmatically en route to promoting prosperity. On inspection they have learned a great deal, though not enough to ensure a trouble-free future. The Party's attention will continue to center on the domestic sphere where its decisions will determine how far and how fast China moves outwardly to redefine the line between inside and outside.

The problem for the rest of the world is that ensuring prosperity at home now pushes China's leaders far afield in search of energy and raw materials. Expanding Chinese influence in countries all over the globe encourages assessments such as those of Juan Pablo Cardenal and Heriberto Araujo, who predict that China is pursuing "an unstoppable and silent world conquest that is set to change the course of human history."[24] This alarmist view ignores the risks China runs in making these investments.[25] Beijing did not seek out Africa or Latin America out of charitable impulses. It observed that Western corporations—after reiterated losses in Africa, for example—have largely come to see investments in such countries as unacceptably risky. That leaves Western aid agencies, national and international, as the only sources of significant funds for these countries outside of China. China, identifying a void worth exploiting, has stepped in to ensure its own ongoing economic growth. Its secret is not just having large amounts of money to invest but also its refusal, unlike the West, to prescribe how local governance should be organized. In these instances, the PRC's insistence on noninterference in matters of internal sovereignty is in sharp contrast to the missionary impulses characteristic of many Western nations in their interactions with developing countries.[26] The risks involved, in any case, remain much the same for China as they have been historically for the West, as exemplified by the uncertain future of their investments in post-Chavez Venezuela.[27]

One litmus test for how the PRC asserts inside policies in outside circumstances is its ongoing use of influence to constrain international recognition and sponsorship of the Dalai Lama. Given that China insists that Tibet, as part of the PRC, must have no distinctive cultural identity of its own, periodic "negotiations" have dragged on for years. There are no compromises in sight that might acknowledge the Dalai Lama's search for limited cultural and religious autonomy within that region. During the same time, strong diplomatic pressure from the PRC, backed by threats of economic or other reprisals, has in recent years led nations as diverse as Norway, South Africa, and Brazil—and in late 2014 even the Vatican—to downgrade contacts or even refuse visits with the Dalai Lama.[28]

As for China's future actions, they will remain elusive to Western analyses based on probability calculations. Chinese policies may often seem contradictory, depending on how they define their own imperatives. As instanced above, "outside" concerns are often driven by "inside" exigencies. In any case, in a world where everything is connected and everything changes, consistency and continuity are not likely to be primary values. As always, Chinese governance, like Chinese culture itself, emphasizes stability and order as first priorities; action and achievement are secondary, determined by the pragmatic decision making of the day.[29] While outsiders may not be privy to the turmoil that lies behind such decision making at the highest level, we can at least assess carefully what shows up in (re)definitions of the line between inside and outside China as the basis from which many such policy decisions will eventually evolve.

NOTES

1. Prominent examples include Martin Jacques, *When China Rules the World: The End of the Western World and the Birth of a New Global Order* (New York: Penguin HC, 2009); Stefan Halper, *The Beijing Consensus: How China's Authoritarian Model Will Dominate the Twenty-First Century* (New York: Basic, 2010); and Ian Morris, *Why the West Rules—for Now: The Patterns of History and What They Reveal about the Future* (New York: Farrar, Straus and Giroux, 2010).

2. To view this image, see http://gaaagle.com/blog/wp-images/movies/homergaaagled. jpg, accessed April 18, 2015. It comes from the *Simpsons* episode titled "Goo Goo Gai Pan," episode 347, season 16, number 12, first shown March 13, 2005.

3. See chapter 12, "Question Two: Human Rights?"

4. A book based on a recent doctoral thesis in anthropology at Boston University shows that among the Tibetan minority in Sichuan Province, community leaders show no interest in independence movements. Instead, they are scrambling for favorable placement in the lucrative future they see for domestic Chinese tourism. Tenzin Jinba, *In the Heartland of the Eastern Queendom: The Politics of Gender and Ethnicity on the Sino-Tibetan Border* (Seattle: University of Washington Press, 2013).

5. This reflex dominates public statements by the PRC, which dates its explicit hegemony in Tibet to the time of the Qian Long emperor in the eighteenth century. Nonetheless, recent press reports point to discreet investment in refurbishing the Dalai Lama's birthplace in Qinghai Province, where he lived till age three. "An Ambivalent China Affirms the Charisma of the Dalai Lama," *New York Times*, February 18, 2012. There are as well current signs of subtle shifts in policies that may separate out issues of religion from those of politics. See Didi Tatlow, "Dalai Lama: No More 'Wolf in Monk's Robes?'" *New York Times*, June 27, 2013, http://rendezvous.blogs.nytimes.com/; and "Watching Cautiously amid Signs of Shift towards Tibet," *South China Morning Post*, July 1, 2013. As often in Chinese policy making, contradictory impulses prevail. In early February 2015, the PRC protested Barack Obama's praise for the Dalai Lama at a national prayer breakfast in Washington. The Chinese goal remains explicit: that no foreign governments should meet with or lend credence to the Dalai Lama. Thus *inside* governs *outside* to whatever extent others are willing to accept Chinese-imposed constraints. See "Obama Triggers Beijing's Wrath after Tribute to Dalai Lama," *South China Morning Post*, February 6, 2015.

6. For an image of a page from PRC passports new in 2012, see Yohanna Ririhena and Novan Iman Santosa, "RI Concerned about Map in New Chinese Passports," *Jakarta Post*, November 29, 2012, accessed November 30, 2012, http://www.thejakartapost.com/. To an outline of the PRC is added a large loop south and east of Hainan Island, representing Chinese claims in the South China Sea. Vietnam, for one, refused to stamp its approval of visas on such pages for fear that such an action might imply acceptance of the Chinese claims. Note that the "Nine-Dash Line" dates from the Republic of China under Chiang Kai-shek. As in relation to the boundaries inherited from the Qing dynasty, as in Tibet and Xinjiang, the PRC has never repudiated the territorial claims of the earlier regimes it so eagerly condemned in all other ways.

7. William A. Callahan, *China: The Pessoptimist Nation* (Oxford: Oxford University Press, 2010), 10.

8. These gestures are important as ones of mutual recognition. As philosopher Zhao Tingyang of the Chinese Academy of Social Sciences (CASS) phrases his arguments for intercultural interchange, "It is evident that the knowledge of the other will never become a truth unless approved by the other. I would thus say that knowledge of life is nothing but dialogue itself and that the other provides the criterion of truth." See "Dialogue between Knowledge Communities" (2003), in *CCCW*, 552–57, esp. 553–54.

9. This strategy is analyzed in detail in Halper's *Beijing Consensus*. A useful counterbalancing view on how this influence is accomplished on the Chinese side is Henry Sanderson and Michael Forsythe, *China's Superbank: Debt, Oil and Influence; How China Development Bank Is Rewriting the Rules of Finance* (Singapore: Wiley, 2013).

10. Soft power as a concept was first elaborated by Harvard professor Joseph Nye, as in his 1990 book *Bound to Lead: The Changing Nature of American Power* (New York: Basic, 1990). Ironically, as the United States in post–Cold War times decided it no longer had a need to explain American policies, the PRC has made effective use of such tools to enhance international

credibility, focusing primarily on Chinese language and culture. The Ministry of Education through its Hanban plans to sponsor one thousand Confucius Institutes by 2020 (Confucius Institute Headquarters [Hanban], home page, accessed November 22, 2012, http://english .hanban.org/).

11. In 2009–2010, more than 125,000 Chinese students studied in the United States, while only one-tenth as many Americans went to China to study. This kind of imbalanced attention is typical; Americans and Westerners in general have yet to realize that they have a lot to learn in and from China. For a recent study of the attitudes of Chinese students abroad, see Vanessa L. Fong, *Paradise Redefined: Transnational Chinese Students and the Quest for Flexible Citizenship in the Developed World* (Stanford, CA: Stanford University Press, 2011).

12. For a fascinating study of the mentality of diaspora Chinese, see Callahan, "Who Is China? (1) Foreign Brothers and Domestic Strangers," in *China*, 127–60.

13. The confrontation is recounted in Shaila Dewan, "Chinese Student in U.S. Is Caught in Confrontation," *New York Times*, April 17, 2008, accessed August 21, 2011, http:// www.nytimes.com/. Grace Wang told her own story soon after the events on http://china digitaltimes.net/2008/05/grace-wang-the-old-man-who-lost-his-horse-video-added/, accessed April 13, 2015. The website title invokes the story of the old man who lost his horse, re-counted below in Part III, "Rethinking the West."

14. In such international forums, the PRC habitually calls for negotiations and opposes direct action.

15. The importance of this motivation for Chinese public opinion is hard to exaggerate. The most inclusive study is Zheng Wang, *Never Forget National Humiliation: Historical Memory in Chinese Politics and Foreign Relations* (New York: Columbia University Press, 2012).

16. For an attempt to situate his political stance within a Chinese context, see the section titled "How to Understand Chinese Dissidents" in chapter 12, "Question Two: Human Rights?"

17. Callahan, *China*, 66, 83, 116.

18. Callahan, *China*, 10. See also chapter 5, "Who Is China (1): Foreign Brothers and Domestic Strangers" and chapter 6, "Who Is China (2): Trauma, Community, and Gender in Sino-Japanese Relations."

19. Lucian W. Pye, *Asian Power and Politics: The Cultural Dimensions of Authority* (Cambridge, MA: Belknap, 1985), 40.

20. For a recent assessment of these challenges, see Timothy Beardson, *Stumbling Giant: The Threats to China's Future* (New Haven, CT: Yale University Press, 2013).

21. See the section titled "Layer 4: The Zone of 'Allied Barbarians'" earlier in this chapter.

22. Callahan, *China*, 98. In our own ignorance of the emotionally loaded character of maps in China, we provoked official consternation by seeking to publish in our sourcebook on comparing civilizations (*CCCW*) a map of the PRC—a standard version bought in a mainline Chinese bookshop in Beijing. Any maps, one textbook publisher told us, would have to go to a special section of the Censorship Bureau dedicated to maps, which would take months to respond. Without their approval, all maps involving China would have to be eliminated. Thus we learned the hard way that maps in China are neither "scientific" nor impartial. They are normative and cultural, defining space in terms of how one feels about it, not how it might appear from a satellite in space. *Xin* prevails, again.

23. According to Lucian Pye, the Chinese feel less threatened by cognitive dissonance than Westerners and hence are more capable of living with the kind of ambiguities and contradic-

tions that saturate not only China's foreign policy statements but their everyday life as well. Pye, *Asian Power and Politics*, 60.

24. Juan Pablo Cardenal and Heriberto Araujo, *China's Silent Army: The Pioneers, Traders, Fixers and Workers Who Are Remaking the World in Beijing's Image*, trans. Catherine Mansfield (New York: Crown Publishing, 2013), xiv.

25. Chinese interactions in Africa are not always trouble free. In June 2013, police raids in Ghana picked up more than one hundred Chinese people mining gold illegally, some of whom were blamed for rapes and other abuses of local people. "Gold Mine Raids in Ghana Seize 124 Suspected Illegal Chinese Workers," *South China Morning Post*, June 6, 2013.

26. As is well known, Western aid often sets out political parameters that stipulate, for instance, that "democracy" is to be promoted along with "free markets."

27. Venezuela currently offers the severest test case for major Chinese investments. The threat comes not from internal rebellion but from an uncertain succession following the death of Hugo Chavez. Strongman leaders may easily be succeeded by others with different priorities. The China Development Bank (CDB) has bet forty billion dollars and more on the continuity of oil revenues in Venezuela. Time will tell. Sanderson and Forsythe, *China's Superbank*, esp. 123–39.

28. Alan Cowell, "Pope Declines to Meet with Dalai Lama," *New York Times*, December 12, 2014, accessed December 13, 2014, http://www.nytimes.com/; "Dalai Lama Visa Row Halts Nobel Forum in South Africa," *BBC News*, October 2, 2014), accessed December 10, 2014, http://www.bbc.com/; Rick Gladstone, "Norway's Leaders Snub Dalai Lama in Deference to China," *New York Times*, May 8, 2014, accessed December 10, 2014, http://www.nytimes.com/; Robin Yapp, "Dalai Lama Snubbed in Brazil after Chinese Fury at Mexico Talks," *Telegraph*, September 18, 2011, accessed December 10, 2014, http://www.telegraph.co.uk/.

29. A paraphrase of Pye, *Asian Power and Politics*, 61.

III

RETHINKING THE WEST

THE WEST IS *WEIRD*

Up to now, we in the West have persisted in trying to frame the world through our own habitual models. These have so dominated our thinking that (in the words of three social scientists) "behavioral scientists routinely publish broad claims about human psychology and behavior in the world's top journals based on samples drawn entirely from Western, Educated, Industrialized, Rich, and Democratic [WEIRD] societies."[1] Thus, they claim, typical studies by social scientists "often implicitly assume that either there is little variation across human populations, or that these 'standard subjects' are as representative of the species as any other population."

Are such assumptions justified? Hardly. Taken from across the behavioral sciences, this review of comparative databases suggests that there is in fact substantial variability in experimental results across populations. More significantly, the authors conclude that WEIRD subjects are "particularly unusual" compared with the rest of mankind—to the extent that they register as "frequent outliers." In the domains of visual perception, fairness, cooperation, spatial reasoning, categorization and inferential induction, moral reasoning, reasoning styles, self-concepts, and related motivations, these findings actually "suggest that members of WEIRD societies, including young children, are *among the least representative populations* one could find for generalizing about humans."

What these authors are explicitly challenging is the belief that Western assumptions about psychology, motivation, and behavior may be used to explain the behavior of *all* of humanity. In contesting previous research conducted on such grounds, they go even further, arguing that we, as Westerners, may in fact be the exotic ones. But being rich and powerful, we in the West have tended to regard our assumptions as "universal"—and thus to dominate the discourse about how other people think

255

and live, making ourselves into the models for all "human nature." Accordingly, when we speak of the world being "globalized," in fact most of us presume it to mean "increasingly Westernized": another indication that we are, in fact, so fully embedded in our own cultural premises that we take it for granted that they reflect a global common ground.

Such assumptions of universality are, as we have seen, radically interrogated by China, which consistently offers alternative ways of looking at things. While many assume that China is on the way to developing moral and political commitments cognate with those of the West, China in fact is continuing to follow its own distinctive trajectory, along lines established often millennia ago. Even where the same words are routinely used (such as "capitalism," "democracy," "equality," or "human rights"), there are crucial differences in the way their meanings are derived and deployed.

Given such a degree of divergence, is it inevitable that there will be, at least intellectually, permanent conflict between the Christian-based values of Euro-America and Confucian China? It is still true today that, for all too many Westerners, the model of our relations with China remains the Cold War, itself prolonging the idea of the West as separate and superior in its rise to power over the last centuries. Western key words, and the models that attend them, grew out of a distinctly Western experience, above all, the Enlightenment. From its intellectual ferment emerged the present value-laden concepts such as "democracy," "equality," "freedom," "progress," "reason," and "science." Because the rise of the West depended on a particularly aggressive form of colonization, we took these words with us as we set out to shape the minds of those we dominated. Now, centuries later, most Westerners assume these are still the best words, implying the best models, for coping with a world in crisis. Yet, over the last few hundred years in the West, key concepts such as capitalism and democracy have already radically changed in meaning—and doubtless will continue to change. Moreover, in present-day Euro-America, just about every one of its key categories—from God to equality to the notion of progress—have come under intense scrutiny, by political scientists and psychologists and philosophers—in fact, from inquiring thinkers from many walks of life.

A CHINESE PARADIGM?

In contrast to the cultural discontinuities of the West, Chinese civilization often exhibits amazing continuities. To what may these be attributed? The tale of Old Saiweng might suggest a few reasons for China's exceptional resilience. One of its most venerable stories, written down first in the third century BCE and still widely known in China, involves a frontiersman who lost his horse:

> A man who lived on the northern frontier of China was skilled in interpreting events. One day for no reason, his horse ran away to the nomads across the border. Everyone

tried to console him, but his father said, "What makes you so sure this isn't a blessing?" Some months later his horse returned, bringing a splendid nomad stallion. Everyone congratulated him, but his father said, "What makes you so sure this isn't a disaster?" Their household was richer by a fine horse, which the son loved to ride. One day he fell and broke his hip. Everyone tried to console him, but his father said, "What makes you so sure this isn't a blessing?"

A year later the nomads came in force across the border, and every able-bodied man took his bow and went into battle. The Chinese frontiersmen lost nine of every ten men. Only because the son was lame did father and son survive to take care of each other. Truly, blessing turns to disaster, and disaster to blessing: the changes have no end, nor can the mystery be fathomed.[2]

Given its own internal logic, the tale will never end: as Westerners, we recognize it as a "shaggy dog" story. Things will just go on happening, sometimes apparently good, sometimes apparently bad. But good luck, bad luck, who knows? It is impossible to assess—unless one decides quite arbitrarily to stop at one point or another. Within such a world, it makes better sense to keep one's equilibrium. Things change and they are connected. One does not know where they will end.

Today, a key word in both China and the West is "progress." It is treacherous. Its treachery lies in the way both modern China and the West have used it to assess the shape of "history." Currently, Western thinking is captive to a vision of unilinear growth. First developed in the late eighteenth-century Enlightenment, by the time of the nineteenth century a veritable religion of progress was promoted by both capitalists and communists alike. In the West, it is still among the most popular of fictions—despite being vividly belied by current trends. As so often, the extreme Western case is the United States. Countering its belief in the "American Dream," recent studies of social mobility confirm that class status tends to be frozen from one generation to another—to an even greater extent than in most European countries.[3] Yet it is hard to dislodge American faith in the possibilities of rising in the world, even as they are becoming less and less obtainable.

For its own part, China imported the affirmation of inevitable progress along with Marxism-Leninism. Like many of these importations, it overlies, but does not obliterate, the more traditional credences contained in the parable of Old Saiweng. Today Xi Jinping's mantra of the "Chinese Dream" seeks to transplant the fantasy of America that lured generations of Chinese emigrants to the West. Bringing that fantasy back to China, this mantra now implicitly places its future on a par with that of the United States. As mantra, it contributes largely to the stubborn optimism characteristic of most Chinese today.[4] One can only observe that, in a developing nation, it is easier for people to believe life will always become better—even though the costs in terms of the environment and social disruption are now becoming painfully clear.

Undeniably, that expectation of unlimited economic growth is leading both the West and China into calamity.[5] Progress is a bankrupt model, as evidenced not only by a stubborn—and now worldwide—economic crisis but also by rapidly spreading environmental degradation. Furthermore, economic crises will worsen with climate change—an issue that promises to dominate our concerns (if not actual emergencies) over the decades to come.[6] Could the more pragmatic view of Old Saiweng be more useful now? Unlike the dramatic and unilinear Western view of history, from the Creation to the Apocalypse, the Chinese version entails no beginning and anticipates no set end.[7] Therefore the focus is on coping with today as it leads toward tomorrow, never quite sure where it will lead.

Meanwhile, in the West, could it be possible that our pervasive belief in a dramatic ending—an apocalypse—may actually lead to a certain indifference to the possibility of a world ecological catastrophe? Do we need to rethink our own premises more radically?

RETHINKING OUR THINKING

In challenging our own premises, China also gives us another ground from which to examine them. In facing such challenges, the Western tradition has one great advantage—a tradition of self-criticism that makes us ready to call into question even our most basic presumptions. In an exemplary instance, standard American formulations of foreign policy toward China can and have been sharply criticized as outmoded. Perhaps one of the sharpest critiques comes from Josh Kerbel, during a time when he worked for the CIA. Spelling it out in a blog titled "Thinking Straight: Cognitive Bias in the US Debate about China," Kerbel remarks that

> of the axioms, dictums, and mantras echoing through the US foreign policy and in-telligence debates in the wake of controversy over estimates of Iraqi weapons of mass destruction, none reverberates more than: *be wary of mind-set and bias and constantly reexamine assumptions.* The fact is, however, that genuine wariness and *thorough* reexami-nations [of assumptions] have been rare.[8]

In undertaking such a reexamination, Kerbel concludes that the most dysfunctional is the "application of linear approaches to nonlinear systems," a recurring theme in America's national security debate. Kerbel goes on:

> Nowhere is this tendency more clearly evident than in the continuing US debate over China, which has long been conducted as if single-outcome predictions of China's long-term future are possible and that the United States is capable of promoting or altering a predicted outcome. I will argue here that these two assumptions are largely the result of an unrecognized, deeply ingrained, and enduring cognitive bias that results in the misapplication of a linear behavioral template to China which, like all nation-states, in reality behaves "nonlinearly."

To behave "nonlinearly" is to elude the strict analysis of cause-and-effect trajectories so dear to Western, and particularly American, thinking. It is held dear because it reduces the world to something that is predictable. Nonlinear systems, on the other hand, embody complex interactions that resist both analysis into parts (as everything is connected) as well as cause-and-effect calculations (because change emerges unforeseeably from such complex interactions—as illustrated vividly by the story of Old Saiweng).

What Kerbel argues is that American foreign policy in regard to China is failing because of a failure in its *thinking*, preferring the language of Newtonian physics to the more blurred big-picture sensibilities of Chinese *xin* (although he does not name it as such). Accordingly, in its discourse, American foreign policy habitually uses such metaphors as *leverage, traction,* and *trajectories* leading to *outcomes*. In response, the Chinese view of relations with others is in terms of influence, relationship building, mutual respect, and maintaining *mianzi*—both internationally and at home. In short, America treats China as a "what," an object to be manipulated, whereas China would respond differently if treated in terms of its own culture, that is, as a "who" or an embodied presence that will emerge according to its own propensities.[9] The underlying issues concern negotiation and compromise as opposed to control. The time available to learn this lesson is short.

In rethinking the biases of Western thinking about China, Kerbel's essay proposes a Chinese view of how relationships between the West and China might most fruit-fully emerge—by implicitly adapting Chinese concepts of *mianzi* and *xin* to the discourse of international relations. What Kerbel pinpoints is a clash of paradigms: the Americans here invoking the model of science (with its reliance on "universal" laws of cause and effect) as against the Chinese model of humanity (with its reliance on presence, personal influence, and the rituals that preserve a smooth social surface). How can these in fact be mediated?

OPENING UP TO CHINA

When people hear us describing our work in this book, they think it is about understanding China. But strictly speaking, it is not about understanding China. It is about creating the conditions for understanding styles of thinking that are in fact quite alien to our own. To rephrase the words of one Chinese intellectual, Zhao Tin-gyang, the aim of this book is less about the need of the West to understand China than about the need to accept that Chinese ways of thinking are, in many ways, radically other—but also just as fundamentally valid. In other words, the West needs to accept the *legitimacy* of a Chinese perspective.[10]

Many Westerners do not recognize the need for change. Their thinking rests on a belief that all humans are rational creatures, so that one simply presumes that "other" minds work as ours are trained to do, that is, along the lines of logical argument. By thinking logically, we in the West believe we will discover those laws that govern the world and thus ourselves. We also believe that those laws have an order that can be articulated in words and numbers. This is what we call "the truth" about things, and it defines our relationship to the world. Little of this makes sense to most Chinese people, who, in thinking through *xin*, are seeking not *a relation to the world* but *a relationship between one human and another*, as defined by practical concerns, specifically, a reciprocal exchange involving both parties. As demonstrated in these pages, this kind of thinking is dramatically different, based as it is on the central value of *xiao* as achieving *ren* 仁 or "humanness."

Only now, research that identifies the West as WEIRD endorses such a radical decentering. But more is required. Comparative cultural studies, such as those exemplified in this book, clearly demonstrate that such recognition emerges not merely from translating the words—but also from translating persons themselves into the premises from which those words have evolved.

In making that translation, elusive as it may be, what emerges is a new mode of assessing, one that moves away from a rhetoric of finding "the truth" about a situation to one that acknowledges, Chinese style, that one is continuously situated differently in relation to "truth." That shift may be defined more simply as pragmatism. As a way of thinking, pragmatism has long played a significant role in Western cultural history. Articulated within the American tradition by William James (1842–1916), John Dewey (1859–1952), and Richard Rorty (1931–2007), each in their successive generations has agreed on the importance of a major shift in philosophical thinking: from *Truth* to *truths*. Using a contingent vocabulary of *truths* allows words to be recalibrated in such a way that they can be used to initiate conversations between civilizations. It allows us to engage with everyone who inhabits today's world on terms that all may recognize and learn to live with.

As for the Chinese, not having an intellectual tradition that perforce appeals to "eternal" first principles, they have in a sense always been pragmatists.[11] Only their deftness in strategizing could have maneuvered a huge nation such as China from the regime of Maoist dictates toward the new "socialism with Chinese characteristics" of Deng Xiaoping. In our own present circumstances, reaching for understanding between Chinese and Western modalities of thinking, pragmatism allows one *not* to leap to judgment. In turn, that strategic reticence can in itself elicit a new kind of attention—a leap of the imagination, if you will—extending recognition, and along with it, a new acceptance of Chinese ways of thinking. As William James put it, in a phrase appropriated for one of our epigraphs, "There should be no premature closing of our account with reality."

IMAGINE

At the moment, in today's world, the West and China are caught up in a race to the bottom. China and America are neck and neck as among the biggest economies in the world. But with China's adoption of the "American Dream," after four decades of breakneck economic growth, the country's air, water, and land have all become heavily polluted.[12] America and China are still the world's biggest emitters of CO_2 emissions. Meanwhile, droughts and floods in America have been matched in mainland China by increasing desertification and drastic water shortages, particularly in the north and northwest. According to official statistics, only 1 percent of China's five hundred largest cities can meet World Health Organization (WHO) air-quality standards; 90 percent of its groundwater is polluted. Soil pollution is so serious that official figures are not even being released.

On the other side of the world, although there is no end to official reports, Western science, once its greatest glory, has singularly failed to redress the crisis.[13] As it has deepened, science itself, increasingly specialized as a "discipline," has become correspondingly detached, allowing a host of "climate deniers" to convince the electorate that the science is, in any case, questionable. Inured by apocalyptic rhetoric (biblical as well as political), some Americans now find it easier to imagine the end of the world than to take the practical measures necessary to keep human life afloat. Most crucially, authorities in the West have been unable to convince people of the necessity of modifying their privileged lifestyles, based on exorbitant energy use and the manifold consumer products that result. As Westerners they seem to believe it is their *right* to be privileged. As a consequence, although the United States is still producing the best data for what is happening in the world, this information has not been incorporated into public policy or become effective as the rationale for the most immediate, necessary, and practical measures. Such measures as have been implemented have been applied only locally and haphazardly.

Failures such as these are significantly concentrated among the WEIRD countries; democratic governments (both parliamentary and republican)—at first unwilling and then unable to deal effectively with the unfolding crisis—have found their regimes are increasingly fragile, riven by partisan dissent. China, on the other hand, has managed to retain some resilience in the face of an escalating global crisis. Here, Beijing's system of decentralized authoritarian governance, so crucial to spurring China's economic growth, has now begun to use its decentralized model to conduct experiments at the local level to learn how to counter the worst of its environmental damage.[14]

Above all, ideologies in both polities are beginning to shift, as the idea of progress has evolved into a fresh recognition of the necessities of sustainable lifestyles, such as the necessity of providing food for the world's growing population. This perceptual shift is crucial to our survival over the next decades. Only by these means, as now commonly acknowledged, can human rights be transformed into the right to remain human, that is, the right of all mankind to live at a level of civilization above that of the merely animal.

With China and the United States as among the richest—and also among the world's worst polluters—the space between them has narrowed. Bound into a net of mutual competition, they know that, economically as well as diplomatically, they must now cooperate—or perish.[15] Of necessity, Western authorities have to become more relentlessly pragmatic, first principles being something of an intellectual luxury of the past. Chinese authorities, for their part, must learn to put aside their own paranoia about the West sufficiently to assume a new leadership role on terms of global necessity. Above all, both must acknowledge, the greatest value has to be simple human solidarity, as achieved through the real presence of face-to-face negotiation. In this newly fragile world, as they are only now beginning to realize, both civilizations need each other, not simply in the economic or political sense but also as resources for understanding—both of themselves and of each other. Human survival itself depends on nothing less than such a transformation in the way each thinks of the other.

So this book closes once again in the imaginary. Because the future now includes the clear probability of such calamities but without any equally clear answers as to how they might be addressed or, at least, ameliorated, our work cannot conclude in any proper sense of the word. In not concluding, it turns to the reader to ask, What kind of quantum leap can China and the West take into the new world that is opening up before us? For without that leap, the globe itself will progressively lose its ability to sustain human life. Could there be a stronger argument for starting to open up our Western thinking to Chinese perspectives?

Imagine.

NOTES

1. Joseph Henrich, Steven J. Heine, and Ara Norenzayan, "The Weirdest People in the World?" *Behavioral and Brain Sciences* 33 (2010): 61–135. The following quotations are from this source (emphasis added).

2. "The Lost Horse," YellowBridge, accessed April 13, 2015, http://www.yellowbridge .com/. The earliest recorded version of this story dates from the second century BCE in John S. Major et al., trans. and eds., *The Huainanzi: A Guide to the Theory and Practice of Government in Early Han China* (New York: Columbia University Press, 2010), 18.7, 728–29. Most Chinese people think of this story as consolation in case of calamity, but it obviously counsels also against attributing good fortune to one's own efforts.

3. Jason DeParle, "Harder for Americans to Rise from Lower Rungs," *New York Times*, January 4, 2012, assembles the latest data on class mobility in the United States compared to Western Europe.

4. This optimism may have limits, notably among the newly rich. "Half of China's Millionaires 'Plan to Leave Country within Five Years,'" *South China Morning Post*, September 15, 2014. What do these well-placed individuals know?

5. The Club of Rome pointed this out in 1972 in *The Limits to Growth*, nearly half a century ago. Its dire predictions have been postponed but never refuted. This organization continues to sponsor major studies of the earth to come. See Jorgen Randers, *2052: A Global Forecast for the Next 40 Years* (White River Junction, VT: Chelsea Green Publishing, 2012). The book website is http://www.2052.info/, accessed April 14, 2015.

6. The Intergovernmental Panel on Climate Change's (IPCC) Fifth Report assessing the causes and prospects for the global climate crisis now confirms the seriousness of the situation for all life on earth. A brief summary is available on the following website: IPCC, "Climate Change 2014: Synthesis Report; Summary for Policymaker," 2014, accessed April 13, 2015, http://ipcc.ch/report/ar5/syr/.

7. One classic description of this mindset comes from the *Zhuangzi*: "When we try to find out the source of the world, we trace back into infinity; when we try to find out the end, we look into infinity. Infinity into the past and into the future implies that it is beyond description." Wang Rongpei, trans., *Zhuangzi*, 2 vols., Library of Chinese Classics (Changsha, China: Hunan People's Publishing House, 1999), 2:25, 456–57.

8. Josh Kerbel, "Thinking Straight: Cognitive Bias in the US Debate about China: Rethinking Thinking," *Studies in Intelligence: Journal of the American Intelligence Professional* 48, no. 3 (2004), accessed March 25, 2013, https://www.cia.gov/. The following quotations are also from this source.

9. See the section titled "*Mianzi* as Identity Performance," in chapter 2, "Locating a Self through Others: *Miànzi*."

10. Zhao Tingyang, "Dialogue between Knowledge Communities," in *CCCW*, 515–18.

11. See Lucian W. Pye, "On Chinese Pragmatism," in *The Mandarin and the Cadre: China's Political Cultures* (Ann Arbor: University of Michigan Center for Chinese Studies, 1988), 75–108, for an in-depth discussion of the characteristics of pragmatism as practiced in China.

12. Observations in this paragraph are drawn from Elizabeth Economy, "Environmental Governance in China: State Control to Crisis Management," *Daedalus* 143, no. 2 (Spring 2014): 186. The following statistics are from this source.

13. This observation as well as those in the next paragraph are indebted to the scenario detailed by Naomi Oreskes and Erik M. Conway, *The Collapse of Western Civilization: A View from the Future* (New York: Columbia University Press, 2014), 14–18, 51.

14. See Economy, "Environmental Governance," 184–97, for an analysis of how China's system of governance both has fostered and is now instrumental in countering the drastic environmental damage of its rapid economic growth.

15. On November 12, 2014, the presidents of the People's Republic of China (PRC) and the United States announced an unprecedented agreement on how and how much to limit or reduce carbon emissions over the next decade and more. Given our emphasis on pragmatic adaptations as the way forward for these two leading polluters, we welcome this announcement as a major step in the right direction. The importance of the agreements cannot be denied, particularly for China, which for the first time promises a cap on emissions and not just increased efficiency of energy use per unit of gross domestic product (GDP). Nonetheless, the workability of these forward-looking commitments will only become clear over time. In both cases implementation efforts will encounter opposition from long-standing civilizational patterns. In China, it is assumed that everything is subject to change. Therefore, though present central authorities have the power to impose their will, leaders a few years from now will find it easy to assert that conditions have changed, requiring a change in policies. In the United States, the president's power is always constrained by the multiple factors inherent in Western-style politics; when his term is over, the mandate for this agreement may be deemed to have expired as well. In the long run, no policy involving constraint can succeed unless restrictions on energy use appear to be broadly consonant with enduring imperatives.

Appendix

Glossary of the Ten Chinese Characters

Cèlüè 策略. These two characters both carry a downward intonation (fourth tone). The character *ce* 策, pronounced "suh," on top incorporates the sign for "bamboo," as in the strips originally used for writing in China before it invented paper two thousand years ago. The second character *lüe* 略, pronounced "lway," contains the sign for *field* at the left, originally implying marking boundaries, hence suggesting an outline or plan.

Dào 道. The character is pronounced as it appears with a downward intonation (fourth tone). It combines two elements: on the right a sign for *head*, with a prominent place for the eyes. The left and lower sides of the character signify *walking* or *moving about*. Combining these two elements implies *moving about using your head.*

Guānxi 关系. To be accented on the first syllable "gwan" with a high flat intonation (first tone) followed by a lighter weight on "she." *Guan* 关, meaning, as an isolated noun, a (mountain) pass, a critical juncture, a barrier, or a turning point, originally depicted gates with threads being woven inside. By implication, weaving together helps one *over* a barrier or *through* a gate or a difficult situation. *Xi* 系, taken by itself, means "to tie together," depicting silk threads with the vestiges of a hand above them; it may now be taken to mean a system, a series, or a family. Together these characters redouble the associations with woven threads by signifying those relationships that help one overcome obstacles, including, by implication, "backdoor connections."

Hé 和. The *e* is pronounced like the *e* in "her," the whole with a rising intonation (second tone). The character for *hé* 和 combines the sign for *grain* on the left with *mouth* on the right. From its etymology, the character implies eating, singing, or talking together.

Luàn 乱. Pronounced "looahn" with a downward intonation (fourth tone). In iconographic terms, the characters evolved from signs showing two hands and silk thread hung on a stand. It used to mean *unraveling* before evolving to signify that idea of pervasive disorder known in the West as *chaos*.

Miànzi 面子. The expression is pronounced "miyen-zuh," with a downward intonation (fourth tone) accented on the first syllable. The Chinese character 面 in one of its earliest oracle-bone inscription forms was 𡇥, depicting an eye within a facial frame. The 子 *zi* serves primarily to differentiate this expression from other uses of *mian*.

Qì 气. Pronounced "chee" with a downward intonation (fourth tone). Originally designating steam rising from rice as it cooks, *qi* refers in a physical sense to air, vapor, or breath; but its more important signification in the present context is that of vital energy, understood as animating everything that exists.

Xiào 孝. Pronounced "sheow" with a downward intonation (fourth tone). The character combines an abbreviation of *lao* 老 (elder) above with *zi* 子 (child, originally, son) below.

Xīn 心. This character depicts a stylized heart, surrounded by three drops of blood. It is pronounced "sheen" with a high flat intonation (first tone).

Yì 易. Pronounced "eee" with a downward intonation (fourth tone), this character is etymologically related to the ancient character for "chameleon."

Acknowledgments

We begin with a bow to our teachers, in particular to two who have become honored ancestors: Charles O. Hucker in the United States and Ding Wangdao in China. To Gu Zhengkun, professor at Peking University, who showed us how large cultural comparisons can be configured for a Chinese audience. To Roger Ames, who taught as much through his exemplary conduct as through his thoughtful lectures. And to Henry Rosemont, first as a colleague in the 1960s and then as a mentor guiding our entry through the tangles of comparing civilizations.

As our thinking has evolved, Walt Verhoeven in Geneva and Donald B. Gibson in Princeton have offered precious feedback on successive texts as they emerged. Our original course on comparing China and the West could not have been developed without the dynamic support of Sun Youzhong, professor and long-serving dean of the School of English and International Studies at Beijing Foreign Studies University. The text for our comparative course was first recommended to Fudan University Press by Professor Zhang Chong. Under the skillful guidance of our editor there, Tang Min, this sourcebook, now titled *Comparing Civilizations: China and the West*, has improved steadily in focus and organization, edition by edition. The brave soul who has now undertaken the task of translating that book into Chinese, Li Yanru in Hohhot, has given us a second chance to make sense by querying any and all passages in which our own prose lapsed from clarity.

Since we began our comparative work more than a decade ago, several of our most promising students have become teachers as well. Of these, two have made singularly generous contributions to the manuscript by discussing it with us in detail. First is Ma Liyuan of Beijing Foreign Studies University, a lecturer in the School of English and International Studies, who helped us incorporate the perspective of a highly educated Chinese woman. The second is John Flood, senior lecturer in the English Department of Groningen University, the Netherlands. His scholarly commentary and sharp questions often kept us scrambling, either to add an erudite footnote or to rephrase a woolly paragraph. Other readers who challenged what they sometimes saw as fuzzy thinking include Thomas McCormack and one of our very helpful, if anonymous, readers for Rowman & Littlefield. We must also single out Li Hui, a former student whose scholarship in both traditional and contemporary Chinese culture helped us to locate and translate documents otherwise inaccessible to us.

Finally, singular among our academic colleagues, the one who has provided the most constant support, particularly in relation to library resources, has been Professor Ann Blair of the History Department at Harvard University.

Of all of these, however, perhaps our best teachers over the last decade and more have been our students, both in the West and in China. It is they who, by their attention, curiosity, and quick minds, have challenged us at every turn in explaining China to the West and the West to China. Without their constant presence in our lives, we might never have developed either the methods or the language for helping people in one world to make sense of the other. Their papers together with their persistent questions have offered vivid examples for or valuable reformulations of key concepts. Without them, it would be hard to imagine this book coming about.

Few in the West understand how differently Chinese people tend to think. Many deny there is any difference at all, as we are all human. However, those valuable colleagues who have given us the courage to make this unpopular case are, as we finish this book, very much in mind. They include, among others, Peimin Ni, professor of comparative philosophy, Grand Valley State University in Michigan, who remains a source of constant support and encouragement.

Finally, we must include our children. Already caught up in the academic world, as students, graduate students, or faculty, David, Thomas, and Ann have proved a source of steady support and encouragement. Over the years, they have allowed us to transport them to China through our daily engagement with this project. They have followed our various adventures with a keen, if sometimes anxious, interest and with many stubborn questions. To them, ultimately our best teachers, if not about China then certainly about life, we extend not only thanks but also the hope that they too might someday encounter something so strange, so overwhelming, and so hard to explain that it may for them become, if not China, then something just as big, as demanding—and life enriching.

Works Cited

BOOKS AND ARTICLES

Adams, Hajo, and Adam J. Galinsky. "Enclothed Cognition." *Journal of Experimental Social Psychology* 48 (July 2012): 918–25.

Agee, James, and Walker Evans. *Let Us Now Praise Famous Men: Three Tenant Families*. 1941. Boston: Houghton Mifflin, 1960.

Ai Weiwei. *Never Sorry*. Directed by Alison Klayman. 2012. Accessed March 13, 2013, http://aiweiweineversorry.com/.

Ames, Roger T., and David L. Hall, trans. *Daodejing: Making This Life Significant; A Philosophical Translation*. New York: Ballantine, 2003.

Ames, Roger T., and Henry Rosemont Jr., trans. *The Analects of Confucius: A Philosophical Translation*. New York: Ballantine, 1998.

———. *The Chinese Classic of Family Reverence: A Philosophical Translation of the* Xiaojing. Honolulu: University of Hawaii Press, 2009.

Asma, Stephen T. *Against Fairness*. Chicago: University of Chicago Press, 2013.

Beardson, Timothy. *Stumbling Giant: The Threats to China's Future*. New Haven, CT: Yale University Press, 2013.

Bell, Daniel A. "Taking Elitism Seriously: Democracy with Confucian Characteristics." In *Beyond Liberal Democracy: Political Thinking for an East Asian Context*, 152–79. Princeton, NJ: Princeton University Press, 2006.

Bell, Daniel A., and Yingchuan Mo. "Harmony in the World 2013: The Ideal and the Reality." Accessed April 16, 2015. https://www.academia.edu/.

Bernstein, Peter L. *Against the Gods: The Remarkable Story of Risk*. New York: Wiley, 1996.

Billeter, Jean François. *The Chinese Art of Writing*. Geneva: Skira, 1990.

Blackman, Carolyn. "Coming Out of China Crying: A Case of Failed Negotiations." In *Negotiating China: Case Studies and Strategies*, 106–21. Crow's Nest, Australia: Allen & Unwin, 1997.

Blair, John G., and Jerusha McCormack. *Comparing Civilizations: China and the West; A Sourcebook.* New York: Global Scholarly Publishing, 2013.

———. *Western Civilization with Chinese Comparisons.* 3rd ed. Shanghai: Fudan University Press, 2010.

Blake, William. "The Marriage of Heaven and Hell." 1790. From the original plates, number 3. William Blake Archive, Bodleian Library. Accessed March 31, 2015. http://www.blakearchive.org/.

Blum, Susan. *Lies that Bind: Chinese Truth, Other Truths.* Lanham, MD: Rowman & Littlefield, 2007.

Bond, Michael Harris. *Beyond the Chinese Face: Insights from Psychology.* Oxford: Oxford University Press, 1991.

Boorstin, Daniel. *The Image: A Guide to Pseudo-Events in America.* 1961. New York: Harper & Row, 1964.

Bruner, Jerome. *Making Stories: Law, Literature, Life.* Cambridge, MA: Harvard University Press, 2002.

Callahan, William A. *China: The Pessoptimist Nation.* Oxford: Oxford University Press, 2010.

Cardenal, Juan Pablo, and Heriberto Araujo. *China's Silent Army: The Pioneers, Traders, Fixers and Workers Who Are Remaking the World in Beijing's Image.* Translated by Catherine Mansfield. New York: Crown Publishing, 2013.

Chang, Leslie T. *Factory Girls: Voices from the Heart of Modern China.* New York: Spiegel and Grau, 2008.

Chen, Xiaoyang, and Ruiping Fan. "The Family and Harmonious Medical Decision Making: Cherishing an Appropriate Confucian Moral Balance." *Journal of Medicine and Philosophy* 35 (2010): 573–86.

China Rises. 2 DVD set. Coproduced by the Canadian Broadcasting Corporation, the *New York Times*, and Zweites Deutsches Fernsehen, 2007.

Chomsky, Noam. "Human Rights in the 21st Century." London School of Economics and Political Science. October 29, 2009. Accessed August 20, 2011. http://www.lse.ac.uk/.

———. "The United States and the Challenge of Relativity." In *Human Rights Fifty Years On: A Reappraisal*, edited by Tony Evans, 24–57. Manchester, UK: Manchester University Press, 1998.

Chow, Rey. "How (the) Inscrutable Chinese Led to Globalized Theory." Special Topic: Globalizing Literary Studies, *PMLA* 116, no. 1 (January 2001): 69–74.

Chua, Amy. *Battle Hymn of the Tiger Mother.* New York: Penguin, 2011.

Ci, Jiwei. "What Is in the Cloud? A Critical Engagement with Thomas Metzger on *The Clash between Chinese and Western Political Theories.*" *Boundary* 2, no. 34 (2007): 61–86.

Coates, Austin. *Myself a Mandarin: Memoirs of a Special Magistrate.* London: Heinemann, 1977.

Cohen, Paul A. *Speaking to History: The Story of King Goujian in Twentieth-Century China.* Berkeley: University of California Press, 2008.

Comerford, Patrick, and Richard O'Leary. "'Heroism and Zeal': Pioneers of the Irish Christian Missions to China." In *China and the Irish*, edited by Jerusha McCormack, 73–78. Dublin: New Island, 2009.

Dabrock, Peter. "Drawing Distinctions Responsibly and Concretely: A European Protestant Perspective on Foundational Theological Bioethics." *Christian Bioethics* 16, no. 2 (2010): 128–57.

de Bary, William Theodore, and Irene Bloom, eds. *Sources of Chinese Tradition.* 2nd ed. Vol. 1. New York: Columbia University Press, 1999.

Delury, John. "'Harmonious' in China." *Policy Review* (Hoover Institution) (April–May 2008): 35–44.

Derrida, Jacques. *Of Grammatology.* Translated by Gayatri Chakravorty Spivak. Baltimore: Johns Hopkins University Press, 1998.

Detienne, Marcel, and Jean-Pierre Vernant. *Cunning Intelligence in Greek Culture and Society.* Atlantic Highlands, NJ: Humanities Press, 1978.

Deutscher, Guy. *Through the Language Glass: Why the World Looks Different in Other Languages.* New York: Metropolitan Books, 2010.

Dikötter, Frank. *Mao's Great Famine: The History of China's Most Devastating Catastrophe, 1958–62.* London: Walker, 2010.

Ding Wangdao. *A Continuing Climb.* Beijing: Foreign Languages Teaching and Research Press, 2000.

———. *A Turning Point.* Beijing: Foreign Languages Teaching and Research Press. 2007.

Dobriansky, Paula. "U.S. Human Rights Policy: An Overview." Accessed August 20, 2011. http://www.disam.dsca.mil/.

Document of the General Office of the Central Committee of the Communist Party of China (Zhong Ban Fa), 2011, no. 18, 2. Accessed December 20, 2012. http://www.chinaaid.org/.

Donne, John. "The Second Anniversary of the Progress of the Soul." In *The Complete Poetry of John Donne,* edited by John T. Shawcross. New York: Doubleday, 1967.

Ebrey, Patricia Buckley. "Northern Song Landscape Painting." Visual Sourcebook of Chinese Civilization. Accessed December 27, 2011. http://depts.washington.edu/.

Economy, Elizabeth. "Environmental Governance in China: State Control to Crisis Management." *Daedalus* 143, no. 2 (Spring 2014): 184–97.

Eliot, T. S. *The Complete Poems and Plays, 1910–1950.* New York: Harcourt, Brace, 1952.

———. "The Metaphysical Poets." In *Selected Essays, 1917–1932.* 1934. New York: Harcourt, Brace, 1964.

Elvin, Mark. "Personal Luck: Why Premodern China—Probably—Did Not Develop Probabilistic Thinking." In *Concepts of Nature: A Chinese-European Cross-Cultural Perspective,* edited by Hans Ulrich Vogel et al., 400–68. Leiden, Netherlands: Brill, 2010.

Emerson, Ralph Waldo. "The American Scholar." In *Selections from Ralph Waldo Emerson.* Edited by Stephen E. Whicher. Boston: Houghton Mifflin, 1957.

———. *Nature.* Boston: James Munroe, 1849.

Encylopaedia Britannica. "Soul." Accessed June 13, 2013. http://www.britannica.com/.

Felski, Rita, and Susan Stanford Friedman, eds. *Comparison: Theories, Approaches, Uses.* Baltimore: Johns Hopkins University Press, 2013.

Fincher, John H. *Chinese Democracy: The Self-Government Movement in Local, Provincial, and National Politics, 1905–1914.* New York: St. Martin's Press, 1981.

Fong, Vanessa L. *Paradise Redefined: Transnational Chinese Students and the Quest for Flexible Citizenship in the Developed World.* Stanford, CA: Stanford University Press, 2011.

Forbus, David. "Yin Yang in 3D." YouTube, February 25, 2007. Accessed September 8, 2014. https://www.youtube.com/.

Fu, Shen. *Six Records of a Floating Life.* Translated with notes by Leonard Pratt and Chiang Su-hui. London: Penguin, 1983.

Gaddis, John Lewis. *We Now Know: Rethinking Cold War History.* Oxford, UK: Clarendon, 1997.

Gardner, Howard. *To Open Minds: Chinese Clues to the Dilemmas of Contemporary Education.* New York: Basic, 1989.

Gernet, Jacques. *China and the Christian Impact: A Conflict of Cultures.* Cambridge: Cambridge University Press, 1985.

Gladwell, Malcolm. *Blink: The Power of Thinking without Thinking.* Boston: Back Bay Books, 2007.

Goffman, Erving. *The Presentation of Self in Everyday Life.* 1959. Harmondsworth, UK: Penguin, 1971.

Goldin-Meadow, Susan. *Hearing Gesture: How Our Hands Help Us Think.* Cambridge, MA: Harvard University Press, 2003.

Grandin, Temple, and Richard Panek. *The Autistic Brain: Thinking across the Spectrum.* Boston: Houghton Mifflin Harcourt, 2013.

Grange, Joseph. "An Irish Tao." *Journal of Chinese Philosophy* 29, no. 1 (March 2002): 21–34.

Guo Jujing. *The Twenty-Four Paragons of Filial Piety.* Accessed November 24, 2012. http://www.rice.edu/.

Guo Xi [Kuo Hsi]. "Advice on Landscape Painting." In *Early Chinese Texts on Painting*, edited by Susan Bush and Hsio-yen Shih. Cambridge, MA: Harvard University Press, 1985.

Hall, David L., and Roger T. Ames. *Thinking from the Han: Self, Truth, and Transcendence in Chinese and Western Culture.* Albany: State University of New York Press, 1998.

Halper, Stefan. *The Beijing Consensus: How China's Authoritarian Model Will Dominate the Twenty-First Century.* New York: Basic, 2010.

Hansen, Chad. "Daoist-Oriented Interpretations." Chad Hansen's Chinese Philosophy Pages. Accessed November 25, 2012. http://www.hku.hk/philodep/ch.

Hanson, Victor Davis. *The Western Way of War.* New York: Knopf, 1989. Second edition with John Keegan. Berkeley: University of California Press, 2009.

Harvard Educational Review. "Two Million Minutes: A Global Examination." Accessed June 29, 2013. http://hepg.org/.

Hazony, Yoram. *The Philosophy of Hebrew Scripture.* New York: Cambridge University Press, 2012.

Heaney, Seamus. *North.* London: Faber and Faber, 1975.

Henrich, Joseph, Steven J. Heine, and Ara Norenzayan. "The Weirdest People in the World?" *Behavioral and Brain Sciences* 33 (2010): 61–135.

Hessler, Peter. "At Night You're Not Lonely." In *Oracle Bones*, 149–68. New York: HarperCollins, 2006.

"The Higgs Boson." Origins, CERN. Accessed January 2, 2012. http://www.exploratorium.edu/.

Hobbes, Thomas. *Leviathan; or, The Matter, Form, and Power of a Commonwealth, Ecclesiastical and Civil.* London: A. Crooke, 1651.

Huang Yongyu. "A Beneficial Bird." In *Huang Yongyu and His Paintings*, translated by Yang Xianyi et al., edited by Zheng Xiaojuan and Xiao Shiling. Beijing: Foreign Languages Press, 1988.

Hu Wenzhong and Cornelius Grove. "The Concept of 'Face' in Chinese-American Interaction." In *Encountering the Chinese: A Guide for Americans*, 117–32. Boston: Nicholas Brealey Publishing, 1999.

Huff, Darrell. *How to Lie with Statistics.* New York: Norton, 1954.

Hutton, Will. *The Writing on the Wall: China and the West in the 21st Century.* Boston: Little, Brown, 2007.

Ikels, Charlotte, ed. *Filial Piety: Practice and Discourse in Contemporary East Asia.* Stanford, CA: Stanford University Press, 2004.

Intergovernmental Panel on Climate Change (IPCC). "Climate Change 2014: Synthesis Report; Summary for Policymaker." 2014. Accessed April 13, 2015. http://ipcc.ch/report/ar5/syr/.

"International Human Rights Law." United Nations Human Rights, Office of the High Commissioner for Human Rights. Accessed August 13, 2011. http://www.ohchr.org/.

Ivanhoe, Philip J., and Bryan W. Van Norden, trans. *Readings in Classical Chinese Philosophy.* Indianapolis: Hackett, 2001.

Jackall, Robert. *Moral Mazes: The World of Corporate Managers.* New York: Oxford University Press, 2009.

Jacques, Martin. *When China Rules the World: The End of the Western World and the Birth of a New Global Order.* New York: Penguin HC, 2009.

Jen, Gish. *Tiger Writing: Art, Culture, and the Interdependent Self.* Cambridge, MA: Harvard University Press, 2013.

Jenkins, Philip. *The Lost History of Christianity: The Thousand-Year Golden Age of the Church in the Middle East, Africa, and Asia—and How It Died.* New York: HarperCollins, 2008.

Jinba, Tenzin. *In the Heartland of the Eastern Queendom: The Politics of Gender and Ethnicity on the Sino-Tibetan Border.* Seattle: University of Washington Press, 2013.

Johnson, Mark. *The Meaning of the Body: Aesthetics of Human Understanding.* Chicago: University of Chicago Press, 2007.

Jullien, François. *Detour and Access: Strategies of Meaning in China and Greece.* Translated by Sophie Hawkes. New York: Zone Books, 2000.

———. *A Treatise on Efficacy: Between Western and Chinese Thinking.* Translated by Janet Lloyd. Honolulu: University of Hawaii Press, 2004.

Jung, Carl Gustav. *Memories, Dreams, Reflections.* New York: Vintage, 1989 (reprinting final revised edition, 1973).

———. Preface. In *The Book of Changes.* Translated by Richard Wilhelm and Cary Baynes. Princeton, NJ: Princeton University Press, 1950.

Kahneman, Daniel. *Thinking, Fast and Slow.* New York: Farrar, Straus and Giroux, 2011.

Kazlev, M. Alan, and Christián Begué. "The I Ching and Genetic Code." Last updated November 19, 2005. Accessed February 9, 2013. http://www.kheper.net/.

Kerbel, Josh. "Thinking Straight: Cognitive Bias in the US Debate about China: Rethinking Thinking." *Studies in Intelligence: Journal of the American Intelligence Professional* 48, no. 3 (2004). Accessed March 25, 2013. https://www.cia.gov/.

Kleinman, Arthur. "Introduction: Remaking the Moral Person in a New China." In *Deep China: The Moral Life of the Person; What Anthropology and Psychiatry Tell Us about China Today*, by Arthur Kleinman et al., 1–35. Berkeley: University of California Press, 2011.

Kostelanetz, Richard. *Conversing with* [John] *Cage.* 2nd ed. New York: Routledge, 2003.

Kövecses, Zoltan. *Metaphor in Culture.* New York: Cambridge University Press, 2005.

Kurtz, Joachim. *The Discovery of Chinese Logic.* Leiden, Netherlands: Brill, 2011.

LaFargue, Michael. "The Semantic Structure of Aphorisms: The Proverb as a Special Genre of Speech." In *Tao and Method: A Reasoned Approach to the Tao Te Ching*, 133–44. Albany: State University of New York Press, 1994.

Lakoff, George. *Ten Lectures in Cognitive Linguistics.* Beijing: Beihang Linguistics Lecture Series, 2004.

Lakoff, George, and Mark Johnson. "Introduction: Who Are We?" In *Philosophy in the Flesh: The Embodied Mind and Its Challenge to Western Thought*. New York: Basic, 1999.

Lan, Chun. *A Cognitive Approach to Spatial Metaphors in English and Chinese*. Beijing: Foreign Language Teaching and Research Press, 2003.

Lao Tzu [Laozi]. *The Book of Tao and Teh* [*Daodejing*]. Translated by Gu Zhengkun. 2nd ed. Beijing: Peking University Press, 2006.

Lee, Lee C. "Day Care in the People's Republic of China." In *Child Care in Context: Cross-Cultural Perspectives*, edited by Michael E. Lamb, Kathleen J. Sternberg, Carl-Philip Hwang, and Anders G. Broberg, 355–92. Hillsdale, NJ: Lawrence Erlbaum, 1992.

Li Gang. *The Way We Think: Chinese View of Life Philosophy*. Beijing: Sinolingua, 2009.

Lian Xi. *The Conversion of Missionaries: Liberalism in American Protestant Missions in China, 1907–1932*. University Park: State University of Pennsylvania Press, 1997.

Lim, Louisa. *The People's Republic of Amnesia: Tiananmen Revisited*. New York: Oxford University Press, 2014.

Little, Stephen, and Shawn Eichman, eds. *Taoism and the Arts of China*. Chicago: Art Institute of Chicago, 2000.

Liu, Lydia. *Translingual Practice: Literature, National Culture, and Translated Modernity—China, 1900–1937*. Stanford, CA: Stanford University Press, 1995.

Liu Xiaobo. *No Enemies, No Hatred*. Edited by Perry Link, Tienchi Martin-Liao, and Liu Xia. Cambridge, MA: Harvard University Press, 2012.

Liu, Yang. *Ost trifft West* [East meets West]. 10th ed. Mainz, Germany: Hermann Schmidt Verlag, 2014.

Li Zhenshen. "Red-Color News Soldier." Accessed October 14, 2014. http://www.contactpressimages.com/.

———. *Red-Color News Soldier: A Chinese Photographer's Odyssey through the Cultural Revolution*. New York: Phaidon, 2003.

"The Lost Horse." YellowBridge. Accessed April 13, 2015. http://www.yellowbridge.com/.

Lovelock, James. *Gaia: A New Look at Life on Earth*. Oxford: Oxford University Press, 1989.

Loyalka, Michelle Dammon. *Eating Bitterness: Stories from the Front Lines of China's Great Urban Migration*. Berkeley: University of California Press, 2012.

Lu, Shigong. *Studies on the Contemporary Chinese Party and Government Relation* [in Mandarin]. Shanghai: People's Press, 2001.

Luo, Weihong. *Christianity in China*. Beijing: China Intercontinental Press, 2004.

Machiavelli, Niccolò. *The Prince*. 1513. Translated by W. K. Marriott. London: D. Nutt, 1905. Accessed January 24, 2012. http://www.gutenberg.org/.

Major, John S., et al., trans. and eds. *The Huainanzi: A Guide to the Theory and Practice of Government in Early Han China*. New York: Columbia University Press, 2010.

Markus, Hazel Rose, and Shinobu Kitayama. "Culture and the Self: Implications for Cognition, Motivation, and Emotion." *Psychological Review* 98, no. 2 (April 1991): 224–53.

"Matteo Ricci, Li Zhizao, and Zhang Wentao: World Map of 1602." James Ford Bell Library, University of Minnesota Libraries. Accessed October 3, 2013. https://www.lib.umn.edu/.

McCormack, Jerusha. "Framing Academic Discourse: East and West." In *English Education and Liberal Education*, edited by Sun Youzhong et al., 307–20. Beijing: Foreign Language Teaching and Research Press, 2008.

McGregor, Richard. *The Party: The Secret World of China's Communist Leaders*. New York: HarperCollins, 2010.

McNeill, David, ed. *Language and Gesture.* Language, Culture and Cognition. Cambridge: Cambridge University Press, 2000.

Mead, George Herbert. *Mind, Self, and Society.* Edited by Charles W. Morris. 1934. Chicago: University of Chicago Press, 1963.

Merleau-Ponty, Maurice. *Sense and Non-sense.* Translated by Hubert L. Dreyfus and Patricia Allen Dreyfus. Evanston, IL: Northwestern University Press, 1964.

Miller, Jean Baker. *Towards a New Psychology of Women.* 2nd ed. Boston: Beacon, 1986.

Mittag, Achim. "Historical Consciousness in China: Some Notes on Six Theses on Chinese Historiography and Historical Thought." In *New Developments in Asian Studies: An Introduction,* edited by Paul van der Velde and Alex McKay, 47–76. London: Kegan Paul, 1999.

Morris, Ian. *Why the West Rules—for Now: The Patterns of History and What They Reveal about the Future.* New York: Farrar, Straus and Giroux, 2010.

Mungello, David E. *The Great Encounter of China and the West, 1500–1800.* 3rd ed. Lanham, MD: Rowman & Littlefield, 2009.

Needham, Joseph. *Mathematics and the Sciences of Heavens and Earth.* Science and Civilisation in China 3. Cambridge: Cambridge University Press, 1959.

Nisbett, Richard E. *The Geography of Thought: How Asians and Westerners Think Differently— and Why.* London: Nicholas Brealey, 2003.

Nye, Joseph. *Bound to Lead: The Changing Nature of American Power.* New York: Basic, 1990.

O'Leary, Richard. "An Irish Mandarin: Sir Robert Hart in China, 1854–1908." In *China and the Irish,* edited by Jerusha McCormack, 26–39. Dublin: New Island, 2009.

O'Leary, Richard, and Lan Li. *Mainland Chinese Students and Immigrants in Ireland and Their Engagement with Christianity, Churches and Irish Society.* Dublin: Agraphon, 2008.

Oreskes, Naomi, and Erik M. Conway. *The Collapse of Western Civilization: A View from the Future.* New York: Columbia University Press, 2014.

Oxford English Dictionary. 2nd ed. Oxford, UK: Clarendon, 1989.

Pearsall, Paul, et al. "Changes in Heart Transplant Recipients That Parallel the Personalities of Their Donors." *Near-Death Studies* 20, no. 3 (Spring 2002): 191–206.

Plato. *Cratylus.* Translated by Benjamin Jowett. Project Gutenburg, January 1, 1999. Accessed November 23, 2012. http://www.gutenberg.org/.

Poovey, Mary. *A History of the Modern Fact: Problems of Knowledge in the Sciences of Wealth and Society.* Chicago: University of Chicago Press, 1998.

Pye, Lucian W. *Asian Power and Politics: The Cultural Dimensions of Authority.* Cambridge, MA: Belknap, 1985.

———. *The Mandarin and the Cadre: China's Political Cultures.* Ann Arbor: University of Michigan Center for Chinese Studies, 1988.

Randers, Jorgen. *2052: A Global Forecast for the Next 40 Years.* White River Junction, VT: Chelsea Green Publishing, 2012.

Raphals, Lisa. *Knowing Words: Wisdom and Cunning in the Classical Traditions of China and Greece.* Ithaca, NY: Cornell University Press, 1992.

Robinet, Isabelle. *Taoism: Growth of a Religion.* Stanford, CA: Stanford University Press, 1997 [French original, 1992].

Roosevelt, Eleanor. *The Autobiography of Eleanor Roosevelt.* New York: Harper and Brothers, 1958.

Rousseau, Jean-Jacques. *The Social Contract; or, Principles of Political Right.* Translated by G. D. H. Cole. 1762. London: J. M. Dent, 1955. Accessed October 3, 2013. http://archive.org/.

Sanderson, Henry, and Michael Forsythe. *China's Superbank: Debt, Oil and Influence; How China Development Bank Is Rewriting the Rules of Finance.* Singapore: Wiley, 2013.

Schell, Orville, and John Delury. *Wealth and Power: China's Long March to the Twenty-First Century.* New York: Random House, 2013.

Scott, James C. *The Art of Not Being Governed: An Anarchist History of Upland Southeast Asia.* New Haven, CT: Yale University Press, 2009.

Secord, James A. "Knowledge in Transit." *History of Science Society* 95, no. 4 (December 2004): 654–72.

Shaughnessy, Edward J., ed. *Confucian and Taoist Wisdom.* London: Duncan Baird, 2010.

Smail, Daniel Lord. *On Deep History and the Brain.* Berkeley: University of California Press, 2008.

Smith, Richard J. *The "I Ching": A Biography.* Lives of Great Religious Books. Princeton, NJ: Princeton University Press, 2012.

Spence, Jonathan. *Emperor of China: Self-Portrait of K'ang-hsi* [Kangxi]. New York: Vintage, 1988.

Stark, Rodney. *For the Glory of God: How Monotheism Led to Reformations, Science, Witch-Hunts and the End of Slavery.* Princeton, NJ: Princeton University Press, 2003.

Stearns, Peter. *American Fear: The Causes and Consequences of High Anxiety.* New York: Routledge, 2006.

Struhl, Karsten J. "No (More) Philosophy without Cross-Cultural Philosophy." *Philosophy Compass* 5, no. 4 (2010): 287–95.

Sullivan, Michael. *The Arts of China.* Berkeley: University of California Press, 1999.

Sunzi. *The Art of War.* Translated by Samuel G. Griffith. New York: Oxford University Press, 1963.

Teachout, Zephyr. *Corruption in America: From Benjamin Franklin's Snuff Box to Citizens United.* Cambridge, MA: Harvard University Press, 2014.

Teilhard de Chardin, Pierre. *The Phenomenon of Man.* New York: Harper & Row, 1959.

Thoreau, Henry David. "Civil Disobedience." In *Walden and Civil Disobedience,* edited by Sherman Paul. Boston: Houghton Mifflin, 1960.

———. "What I Lived For." In *Walden; or, Life in the Woods.* 1854. Boston: Houghton Mifflin, 1960.

Trilling, Lionel. *Sincerity and Authenticity.* New York: Harcourt Brace Jovanovich, 1971.

Trompenaars, Fons, and Charles Hampden-Turner. *Riding the Waves of Culture: Understanding Cultural Diversity in Business,* 2nd ed. London: Nicholas Brealey, 1997.

Two Million Minutes (documentary). Directed by Chad Heeter. Arlington, VA: Broken Pencil Productions, 2007. Accessed November 24, 2012. http://www.2mminutes.com/.

Ulaby, Neda. "Muybridge: The Man Who Made Pictures Move." National Public Radio, April 13, 2010. Accessed September 5, 2014. http://www.npr.org/.

"The Universal Declaration of Human Rights." United Nations. Accessed April 2, 2015. https://www.un.org/.

"The Universal Declaration of Human Rights: History of the Document." United Nations. Accessed August 16, 2011. http://www.un.org/.

Vattimo, Gianni. *After Christianity.* New York: Columbia University Press, 2002.

Veblen, Thorstein. *The Theory of the Leisure Class.* 1899. New York: Penguin, 1979.

von Neumann, John, and Oskar Morgenstern. *Theory of Games and Economic Behavior.* Princeton, NJ: Princeton University Press, 1944.

von Senger, Harro. *The Book of Stratagems.* New York: Viking, 1991.

Waley, Arthur. *Three Ways of Thought in Ancient China*. 1939. London: Routledge, 2012.

Wang, Eugene Y. "The Winking Owl: Visual Effect and Its Art Historical Thick Description." *Critical Inquiry* 26, no. 3 (Spring 2000): 435–73.

Wang, Keping, trans. *The Classic of the Dao [Daodejing]: A New Investigation*. Beijing: Foreign Languages Press, 1998.

Wang, Qi. "Are Asians Forgetful? Perception, Retention, and Recall in Episodic Remembering." *Cognition* 111 (2009): 123–31.

———. "Culture Effects on Adults' Earliest Childhood Recollection and Self-Description: Implications for the Relation between Memory and the Self." *Journal of Psychology and Social Psychology* 81 (2001): 220–33.

Wang, Rongpei, trans. *Zhuangzi*. 2 vols. Library of Chinese Classics. Changsha, China: Hunan People's Publishing House, 1999.

Wang, Zheng. *Never Forget National Humiliation: Historical Memory in Chinese Politics and Foreign Relations*. New York: Columbia University Press, 2012.

Waswo, Richard A. *The Founding Legend of Western Civilization: From Virgil to Vietnam*. Middletown, CT: Wesleyan University Press, 1997.

Weir, David. *Brahma in the West: William Blake and the Oriental Renaissance*. Albany: State University of New York Press, 2003.

Weller, Robert P. "The Politics of Increasing Religious Diversity in China." *Daedalus* 143, no. 2 (Spring 2014): 135–44.

Westad, Odd Arne. *Restless Empire: China and the World since 1750*. London: Bodley Head, 2012.

Whitehead, Alfred North. *Process and Reality*. New York: Macmillan, 1929.

———. *Science and the Modern World*. 1925. New York: Simon and Schuster, 1997.

Wikipedia. "Charter 08." Accessed February 13, 2012. http://en.wikipedia.org/.

———. "Confucius: Descendants." Accessed January 31, 2013. http://en.wikipedia.org/.

———. "Constitution of the People's Republic of China." *Wikipedia*. Accessed August 16, 2011. http://en.wikipedia.org/.

———. "Gini since World War II." *Wikipedia*. Accessed February 4, 2012. http://en.wikipedia.org/.

———. "River Crab (Internet Slang)." *Wikipedia*. Accessed November 24, 2012. http://en.wikipedia.org/.

Wordsworth, William. "Lines: Written a Few Miles above Tintern Abbey." In *Wordsworth: Poetry and Prose*, edited by W. M. Merchant. Cambridge, MA: Harvard University Press, 1967.

Wu Fei. "Suicide: A Modern Problem in China." In *Deep China: The Moral Life of the Person; What Anthropology and Psychiatry Tell Us about China Today*, by Arthur Kleinman et al., 213–36. Berkeley: University of California Press, 2011.

Wu, Kuang-Ming. *On Chinese Body Thinking: A Cultural Hermeneutic*. Leiden, Netherlands: Brill, 1996.

Xinran. *Witness: Voices from a Silent Generation*. London: Chatto and Windus, 2008.

Xun Zhou, ed. *The Great Famine in China, 1958–1963: A Documentary History*. New Haven, CT: Yale University Press, 2012.

Xunzi. "The Regulations of a King" (section 9). In *Hsün Tzu [Xunzi]: Basic Writings*, edited and translated by Burton Watson. New York: Columbia University Press, 1963.

Yan, Kejia. *Catholic Church in China*. Beijing: China Intercontinental Press, 2004.

Yang, Jisheng. *Tombstone: The Great Chinese Famine 1958–1962.* Translated by Stacey Mosher and Gui Jian. New York: Farrar, Straus and Giroux, 2012 [original Chinese edition 2008].

Yoshioka, Yoshitoyo. "Taoist Monastic Life." In *Facets of Taoism,* edited by Holmes Welch and Anna Seidel, 229–51. New Haven, CT: Yale University Press, 1979.

Zhang Longxi. "The Complexity of Difference: Individual, Cultural, and Cross-Cultural." *Interdisciplinary Science Reviews* 35, nos. 3–4 (2010): 341–52.

———. "Crossroads, Distant Killing, and Translation: On the Ethics and Politics of Comparison." In *Comparison: Theories, Approaches, Uses,* edited by Rita Felski and Susan Stanford Friedman, 46–63. Baltimore: Johns Hopkins University Press, 2013.

———. "The 'Tao' and the 'Logos': Notes on Derrida's Critique of Logocentrism." *Critical Inquiry* 11, no. 3 (March 1985): 385–98.

Zhao Zhentao, Zhang Wenting, and Zhou Dingzhi, trans. *Mencius.* Bilingual ed. Library of Chinese Classics. Changsha, China: Hunan People's Publishing House, 1999.

Zhou, Xun. *The Great Famine in China, 1958–1963: A Documentary History.* New Haven, CT: Yale University Press, 2012.

PRESS REPORTS

BBC News. "China 'Detains' Shanghai Bishop Who Quit Official Post." July 10, 2012. http://www.bbc.co.uk/.

———. "China Law to Make Children Visit Parents." January 6, 2011. Accessed April 8, 2015. http://www.bbc.co.uk/.

———. "Dalai Lama Visa Row Halts Nobel Forum in South Africa." October 2, 2014. Accessed December 10, 2014. http://www.bbc.com/.

Blakeslee, Sandra. "Mind Games: Sometimes a White Coat Isn't Just a White Coat." *New York Times,* April 2, 2012.

Bradsher, Keith. "Chinese Titan Takes Aim at Hollywood." *New York Times,* September 22, 2013.

China Daily. "Civil Servant Sorry for Beating Parents." November 1, 2011. Accessed November 18, 2012. http://www.chinadaily.com.cn/.

———. "*Laojiao* System to Be Phased Out." January 21, 2013. Accessed March 15, 2013. http://www.chinadaily.com.cn/.

China View. "Window of China: National Human Rights Action Plan of China (2009–2010)." April 13, 2009. Accessed August 16, 2011. http://news.xinhuanet.com/.

Clark, Andy. "Out of Our Brains." Opinionator. *New York Times,* December 12, 2010.

Cohen, Paul A. Interview in "Coming Distractions" by *China Beat.* September 26, 2008. Accessed November 11, 2012. http://thechinabeat.blogspot.ie/.

Cowell, Alan. "Pope Declines to Meet with Dalai Lama." *New York Times,* December 12, 2014. Accessed December 13, 2014. http://www.nytimes.com/.

Crampton, Thomas. "Chasing the Rumors to Chase Down SARS." *International Herald Tribune,* June 4, 2003.

DeParle, Jason. "Harder for Americans to Rise from Lower Rungs." *New York Times,* January 4, 2012.

Deutscher, Guy. "Does Your Language Shape How You Think?" *New York Times,* August 26, 2010. Accessed March 25, 2013. http://www.nytimes.com/.

Dewan, Shaila. "Chinese Student in U.S. Is Caught in Confrontation." *New York Times*, April 17, 2008. Accessed August 21, 2011. http://www.nytimes.com/.

Feng Shu. "A National Conundrum." *People's Daily Online* (English ed.), February 10, 2012. Accessed July 8, 2012. http://en.people.cn/.

Fish, Stanley. "Favoritism Is Good." Opinionator. *New York Times*, January 7, 2013. Accessed March 24, 2013. http://opinionator.blogs.nytimes.com/.

Fisher, Max. "How China Stays Stable Despite 500 Protests Every Day." *Atlantic*, January 5, 2012.

Gladstone, Rick. "Norway's Leaders Snub Dalai Lama in Deference to China." *New York Times*, May 8, 2014. Accessed December 10, 2014, http://www.nytimes.com/.

Guardian. "China Media Watchdog Bans Wordplay Puns." November 28, 2014. Accessed December 8, 2014. http://www.theguardian.com/.

———. "Chinese Toy Factory Boss Commits Suicide over Lead Paint Scandal." August 13, 2007. Accessed February 4, 2013. http://www.guardian.co.uk/.

International Herald Tribune. "Business Etiquette for Hong Kong and the Mainland." December 7, 2010.

———. "Saving Face in China." December 13, 2010.

Irish Times. "Beijing Removes Controversial 'Confucius.'" April 22, 2011.

Larouche PAC. "President Xi Jinping Works to Revive Confucianism in China." September 26, 2014. Accessed October 14, 2014. http://larouchepac.com/.

Law, Andy. "Out of Our Brains." Opinionator. *New York Times*, December 12, 2010.

Ludlow, Peter. "The Banality of Systemic Evil." *New York Times*, September 15, 2013.

New York Times. "An Ambivalent China Affirms the Charisma of the Dalai Lama." February 18, 2012.

———. "China Reportedly Strips Shanghai Bishop of His Title." December 12, 2012. Accessed March 26, 2013. http://www.nytimes.com/.

———. "Chinese Student in U.S. Is Caught in Confrontation." April 17, 2008.

———. "He May Have Nothing to Hide, but He's Always Under Watch." February 24, 2013.

———. "Illicit Church, Evicted, Tries to Buck Beijing." April 18, 2011. Accessed March 26, 2013. http://www.nytimes.com/.

———. "Vatican Condemnation of New Chinese Bishop Worsens Tensions." July 8, 2011. Accessed March 26, 2013. http://www.nytimes.com/.

People's Daily Online (English ed.). "Bourgeois Liberalization Means Taking the Capitalist Road." May/June 1985. Accessed November 3, 2012. http://en.people.cn/.

———. "Raising a Child in Today's China." December 2, 2004. http://en.people.cn/.

Ririhena, Yohanna, and Novan Iman Santosa. "RI Concerned about Map in New Chinese Passports." *Jakarta Post*, November 29, 2012. Accessed November 30, 2012. http://www.thejakartapost.com/.

Schueler, Linda. "More Options Than Ever: Educating Your Child in Beijing." *Beijing This Month*, May 23, 2006. Accessed August 29, 2011. http://www.btmbeijing.com/.

South China Morning Post. "China's Slow but Sure Democratization." March 20, 2013. Accessed March 20, 2013. http://www.scmp.com/.

———. "Cirque du Soleil Pulls Tiananmen Image from China Shows after 'Collective Gasp.'" August 14, 2013.

———. "Gold Mine Raids in Ghana Seize 124 Suspected Illegal Chinese Workers." June 6, 2013.

———. "Half of China's Millionaires 'Plan to Leave Country within Five Years.'" September 15, 2014.

———. "Obama Triggers Beijing's Wrath after Tribute to Dalai Lama." February 6, 2015.

———. "Tradition of Filial Piety Needs the Force of Law." July 2, 2013.

———. "Watching Cautiously amid Signs of Shift towards Tibet." July 1, 2013.

———. "Wealth Gap Puts China among World's Most Unequal Nations, Survey Reveals." December 11, 2012. Accessed December 22, 2012. http://www.scmp.com/.

———. "Wukan Democracy Leaves Village Divided." February 15, 2013.

———. "Wukan Villagers Decry Vice-minister's Mixed Message on Free Polls." March 14, 2013.

Tatlow, Didi. "Dalai Lama: No More 'Wolf in Monk's Robes?'" *New York Times*, June 27, 2013. http://rendezvous.blogs.nytimes.com/.

Wang, Grace. "Grace Wang: The Old Man Who Lost His Horse." Accessed April 13, 2015. http://www.chinadigitaltimes.net/.

Washington Post. "How China's Richest Man Made It." November 3, 2012.

Wines, Michael. "China's Censors Misfire in Abuse-of-Power Case." *New York Times*, November 17, 2010.

———. "Crackdown on Chinese Bloggers Who Fight the Censors with Puns." *New York Times*, May 28, 2012.

———. "In China, 'Audi' Means 'Big Shot.'" *New York Times*, November 16, 2012.

———. "Tank Cartoon Censored on Eve of Anniversary of Tiananmen Square." *New York Times*, June 2, 2010.

Xinhua. "Seems Money Can't Buy Happiness, as Saying Goes." *People's Daily Online* (English ed.), August 31, 2004. Accessed June 1, 2007. http://en.people.cn/.

Yapp, Robin. "Dalai Lama Snubbed in Brazil after Chinese Fury at Mexico Talks." *Telegraph*, September 18, 2011. Accessed December 10, 2014, http://www.telegraph.co.uk/.

Yu Hua. "When Filial Piety Is the Law." *New York Times*, July 7, 2013.

Index

Page numbers indicating illustrations are italicized.

About the Authors

Jerusha McCormack and **John Blair** were born and educated in the United States, then with PhDs in hand (from Brandeis and Brown Universities), they moved independently to Western Europe. As academics, each taught for thirty years in English Departments at University College, Dublin, and the University of Geneva, respectively. As immigrants to Europe they gained first-hand experience of cross-cultural issues. As teachers of American literature and culture, they learned how to make that experience meaningful for international audiences.

Over the last twelve years, teaching frequently as Foreign Experts in China, they designed—initially for Beijing Foreign Studies University—a course called "Western Civilization with Chinese Comparisons." Their sourcebook under that title published by Fudan University Press is now in its fourth edition. Since 2003 the course based on this book has been required for graduate students in the School of English and International Studies at BFSU. It is being adopted in universities from Beijing to Chengdu to Hohhot. Published in the United States under the title *Comparing Civilizations: China and the West*, this sourcebook serves as a platform for this, their latest book—as well as for the comparative civilizations course they have been invited to teach in the autumn semester of 2015 as distinguished visitors at the Institute of World Literature at Peking University.